THE NEW BOOK OF KNOWLEDGE ANNUAL

1975

HIGHLIGHTING EVENTS OF 1974

THE NEW BOOK OF KNOWLEDGE ANNUAL

THE YOUNG PEOPLE'S BOOK OF THE YEAR

Grolier
INCORPORATED
NEW YORK

ISBN 0-7172-0606-8
The Library of Congress Catalog Card Number: 40-3092

COPYRIGHT © 1975 BY  Grolier
INCORPORATED
NEW YORK

Copyright © in Canada 1975 BY GROLIER LIMITED

JOHN RATTI
MANAGING EDITOR

BARBARA EFFRON
ART AND PRODUCTION DIRECTOR

FERN L. MAMBERG
ASSOCIATE EDITOR

MARTHA GLAUBER SHAPP
DIRECTOR, YOUNG PEOPLE'S PUBLICATIONS

WALLACE S. MURRAY
VICE-PRESIDENT AND EDITORIAL DIRECTOR

EDITORIAL STAFF

EDITORS	**SUE R. BRANDT**
	JOHN COX
	PATRICIA ELLSWORTH
	ELEANOR FELDER
	WAYNE JONES
	LEO SCHNEIDER
	MARY LOU SITTLER
	RUTH SKODNICK
	LYDIA STEIN
	JANET STONE
COPY EDITORS	**J. MICHAEL RAIKES**
	PATRICIA M. GODFREY
INDEXER	**VITRUDE DE SPAIN**

ART AND PRODUCTION STAFF

PRODUCTION SUPERVISOR	**HARRIET L. SMITH**
LAYOUT ARTIST	**JACQUES CHAZAUD**
PICTURE EDITOR	**JOYCE DEYO**

MANUFACTURING

DIRECTOR	**JAMES W. HINKLEY IV**
ASSISTANT DIRECTOR	**ANTHONY LEONARDI**

CONTENTS

CONTRIBUTORS

ASIMOV, Isaac
Scientist; author, *I, Robot; Stories from the Rest of the Robots; ABC's of Space; David Starr: Space Ranger; Fantastic Voyage; From Earth to Heaven*   THE ROBOT PIONEERS

BARBER, Alden G.
Chief Scout Executive, Boy Scouts of America
                                    BOY SCOUTS

BENNETT, Jay
Author, *The Long Black Coat; The Dangling Witness: A Mystery; Deadly Gift; The Killing Tree;* 1974 Edgar Award winner
                        THE GUICCIOLI MINIATURE

BOHLE, Bruce
Usage Editor, American Heritage Dictionaries
                   NEW WORDS IN DICTIONARY INDEX

COLBY, Constance Taber
Author, *A Skunk in the House;* instructor, Barnard College (Columbia University)
        WHEN YOU TALK TO YOUR PLANTS, SMILE!

CRONKITE, Walter
CBS News Correspondent
                          OUR CHANGING WORLD

DAUER, Rosamond
Author and poet; Vice-President, Staten Island Council on the Arts
                                    IF SPRING
                             MY OLDER SISTER
                       PLEASE DON'T INTERRUPT

GOLDBERG, Hy
Co-ordinator of sports information, NBC sports; winner of New Jersey Sports Writer of the Year award   SPORTS

HAHN, Charless
Stamp Editor, *Chicago Sun-Times*
                             STAMP COLLECTING

HAIMOWITZ, Benjamin
Science writer   COMPUTER CHIMPS

HALLIDAY, William R.
Author, *American Caves and Caving; Depths of the Earth; Adventure Is Underground;* Director, Western Speleological Survey; physician
                      ADVENTURE UNDERGROUND

HARP, Sybil C.
Editor, *Creative Crafts* magazine
                        A BAKER'S CLAY FRAME

8

KHADDURI, Majid
Director, The Middle East Center, School of Advanced International Studies, The Johns Hopkins University   BAHRAIN
                                      OMAN
                       UNITED ARAB EMIRATES
                                      QATAR

KNOX, Richard G.
Director of Public Relations Department, Girl Scouts of the United States of America
                       GIRL SCOUTS AND GIRL GUIDES

KURTZ, Henry I.
Author, *John and Sebastian Cabot; Captain John Smith;* contributor to *History Today* and *American Heritage* magazines
              WONDERFUL, WONDERFUL TIVOLI
                     THE "MONITOR" REAPPEARS

MACDONALD, M. A.
Author, *The Royal Canadian Mounted Police;* co-author, *Growing Up*
                           THE CANADIAN NORTH

MARGO, Elisabeth
Author, *Taming the Forty-niner*
                           THE WITCHES OF SALEM

MENUEZ, Mary Jane
Poet   MARCH; CRAB MEADOW BEACH

MISHLER, Clifford
Senior Editor, *Numismatic News Weekly*
                              COIN COLLECTING

NEIBRIEF, Jerome Z.
Managing Editor, *Lands and Peoples* encyclopedia
                             THE MIDDLE EAST

REINSTEIN, R. A.
Co-director, ISAR (Institute for Scientific and Artistic Research); science writer and editor
                       NEW EYES ON THE SKIES

ROSENTHAL, Sylvia
Managing Editor, *Disney's It's a Small World* encyclopedia; Author, *Live High on Low Fat*
                       A MIDDLE EAST SUPPER

SCHMITT, Harrison H.
Scientist-Astronaut, Apollo 17 Mission, National Aeronautics and Space Administration
                                  ON THE MOON

SHAW, Arnold
Author, *The Rockin' 50's; Honkers and Shouters: The Rhythm and Blues Years; The Rock Revolution; The World of Soul; The Street That Never Slept*   THE MUSIC SCENE

TAFT, Henry W.
President, Outward Bound, Inc.
                              OUTWARD BOUND

USTINOV, Peter
Actor, author, and director
                       THE LITTLE PRESIDENT

WILSON, Marion B.
Writer, artist, and collector
                       THE STORY OF SCRIMSHAW

OUR CHANGING WORLD

The keynote of 1974 was change. Many of the world's nations gained new leaders in 1974. The United States, France, Israel, Greece, Japan, Britain, West Germany, and Portugal were among the nations with major changes in political leadership. Perhaps the most dramatic of these political changes was the resignation from office of President Richard M. Nixon, the first president of the United States to leave office by resignation. President Nixon made his decision after months of political controversy touched off by the Watergate scandal. He resigned at a point when it seemed certain that articles of impeachment would be voted in the House of Representatives. Gerald R. Ford, who had been appointed vice-president by Mr. Nixon after the resignation of Spiro Agnew, became the first unelected president of the United States. Mr. Ford appointed former New York governor Nelson A. Rockefeller as his vice-president.

The governmental changes of the year seemed especially unsettling when viewed against the backdrop of a world plagued by severe economic and political problems. There was economic recession in many of the industrialized countries, famine in various parts of the world, and continuing tension in the Middle East between the Arab nations and Israel. Although the Arab oil embargo established in 1973 was ended in 1974, there was no guarantee that it would not be re-established—especially if the precarious ccasefire should fail or if some other Arab-Israeli conflict should develop. And the economic chaos caused by the oil embargo in many of the industrialized nations was a reminder of how much political and economic power the oil producers could wield in the 20th century. If there was one benefit gained from the oil embargo, it was the general realization that a worldwide energy shortage was a reality. And it was a reality with which each nation of the world would have to cope.

A lesson learned in 1974 was that the world had shrunk more rapidly than anyone had imagined. It was apparent that the political and economic relations among countries were even more intricately interwoven than had been thought.

And war continued in the world. Although direct United States involvement in Vietnam was over, the war between North and South continued. Trouble flared up again on the island of Cyprus over the rights of the Turkish-Cypriot minority. Although there was peace for the time being between Israel and its Arab neighbors, there was the continuing danger that incidents could easily touch off another war.

But there was hope at the end of 1974. Many of the world's nations with their new governments were trying sincerely to find solutions to their problems. And because so many governments were new, it was hoped that there might be fresh solutions that might work better than the old ones had.

WALTER CRONKITE

THE MIDDLE EAST

The Middle East has long been considered one of the world's major trouble spots. Time and again newspaper headlines have called attention to a new crisis threatening that part of the globe. Since 1973 alone the Middle East has twice erupted into armed conflict. In October, 1973, war broke out between Israel and the Arab states of Egypt and Syria. It was the fourth Arab-Israeli war in the past 25 years and the latest chapter in the long history of hostility and distrust between Israelis and Arabs. The 1973 war was hard fought but relatively short. Intensive diplomatic efforts eventually succeeded in bringing about a ceasefire and a pullback of forces, but not before a further complication had been added—an oil embargo. The Middle East is the world's leading producer of oil, the lifeblood of modern industry. In support of the Arab cause, the chief Arab oil-producing states briefly cut off supplies of oil to countries they considered unsympathetic. The result was an energy shortage that for a time threatened to paralyze a number of the nations of the world.

After peace had been restored, at least temporarily, to one part of the Middle East, a new crisis developed in another—Cyprus. An island country inhabited by people both of Greek and of Turkish descent, Cyprus has been another area of strife, largely because of the antagonism between the two groups. Its strategic location just off the coast of Turkey, and the desire on the part of some Greeks and Cypriots for union of the island with Greece, added to the explosiveness of the problem. In the summer of 1974, seemingly without warning, Greek Cypriot forces led by army officers from Greece overthrew the government of Cyprus. Turkey, fearing that Greece meant to take over the island, responded by sending troops to invade Cyprus. It seemed as if something long feared was about to happen—a Middle East crisis that would expand beyond the Middle East itself into a full-scale war. The fighting finally died down, however, though Turkish forces were left occupying a third of the island. A very shaky truce had once more been achieved in the Middle East.

Considering the location and the history of the Middle East, it is not surprising that the region has been marked by crisis and conflict. It has been called "strategically the most important geographical area in the world." It spans three continents—Asia, Africa, and Europe—and is surrounded by some of the world's most important waterways. For thousands of years the Middle East was a bridge across which countless peoples migrated. Great empires arose here, warred with each other, and fell, to be succeeded by new empires. In modern times the Middle East became a prize for European powers who sought to exert their influence in this most strategic part of the world. More recently, the discovery of oil in vast quantities has given the rest of the world a renewed interest in the affairs of the Middle East.

But the history of the Middle East is not just one of war or oil; it is also a history of civilization. Mankind's earliest civilizations are believed to have been born here. It was here that man first learned to domesticate animals and to cultivate the soil. The invention of agriculture meant that people could live a settled existence. The first towns and cities were built in the Middle East, and here, too, man first learned the art of working metals. The alphabet was invented in the Middle East, and history was recorded here for the first time. Three of the world's great religions—Judaism, Christianity, and Islam—all began in the Middle East. Over the centuries, art, architecture, and science all flourished.

▶ **WHAT IS THE MIDDLE EAST?**

The name "Middle East" is relatively new. It came into popular use during World War II, replacing a somewhat similar term that had been in use until then—"the Near East." The term "Middle East" is one of geographical convenience and has no exact definition. In fact, scholars disagree on which countries make up the Middle East, although the following are usually included in the region: Iran, Iraq, Turkey, Cyprus, Syria, Lebanon, Israel, Jordan, Saudi Arabia, Kuwait, Bahrain, Qatar, the United Arab Emirates, Oman, Yemen (Aden), Yemen (Sana), Egypt, and Libya. Sometimes Algeria, Tunisia, and Morocco are included in the Middle East, and some geographers would also add Sudan, Afghanistan, and Pakistan. In this article, however, only the countries in the first list will be considered as making up the region.

The Middle East covers a large area, almost as large as the United States or China, although it has a smaller population than either. In spite of its great size, vast stretches of the region are unsuitable for human life or can support only a limited number of people. Much of the Middle East consists of immense deserts of sand, rugged mountain ranges, and barren plateaus. The most heavily populated areas are found on the coasts of the Mediterranean Sea, in the fertile valley of the Nile River in Egypt, and in the valley formed by the Tigris and Euphrates rivers of Iraq and Syria. These have been centers of population since ancient times, and it was in the river valleys that Western civilization began.

The climate of the Middle East can be as severe as the landscape. Temperatures are often extreme. In some parts of Turkey and Iran, winters are almost Arctic; along the coast of the Persian Gulf, summer temperatures well over 100 degrees Fahrenheit (38 degrees Celsius) are common. Much of the Middle East is arid and receives little rainfall, particularly the great deserts of North Africa, Syria, and the Arabian Peninsula. Rain is more plentiful in other areas, but lack of water is an age-old problem and various methods of irrigation have been in use since the earliest times.

The Middle East is not rich in mineral resources, except for oil, and this valuable mineral is found in only some parts of the region. Saudi Arabia, Iran, and Iraq are the leading oil producers, and a number of tiny Persian Gulf states, especially Kuwait and the United Arab Emirates, have great reserves of oil. Altogether, the Middle East has over two thirds of the world's known oil deposits.

▶ A VARIED POPULATION

The Middle East is a varied land with a variety of peoples. About half the population is Arab, descended from people who originally came from the Arabian Peninsula. Turks and Iranians are the next largest groups. The ancestors of the modern Turks ruled the last great empire of the Middle East. The Iranians are descended from the ancient Persians, who once held sway over a vast area of the Middle East, too. Jews are the predominent group in the population of Israel, the modern counterpart to the ancient Israelite realm. In the mountain fastnesses of Turkey, Iraq, and Iran live the Kurds, a people who have long fought, unsuccessfully, for an independent state of their own. Their divided homeland is called Kurdistan.

The major languages spoken by the peoples of the Middle East belong to three distinct families. Arabic, the language of the Arabs, belongs to the Hamito-Semitic family. It is closely related to Hebrew, the language of Israel. Another branch of this family, called Hamitic, includes a number of African languages. The ancient Egyptians spoke a tongue that belonged to the Hamito-Semitic family, as do the Berbers of North Africa and many of the people of Ethiopia and Somalia. The Turks, whose origins were in the plains of Central Asia, speak a language, Turkish, that is similar to languages spoken in that part of the world. This language family is called Altaic. Farsi (New Persian), which is the chief language of Iran, and Kurdish both belong to the great Indo-European family, which includes most of the languages of Europe and America.

The influence of Arabic on the non-Semitic languages has been strong. Modern Persian, or Farsi, for example, is written in a modified Arabic alphabet, as was Turkish until fairly recent times.

In a land of different peoples, languages, and customs, it is the religion of Islam that provides the unifying force in the Middle East today. The newest of the great religions that arose here, Islam originated in Arabia, in the 7th century, with the preaching of its prophet, Mohammed. Carried by Arab warriors, the new faith swept out of its desert home and spread quickly across the Middle East. It was eventually carried beyond the borders of the Middle East, into other areas of Asia, into many parts of Africa, and even into southern Europe. The older religions of Judaism and Christianity still have followers in the Middle East: Israel is largely Jewish and Lebanon is half Christian.

Like Judaism and Christianity, from which

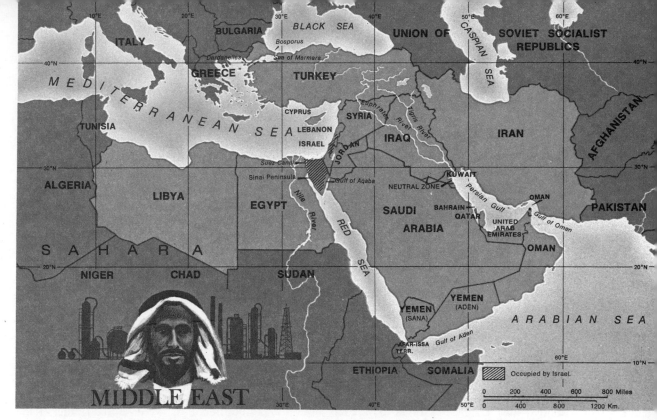

MIDDLE EAST

it drew much of its inspiration, Islam is a monotheistic religion. "Monotheism" means belief in a single, all-powerful God. In Arabic the name for God is Allah. One who believes in Islam is called a Muslim, which means, in Arabic, "one who surrenders himself" to God. The holy book of Islam is the Koran, which Muslims believe contains the word of God as revealed to Mohammed.

▶ FARMERS, CITY DWELLERS, AND NOMADS

Over the centuries the people of the Middle East have developed two distinctive ways of life: that of the settled farmer and town dweller, and that of the wandering nomad. The farmers live in the more fertile areas. The desert and semi-desert regions are the domain of the nomad. Agriculture has long been the mainstay of the economy of the Middle East, and most of the people still cultivate the soil and live in small villages. Town life developed early in the Middle East, and cities have been important since the most ancient times as centers of trade, commerce, and culture. The nomads make up only a fraction of the people, but unlike the farmers, who are clustered densely together in the few fertile areas, the nomads roam freely over the vast, empty, arid parts of the region.

The desert nomads, or Bedouins, live a largely self-sufficient life, with few possessions. Their lives are dependent on the camel, which provides them with food, transportation, and material for clothing and tents. (The nomads of the semi-desert regions keep sheep and goats.) In response to the harsh demands of the desert, the nomads have developed a strict way of life. They follow age-old trails seeking water and pasture for their animals.

The nomadic way of life has been declining over the years. Today, many of the Bedouins have been settled in towns. Some now work in the growing oil industry of Saudi Arabia and the other countries of the Arabian Peninsula; others serve as soldiers.

▶ WHERE CIVILIZATION BEGAN

Civilization was born in the valley between the Tigris and Euphrates rivers, in what is now Iraq, over 5,000 years ago. The people who lived there were the Sumerians, and their land was called Sumer. In later times this region came to be known as Mesopotamia. This name is a Greek word meaning land "between rivers." The Sumerians invented a kind of wedge-shaped writing called cuneiform, which they inscribed on clay tablets. They built carefully laid-out cities, and temples to their

15

gods. They were skilled weavers and craftsmen in metal and pottery, and practiced an intensive form of agriculture.

At almost the same time, in the valley of the Nile, the Egyptians were creating a great civilization of their own. Remains of some of their great accomplishments can still be seen in Egypt today. Great temples to the many gods of Egypt, giant pyramids, and enormous stone statues of their pharaohs, or kings, are scattered through the land. The Great Pyramid at Giza was built almost 5,000 years ago as a tomb for Khufu, or Cheops, an early pharaoh. When it was built it stood 481 feet (147 meters) high and covered an area of 13 acres (5 hectares). It is considered one of the wonders of the ancient world.

The Egyptians were among the first peoples to explore the mysteries of science. They needed to know when the Nile River would rise or fall, so that they could plant their crops, and so they devised a calendar. It was divided into 12 months of 30 days each, not unlike our modern calendar. Egyptian physicians prescribed drugs for illness, set broken bones, and performed surgery.

The land of Mesopotamia was dominated for 2,000 years by various Semitic peoples—the Akkadians, Babylonians, and Assyrians. Babylon, the capital of the Babylonians, was famous in the ancient world for its wealth and beauty. The semi-legendary Tower of Babel was probably one of the tower-like temples of the Babylonians. One of their most famous kings, Hammurabi, compiled the first known code of laws. The Assyrians, who succeeded the Babylonians, were a military people who forged a strong empire. They recorded their exploits in a form of sculpture called bas-relief, in which the carved figures are slightly raised from the surface. The Assyrians were themselves to be conquered, in the 7th century B.C., by a new Babylonian kingdom (the Chaldean) under Nebuchadnezzar.

▶ PHOENICIANS, HEBREWS, AND PERSIANS

Along the eastern coast of the Mediterranean, in what is today Lebanon, lived the Phoenicians. They were the great traders and sailors of the ancient world. The Phoenicians gave the world its alphabet.

The Hebrews, neighbors of the Phoeni-

cians, claimed descent from Abraham, who is considered the father of Judaism. In a land where many gods were worshipped, he was the first to believe in a single God. The Arabs also consider themselves descendants of Abraham, through his son Ishmael. The kingdom of the Hebrews, or Israelites, was at its height during the reign of King Solomon, in the 10th century B.C. Later, the Israelites suffered the repeated destruction of their state and dispersal of their people. Christianity was a continuation of the monotheism of the Jews. The faith of the Christians originated in the teachings and person of Jesus, who was himself born a Jew, and his disciples. Jerusalem, the capital of the Jewish realm, is still a holy city for Jews, Christians, and Muslims.

The ancestors of the people whom we today call the Persians arrived in the Middle East and settled on the Iranian plateau, possibly around 1500 B.C. They included a number of related tribes, two of which, the Medes and the Persians, were united under King Cyrus I (the Great) in the 6th century B.C. Cyrus defeated the Babylonians under King Nebuchadnezzar and established the first Persian empire, the greatest empire of its time. The Persians were efficient and cultured rulers, and under their reign art and science flourished. Their religion was Zoroastrianism. Its god is called Ahura Mazda, and his symbol is fire. Central to this faith is a belief in the perpetual battle between the forces of good and evil. Zoroastrianism was later overwhelmed by the advance of Islam. The religion still has a handful of followers in Iran today, but many more live in India, where they are called Parsis.

The empire of the Persians was overthrown by the Macedonian-Greek army of Alexander the Great in the 4th century B.C. In just a few years Alexander conquered lands stretching from Greece to Egypt and across the Middle East to what is now Pakistan. After Alexander's death, his empire was divided among his generals. They established Greek dynasties that ruled until the arrival of the Romans and the rise of new Persian kingdoms.

▶ BYZANTINES, ARABS, AND TURKS

In A.D. 330 the Roman emperor Constantine I (called the Great) established a new

fertile river valleys . . .

desert . . .

THE MIDDLE EAST—LAND OF DIVERSITY

and mountain ranges

FACES OF THE MIDDLE EAST

Bedouins from Syria

The ancient face of Egypt

Israelis—old and young

A tribal girl of Iran

A Turk

A Palestinian

capital on the site of an earlier Greek city called Byzantium. The new city, situated in what is now western Turkey, was named Constantinople (city of Constantine). As the Roman Empire in the West declined, Constantinople came to be considered the "New Rome" and the center of the Eastern, or Byzantine, Empire. The Byzantines were Christian in religion and Greek in culture. Their empire was to survive for over a thousand years, until the capture of Constantinople in 1453 by the Ottoman Turks, who renamed the city Istanbul.

The Arabs remained largely outside the historical events of the Middle East until the 7th century when, united by Islam, they overran the region. Within a short time they had spread across North Africa and into Spain. Islamic culture absorbed much from earlier cultures, especially from the Persian and the Greek. It reached its height during the period when Baghdad was the capital of the Islamic world. Perhaps the most famous of the caliphs (who were both rulers and religious leaders) was Harun al-Rashid, who reigned during the late 8th and early 9th centuries. During this period Arabic literature flourished. Translations were made of Greek philosophical, scientific, and mathematical works, thereby preserving knowledge that might otherwise have been lost. Algebra was invented and Arabic numerals were introduced into the West.

Over the next centuries other people were to invade the Middle East—Crusaders from the West and Turks and others from the East. The Crusaders were European knights who hoped to free the Christian shrines of the Middle East from the grip of Islam. The First Crusade, in the 11th century, was successful. Jerusalem was captured and the Crusaders established several small kingdoms, but eventually they were driven out.

The Turks had already been converted to Islam when they arrived in the Middle East. The first tribe, the Seljuks, settled in what is now Turkey. They were succeeded by the Ottomans, named for their legendary ancestor, Othman or Osman. They were a well-disciplined, soldierly people, who easily conquered the already weakened empires and kingdoms that were there. Ottoman power reached its height in the 16th century, when Turks ruled most of the Middle East and much of eastern and southern Europe. But though their empire was to last, in greatly reduced form, until 1918, decline set in much earlier. By the 19th century the Ottoman Empire was referred to as a "sick man," and the Turkish sultans continued to hold power only with the help of Britain and France, who feared the southward expansion of Russia. The opening of the Suez Canel in 1869 made the Middle East even more important to the Western powers, particularly Britain.

▶ THE MIDDLE EAST TODAY

By World War I little remained of the once-vast Ottoman realm. Following the war the Ottomans were stripped of their remaining Arab lands in the Middle East, and were reduced to what is now Turkey. The Arab lands became protectorates (called mandates) of Britain and France, who ruled them until about the time of World War II, when they became independent. In 1947 the United Nations voted to divide the British mandated territory of Palestine (the ancient realm of the Hebrews) into separate Jewish and Arab states. Israel was to be a homeland for the Jews, who had suffered grievously in World War II. But the Arabs, who had been subjugated for centuries, felt that they were being deprived of their rightful land. They rejected the United Nations plan and went to war against Israel in 1948. Israel maintained its independence, but at the cost of repeated wars—in 1956, 1967, and in 1973.

The hostility between Israel and the Arab countries remains the single greatest obstacle to peace in the Middle East. One factor in the problem is the plight of the Palestinian Arabs. They were promised their own state at the time of the creation of Israel, but many fled their land during the Arab-Israeli wars and became refugees. The rivalry between the United States and the Soviet Union is a source of possible conflict, and Cyprus remains a powder keg that could explode again.

The Middle East countries have done much to help their people. However, many social and economic problems remain that cannot be solved until peace comes to the area.

JEROME Z. NEIBRIEF
Lands and Peoples encyclopedia

Teheran, Iran's capital and largest city, lies in the shadow of the great Elburz mountain range.

CITIES OF THE MIDDLE EAST

The famous Blue Mosque in Istanbul. The city, Turkey's largest, was once called Constantinople.

Pilgrims from all the Muslim world come to Mecca in Saudi Arabia, Islam's holiest city.

Cairo, Egypt's capital and the largest city in the Middle East, stands on the bank of the fertile Nile River. In the background are the pyramids at Giza.

The ancient city of Jerusalem is holy to Jews, Christians, and Muslims alike.

Damascus, Syria's capital and largest city, is one of the world's oldest cities.

The ruins of Persepolis, seen from the Mount of Mercy. In the background is the modern tent city raised in 1971 for the 2,500th anniversary of the Persian empire.

PERSEPOLIS

As the sun sets on the plain of Marvdasht in southwestern Iran, the stones of Persepolis seem to change color from yellow to pink to deep red. Though in ruins, Persepolis is a very beautiful and strange place.

Persepolis was the ceremonial capital of the great Persian empire. As such, it was the official residence of the emperor and the religious center of the empire. Every New Year's Day—which the ancient Persians celebrated on the first day of spring—a seemingly endless procession of people from all parts of the vast empire came to the city. They came to bring gifts to the emperor. The Persians believed that Ahura Mazda, their supreme god, renewed his blessing of the emperor's rule on New Year's Day. The gifts were intended to show how loyal all parts of the empire were to the ruler. The Persians called their emperor "king of kings." He was truly all-powerful.

The Persian emperors Darius I, Xerxes I, and Artaxerxes I built Persepolis between 520 B.C. and 450 B.C. It was built specifically to be the heart of the empire. The New Year's Day ceremony was to be the central event in the life of the city. The empire lasted from 550 B.C. to 330 B.C. It was by far the largest empire the world had known up to that time. It stretched eastward to India and westward to the Balkans, the shores of the Mediterranean, and Ethiopia. Because the empire was so vast, people in outlying lands became rebellious from time to time. The New Year's Day ceremony was used to remind distant lands of their allegiance to the empire's central government.

Persepolis stands at the foot of the Mount of Mercy. From a distance or from the air, the Mount of Mercy has the look of a crouching lion protecting the city on the east. To the west, the wide plain opens up, ringed by distant mountains. A spur of the Mount of Mercy actually forms the base or foundation of Persepolis. The natural structure was built up to form a 33-acre (13 hectare) platform rising some 50 feet (15.2 meters) above the plain.

On the platform are the ruins of nine structures, several of immense size. Two of these structures were huge audience halls. Some of the columns of these halls are still standing. Another of the structures was a ceremonial, four-walled gateway dedicated to "All Lands" of the empire. The platform's southern half was occupied by palaces, including the famous Palace of Darius. But it is the stairways, the columns, the wall carvings, and the inscriptions that make Persepolis a treasure-house of Persian history.

There is a grand staircase which leads up to the platform from the plain. There are also other staircases, atop the platform, connecting the various levels of the city. Lifelike bas-relief carvings of the men who came on New Year's Day bearing gifts for the emperor from the 23 lands of the empire are carved into the limestone. Each nationality can be recognized by its headdresses, clothing, and gifts. The figures in these carvings have a beauty and humanity that was new in sculpture in 500 B.C., when they were carved. And the animals, carried or led, look exceptionally gentle and dignified. Courtiers and guards also form part of the procession. Some of the courtiers sniff the flowers they carry, while others reach a helping hand to assist a neighbor up the staircase.

Animal themes appear often at Persepolis in the decoration and carving. Huge winged beasts, some with human heads, guard the Gateway of All Lands. In panels under every staircase a marvelously carved lion pounces on the flank of an equally well carved bull. The lion is the symbol of the New Year, and the bull represents the old year.

The extraordinary columns of Persepolis are taller and more slender than traditional Greek columns. Unlike most Greek columns, each of the columns at Persepolis had an animal carving on top of it as a capital, or top portion. Griffins (mythological winged beasts), lions, and bulls were the animals carved most frequently. Many of the animal carvings at Persepolis have fallen off their columns. Some of them can be seen lying on the ground.

Hard as it may be to imagine, the carved friezes of Persepolis were once painted in vivid colors. It is likely that they were also inlaid with gold and copper. Some of the figures in the carvings were decorated with jewels. The figures of kings and the images of the god Ahura Mazda wore earrings. The rulers' beards were made of lapis lazuli (a blue stone) or bronze. At its height Persepolis must have been a blaze of color.

Another sort of blaze destroyed Persepolis. The great halls and palaces were burned in 330 B.C. by Alexander the Great, the Macedonian conqueror of the Persian empire. Everything in the halls and palaces that was made of wood and cloth, including the ceiling beams made of the famous cedar wood of Lebanon, burned in the fire. The debris covered up many parts of the walls. Much that was not covered by ashes from the fire was covered up later by windblown sand. Centuries later, archeologists who came to the site found that only the parts of Persepolis that had been buried under ash and sand had been spared further destruction by later conquerors. What has survived at Persepolis is of great value. Much that we know about the ancient Persian empire has been learned in the fascinating and beautiful ruins of Persepolis.

Carvings of tribute bearers, animals, and guards adorn the Palace of Darius.

BAHRAIN

Bahrain is a country made up of a group of islands lying in the Persian Gulf off the coast of Saudi Arabia. It is the smallest in area of all the states of the Arabian Peninsula. Indeed, it ranks among the smallest of the world's nations. In spite of its size, however, Bahrain has for centuries been one of the more flourishing states of the region and the most economically advanced. Its location made it important as a port and a center of trade for the countries bordering the gulf. It was famed for its pearls and for the skill of its boat builders. The discovery of oil brought further prosperity to Bahrain, although its reserves of oil are not nearly so large as those of some of its neighbors. Over the years Bahrain has used its income from oil to establish an extensive social welfare program for its citizens and to continue its economic development toward the day when its oil will be completely gone.

▶ THE PEOPLE

Bahrain is by far the most densely populated country of the Arabian Peninsula, with some 230,000 people living in an area of only 240 square miles (622 square kilometers). Most of the people are Arabs, some having immigrated to Bahrain from neighboring countries. There are sizable numbers of Pakistanis, Iranians, and Indians, some of whom work as merchants in the cities. It is estimated that about 20 per cent of the people are non-Bahraini. Many came to Bahrain because of the relatively high standard of living and to work in the oil industry. The foreign communities include Europeans (mainly British) and Americans. The Arabs are Muslims, about equally divided between the Sunni and Shi'a sects, the two main branches of Islam.

About half the population is concentrated in the two leading cities of Manama and Muharraq. Manama is the largest city, the capital, and chief port. It is connected with Muharraq, which is on another island, by a 1½ mile (2.4 km.) causeway. The two cities present interesting contrasts. Manama, a commercial city, has been modernized, while Muharraq, with its old houses and narrow streets, retains a traditional look. An important port in its own right, Muharraq is the center of Bahrain's pearling and boat-building industries. The boats are dhows, rather small vessels with triangular sails, which were once commonly found through much of the Arab world.

Traditional ways of life in the Arab states of the Persian Gulf began to change when oil was discovered. Bahrain was the first of the gulf states in which oil was found, and the effects of modernization are most evident here. The country has a growing middle class and a skilled work force. This is largely a result of Bahrain's emphasis on education. Schooling is free and compulsory for all children between the ages of 6 and 16. There are teacher training colleges and a technical school. Bahrain has no university, but students are sent abroad to study.

Social welfare programs include free medical and hospital care and low-cost housing. One of the most striking examples of Bahrain's social planning is Isa Town, located a few miles from Manama. When fully completed, it will provide modern housing for some 35,000 people, with shopping centers, a library, schools, playgrounds, and a sports stadium.

▶ THE LAND

Bahrain is made up of about 33 islands, islets, and sandbars, most of them uninhabited. The largest island, Bahrain, from which the country takes its name, is about 30 miles (48 km.) long and 10 miles (16 km.) wide. Other important islands include Muharraq, Sitra, Umm Nasan (Umm Na'san), and Hawar, which lies near Qatar. The land is mainly flat desert with the only fertile area in the north. The highest elevation, 450 feet (137 meters), is at Jabal Dukhan on Bahrain Island. Dukhan is the site of Bahrain's oil deposits.

Summers are extremely hot and humid. Rainfall is slight, but springs and wells provide some fresh water for cultivation and for drinking. The chief crops are dates, vegetables, and alfalfa. The waters of the surrounding Persian Gulf are one of the world's richest source of natural pearls, which were formerly one of Bahrain's most important products.

ECONOMY

Most of Bahrain's income is derived from oil. It has the second largest oil refinery in the Middle East and refines not only its own crude oil but also oil from nearby Saudi Arabia. Before oil was discovered in 1932, the economy was based on trading and other commercial activities, agriculture, fishing, pearling, and boat building. The last two are not as important as they once were. The development in Japan of cultured, or artificially induced, pearls led to the decline of Bahrain's industry. An important part of the fishing industry is the harvesting of shrimp, which abound in the gulf, and which are exported frozen.

FACTS AND FIGURES

STATE OF BAHRAIN is the official name of the country.

CAPITAL: Manama.

LOCATION: Persian Gulf near Saudi Arabia.

AREA: 240 sq. mi. (622 sq. km.).

POPULATION: 230,000 (estimate).

LANGUAGE: Arabic.

RELIGION: Islam.

GOVERNMENT: Emirate. **Head of state**—emir. **Head of government**—prime minister. **International co-operation**—United Nations, Arab League.

ECONOMY: Agricultural products—dates, vegetables, alfalfa. **Industries and products**—oil, fish, pearls, boat building. **Chief exports**—oil and oil products, shrimp. **Chief imports**—machinery and transportation equipment, manufactured goods, food, chemicals. **Monetary unit**—dinar.

Oil experts predict that Bahrain's deposits of oil, never very large to begin with, will be exhausted before the end of the 20th century. To help diversify the economy, the government has encouraged foreign investment. A new aluminum plant has already been built, port facilities are being enlarged, and new industry is being sought.

HISTORY AND GOVERNMENT

Bahrain's history goes back to very ancient times. In the northern part of Bahrain Island are many thousands of burial mounds, some extremely large, which indicate that people lived here perhaps as long ago as 3000 B.C. The Sumerians, who belonged to one of the world's oldest civilizations, had contacts with ancient Bahrain, which even then was known as an important port. Later the Greeks and Romans visited the islands.

Bahrain was colonized by the Portuguese in the 16th century, and then fell under the rule of the Persians. In the 18th century the al-Khalifa family, who came from the Arabian mainland, became the ruling sheikhs of Bahrain and for a time exercised control over the neighboring region of Qatar. Their descendants rule as emirs, or princes, in Bahrain today.

Early in the 19th century Bahrain came under British influence. A series of treaties were signed with Great Britain similar to the treaties with Britain signed by other gulf states. In return for British protection, Bahrain agreed, among other things, not to engage in slavery or piracy. Bahrain remained a British protectorate until 1971, when it declared itself completely independent. An attempt was made to form a federation of the gulf states—Bahrain, Qatar, Oman, and the United Arab Emirates—but it proved fruitless.

The emir is the chief of state of Bahrain. He appoints the prime minister and the council of ministers. Bahrain's first constitution was approved in 1973. It established a parliament for the country consisting of elected members plus some members of the council of ministers.

Reviewed by MAJID KHADDURI
School of Advanced International Studies
The Johns Hopkins University

These camels wait patiently for new owners in a Kuwait camel market.

THE DESERT DWELLER'S BEST FRIEND

To most people the camel is a comical-looking animal. It is tall and awkward, with a clumsy hump or two on its back, and a small head set on top of an elongated neck. Long, slender legs ending in big feet add to the picture of awkwardness. The camel always seems to look aloof or annoyed, and if it is approached too closely it may show its bad temper by biting or spitting.

Someone seeing a camel for the first time might wonder what such an animal was good for. But to people of desert lands its usefulness is beyond dispute. Camels have served them for thousands of years as a means of transportation and a source of food, clothing, and shelter. The camel is the desert dweller's best friend.

The ancestor of the camel first appeared over 40,000,000 years ago, in North America. It was a small creature that barely resembled the camel of today. Over millions of years different forms of the animal evolved. Gradually the camel-like characteristics that we are familiar with appeared. The early camels slowly migrated to the parts of the world where they are now found, but the North American branch of the family died out.

Today camels are native only to Asia and northern Africa. Their close relatives, and the only other living members of the camel family, are found in South America. These are the llama, alpaca, vicuña, and guanaco. They are smaller and generally more delicate in appearance than the camel, and do not have the distinctive hump. They live in the high mountains of the Andes, where the llama and alpaca are raised for their fine wool and used as beasts of burden.

There are two varieties of camel. The Bactrian camel is found in the arid parts of Central Asia. (In ancient times part of this region was called Bactria.) It is distinguished by two humps; its body is relatively heavy; and it has longer hair to protect it against the cold winters of its homeland. The camel of the Middle East is called the Arabian camel, or dromedary. It has a single hump and is taller and slenderer than its Bactrian cousin. The Arabian camel is found in the desert regions of the Middle East and northern Africa.

The men of Jordan's famous Desert Patrol are mounted on fine Arabian camels.

The camel is remarkably well adapted to life in the desert. Many of the physical characteristics that give the camel its odd appearance actually enable it to thrive in an environment that would kill any other domestic animal. The camel's hump acts as a storehouse for food, in the form of fat. (The camel does not, despite what many people think, store water in its hump.) Its weak-looking legs are really quite strong and help it to carry heavy loads over long distances. Its feet are so constructed that it can move easily over loose, drifting sand. The camel sometimes has a sleepy look because its eyes are covered with three sets of eyelids and have long eyelashes. These protect its eyes against blowing sand. It can go for months without water in cool weather, and for several days during the hot summers. It will eat almost any kind of vegetation, and if necessary can go without food for long periods by absorbing the fat in its hump.

Since it is a creature of the desert, the camel has flourished in the Middle East, much of which is desert and semi-desert. The Arabian camel was first domesticated, or trained to work for people, over 4,000 years ago, probably in what is now Saudi Arabia.

The animal soon became an essential part of the way of life of the nomadic peoples who wandered the vast, empty stretches of the Middle East. The nomads traveled over long distances seeking grass and other vegetation to feed their herds of camels. In return, the camels supplied the desert people with nearly everything needed to sustain life. They supplied transportation in the desert as horses and donkeys did in less harsh climates. The camel was ridden and used as a pack animal (that is, it carried goods). Camels carried desert soldiers into battle; and dromedaries, often bred especially for speed, were used in racing. The female camel provided milk, and the male meat and leather. The fine hair of the camel was woven into cloth for tents and clothing. There was very little wasted. Even dried camel dung was used for fuel.

Over the years, however, the way of life of the nomad has been changing. As more and more desert people have come to live in settled areas, their dependence on the camel has declined. But the day of the appropriately named ship of the desert is not yet over. The camel has served the desert dwellers for a long time, and it will probably do so for some time to come.

A page from the Koran written in the Kufic script.

THE BEAUTY OF THE ARABIC LANGUAGE

Arabic is the language of over 100,000,000 of the earth's inhabitants. It is the most widely used of the Semitic tongues, and the langauge that unites the many and varied peoples of the Arab world. In addition to the many people who speak Arabic itself, there are millions of non-Arabs in Asia and Africa who use the graceful and flowing Arabic alphabet to write their own languages.

Arabic in its modern form originated in the 6th century in northern Arabia. The people who spoke it were desert dwellers, and their language reflected the life around them. Love and war, animals, hunting, desert life—these were the things about which the early Arab poets sang. In the following century, however, something happened that was to have a pro-

found influence on Arabic. This was the development of the religion of Islam. Muslims believe that their religion was received from God by the Prophet Mohammed, and that God's Word, in Arabic, was inscribed in a book called the Koran. Arabic became the language of the new religion, and as Islam swept like fire across Asia and Africa and into Europe, the Arabic language went with it. From a language of simple desert people, it became the language of officials who ruled newly conquered lands. In the centuries that followed the Arab conquests, Arabic also became the language of scholars, philosophers, and scientists. A number of English words are derived from the Arabic, such as *algebra, alchemy, admiral,* and *sherbet.*

This book of Arabic poetry comes from Syria and dates from the 16th century.

Arabic never lost its early poetic and religious qualities. Since the words of the Koran were believed to have come directly from God, they were revered. To make a copy of the Koran was considered a worthy, even a holy, act. The result was that a classical, or standard, form of written Arabic developed that remained constant throughout the Islamic world. Even today, a Syrian and a Moroccan may not understand each other's spoken Arabic dialects, but they can easily understand each other's written Arabic.

Islamic tradition forbids the representation of human or animal figures in art. So Arabic artists turned to their language and made the Arabic alphabet itself a work of art. "Calligraphy" means beautiful handwriting, and Arabic calligraphers were honored for their work much the same way great painters were honored in the West. Arab artists devoted their lives to producing handwritten versions of the Koran, and apprentices spent years of study before becoming master calligraphers. Using reed pens, Arabic calligraphers created a number of elegant and majestic scripts. One, the Kufic, was used especially for copying the Koran. It is square and angular, and somewhat resembles the Gothic script created by monks in Europe during the Middle Ages. Another popular script, called Neskhi, was used in correspondence. Calligraphy became such a fine art that the script was also used to decorate mosques, where Muslims gather to pray, and other buildings.

The Arabic alphabet has 28 letters, and is written from right to left. There are no capital letters. Vowels are indicated by dot-like symbols placed above or below the letters. In recent years a unified alphabet has been devised. If adopted, it is expected to make the complicated script easier to use, and thus make Arabic easier to learn.

OMAN

The Sultanate of Oman has been called "among the least known and least visited places on earth." For many years its rulers, the sultans, resisted outside influences and all attempts at change. The discovery of oil, however, and the coming to power of a young sultan have brought change to Oman.

OMAN

▶ THE PEOPLE

Oman's population, estimated at about 700,000, is mostly Arab. About half belong to the Ibadi sect of Islam; most of the others are Sunni Muslims of the Shafi'i school of law. There are minorities of Pakistanis, Indians, and East Africans whose ancestors came to Oman generations ago. They reflect a period in the country's history when it was an important power, with colonies in both Asia and Africa. Most of the non-Arabs live in the coastal cities of Muscat, the capital, and neighboring Matrah. Most of the Arab Omanis are farmers, who grow dates, limes, coconuts, and various grains and raise livestock. Some engage in fishing or work in the oil industry. There are also nomads who travel from oasis to oasis with their herds of camels and goats.

▶ THE LAND

Oman lies in a wide curve along the southeastern coast of the Arabian Peninsula. Its area is 82,030 square miles (212,457 square kilometers). Part of its border with Saudi Arabia, however, is still undefined. There are two main fertile regions: the Batina, a narrow coastal plain in the northeast, where one third of the people live; and Dhofar (Dhufar) in the southwest. Inner Oman consists largely of mountains and desert. Oman has an extremely hot climate, with temperatures reaching as high as 130 degrees Fahrenheit (54 degrees Celsius). Rainfall is limited.

▶ HISTORY AND GOVERNMENT

Early in the 16th century the Portuguese established themselves in the coastal areas of Oman. The Omanis expelled them a century later and began to build their own empire. By the 19th century Oman was the most powerful state on the Arabian Peninsula.

The present sultan came to power in 1970, after overthrowing his father in a palace coup. The new ruler was faced with enormous problems of poverty, illiteracy, and disease. Using oil revenues, he began a program of economic development and built new schools and hospitals. Since 1967, when oil was first produced in commercial quantities, the per capita income has more than tripled. The sultan also has had to deal with a rebellion against his rule in part of Oman.

The sultan rules as an absolute monarch, assisted by his ministers. The legal system of the country is based on the sacred law (Shari'a) and local custom.

Reviewed by MAJID KHADDURI
School of Advanced International Studies
The Johns Hopkins University

FACTS AND FIGURES

SULTANATE OF OMAN is the official name of the country. It was formerly called Muscat and Oman.

CAPITAL: Muscat.

LOCATION: Southeastern coast of the Arabian Peninsula.

AREA: 82,030 sq. mi. (212,457 sq. km.).

POPULATION: 700,000 (estimate).

LANGUAGE: Arabic.

RELIGION: Islam.

GOVERNMENT: Sultanate. **Head of state and government**—Sultan. **International co-operation**—United Nations, Arab League.

ECONOMY: Agricultural products—dates, limes, coconuts, grains (wheat, barley, millet), livestock. **Industries and products**—oil, fish, hides, handicrafts. **Chief minerals**—oil. **Chief exports**—oil, dates, dried limes, dried fish. **Chief imports**—foods, motor vehicles, textiles, building materials. **Monetary unit**—rial.

Ancient Beersheba has become an important center in the awakening Negev.

MAKING THE DESERT BLOOM

It was the spring of 1943, and the world was at war. The Allied armies battled the armies of the German dictator Adolf Hitler. For no people would the war's outcome be more crucial than for the world's Jews. Adolf Hitler had vowed to destroy the Jews. Indeed, before Hitler was defeated in 1945, more than 6,000,000 Jews were killed by the Nazis.

On the morning of March 23, 1943, in an obscure Middle Eastern desert called the Negev, a single car raised dust as it moved along a rough camel track. The car contained two men. Although they were far from the battlefields, their mission would be of great importance to the Jews of the world. The mission was to establish a Jewish settlement in the Negev. Their ultimate goal was the establishment in the Middle East of a Jewish homeland where Jews would be forever free of persecution.

The car stopped for water at a Bedouin camp. Then it proceeded a few miles more before finally coming to a halt at the top of a small hill. The two men got out. What they saw from the hilltop was hardly encouraging. Not a tree could be seen—not a shrub. But around them was the land they had bought. Here they would plant trees and raise crops, here in the middle of the desert.

Later that day two trucks arrived. One was loaded high with tents, timber, barrels, and barbed wire. The other carried fifteen young men. After centuries of being scattered around the world, Jews were returning to the Negev to live.

▶ WHY THE NEGEV?

The pioneers who arrived in the Negev in 1943 knew they had chosen a hard place in which to settle. But they did not feel they had any choice. Many Jewish settlements had already been made in the northern portions of what is today the state of Israel. The Jews' Arab neighbors resented the newcomers. The Arabs put pressure on the British, who then controlled the region, to restrict Jewish immigration. The Jews knew they had to make inroads as fast as possible. The Negev was simply too big to ignore. Indeed, when the state of Israel was created in 1948, the Negev made up half of its total area.

By 1948, eighteen settlements had been established in the Negev. During the war with the Arabs that followed independence, the soldier-farmers of the Negev were a vital part of Jewish self-defense. Cut off from the Israeli Army, they were kept supplied by parachute. Without them the entire Negev might have been lost.

The Negev pioneers were fighting for a desert that they thought could be made to bloom. Centuries before, farming had been carried on successfully in the Negev. The ruins of these ancient farms were still to be seen in the desert. The ancient farmers had succeeded by channeling water from large collection areas to much smaller growing areas on lower ground. Certainly, if the desert had been tamed centuries before, it could be tamed again.

▶ THE NEGEV IN BLOOM

Today the hopes of the first pioneers of the Negev have been realized. In many places where there was once only barren desert, the Negev is now dotted with farm villages.

How can farming succeed in a place with so very little rainfall? One way is by bringing in water from northern Israel, which gets more rainfall than the Negev. Great concrete cylinders were transported southward by rail and laid end to end. The segments of pipe were so huge and heavy that a single railroad freight car was needed to carry each cylinder.

Finally the huge pipeline was completed. Precious water gushed through to the farms of the Negev.

Important as it is, the water that can be furnished in this way is limited. Even northern Israel does not get a great deal of rain. In many places the farmers of the Negev are making do with the small amounts of rain that fall locally every year. They have studied the runoff systems of the ancient farmers and have adapted them to their own purposes.

The Negev soil in many places lends itself to runoff farming. It is a type of soil that quickly turns into a hard crust when it gets wet. The rain, therefore, runs off instead of seeping into the ground. By channeling the runoff, the farmers can collect enough water from a large area to sustain a much smaller growing area. The hard crust also prevents water from evaporating once it does sink into the ground. The water remains in the soil, where it can be reached by the roots of trees and crops.

The Israelis have found that they get better results by directing runoff rainfall into many small basins rather than into one large basin. In some orchards a small basin surrounds each tree. Each tree, in other words, is at the bottom of its own individual depression.

The Israelis have experimented extensively to find crops that can survive the Negev's drought conditions. A wide variety of fruits and vegetables have been found that can grow with runoff water as their only water source. Particular success has been achieved with certain varieties of almond and pistachio trees. Asparagus, with its deep, dense roots, has also been found to be a very efficient user of water. Various types of grasses have been found to grow well—in particular, wild oats. The Israelis have also pioneered research on crops irrigated with salty water, which sometimes is all that can be obtained from underground wells in the Negev.

Today, with much accomplished, the battle against the desert continues. Experimentation goes on. New settlers arrive, and the words of the prophet Isaiah are not forgotten: "Behold, I will do a new thing; now it shall spring forth; shall ye not know it? I will even make a way in the wilderness, and rivers in the desert."

The lifeline of the Negev—an irrigation pipe carrying water to the fields.

Young plants on a desert farm are shielded from the blazing sun by plastic.

A TURKISH TALE

Nasreddin Hodja and the Honored Guest

First let us say a few words about Nasreddin Hodja. There are scholars who claim that he actually lived at one time, and there are those who claim that he is a completely legendary figure. Even those who say that he existed differ about the time of his existence. Some place the Hodja, as he is at times called, as far back as the 9th century, and others bring him as close to us as five hundred years ago. But one thing is certain about the Hodja—he is Turkey's most famous, most wise, and most comic folk figure. There are hundreds of stories about Nasreddin Hodja, and even today a peasant or a city dweller will pause and smile and say in the middle of a conversation, "Now that reminds me of a Hodja story."

A few more words and then we will begin our tale. Picture to yourself a round figure, with a round face and merry but wise eyes, short white sideburns, and a white turban on a bald head. Set this round figure on an old, patient, and wise donkey and we are ready.

Early one morning, the Hodja left his house, mounted his donkey, rode a little way, and then turned in to his field. He dismounted, tied the donkey to a tree, and then started working. The whole day long he worked under a hot sun, digging and hoeing. When sunset came he was tired and thirsty. The old fellow sighed, straightened himself up, and then leaned his hoe against a gnarled tree stump.

"I'll work another hour, and then I shall go home and eat and rest," he said to himself.

But just then he heard the voice of his wife calling to him.

"Hodja! Come to the house."

The Hodja's wife, who had walked down the road, now stood at the edge of the field, waving to him. She was a small woman with bright little eyes and a voice that was clear and penetrating.

"Don't delay," she called again. "Come at once."

She stood there waiting patiently for him.

"All right," he murmured to himself.

"Hodja, it's late," he heard her call again.

"Late for what?" he said to himself.

He shrugged, mounted his donkey, and made his way slowly and wearily toward her, wondering what she wanted.

"Have you forgotten?" she cried out.

"Forgotten what?"

"Emir Hamil's feast."

"Oh." He had forgotten.

"You will be late. And look how you are dressed."

Anyone looking at him would have seen a round, weary figure in old, torn peasant clothes, face and hands grimy and sweaty.

"I've no time to change," Nasreddin Hodja said. "But I'm sure I'll be welcome as I am."

"I would advise you to change your clothes."

The Hodja shook his head.

"Don't be stubborn. Come to the house."

"I will go as I am."

So, just as he was, he mounted his old, wise, and patient donkey, and the two of them went their slow way to the big banquet. Every now and then the gray donkey would glance back at his rider and look at him with his big round eyes. Then the wise animal would shake his head sadly, as if to say to the Hodja, "You're in for a great surprise, a very great one, dear master."

And sure enough the Hodja was.

For when he entered the large banquet hall and found himself standing among the splendidly attired guests, a strange thing happened. No one seemed to recognize him. And the Emir, who was giving the banquet and who certainly knew Nasreddin Hodja, now pretended that he had never seen him before in all his life.

"Hello," the Hodja said, smiling at him. "Thanks for inviting me to your most . . ."

But the Emir merely turned away—he didn't even wait for the Hodja to finish his sentence—he just turned his back on the grimy old man and began talking to his other guests.

"H'm," thought the Hodja. "This is strange. Strange and most shameful."

And it became even more shameful when he found that there was no place for him to sit.

This was too much for Nasreddin Hodja. So he left the banquet and mounted his donkey and went home.

"What happened?" his wife asked anxiously.

He stood a while, deep in thought, not answering her.

"What happened, Hodja?" she asked again.

"Nothing," he said quietly. "But something is soon going to happen."

Then he left her and bathed and scrubbed himself till his very skin sparkled. He dressed himself in his best clothes. Then he asked his wife to bring him his splendid coat.

"How do I look now?" he asked her.

"Better than the Emir himself," she said.

"Good."

Then he went out to his patient, old, and wise donkey and stood before him.

"Well?"

The old animal inspected the Hodja with his huge round eyes and then slowly nodded, once, then twice.

"Good," the Hodja said. "Now back to the Emir's banquet."

When the Hodja reached the Emir's house the banquet was in full swing. The quests were eating, and talking with great laughter and animation. But when the Hodja entered, all eyes turned to him.

"Ah, here is Nasreddin Hodja," the Emir said.

He hurried over and embraced him.

"How splendid you look. Have you just arrived?"

"Yes," the Hodja said, knowing full well that the Emir knew that he had been there before.

The Emir turned to the gathering and called out in a loud and clear voice.

"All give welcome to our honored guest, Nasreddin Hodja!"

The hall echoed with the welcome.

"And now you must come with me and sit at my side, most honored guest," the Emir said.

"I'll be glad to," said the Hodja.

As he escorted the Hodja to the place of honor he said to him, "Your coat is very admirable. I've never seen one so handsome before."

"I'm glad you like it," the Hodja said.

And so he sat quietly until the food was served to him. And then he did the most extraordinary of things. He took a piece of veal and put it into his coat pocket, saying: "Here, Coat, this is for you."

Then he took some grapes and did the same, saying: "I hope you like these fresh grapes."

By now all the other guests were sitting silent and stunned, watching him.

The Emir's face had turned white with astonishment. But he was speechless.

The Hodja picked up an olive and was about to put it into the pocket of the coat when the Emir cried out, "What are you doing? Have you gone mad?"

The Hodja turned to him and then said calmly:

"No. Not at all. I'm feeding the coat. After all, it was the coat, not me, that you invited to the banquet."

With that, the Hodja got up and left them. He came out to the wise donkey and looked at him triumphantly. The donkey grinned and slowly nodded.

Then they went home.

MIDDLE EASTERN KITCHENS

Visitors to the countries of the Middle East are always impressed by the beautiful relics of the past—the noble statuary, the splendid mosques, the majestic pyramids, and, in contrast to those great monuments, the delicately wrought handicrafts. But a feast for the eyes is not quite enough. People must also eat. And to satisfy this need, Middle Eastern kitchens produce an array of hearty dishes, fragrant with herbs and spices.

Although the Middle East is made up of a number of distinct, independent countries, there is an underlying unity among their various cuisines. The chief influence in Middle Eastern cooking is that of the Turks, whose Ottoman Empire at its most powerful stretched from central Europe to the Arabian Peninsula and included a large part of North Africa. During the period of conquest and expansion, the Turks took their cooking traditions with them. These basic traditions still remain, but over the years they have been mingled with native cooking styles and adapted to suit local tastes.

About half the people of the Middle East are Arabs, united by the religion of Islam and the Arabic language. Muslims consider hospitality and the cooking and serving of food very important. An Arab saying, "The food equals the affection," means, in practice, that the Arab host will serve twice as much food as can be eaten, and guests can prove their fondness for the host only by overeating.

The food staples of the modern Middle Eastern countries are sheep and wheat. When an Arab speaks of meat he means lamb or mutton. Goat, camel, and some fish are eaten, but poultry and meat are more popular. Muslims are forbidden to eat pork or drink alcoholic beverages. On special occasions, small, stuffed whole lambs are roasted on the spit, preferably over charcoal.

The meat of older lambs and of sheep is used in a variety of dishes—stews rich with vegetables; kibbeh, ground lamb beaten together with a cracked wheat cereal called bulgur; couscous, the cereal dish of North Africa, steamed with meat, poultry, or fish; moussaka, a Greek dish made with ground lamb and eggplant. Shish kebab, chunks of meat and vegetables threaded on a skewer and grilled over a fire, is one of the glories of Middle Eastern cooking that has found its way into kitchens all over the world.

For thousands of years a bread called pita has been the mainstay of the Middle East. Made of wheat flour and leavened with yeast, this round, flat Arab bread takes the place of cutlery. Bite-sized pieces are torn from the bread and used to scoop up food.

The hot climates of all the Middle Eastern countries make it difficult to keep foods fresh, so milk is replaced by yogurt, which may appear as a breakfast dish eaten with bread, or as a between-meal snack, or diluted with water as a drink. Clarified butter, known as ghee, can keep for months without refrigeration and is used in cooking and baking.

The most commonly used vegetables are eggplants, tomatoes, green peppers, cucumbers, and onions. Several of them are frequently mixed together into various kinds of salads, called salata. In the Mediterranean area, olives, figs, dates, and lemons grow abundantly and are used lavishly. Pomegranate juice is a first-rate breakfast drink, and the seeds are used in soups, salads, and ground meat. Spices such as cumin, saffron, coriander, cloves, and cinnamon are used in every kind of dish from meats to sweets.

A Middle Eastern dinner begins with appetizers, which may range from a dish of olives and scallions to a wealth of mouthwatering tidbits—hummus bi tahina (a puree of chick-peas and sesame paste); baba ghannooj (seasoned eggplant puree); dolmas (grape leaves stuffed, usually with rice, meat, and seasonings); pickled vegetables.

The Middle East has a king-sized sweet tooth. Crisp cookies bathed in honey and sprinkled with nuts; baklava, flaky pastry oozing with melted butter, honey, and chopped nuts; sweet puddings fragrant with rose water; and halvah, a confection of crushed sesame seeds and honey, are among popular favorites.

No meal ends without many servings of sweet, thick black coffee sipped from tiny cups, or sweet mint tea, drunk iced in summer or hot in winter.

Assorted appetizers from a Middle Eastern kitchen: From left—a plate of olives; salata with dressing; scallions, feta cheese, and olives; kibbeh; pita bread; and hummus bi tahina. In the center are dolmas.

39

THE HARRANIA TAPESTRIES

The tapestries pictured here were made by quite ordinary children—which is one of the extraordinary things about them. Ramses Wissa Wassef, a professor at the University of Cairo, Egypt, built a workshop in the village of Harrania. There he gathered the local children, taught them the mechanics of weaving—and left them alone. The children were not allowed to see any works of art. No one was allowed to criticize their work or advise them about it. They were not allowed to draw any preliminary sketches. They just went ahead and wove the everyday things they saw about them. And these young Egyptians, most of them under ten years of age, made the tapestries pictured here.

The Procession, by Garia Mahmoud

The Land of the Nile, by Chehaba Hamza

Bedouins and Their Herds, by Ali Selim

41

In accordance with custom, these Bedouin males share food from a common bowl.

THE WANDERING PEOPLES

Millions of people in the Middle East today still follow a way of life that is thousands of years old: they are wanderers, or nomads. Among these tribes of wanderers the chief groups are the Arab nomads, who are called Bedouins. They are herders. They raise sheep, camels, and goats, and sometimes cattle, donkeys, horses, and chickens. The Bedouin travels in search of two things: water for himself and his animals to drink; and shrubs and grass for his animals to eat.

The Bedouin lives almost entirely off his animals. They furnish him with meat and milk, and, through trade, with money to buy the other foodstuffs he needs, such as grain, sugar, and tea. The animals also furnish the materials for his garments. Camel and goat hair can be woven into tents and rugs. The camel also provides transportation.

The Bedouin does not wander about for the pleasure of it. His life is hard. Through much of the Middle East, water and grazing land are scarce. If the Bedouin stayed in one place, the animals on which he depends would soon eat up all the grass and shrubs, and then starve. Moving from place to place enables the Bedouin not only to survive, but to maintain fairly large herds.

The Bedouin does not simply wander about at random. There is a very logical pattern to his movements. If there were not, his way of life could not have lasted for thousands of years. Still, there are signs today that the Bedouin way of life is coming to an end.

▶ MOVING WITH THE SEASONS

In the Middle East the amount of water and grazing available varies from season to

42

Not all of the Middle East's nomads are Bedouins. These people are Iranian nomads whose way of life is beginning to change. The children above are going to school for the first time—although classes are held in a tent. The woman below has never been to school, but her daughter will go to a tent school.

season. Throughout much of the region there are three main seasons. The longest of these is a hot, dry season of about five months. It is followed by a cool, wet season of about three months, in which almost all the rain falls. Then there is a cold, dry season. The basic aim of the Bedouin is to get as many animals as possible through the hot, dry season, so that he can take advantage of the other two seasons.

In the hot, dry season, water is scarce. But because of the heat the animals need more water than at other times and can go only a short while without it. During these months, the herds have to be kept in areas where there are wells. Herders can live with their families, since the animals cannot graze very far from the wells. Also, a lot of water has to be brought up from the underground wells by hand, and the herders need the help of their families for this.

Toward the end of the hot, dry season, the herders drive the herds away from the well areas. Perhaps the rains have already started somewhere else. The herders are in a hurry to leave the used-up grazing lands near the wells and move on to fresh pastures where the rain has already begun. Most of the tribe remain behind. They will only leave to join the herders a month or so later, when the rains are falling hard, there are numerous rainpools to furnish all the water the tribe needs, and there is no need to worry about wells.

By about the middle of the rainy season, the households join the herders. This is the easiest time of year. Water is plentiful, and there is no need to move around a lot. The yield of milk is highest at this time. There is plenty for everybody and even an excess that can be made into butter. The women help their husbands with the considerable work involved in the birth of lambs.

When the rains end, the households make their way slowly back to the area where the wells are. It is still far too early for the herds to return, however. If they returned now they would exhaust the pasturage around the wells that must get them through the dry, hot season. Since it is cold now, the herds can go a fairly long time without water. For the next few months the herds wander through the cold desert, grazing on the juicy grasses and herbs that grow there. The herders can drink the animals' milk. The herders put off the return to the wells until the need for water forces them back, at which time the cycle begins all over again.

▶ A DYING WAY OF LIFE

Although millions of people in the Middle East still live in this way, their numbers are diminishing. Indeed, before long, a way of life that has gone on for thousands of years may have died out.

The wanderings of the Bedouin enable him to make a living in a hard land. But the Bedouin way of life does not fit in with the desire of Middle Eastern governments to modernize agriculture as well as life in general. Bedouins need to wander over large areas. They are often careless of property lines or cultivated fields or even national boundaries. Wandering about as they do, Bedouins are a very hard people to educate or supervise.

Recently Middle Eastern governments have been trying to get the nomads to settle down. In Iran, for example, the government has been recruiting young tribesmen and giving them crash courses in education, health, and modern stock-breeding techniques. The young men then go back to their tribes, where, it is hoped, they will introduce higher standards of education and health among the nomads and encourage stock-breeding practices that will make for a more settled life.

Even without programs like these, the attractions of modern life may put an end to the Bedouins' wanderings. The nomadic life is hard, and Bedouins may be more willing than one would expect to give it up. One reporter recently wrote that, in the desert, camels and stallions are being replaced by jeeps as status symbols. Another reporter told about a 1,300-mile (2,100-kilometer) camel trip he had taken across northern Saudi Arabia and Jordan. His Bedouin companions had not ridden camels in 10 years. The camels weakened and had to be replaced during the journey, and the guides constantly lost their way. Even the Bedouins he met along the way were becoming more and more settled and were no longer interested in the ancient work of breeding camels.

UNITED ARAB EMIRATES

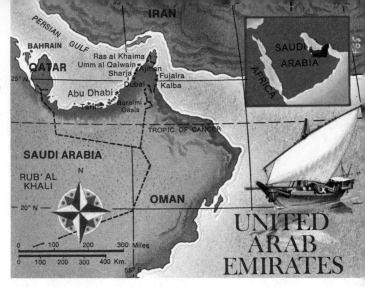

The United Arab Emirates is a union of seven small states, each ruled by an emir, or prince, lying along the Persian Gulf coast of the Arabian Peninsula. The seven states are Abu Dhabi, Dubai (Dibai), Sharja, Ajman, Umm al Qaiwain, Ras al Khaima, and Fujaira. The region has a colorful history. At one time it was known for pearls and for pirates. More recently, oil has been found in enormous quantities, particularly in Abu Dhabi. The discovery of great oil reserves has had a tremendous impact. It has brought great wealth to a country with almost no natural resources, except for oil, and very little usable land. And it has transformed a quiet, traditional society into one trying to modernize itself almost overnight.

▶ THE PEOPLE

The United Arab Emirates has a population estimated at about 300,000. The two most populous emirates are Dubai and Abu Dhabi, which between them have more than half the people in the country. Most of the people are Arabs. A majority belong to the Sunni branch of Islam, which has the greatest number of followers throughout the Muslim world. Indians, Iranians, Pakistanis, and Africans are found in the coastal towns, especially in Dubai, the largest and most important town, and in Abu Dhabi, the provisional capital of the new country. (The chief town of each of the emirates has the same name as the emirate itself.)

Arabic is the language spoken by most of the people of the seven emirates. Other languages, including Persian and English, are also used, particularly in the coastal towns.

The presence of a variety of peoples is due in part to the fact that Dubai has always been an important trading center and a point for the transshipment of goods. Slavery, which was common in past centuries, also brought foreigners to the area. The growth of the oil industry has seen a great rush of immigration to the country in the last few years.

The traditional way of life of the people depended largely on where they lived. In the coastal towns trading, fishing, and pearling were the usual occupations. In the interior lived the settled farmers and the nomadic Bedouin. The farmers eked out a living from the generally inhospitable soil; the Bedouin traveled from place to place seeking grazing land and water for their flocks of sheep and goats.

But traditional ways of life have been radically altered by the oil boom. Farmers and Bedouin alike have been leaving the country to come to the towns and to work in the rapidly expanding oil industry. These changes have been taking place most quickly in Abu Dhabi, where the richest oil deposits have been found, and to a lesser extent in Dubai. The other emirates have been much less affected.

▶ THE LAND

The area of the United Arab Emirates is estimated at 32,278 square miles (83,600 square kilometers). However, as in many of the states of the Arabian Peninsula, some borders are in dispute. It is a sickle-shaped strip of land, largely barren and flat, relieved only by occasional oases and by a mountain range in the eastern part of the country. A low, sandy coastal plain extends for some 400 miles (644 km.) along the Persian Gulf between Qatar and Oman. Most of the towns are situated on this coastal plain. In the interior the land merges into the Rub' al Khali, or Empty Quarter, the vast, forbidding desert of Saudi Arabia.

One of the few fertile areas of any size is the Buraimi oasis, which Abu Dhabi shares

Dinner is served in a home in Abu Dhabi.

with Oman. It has about ten villages consisting of some 12,000 people.

The climate is very hot, with summer temperatures of 120 degrees Fahrenheit (49 degrees Celsius) in the shade not unusual. Rainfall amounts to only a few inches a year, except in the eastern mountains, which is also a relatively fertile region.

▶ ECONOMY

Until the discovery of oil, the economy of the country was based mainly on trading, fishing, and pearling. Agriculture was limited to subsistence farming, in which a farmer grew only enough food to feed himself and his family. Only the emirate of Dubai was developed commercially, because Dubai town was important to Persian Gulf trade. Today oil, especially the oil reserves of Abu Dhabi, has made the United Arab Emirates one of the wealthiest countries in the world. Money from oil has been used to improve health and education and for economic development projects, including a water desalting plant. Some of the oil revenues are shared with the less fortunate emirates, in four of which no oil has yet been found.

▶ HISTORY AND GOVERNMENT

The region in which the United Arab Emirates is located came to the attention of European powers in the 16th and 17th centuries. First the Portuguese, followed by the Dutch, French, and British, sought commercial advantages there. When Great Britain became supreme in the Persian Gulf, it found widespread piracy was interfering with its trade and shipping. The British crushed the activities of the pirates and in the 19th century signed a series of treaties, or truces, with the local sheikhs, the Arab leaders. Because of these truces the seven emirates came to be known as the Trucial States or Trucial Oman. Near the end of the 19th century, the British, to strengthen their influence in the area, signed a more binding treaty with the Trucial States, similar to treaties signed with other Persian Gulf states. Thus the Trucial States came under the protection of Great Britain and remained so until 1971, when the Trucial States became completely independent as the United Arab Emirates. An attempt was made to unite the seven emirates with the small nearby states of Bahrain and Qatar, but nothing came of this.

Upon independence, the emir of Abu Dhabi became the first president of the union. Both the president and vice-president serve 5-year terms. The head of government is the prime minister, who heads a council of ministers. The rulers of all the states are represented in legislative councils, and each ruler has great power in his own emirate.

Reviewed by Majid Khadduri
School of Advanced International Studies
The Johns Hopkins University

Students from different backgrounds mingle at IC in Lebanon.

BEIRUT INTERNATIONAL COLLEGE

The Middle East is at the crossroads of the world. It is the place where many religions, languages, and cultures meet. Because of this, it is a fascinating part of the world. But it is also a troubled place. It is harder for people of diverse backgrounds to understand each other than it is for people of the same background. And the Middle East is a place where young people of different backgrounds are always meeting. The Beirut International College, in Lebanon, is a unique experiment, and one that has worked. It is a place where young people with different religious, ethnic, and cultural backgrounds live, work, and study together. It is living proof that cultures can mix and enrich each other.

IC, as the school has been informally called since it was founded in 1872, has two campuses. One is in Beirut, and the other is outside the city. The students, more than 2,000 girls and boys, ranging in age from four to twenty, come from 40 nationalities and 15 religious groups. Classes are taught in French, English, and Arabic. Teachers at this unusual Middle Eastern school come from Europe, America, and countries throughout the Middle East.

Admission to IC is granted without regard to national or religious background. All the classes and social activities are integrated. As a result, students must soon give up their prejudices or remain alone. Experience has shown that most IC students quickly forget about race, color, and creed. As one young Jordanian said, "When you are studying together you see how ridiculous most of your prejudices are, really."

Youngsters at IC learn each other's languages.

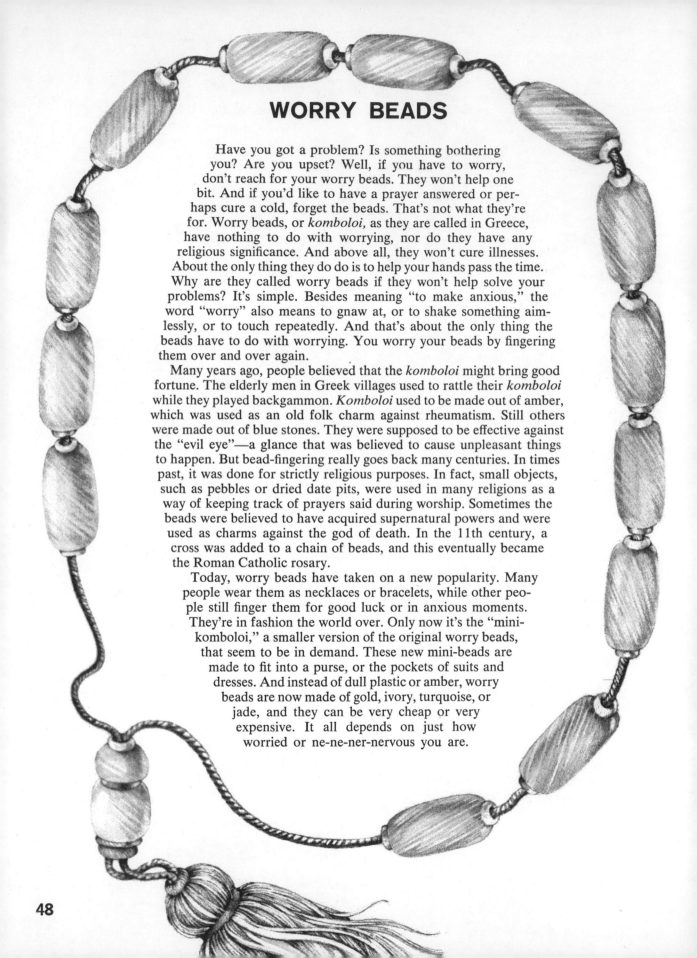

WORRY BEADS

Have you got a problem? Is something bothering you? Are you upset? Well, if you have to worry, don't reach for your worry beads. They won't help one bit. And if you'd like to have a prayer answered or perhaps cure a cold, forget the beads. That's not what they're for. Worry beads, or *komboloi,* as they are called in Greece, have nothing to do with worrying, nor do they have any religious significance. And above all, they won't cure illnesses. About the only thing they do do is to help your hands pass the time. Why are they called worry beads if they won't help solve your problems? It's simple. Besides meaning "to make anxious," the word "worry" also means to gnaw at, or to shake something aimlessly, or to touch repeatedly. And that's about the only thing the beads have to do with worrying. You worry your beads by fingering them over and over again.

Many years ago, people believed that the *komboloi* might bring good fortune. The elderly men in Greek villages used to rattle their *komboloi* while they played backgammon. *Komboloi* used to be made out of amber, which was used as an old folk charm against rheumatism. Still others were made out of blue stones. They were supposed to be effective against the "evil eye"—a glance that was believed to cause unpleasant things to happen. But bead-fingering really goes back many centuries. In times past, it was done for strictly religious purposes. In fact, small objects, such as pebbles or dried date pits, were used in many religions as a way of keeping track of prayers said during worship. Sometimes the beads were believed to have acquired supernatural powers and were used as charms against the god of death. In the 11th century, a cross was added to a chain of beads, and this eventually became the Roman Catholic rosary.

Today, worry beads have taken on a new popularity. Many people wear them as necklaces or bracelets, while other people still finger them for good luck or in anxious moments. They're in fashion the world over. Only now it's the "mini-komboloi," a smaller version of the original worry beads, that seem to be in demand. These new mini-beads are made to fit into a purse, or the pockets of suits and dresses. And instead of dull plastic or amber, worry beads are now made of gold, ivory, turquoise, or jade, and they can be very cheap or very expensive. It all depends on just how worried or ne-ne-ner-nervous you are.

A TALE FROM THE ARABIAN NIGHTS

The Prince and His Magic Horse

Many, many years ago there lived a king, a most powerful king, who had but one son, whom he loved dearly. The Prince was tall and handsome and brave, and every maiden of the land wished to become his bride. But the Prince loved none of them. Not one maiden had gladdened his eye or touched his heart. The Prince would have nothing to do with any of them. The King, who longed for a grandchild, was very unhappy. One day a great festival was held in honor of the Prince's twenty-first birthday. People came from all over the kingdom bearing gifts. Three wise men appeared, each with a wondrous gift. The first gift was a peacock made of shining gold; the second gift was a silver trumpet that sparkled like white fire; and the third gift was a magnificent horse carved from the purest ivory, with a mane and tail of blackest ebony.

It was the horse that appealed to the Prince most of all, for the wise man claimed that it was a magic horse. By pressing a button on the horse's saddle, the rider could make the horse soar into the sky. The wise man urged the Prince to ride the magic horse. But for some strange reason, a reason he could not explain, the King did not trust the wise man. He tried to stop his son from mounting the magic horse. He begged and pleaded with the Prince not to do it. But the prince was a headstrong fellow. Once his mind was made up, no power on earth could stop him. So he leaped into the saddle, pressed the button, and before the astonished eyes of all the onlookers the horse rose lightly into the air and carried the Prince away.

The King turned furiously on the wise man and demanded to know what had become of the Prince. The wise man refused to speak, and the King ordered him thrown into a dungeon. Then the King sat down on his golden throne in despair, waiting for his beloved son to return.

The young Prince sat easily upon his magic horse, and a great joy surged through him. How wonderful it was to ride into the blue sky, passing through the white clouds and listening to the loud song of the wind!

The ivory horse galloped gracefully along through the darkness of the night and into the early hours of the next morning. Finally the sun rose, bright and strong, and there in its rays the Prince saw the golden domes of a magnificent palace. He gently pressed the button and murmured to his magic horse, "Descend, O faithful animal."

The Prince tethered the horse in a small, grassy glade not very far from the palace. He then quietly made his way to the doors of the palace. It was still early morning, and everyone in the palace was asleep. He walked through hallway after hallway, and soon found himself standing before the silken curtains of an inner chamber. The Prince softly drew the curtains aside, looked into the room, and paused, breathless. For there, lying asleep on a golden couch, was the most beautiful maiden he had ever seen.

He just stood and gazed at her for a few moments. Then he walked over and gently touched her. Her large eyes opened. And the instant their eyes met, the two fell in love.

The two happy young people went to the maiden's father, who was also a king. The Prince bowed and said to the King:

"I am a king's son. I should like to take your daughter to my land, and there we shall marry."

The King, who was very pleased with the nobility and grace of the Prince, immediately gave his consent. The very next morning, the Prince and his beloved made their way to the glade where the horse was tethered. They mounted the magic horse together and rose into the sky.

With incredible speed the magic horse brought the lovers closer to the homeland of the Prince. As they approached, the Prince said to his beloved:

"There is a summer palace just on the outskirts of the city. You shall stay there while I go and see my father and prepare for our marriage celebration."

But a great fear came over her.

She said to him, "No. Do not leave me. Please take me with you."

He shook his head sadly.

"It is the custom of my people. The way must be prepared for the bride."

So it was arranged.

The King wept for joy when he saw his returning son. And when the Prince told his father that he had fallen in love and wished to marry, the King cried out in delight.

"You shall have the greatest wedding in the history of our land. I must see your bride. Go bring your maiden to my palace at once."

Now the wise man—who had been released from prison at the safe return of the prince—hurried to the summer palace. He carried a fierce hatred in his heart for the King and the Prince.

When he found the eagerly waiting Princess, he said to her, "I am sent to bring you to the King. And here is the magic horse to take us."

But once they were mounted on the horse the evil wise man pressed the button, and the magic creature carried them high into the heavens. In a short while they were thousands of miles away from the land of the Prince.

When the Prince learned of his loved one's disappearance he cried in grief and despair.

Finally, he rose and said, "I will search the world over for her, search till my hair turns white with age, but I will find my beloved again."

Now when the gods of fortune and love come upon a devotion like this, they are forced to smile in its favor. And so it happened that the Prince came to a city far away. And there he learned that his Princess had been sold to the Sultan. He also learned that she was ill, but that as soon as her illness was cured, she would be forced to marry the all-powerful Sultan.

"Never!" the Prince swore to himself.

He disguised himself as a physician and appeared before the Sultan.

"You have a horse of ebony and of ivory," he said to the Sultan. For the Prince had learned that the cruel Sultan had killed the wise man and taken the horse from him. But the Sultan did not know that the horse was a magic creature.

"What do you want with it?" the Sultan asked.

"I want to place the sick maiden on it. Then I shall show you how she can be cured."

So the horse and Princess were brought to the courtyard of the Sultan's palace.

"I shall now place the maiden on the horse and you shall see the cure, O mighty Sultan," the Prince announced.

As soon as the Princess was on the horse, the Prince mounted behind her. He pressed the button, and the magic creature soared into the air, amid the angry shouts of the Sultan and his people. The magic horse rose higher and higher into the blue sky. Soon the two lovers were home again, and there they had the greatest wedding in the history of the kingdom.

And, of course, they lived happily ever after.

THE OLDEST SONG IN THE WORLD

When did music begin? Until recently, scholars believed that music began in China several thousand years ago. They thought that Western music began independently in Greece somewhat later, about 400 B.C. In 1974, however, the oldest known song in the world was performed for the first time since 1800 B.C. And it was clearly Western music. With that single performance the beginning of Western music history was pushed back at least 1,400 years.

The extraordinary event became possible about twenty years ago, when archeologists discovered the fragments of a clay tablet at a place called Ras Shamra, in Syria. The tablet had inscriptions in the cuneiform writing that was used in Assyria and Babylonia. Assyria and Babylonia were ancient civilizations in the Middle East.

In 1972 an expert on Assyrian civilization was finally able to decipher the symbols. The first four of the ten lines of writing on the tablet are the words of what is believed to be a song written to gods and goddesses. The last six lines on the tablet describe how the music is to be played. When the melody was reconstructed from these musical notations, it was found to be written in the familiar seven-tone scale of Western music.

Next, a physicist built a working reproduction of a lyre, an ancient musical instrument. He based his reconstruction on fragments of a lyre dating back to 2600 B.C. that had been discovered 50 years earlier in Iraq. Now the preparations were complete.

The historic performance took place on March 25, 1974, at the University of California at Berkeley. There, before a specially selected audience, Professor of Music History Richard L. Crocker seated himself at the lyre. He began to play and sing.

"Hamutu niyasa ziwe sinute," he sang. The words were certainly strange, but the soft music sounded like a lullaby. The music continued for three minutes, returning again and again to the chorus, "Kalipanil nikala." Some of the strange words have been translated and

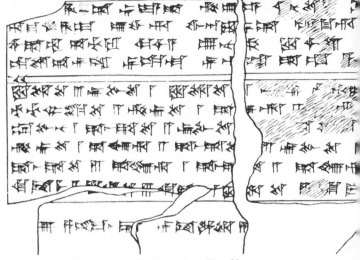

Part of the clay tablet found at Ras Shamra.

found to be terms of love and references to gods and goddesses.

The performance was a huge success. It established without question that the Western music tradition arose in the Middle East.

Is the song destined to become a classic? Well, most agree that it is definitely "number one" chronologically, if not on the Hit Parade.

Richard L. Crocker plays the oldest song.

QATAR

Qatar is a small Arab country in the part of the world known as the Middle East. It is situated on the eastern—or Persian Gulf—side of the Arabian Peninsula. Officially, it is the State of Qatar. It covers a desert peninsula, also named Qatar, that juts northward into the gulf. To the south Qatar is bordered by the Kingdom of Saudi Arabia and by Abu Dhabi, which belongs to a union of small states known as the United Arab Emirates.

Like its neighbors, Qatar has rich oil deposits. And the production of oil, since the 1950's, has made Qatar a prosperous country. This prosperity, in turn, has changed the way of life of the people. For centuries the people had lived in small fishing villages along the coast or tended herds of camels in the dry inland areas. Now the majority of the people live and work in the bustling capital city of Doha (al-Dawha).

▶ THE PEOPLE

All the activity that is changing Qatar into a modern state has brought a steady stream of immigrants, mostly from other Arab countries. In the total population of some 150,000, people born in Qatar and other Arabs far outnumber the groups that have come from Iran, India, Pakistan, and other countries of the world. Arabic is the official language of Qatar, as well as the language of the majority of the people. But English also is used, especially in government and business. Most of the people are Muslims, or believers in Islam, which is the official religion.

Most Qataris prefer the traditional dress of the Arab countries—long, loose, light-weight robes and head coverings, which give protection from the sun and windblown sand. But workers in the oil industry and in government and business offices in Doha often wear Western-style dress. In Doha, which is situated on the eastern coast of Qatar, many changes have been made since the 1950's. Doha has a new deepwater port, desalting plants to provide fresh water, wide streets crowded with traffic, modern air-conditioned shops, and gracefully designed public buildings. Other main centers of activity in Qatar are Dukhan, a town on the western coast surrounded by oil fields, and Umm Said, a port for oil tankers, south of Doha. Umm Said's industries include a flour mill and a fertilizer plant.

Income from oil has made it possible for the government to provide a growing number of services for the people of Qatar. The system of free public schools is divided into three levels—primary (6 years), preparatory (3 years), and secondary (3 years). Students in the secondary schools may receive training in technical or commercial subjects, so that they will be prepared to work in various trades or in business and government offices. Colleges for the training of teachers were opened in 1973, and the government pays the expenses of qualified students who wish to study at universities in foreign countries. Other services include medical and hospital care and housing for low-income families.

▶ THE LAND

The Qatar peninsula, which is about 100 miles (160 kilometers) long and less than half as wide, contains an area of about 4,000 square miles (10,400 square kilometers).

FACTS AND FIGURES

STATE OF QATAR is the official name of the country.

CAPITAL: Doha.

LOCATION: Eastern coast of the Arabian Peninsula.

AREA: About 4,000 sq. mi. (10,400 sq. km.).

POPULATION: 150,000 (estimate).

LANGUAGE: Arabic.

RELIGION: Islam.

GOVERNMENT: Emirate. **Head of state and government**—emir. **International co-operation**—United Nations, Arab League.

ECONOMY: Agricultural products—vegetables. **Industries and products**—oil, natural gas, fertilizer, cement, flour, fish. **Chief minerals**—oil, natural gas. **Chief exports**—crude oil. **Chief imports**—construction machinery, foodstuffs, motor vehicles, building materials, cloth and clothing, electrical goods, air-conditioning machinery, livestock, radio and television sets. **Monetary unit**—Qatar riyal.

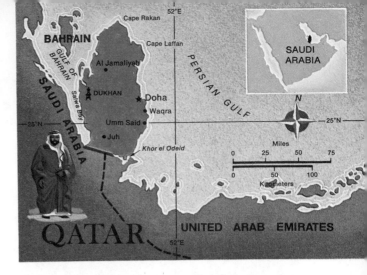

The state also includes some small islands. On the west Qatar is bordered by parts of the Persian Gulf called Salwa Bay and the Gulf of Bahrain. The State of Bahrain, an Arab country made up of islands, is situated in those waters northwest of Qatar.

Except for limestone ridges on the western coast, the land surface of Qatar is flat. Loose sand covers much of the southern half of the peninsula. Rainfall, which is very slight, comes only in the winter months of December through March. The summer months are hot and humid.

Natural vegetation is found around wells in the northern part of the country and in low places after rains. Elsewhere there are only small patches of a shrub called camel thorn and a few date palms. The main kinds of animal life are camels and birds such as flamingos and ospreys. The chief natural resource is oil, which is found both on the land and offshore. Other resources are natural gas, limestone, and clay.

ECONOMY

Qatar's national income is obtained almost entirely from the production of oil. But the government is taking steps to establish a variety of industries so that the country will have other sources of income. Factories for packaging frozen fish and for producing fertilizer, flour, and cement were in operation by the early 1970's. Plans then were made for refining oil and making various products based on oil and natural gas. Although the development of agriculture is difficult in a desert country, the government provides free seeds and insecticides and helps the people find ways to manage the land so that some crops can be grown. As a result, Qatar produces enough vegetables for its own use and also exports some, especially tomatoes, to neighboring countries.

The development of transportation, communications, and electric power has been a great help to the economy. Doha's man-made port can accommodate oceangoing ships, and jumbo jets can land at the Doha international airport. New roads connect the capital city with other parts of the country and with Saudi Arabia, and a system of pipelines has been built to carry oil and gas. A government-owned radio and television station broadcasts within Qatar and to other states on the shores of the Persian Gulf.

HISTORY AND GOVERNMENT

Qatar became a completely independent country in 1971. Between that time and 1916, it had been under the protection of Great Britain. That is, Qatar had signed a treaty giving Britain control of its foreign affairs in return for British defense of its territory. The treaty recognized a sheikh (Arab chief) of the al-Thani family as the ruler of the country. Members of that family had been leaders in Qatar since the early 1800's. When Britain announced that it would end the treaty, Qatar prepared for independence by drawing up a provisional constitution in 1970. This constitution, which was later revised, states that the emir, or ruler, shall be a member of the al-Thani family. It provides for a council of ministers, or cabinet, to assist the emir, and an advisory council.

In earlier times the rulers of Bahrain had governed Qatar, but in 1868 the British helped in negotiations that brought an end to Bahrain's claims to Qatar. Then in the 1870's the Ottoman Turks, who controlled what is now Saudi Arabia, extended their control into Qatar and established a garrison, or military post, at Doha. The British expelled this garrison in 1916 and signed the treaty that brought Qatar under British protection. This treaty was ended in 1971, and Qatar declared its independence on September 3 of that year.

Reviewed by MAJID KHADDURI
School of Advanced International Studies
The Johns Hopkins University

WORLD OF SCIENCE

EXPO'74 · US1
PRESERVE THE ENVIRON

A United States stamp honoring EXPO '74.

Expo '74, seen from across the Spokane River.

Exuberant crowds at the opening-day ceremonies.

EXPO '74

On May 4, 1974, an international exposition opened in Spokane, Washington. There have been many international expositions and fairs in the last few years—but Expo '74 was truly unique. The theme of the exposition was Celebrating Tomorrow's Fresh New Environment. Ecology, in fact, was what Expo '74 was all about. The participating nations had exhibits and demonstrations of their latest methods of dealing with environmental problems at home. Expo '74 was really a forum, in which people from all over the world could trade ideas about their common problems and, in so doing, learn a great deal.

But Expo '74 was also a lot of fun. There was delicious food from all over the world and there were unusual rides and games. There were also performances by leading actors, dancers, and singers from countries all over the world. In fact, Expo '74 was a special world in itself.

Although the host nation of Expo '74 was the United States, a number of other countries were deeply involved in making it possible. Australia, Canada, the Republic of China (Taiwan), Iran, Japan, Korea, the Philippines, the Soviet Union, and the German Federal Republic (West Germany) all had pavilions at Spokane. Each national or regional pavilion treated ecology and the environment in a different and often unique way.

▶ THE UNITED STATES AND CANADA

Each of the pavilions at Expo '74 had something special to say about the environment. The exhibits set up by the United States and Canada were especially elaborate—and interesting. Both countries still have vast wilderness areas that they are struggling to preserve. Both countries are also interested in industrial development and in finding ways to move forward without further destroying the ecological balance.

The United States pavilion (it would cover two football fields) was divided into three basic areas, each with a different theme. One section was devoted to Environmental Problems and another to The Consumer and the Environment, and a third was an Environmental Action Center. Each section had exhibits and films. The Consumer and the Environment actually had a 1-acre (0.4-hectare) garden in which several environmental problems were illustrated. One of the most popular features of the United States pavilion was an 800-seat theater. In it, films dealing with the environment were shown on a giant screen 65 feet (20 meters) high and 95 feet (29 m.) wide.

In addition to the main United States pavilion, there were many other American exhibits of interest to everyone. The Vanishing Animals Exhibit was especially appealing. Members of endangered species of animals were exhibited there. They included the Siberian tiger; the gray, or timber, wolf; and the nene, or Hawaiian goose. There was also a special nursery for baby animals that had been deserted by their mothers. Visitors could actually watch the staff feeding and caring for the little animals.

The United States also sponsored a Folk Life Festival. The theme of this festival was the life of people who still make their living from the land. Sheep herders, lumberjacks, farmers, and other outdoor workers were actually on hand to greet visitors and explain their jobs.

Another popular United States exhibit was a transportation center set up by the General Motors Corporation. The most popular part of the exhibit was the "people mover," a new means of mass transportation designed to reduce pollution by decreasing the use of cars and buses. This odd-looking vehicle, a 5-foot-long (1.5-meter-long) capsule, carried four to six passengers. It was powered by electricity, and its operation was computerized so that no driver was necessary.

Expo '74 was built on the banks of the Spokane River. The Canadian pavilions were on an island in the river's rapids. The island was planted with trees and shrubs from all over Canada.

Two Canadian provinces, British Columbia and Alberta, had their own pavilions on the island. The British Columbia pavilion contained a spectacular photographic exhibit of the province's natural environment—including everything from tiny insects to breathtak-

"THE EARTH DOES NOT BELONG TO MAN, MAN BELONGS TO THE EARTH"

"THE LAND, ITS MINERAL WEALTH, WATERS, FORESTS, FACTORIES... ARE STATE PROPERTY, THAT IS, BELONG TO THE WHOLE PEOPLE." CONSTITUTION OF THE USSR, ARTICLE 6

Both the United States pavilion (*left*) and the Soviet pavilion (*right*) expressed the theme of Expo '74—save our environment.

ing aerial views of vast stretches of wilderness. British Columbia also brought together an exhibition of local crafts and craftsmen. There were artists of all kinds, carvers, and weavers—all of whom gave demonstrations of how they worked.

The province of Alberta made a unique contribution to Expo '74. Alberta built two unusual theaters. A man-made hill was constructed. An indoor theater was concealed inside the hill, and an outdoor amphitheater was built against the hill. These theaters provided stages for performers from Alberta and other parts of Canada. Documentary films on the environment were made in Alberta and

shown in the theaters. Canada's famous Royal Canadian Mounted Police performed their popular display of horsemanship, the "musical ride," in the amphitheater.

ECOLOGY AROUND THE WORLD

Everyone who visited Expo '74 had a favorite exhibit. Many people who visited Expo were fascinated by the pavilion set up by the Soviet Union. One of the major themes of the Soviet exhibition was the importance of international co-operation in preserving the environment of the world as a whole. But the exhibit that really caught the eye of most visitors was the fascinating display of maps

Above: The dramatic United States pavilion—topped with a translucent vinyl canopy. Below: The Energy Cube—consisting of 85 energy-consuming appliances found in the average U.S. home.

The Canadian exhibits occupied a whole island in the Spokane River.
Their children's playground featured these delightful animal amusements.

and photographs of the Soviet Union's vast land area. There were views of Soviet forests and mountains and streams—and the wildlife to be found there. And there were exhibits showing the ways in which the Soviets are trying to develop industry without destroying the natural environment. There was a fascinating series of scale models that showed the way in which Russia's vast forests contribute to purer air.

Iran's pavilion was of interest because of that country's special position in the world of ecology. Until recent years, Iran has been a largely non-industrial nation. Because of this, Iran has not yet experienced many of the problems that have beset the nations of Europe and North America. All of Iran's exhibits illustrated ways to begin developing modern industry and transportation without damaging or destroying as yet untouched natural beauty and resources. There was also a dazzling exhibit of Iranian art and architecture, both ancient and modern.

The Japanese pavilion attracted visitors because of its success in capturing the Japanese way of life. Stepping into the Japanese pavilion was, in many ways, like visiting Japan. The Japanese exhibits were all planned to show how the Japanese, a people crowded onto small islands, have learned to live with their environment. To a great extent, Japanese tradition and culture are based on man's relation to nature. The exhibits showed the beautiful and the practical ways this relationship has expressed itself. There was a traditional Japanese garden. And there was also an interesting exhibit on the traditional and modern ways the Japanese enjoy their fields, mountains, and streams. Activities ranged from traditional kite flying to baseball games in city parks.

The pavilion of the Republic of Korea was popular because the food was so good. There were, among other things, an outdoor and an indoor restaurant, both featuring traditional Korean barbecued food. Another unique feature of the Korean pavilion was a tape-recorded "sound environment." Tapes had been made of all of the sounds one can hear in Korea—the sound of birds, wind chimes and gongs, people talking and singing, wind, rushing water, and even a little city noise.

▶ FUN AND GAMES

But not everything at Expo '74 was serious or thought-provoking. Some of it was just plain fun.

People at international fairs always enjoy the food. No matter how busy a traveler you are, you could never taste so many national treats in so short a time in any trip you might take. There were specialties of many countries at Expo '74—and not just the countries with pavilions. Belgian waffles and Italian pizza were special favorites with young people who visited the fair.

And the shops of Expo '74 were like a vast bazaar: crafts and manufactured goods were on sale from all over the world. The shops featured an endless procession of toys. There were Swiss watches and Japanese kites and Mexican clay toys and carved jade from the Orient.

The rides at Expo '74 were most unusual. In fact, some of the young people who visited Expo felt they had found their true home in Universa, the area where most of the rides and games were located. There was a cable car that rose above the fair and then dipped down low into the spray from Spokane Falls—near which the fair site was located. There was also an exciting toboggan ride on artificial snow, and many, many more.

Expo '74 closed on November 3 after an 184-day run. It was estimated that more than 5,000,000 people had visited this world's fair dedicated to the environment. At the closing ceremonies, President Gerald Ford, in a taped message, asked people to preserve the land for future generations. Now that Expo '74 has closed, the fairgrounds will become an environmentally planned park for the use of Spokane residents.

Those who visited Expo '74 felt that they had enjoyed a new and worthwhile experience. It was unique and exciting because it was a place where there was not only a great deal to learn, but also a great deal to enjoy. Unlike many other large expositions, Expo '74 had a feeling of warmth, friendliness, and cooperation. The theme of the fair may have had something to do with this feeling, for its theme was the thing all men and women and children share in common—the fascinating planet earth on which we all live.

PROBING THE PLANETS

Space scientists enjoyed a long Christmas season in 1973. Their earliest "gifts" arrived in November, as Pioneer 10, a probe launched 21 months earlier by the United States, began to send television pictures of the giant planet Jupiter. The flow of pictures, and of information about conditions on Jupiter, continued through December and into 1974. In February, 1974, Mariner 10, another U.S. probe, flew close to the planet Venus. It traveled on, flying by the planet Mercury in March. The probes revealed enormous amounts of information about the three planets.

▶ **JUPITER**

Jupiter is the largest planet in the solar system. It was approached by Pioneer 10 after a flight of 620,000,000 miles (1,000,000,000, or one billion, kilometers). Cameras on the probe sent back the clearest pictures ever made of Jupiter. A variety of instruments collected information about conditions on the planet. What appears to be the surface of Jupiter is really the top of its thick, cloudy

atmosphere. Most of the atmosphere, which may be thousands of miles thick, is hydrogen. Beginning at 600 miles (960 km.) down into the atmosphere, the hydrogen starts to turn into liquid form. The temperature at the top of the atmosphere is extremely cold—about 200 degrees below zero Fahrenheit (130 degrees below zero Celsius). But a few hundred miles down in the atmosphere the temperature may be as high as 3,500 degrees F. (1,900 degrees C.). Pioneer 10 also detected a strong magnetic field surrounding Jupiter. Even as Pioneer 10 sent back its information, a second probe, Pioneer 11, was on its way to Jupiter. In the meantime, an astronomer at the California Institute of Technology, using a telescope, found a tiny object that appears to be a moon of Jupiter. If this is correct, it will be the thirteenth known moon of the giant planet.

▶ **VENUS**

Venus comes closer to the earth than any other planet does. Yet the surface of Venus is almost impossible to observe, because it is hidden by a thick layer of clouds. Scientists learned about the surface of the planet by beaming radar waves from the earth to Venus, and by mapping the pattern of the reflected waves. This method revealed that there are large craters on Venus. These cra-

Photo of Jupiter shows its atmospheric bands, the Red Spot (*left*), and the shadow of Io, one of Jupiter's moons (*right*).

Cameras aboard the space probe Mariner 10 took nearly 3,500 photographs of the cloud-covered planet Venus.

ters are rather shallow compared with those on the moon.

Mariner 10 was launched on November 3, 1973. It came within 3,600 miles (5,800 km.) of Venus in February, 1974. Like telescopes on the earth, Mariner's cameras could not photograph through the clouds. However, the 3,500 pictures that were sent showed that the clouds are driven into spiral patterns by winds of up to 200 miles (320 km.) an hour.

The clouds of Venus are made up mainly of carbon dioxide gas. Very small amounts of hydrogen and oxygen are also present in the Venusian atmosphere. The thick, heavy clouds cause tremendous pressure on the planet's surface, perhaps 90 times as great as the pressure of the earth's atmosphere. The clouds also slow the escape of heat from the surface, where the temperature reaches nearly 900 degrees F. (480 degrees C.). Unlike the earth, Venus has no magnetic field.

▶ MERCURY

Mercury is hard to observe because it is small and close to the sun in the sky. Even the most powerful telescopes reveal very little of the planet's surface. The pictures taken and transmitted by Mariner 10 gave scientists their first clear, detailed look at the surface. The probe began to send its pictures of Mercury on March 23, 1974. By March 29 it was less than 500 miles (800 km.) above the surface of the planet. In all, more than 2,000 pictures of Mercury were received.

The photographs show a surface that closely resembles that of the moon. It is covered with craters of all sizes. There are also long, narrow valleys. But, unlike the moon, Mercury has no great mountain ranges. Neither does it have widespread "seas," the dark flat areas that are the moon's most easily seen features.

Instruments aboard Mariner 10 gathered a great deal of new information about the planet, and confirmed some facts that had already been suspected. As had been believed, Mercury has an atmosphere of helium gas. This atmosphere is very thin, with a density less than one hundredth the density of the earth's atmosphere. The probe also detected traces of two other gases, neon and argon.

Closeup photo taken by Mariner 10 shows that the planet Mercury is covered with craters.

Temperatures on Mercury cover a great range. On the side facing away from the sun, the temperature falls to about 300 degrees below zero F. (185 degrees below zero C.); on the sunlit side the temperature reaches above 750 degrees F. (400 degrees C.).

Mariner 10 also detected a magnetic field around Mercury, with perhaps one tenth the strength of the earth's magnetic field.

In a few days, Mariner 10 told more about Mercury than had been learned in hundreds of years of observation by telescope. Scientists were pleased when the probe survived the intense heat of that part of the solar system, and sent more pictures and information when it again crossed the orbit of Mercury, in September, 1974.

SCIENCE EXPERIMENTS

The moon is a sphere, like the earth. Sometimes the moon looks like a round circle. At other times the moon seems to have the shape of a crescent, a half circle, or a nearly full circle. These different shapes are called the *phases* of the moon.

We see the moon only because it reflects the light of the sun. The moon does not give off any light of its own. The moon moves in an orbit around the earth. An easy experiment will show you how these facts combine to cause the phases of the moon.

PHASES OF THE MOON

You will need a light-colored ball and an unshaded lamp with a 100-watt bulb. It is important that you work in a darkened room. The ball represents the moon, the lamp is the sun, and you are an observer on the earth. Face away from the lighted lamp. Hold the ball at arm's length, high enough to keep your own shadow from falling on the ball. You will see that the entire half of the ball is lighted. This is "full moon," the time when the moon is on the side of the earth away from the sun.

Now turn very slowly, to copy the moon's monthly motion around the earth. You will see that the lighted part of the ball will shrink, and so you will observe a shape like that of a nearly full moon. This is called a gibbous moon. Keep turning, and you will see a half moon, then a crescent. The shrinking of the lighted part of the moon is called the "waning of the moon."

Keep turning until you face the lighted lamp, when no part of the ball will appear lighted. This is "new moon." Go on turning, and a crescent, facing the opposite way from the first one, will appear. It will be followed by a half moon and then a gibbous moon. Finally you will again have a full moon. The growth of the lighted part of the moon is called the "waxing of the moon." The entire cycle from one full moon to the next full moon takes 29½ days.

From left to right: early crescent, gibbous, full moon, half moon, late crescent.

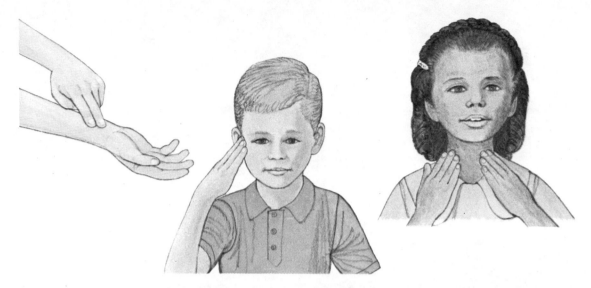

Your body is composed of billions of cells. There are muscle cells that move you about, and bone cells that support your weight. There are many other kinds of cells, too. All these billions of cells need a constant supply of food and oxygen. This supply is brought to the cells by the blood.

The blood is kept moving by the heart, a living pump made of powerful muscle. Each time the heart muscle tightens, it pushes the blood along through vessels called arteries. When you work hard the cells need more food and oxygen. At such times the heart beats faster, sending more blood to the cells.

Arteries branch to form smaller arteries, and still smaller ones that lead to the smallest blood vessels, called capillaries. These form a network that reaches all of the body cells.

You can't see your heart beating, but you can feel the blood as it is pumped. Wherever arteries run close to the skin you can feel the blood being pumped along.

Feel your temple (the side of your forehead), the inside of your wrist, and the side of your throat. The throbbing you feel is the beating of the blood in your arteries. This throbbing is the pulse. You can also *see* the pulse.

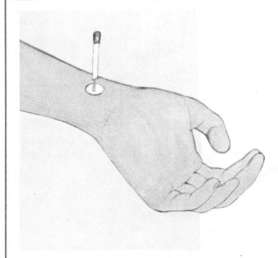

CHECK YOUR PULSE

You will need a thumbtack, a paper match, and a watch with a second hand.

1. Stick the tack into the end of the match, as shown in the diagram.

2. Rest the head of the tack on your wrist, where you can feel your pulse. You may have to move the tack around a bit until you get the right spot. Watch the match as it bobs back and forth. It bobs once for each beat of your heart.

3. With the watch, time the number of heartbeats per minute. This is your pulse rate.

4. Observe the effect of exercise on the pulse rate. Do knee bends for several minutes, then check your pulse rate. Compare it with the first pulse rate.

THE ROBOT PIONEERS

Both the United States and the Soviet Union have, in the last five years, sent explorers moving over the surface of the moon. Both nations have had rock samples brought back to earth.

The two nations explored in different ways. The United States sent human beings to the moon. In fact, it sent humans on six occasions. The twelve Americans who set foot on the moon took many photographs, ran experiments, and scooped up samples of the lunar surface.

The Soviet Union landed several unmanned vehicles on the moon. They were equipped to scoop up and analyze lunar material and transmit the information back to earth.

So it's a case of human beings versus mechanical devices. There is no question that the human explorer is superior to any mechanical explorer. The human being is more intelligent, of course. Humans are more capable of reacting properly to the unexpected and of correcting something that goes wrong. A human space explorer can go beyond his instructions in order to take advantage of some unforeseen event.

On the other hand, sending a mechanical explorer out from earth is cheaper and simpler than sending men. A non-living device doesn't require the expense and complication of life-support systems. It doesn't need air, food, or water. No provision need be made for eliminating or storing wastes. And if something goes wrong—if the mechanical explorer misses contact or is damaged on landing—it's only money that's lost. If scientists lose a mechanical device, they can try again, learning lessons from the first failure. They do not experience the misery of losing a brave human being.

Yet on the whole, the American manned missions have been successful. They accomplished a great deal more than the unmanned missions of the Soviet Union. This seems to indicate that in the future, men will return to the moon. Better and better mechanical devices will go along with them—but men will be there.

BEYOND THE MOON

That is all very well for the moon. But the moon, you know, is practically in our backyard. Astronauts can get there in three days. They can travel to the moon and back in a week, even allowing for exploration.

The nearest sizable worlds beyond the moon are the planets Venus and Mars. Venus is never closer to earth than 25,000,000 miles (40,200,000 kilometers). That is over 100 times as far as the moon. Mars is never closer than 36,000,000 miles (57,900,000 km.). That is nearly 150 times as far as the moon. Astronauts going to either world would have a one-way trip of six to nine months and an equally long return trip.

A manned voyage to even the nearest planet would be a far more difficult job than reaching the moon was. Might it not be better to send mechanical explorers?

Without the need for carrying food, air, and water, a spaceship could carry more fuel and build up higher accelerations so that the trip would take less time. A mechanical explorer could be designed to stand higher accelerations than a human being could stand. A mechanical explorer would also be better able to endure the long zero-gravity condition during the coasting portion of the trip.

The Soviet Union has already sent devices that have landed on the surface of Venus and Mars. They were very simple devices designed to take photographs and test the nature of the atmosphere. As it happened, the devices reaching Venus were put out of action after a short while by the high temperatures and the atmospheric pressure. The device reaching Mars got there in the middle of a sandstorm and could do nothing.

However, in the future, human beings may well send better devices to the nearby planets. They will send devices better designed to cope with the conditions on those planets and equipped to gather all kinds of information.

ROBOTS

It would be best if we could send a very versatile device to a new world—a device that could absorb information quickly and react on the basis of that information. That's just another way of saying that it would be nice to be able to send an "intelligent" device to the new world, one that is capable of making decisions. It has long been customary to speak of an intelligent mechanical device as a "robot."

In 1920 a Czech writer named Karel Čapek wrote a play titled *R.U.R.* In the play, a man named Rossum designed and built intelligent mechanical men and women to do the work of mankind. The "R.U.R." of the title were the initials of Rossum's company, which was called "Rossum's Universal Robots." *Robota* is a Czech word for "work."

In the play, of course, the robots had human shapes. They had to have them because they were played by human beings. In real life, though, must robots have human shapes?

Not really. You can imagine robots on wheels for rapid movement on flat surfaces. You can also imagine robots with long tentacles rather than arms—or robots like turtles in shape, and with eyes all over their bodies. You could imagine robots with hundreds of different shapes, each suitable for some special job.

Yet there are advantages to the human shape.

The human shape, after all, is the product of billions of years of evolution. It is a very generalized product—it is designed to do many different things quite well. That is part of the reason humans have been successful in the world. Wheels might move us faster, but they would not be as good on rough ground. Tentacles might be more useful for some jobs, but they're no good for pushing. Flying would be useful, but it is wasteful of energy for a large object to fly.

If you want an intelligent mechanical device—a robot—to land on a world we don't know very well, and you want it to be ready for the unexpected, it is better not to make it too specialized. If it is specialized, it will be very good at whatever the specialty is. However, it would be poor in other directions. It just might be in those other directions that the robot will have to act. However, if you make it human-shaped, it will be ready for just about anything.

Then, too, we have built a whole technology based on the human shape. All our furniture is designed to be used by beings of human size and shape that bend at certain joints. Our machines are designed to be run conveniently and comfortably by such beings. If we build our robots in human design, they can take advantage of human technology.

But how can we make human-shaped robots intelligent? How can we give them brains?

We already have "brains" of a sort in the form of computers. The computers we have today can work out certain kinds of problems with almost unimaginable speed. But this is not intelligence. Computers can do certain arithmetical operations in a certain sequence, provided some human being tells them exactly what to do. But they are no more intelligent in doing this than an ordinary hand-cranked adding machine would be.

But look to the future. The first modern computer was built during World War II. It was immensely large, very limited in what it could do, and quite slow. In only 30 years, we have progressed enormously. Computers have become much smaller, much faster, and much more capable.

Remember that 30 years is a very brief time. It took 3,000,000,000 (billion) years or more for the human brain to develop. Perhaps we ought to be patient and allow computer scientists another 30 years, to see if they can come up with something suitable for robots.

It isn't at all likely, of course, that even in another 30 years, scientists will come close to making a computer as complicated as the human brain. The cells that make up the brain are so tiny they can only be seen in a microscope. The brain is made up of 10,000,000,000 (billion) complicated brain cells. It also has 100,000,000,000 (billion) smaller and less complicated cells. And all of that is crammed into a container (the human skull) weighing only 3 pounds (1.36 kilograms). We can't possibly expect to build computers with that many units crammed into a space so small in only 30 years.

A robot, however, doesn't really have to be as smart as a man to do a good job exploring another world. It doesn't have to be able to make speeches or write poetry or understand a football game or have political opinions. A brain far simpler than the human brain will hold enough information to enable a robot to absorb what it needs to know to make the decisions it must make.

▶ ROBOT–HUMAN TEAMS

But must we depend only on robots? Will human beings never see these other worlds?

In some some cases, human beings may not see them. Venus, for instance, beneath its blanket of clouds, is a dim world of ferocious heat. Temperatures on Venus are far above the boiling point of water. Perhaps human beings will never try to land on Venus, or on Mercury either.

The satellites of Jupiter, on the other hand, are worlds that may be very much like our moon in some ways. They are so far away that it might take two years for manned spaceships to reach them. That's not the bad part, though. The satellites of Jupiter are inside Jupiter's magnetosphere, a belt of radiation and energetic particles that is deadly to life. It may be a long time before human beings venture that close to mighty Jupiter.

Robots, however, will serve as our pioneers, telling us more and more about these strange deadly worlds. They can satisfy our curiosity and increase our knowledge. As science advances (partly because of the knowledge our robots will bring us), we will learn how to build larger and better spaceships. The spaceships will be manned by astronauts equipped to deal with conditions on other worlds.

These worlds would include Mars to begin with, and then perhaps some of the larger asteroids. There might also be robot probes and then manned expeditions to comets that move past the earth.

With the aid of robots, it may become possible to build houses on the moon while the rest of the solar system is being explored. Caverns may be dug out underneath the lunar surface and made into a comfortable town for human beings. Robots could do the rougher part of the work of digging. They could also do riskier jobs on the moon's hostile surface. One day a full-fledged human colony might exist on the moon.

The lunar colony would have to begin with supplies from earth: food, water, plants, energy-producing devices. If the supplies were carefully conserved, and if ways of getting energy from the sunlight that bathes the moon were worked out, the colony might learn how to support itself. The colony could derive some materials from the lunar crust, and grow its own food, too.

A hundred years from now, there may be human beings who were born on the moon. They would probably be humans whose bodies had adapted to the low gravity there (only one sixth the earth's gravity). By that time, robots will have sent back information from their pioneering journeys to every large body in the solar system.

New advanced ships could then be manned by crews composed of robots and lunar colonists. Lunar colonists, used to low gravity, to living in an enclosed area, to working with robots, would find it easier to withstand long journeys through space than earthmen would.

The space explorers of the future will move outward, in greater comfort than is possible today, and with higher confidence, toward better-known destinations. The solar system will offer a new horizon for mankind. It will be a greater, wider, and more distant horizon than any we have ever known.

Need we fear the robots? Will they become too intelligent? Will they "take over"?

Probably not. For a while, anyway, robots will be designed by people to fulfill certain specific purposes. It may never be necessary to make them more intelligent than mankind. In fact, we may end up with robots that are not more intelligent than humans, but intelligent in different ways. Robots and people, thinking in different ways but working together, may well prove far more intelligent and capable as teams than either would be alone.

It has happened before. Human beings tamed dogs and horses, and it turned out that the human-and-dog combination was excellent for hunting. The human-and-horse combination was good for farming and traveling.

It may be the human-and-robot combination that will turn out to be excellent for exploring the solar system. It may even be that the exploration of the solar system can't be done until the human-and-robot combination is worked out.

ISAAC ASIMOV
Scientist and Author

The struggle for survival: these people are eating food meant for cattle.

DROUGHT IN THE SAHEL

It covers an area of Africa about one half the size of the continental United States and is—or was—home to some 25,000,000 people. It is called the Sahel. The name comes from Arabic and means "edge" or "shore," as in the shore of the sea. But the "sea" is a vast sea of sand, and the only ship to be seen is the age-old ship of the desert—the camel. The sea of sand is the great Sahara, the largest desert in the world, and the Sahel is its shore.

Extending in a belt from the Atlantic Ocean to the Red Sea, the Sahel crosses the African continent without regard for national boundaries. Running parallel to the Sahara, it passes through the six traditional Sahelian countries—Senegal, Mauritania, Mali, Upper Volta, Niger, and Chad—and into the Sudan. The land of the Sahel is distinct. It is neither as arid and lifeless as the desert to the north,

nor as green as the savannah, or grassland, to the south. It is the dividing line between tropical Africa and the Africa of the Sahara. More than that, it is the last line of resistance to the slow but steady southward movement of the desert.

The Sahel is a land of scattered grasses, scrubby bushes, and stunted trees. Over the centuries it has afforded the people who live there only a bare and uncertain livelihood. A hardy people who have adapted themselves to a harsh land, the Sahelians live in a delicate balance with their environment. But their precarious existence depends on the regularity of the region's limited rainfall. When the rains are late or there is less rainfall than usual, there is drought—vegetation withers, animals die, and the desert creeps closer. For the last six or seven years the rains in the Sahel have been scanty. The result has been the worst drought the region has seen in this century. For the countries of the Sahel, which are already among the world's poorest, the drought has been a tragedy.

It has caused the death, by famine and disease, of many thousands of Sahelians. Cattle by the million and entire crops have been wiped out. Masses of people have left the land and migrated to the towns to avoid starvation.

Nor has the tragedy been limited to the Sahel. Some of the neighboring countries have begun to feel the effects of the drought as it moves relentlessly into other parts of Africa. One of the countries particularly hard-hit has been Ethiopia. It has experienced a famine in which 100,000 people are believed to have died.

▶ **THE PEOPLE OF THE SAHEL**

The people of the Sahel may be divided into two groups—the settled farmers and the nomads. Among the nomads, the Tuareg is lord of the desert. He is an imposing figure, mounted on a camel and silhouetted against the desert sky, swathed from head to foot in dark blue robes and veiled so that only his eyes can be seen.

The Tuareg are one of the peoples of the Sahel. Nomads of Berber stock from North Africa, they are a tall, proud people, famed as warriors. Although they were converted to the Muslim faith when the Arabs swept across northern Africa, the Tuareg were never completely conquered. Even when the French colonized the region, the Tuareg maintained much of their independence and their own culture. They live mainly in Mali and Niger, but they have little respect for borders and they travel time-honored routes seeking water and pasture for their camels, sheep, and goats. During the "wet" season they travel the Sahara itself. But during the dry months they move down into the Sahel, for then the Sahara is unlivable, even for the Tuareg.

Related to the Tuareg are the Moors. A nomadic people of mixed Berber and Arab stock, they make up much of the population of Mauritania, which takes its name from them. (*Maure* is the French word for "Moor.") Livestock raising is vital to the economy of Mauritania, which has more cat-

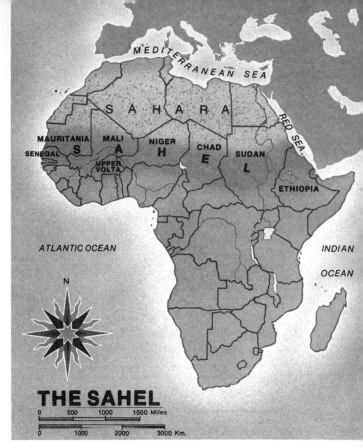

THE SAHEL

The Sahel is home for this Tuareg. The arid soil, occasional stunted trees, and scrubby bushes are typical of the Sahel region.

73

tle than people. Probably 80 per cent of its cattle have died as a result of the drought, a disaster for the country.

The Sahel has been a meeting place of black and white Africa. In earlier times the blacks were taken as slaves by the Tuareg and Moors. Intermarriage occurred and today there are "black" and "white" Moors, and many of the Tuareg show a mixture of the two racial strains.

Generally, the black Africans inhabit the southern part of the Sahel, where many live as settled farmers. Here the rainfall is relatively heavier, permitting the cultivation of certain crops. The two basic food crops are millet and sorghum. These grains, which in the more developed countries of the world are often used as feed for animals, are basic to the life of the people of the southern Sahel. When the crops were destroyed by drought, the people ate the seed set aside for the next year's planting. When that too was gone, they were forced to abandon their land.

A distinctive black nomadic people of the Sahel are the Fulani (or Fulbe), who are great herders of cattle. The Fulani maintain enormous herds, which to them represent both wealth and prestige. The cattle are rarely slaughtered for food. Instead, the Fulani live from their milk and from milk products, which they sometimes trade with the farmers for grain. The Fulani have suffered badly from the drought. They have watched their great herds die off as the land grew parched and the pasture shriveled from lack of rain.

Even before drought struck the Sahel, the traditional ways of life of its peoples, especially the nomads, were under attack by the forces of modernization in Africa. Now the forces of nature may hasten the end not only of a way of life, but possibly of the Sahel itself.

▶ **WHAT CAN BE DONE**

The magnitude of the disaster in Africa first came to the attention of the world

The result of years of drought. The vegetation has died and the soil has cracked.

in 1973. By then the effects of the drought had reached epidemic proportions. The economically hard-pressed countries of the region could do little themselves to relieve the suffering of their people, and an international program of aid was begun. Food and medicines were shipped to the drought-stricken areas, but these efforts were hampered by a number of obstacles. The amounts of food sent were not enough to feed the enormous numbers of people involved. Supplies could not be easily moved to where the people were because transportation was lacking. Roads were few and were sometimes made impassable by short but heavy rain showers, which were too brief to moisten the dry soil. By 1974 the situation was still desperate, and the United Nations warned that more help was needed if even greater loss of life was to be prevented.

Can anything be done to avert similar tragedies? Some scientists think that the Sahel drought is part of a change in world weather patterns. The movement of the rain-bearing monsoon winds, they believe, has shifted, so that the affected areas are not receiving as much rain as before. This has caused similar droughts in places as distant as Asia and South America. Little can be done about this, but some steps can be taken to restore the land so that it will be livable.

One problem is that the ecological balance of the Sahel has tipped. Improved health care has increased the population. With more people have come larger herds of cattle, sheep, and goats, which have overgrazed the land. The cattle are lean and poor producers of milk, but their numbers are important to the herders since they represent wealth. The people have to be persuaded that it is to their own interest to limit the size of their herds and to increase their quality. Goats present perhaps the worst problem, for they eat the grass to the roots, which causes it to die. One government leader of a Sahel country has even suggested that the goats must be gotten rid of entirely. This will be difficult, for most of the people of the region keep them and they are an important source of food.

The nomads, too, may have to change their ancient way of life, and perhaps live in more settled communities rather than constantly moving from place to place. And finally,

An international aid program was begun in 1973. These Tuareg women and children are preparing food sent by the United Nations.

methods of irrigation must be developed if the Sahel is to be able to support life again. Some rain finally came to the Sahel in the summer and fall of 1974, bringing a measure of relief to the parched land. However, it remains to be seen if the long drought is over. For if the scientists are correct, the rains will continue to be scanty, and without irrigation the land will again become desert.

There is hope for the Sahel, but much will have to be done. People will have to be persuaded to discard their traditional ways, which until recently have served them well. And equally important, the more developed and prosperous nations of the world will have to provide more help for the people of the Sahel.

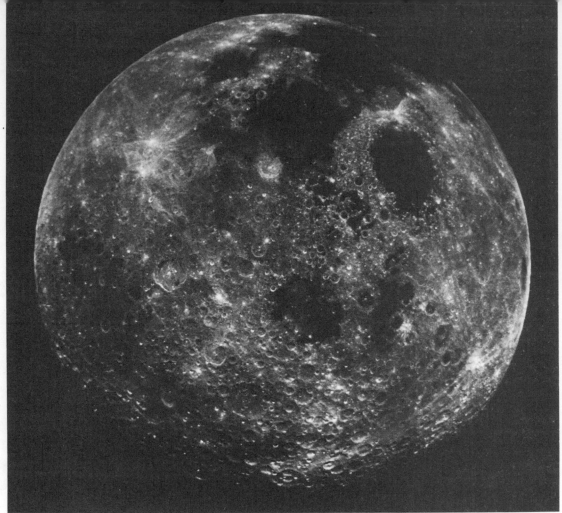

The far side of the moon, seen from Apollo 17.

ON THE MOON

People have wondered for thousands of years how the moon came into being. Many explanations have been offered. One theory is based on the idea that the moon was once a planet, moving in an orbit around the sun, as the earth does. The earth, with its greater force of gravitation, "captured" its nearby neighbor, pulling it into earth orbit.

A second theory suggests that at one time the earth spun so fast a portion of it was torn away and thrown out into space. This portion became the moon.

Still another theory states that the whole solar system was formed from a huge cloud of dust and gas. More than 99 per cent of this cloud collected into one mass that became the sun. The rest of the cloud collected into smaller masses that formed the earth, its moon, and all the other planets and their satellites.

These theories were developed at a time when scientists could study the moon only from a distance. What kinds of rock make up the moon? How old are they? Is there volcanic activity, or is the moon "dead"? These questions and many others could not be answered until space probes and the Apollo astronauts reached the moon.

Between mid-1969 and late 1972, six Apollo craft landed at various places on the moon. The astronauts who manned these craft conducted experiments to collect samples and information about the moon's crust, its gravity, its magnetic field, and the temperatures beneath its crust. They also set up instruments to detect moonquakes. The astronauts brought back to earth over 800 pounds (over 360 kilograms) of moon rocks and soil. Scientists are testing and studying this material to learn its origin, age, and chemical composition. These studies, and other measurements and experiments, have suggested new ideas about the way in which the moon and the earth might have begun and then evolved or changed with time.

Most scientists think that the moon, the earth, and the other planets in the solar system originated at about the same time, 4,600,000,000 years ago. This idea was strengthened when the Apollo 17 astronauts returned from the moon. Tests showed that one of the rocks they brought back is 4,600,000,000 years old. It is the oldest known rock other than meteorites.

The first stage in the development of the solar system may have been a vast cloud of gases and dust. As parts of the cloud cooled, they condensed into rock. Some of the larger rocks, having more gravitational attraction, pulled other rocks toward them. The larger rock masses attracted still other rocks. In time some of these ever-growing masses collected to form the moon. The moon's growth was unimaginably violent. Rocks ranging from pebble size to boulders miles in diameter crashed onto the moon's surface. The energy of these crashes heated up the surface. This tremendous production of heat melted the rocks. The moon's surface became a sea of glowing liquid rock (lava).

After many thousands of years fewer rocks were left in space, so fewer rocks fell on the moon. The lava cooled slowly. Crystals of solid minerals formed in the cooling liquid. These crystals were not all alike. The lighter, or less dense, ones floated. In time they formed the moon's outer layer, or crust. The denser crystals sank, forming a lower layer of the moon, called the mantle. The chemical composition of the crystals was different, so the rocks of the moon's crust and its mantle are different.

After the crust cooled, some rocks continued to fall on the moon, blasting open huge craters in the solid crust. Some of the craters were 30 miles (50 kilometers) or more in diameter. A few, called basins, were many times that width. During this violent time the upper part of the moon's crust was ground, broken, remelted, and mixed almost completely.

About 4,000,000,000 (billion) years ago, after the moon's outer crust was cool and solid, the mantle was heating up. This happened because the rocks in the deeper part of the moon contained radioactive elements such as uranium. A radioactive substance is unstable. The atoms of which it is composed break down at a constant rate. In one type of uranium, for example, the atoms break down to form atoms of another element, lead. Heat is produced during this process of radioactive decay.

The heat of radioactive decay built up within the moon until portions of the interior rocks melted to form lava. The heating up went on for millions of years. At last the lava worked its way up through the moon's crust. In some places the lava spilled across the surface, forming great plains. It also burst into the basins from below, in flow after flow of hot lava. These gigantic eruptions took place again and again, for a period of nearly 1,000,000,000 (billion) years. After they ended, about 3,000,000,000 (billion) years ago, the lava cooled. The rock that crystallized in the basins was mainly basalt. It was this dark, almost black, rock that led Galileo to call the basins "maria," or "seas."

Except for the continuing impact of meteors, asteroids, and comets, the moon has changed little since the last flows of basalt cooled. Great craters like Copernicus were formed during this "quiet" time.

Most scientists now believe that the earth began and developed in the same general way and at the same time as the moon. But a great difference between the two bodies began to appear soon after the time of their formation. Millions of tons of nitrogen, carbon dioxide, water vapor, and other gases formed a shell or blanket around the earth, held in place by the earth's gravity.

Over millions of years, as the earth's crust cooled, the water vapor condensed into drops of water and fell as rain. Torrents of water poured across the face of the earth. The rushing waters, violent winds, and changes in

Exploring: Scientist-Astronaut Harrison H. Schmitt has reached his destination in his lunar Rover, and is collecting lunar rocks.

the earth's crust itself, wore away the large craters and other evidence of the world's early history. It was the atmosphere and the oceans of water that made life on earth possible.

No atmosphere collected on the moon. Gases did not remain around it because its gravitational attraction was not strong enough to hold on to them. Without gases to provide an atmosphere or water, no great changes took place on the moon. The changes that have occurred in the last 3,000,000,000 (billion)

years have been caused mainly by asteroids, comets, and meteors that have crashed on the moon's surface. These objects dug out craters of all sizes, and threw up rocks that fell back, digging smaller craters. In some places, where objects fell close together, overlapping craters were formed.

For these billions of years the moon has looked much as we see it today. Its surface, cratered and mountainous, is like a partial portrait of our earth when it was young, billions of years ago.

EXPLORING

An astronaut climbs down slowly from the *Challenger*, the lunar module of Apollo 17. Some minutes later a second astronaut descends from the module. The two men stand on the moon's surface in their bulky space suits, looking up at the black sky. There they see the faraway shining earth, with its blue oceans and bright white clouds. The colors of the earth contrast strangely with the gray rocks and soil of the moon.

On the moon, away from the lunar module, the space suit is the astronaut's world. It supplies him with oxygen for breathing for up to 8 hours. Then he must return to the lunar module for a fresh supply of oxygen. The suit has a built-in air-conditioning system, needed to protect the astronaut from extremes of heat and cold unknown on the earth. The special fabrics of the space suit are the astronaut's shield against the solar heat and the vacuum of space. The communications systems in the suit are the astronaut's link to the earth and to his fellow astronaut. All this equipment makes the suit heavy. But on the moon, whose gravity is only one sixth that of the earth, the suit seems light.

Walking on the moon is fun. Some astronauts prefer a skiing kind of walk, while others make giant kangaroolike hops. On the earth the suit and backpack weigh nearly 200 pounds (90 kg.) but on the moon one can walk a long way in it without tiring. The moon has no atmosphere to carry sound waves, but the astronaut, sealed within his suit, always hears some sounds. Even when his radio is silent, there is the hum of the oxygen blower fan and of the pump that circulates cooling water through the suit. In fact, the entire trip to the moon and back is never free of the sound of motors, fans, and pumps of all kinds.

The sounds are soon forgotten, for there is much work to be done. Equipment for some of the experiments must be checked and set up on the ground. Other equipment is checked and loaded aboard the battery-powered lunar roving vehicle, or "Rover." The Rover itself must be checked before starting out on the first of three moon rides, or "traverses."

The Rover is a very dependable exploration vehicle, but it is not exactly a racing car. On level ground its top speed is about 7½ miles (about 12 km.) per hour. On their three traverses, the Apollo 17 crew drove a total distance of about 20 miles (about 32 km.).

The Rover is usually driven first to the most distant place on the traverse. The astronauts dismount and unload their equipment. Their aim is to gather all the facts they can about the spot. But for safety's sake, many "housekeeping" jobs must be done first. For example, dust thrown up by the wheels must be carefully removed from the surface of the Rover's batteries to prevent overheating. Checks must be made on the space suit batteries, air conditioners, and the supply of oxygen and water within the suit.

The moon explorers use a small hammer to chip off rock samples. They also use a device that drills into the soil. It removes cores of soil that are studied with great interest by scientists. Different layers in the core date from different periods in the history of the moon.

In addition to collecting samples of rocks and soil, the astronauts take many photographs at each stopping place. Their cameras, of a type used by many photographers on earth, are fitted with special controls. These make it possible to operate the camera through the bulky gloves of the space suit. Photography is important in moon exploration. Often the position of rocks and boulders in relation to one another and to the general area can give scientists clues to past events. The astronauts also describe what they see as they move about an area. Their words are recorded for use when the photographs and samples are studied. When the work is done, the Rover is driven to the next work area. Elapsed time must be watched with great care, for the oxygen supply in the space suit is limited, and a breakdown of the Rover could force a long walk back to the lunar module. Fortunately this has never happened.

The astronauts are part of a large group of scientists working together. The scientific team on earth follows the astronauts by television, ready to give suggestions or make changes in the planned programs quickly, if they are made necessary by new information.

Some members of the scientific team are geologists. There are also astronomers, biologists, engineers, and specialists in various other branches of science. They plan the program of experiments for the trip. The experiments, and the rocks and soil that the astronauts bring back to earth, tell us what the moon is like. They also tell much about the moon's past. Most important, they give us a better understanding of the origin and history of our home planet, the earth.

Harrison H. Schmitt
Scientist-Astronaut
Apollo 17 Mission

A plant will make you happy.

A plant will beautify your home

A plant will Freshen the air.

A plant will make a friend feel good.

A plant will never talk back to you.

A plant will never mess on your rugs.

A plant will love you if you water it.

A plant will give you something to talk about.

And best of all— you don't have to walk a begonia.

WHEN YOU TALK TO YOUR PLANTS, SMILE!

Have you ever talked to a tulip? A tulip that listened? Have you ever watched a vine curl to the sound of rock music? Plants obviously don't have ears. But do they still react to sound? Some people think so.

The idea is far from new. Primitive man often used music to help his crops grow. He had special songs for planting seeds, and indeed for every stage of growth. Often he used sacred drums or a magic rattle to add power to his songs.

European peasants still followed such customs during the Middle Ages and even after the Renaissance. People danced along the barley furrows and between the grapevines, chanting songs as their ancestors had done to bring a successful harvest.

The first scientific tests of these old folk beliefs took place in the 19th century. In one early experiment, the great naturalist Charles Darwin played his bassoon to a small plant called the sensitive plant (*Mimosa pudica*). The feathery leaflets of this plant are sensitive to even the slightest touch. Darwin wondered whether they might also react to sound waves. So the eminent scientist tootled earnestly away to his little plant. Unfortunately, it did not respond.

Although this experiment was unsuccessful, it aroused the interest of other European scientists. However, their experiments, like Darwin's, produced no positive results. Eventually, the research was dropped. Not until the mid-20th century did the subject again catch the scientific eye.

In the 1950's, a botanist in Madras, India, became interested in Hindu legends that told of the gods' playing music to create plants and make them bloom. He decided to run an experiment to test the ancient stories.

Using loudspeakers, he broadcast a sacred song across a special section of rice paddies. He did this for several hours every day. Apparently, the rice loved it. According to his report, the harvest was from 25 to 60 per cent larger than normal.

American scientists were not impressed. How could plants, without anything like an ear, react in this way to sound? And even if it could affect them, could it cause them pleasure? Do plants have feelings? The whole question, most experts felt, belonged in the area of magic, superstition, and folklore.

Yet news stories began to appear, in both the United States and Canada, describing some very curious events. A florist started piping music into his greenhouse. His flowers, he said, grew bigger than before. Their colors were brighter, and they lasted longer.

A minister recited prayers over a patch of young beans. They flourished. A housewife shouted angrily at her ivy. It wilted as if under a curse. A farmer broadcast classical music to a test plot of wheat. He claimed a 66 per cent crop increase.

After reading many of these stories, an Illinois botanist set up a controlled experiment. He planted a mixture of corn and soybeans in two identical growing trays. He kept both trays at the same temperature and gave them the same amount of water and light. But he kept one in silence, while playing music to the other (George Gershwin's *Rhapsody in Blue*).

The serenaded seedlings were clearly bigger, thicker, and healthier than those grown without music. What was the explanation? The botanist thought that perhaps sound energy had increased the molecular activity in the plants.

By the late 1960's similar investigations were going on everywhere. One of the most interesting was begun in 1968 by a Colorado soprano who also happened to be a graduate student in biology.

Using a mixture of plants, she tested their reactions to different types of sound. In one case, she used a tape recorder to play the note of F over and over for eight hours a day. Within two weeks, all the plants were dead. "Almost," she said, "as if they were driven out of their minds." An identical assortment

A green thumb is simply
a positive state of mind.

Just the intent of harming it seemed
to trigger a response in the plant.

that had been left in peace continued to grow.

A group of squash plants twined lovingly around a loudspeaker that played Mozart to them, while another group grew as fast as possible *away* from a loudspeaker playing rock music.

In other tests Beethoven, jazz, and tapes of jet airport noise have been used. The plants have responded in different ways. But they have always responded.

Why? How? One explanation, suggested by a research chemist in California, is that all living things, plant and animal, share a still unknown type of electrical energy. This energy enables them to communicate with one another and to influence one another. What is more, they may be able to do this without sound.

Plant experiments sometimes fail, this man asserts, because the plants have grown tired or are simply in a bad mood. Or a plant may take a dislike to one human being and refuse to co-operate with him.

The same researcher tries to get reactions from his own plants by capturing their interest. He believes that one of his philodendrons likes spooky stories told in a dark room. At tense moments—"Charles bent down and raised the lid of the coffin"—the plant seems to pay special attention.

How can you tell whether a plant likes you or enjoys your ghost stories? Well . . . you could use a lie detector.

Late one evening, in 1966, a New York expert in the use of the polygraph, or lie detector, was checking his equipment. Out of curiosity, he attached a set of electrodes to one of the large leaves of a palm-like plant in his office.

He wanted to see if the polygraph would record any response when water was poured on the dry soil at the roots.

He did not expect an emotional response. He thought the polygraph might register an upward line. This would show that as the plant became more moist, it conducted more electricity. But to his surprise, the line began to move jerkily downward, just as it does when a human subject is experiencing a strong emotion.

Was it possible that the plant felt emotion when he watered it? If so, then a threat should cause a stronger emotion. He dipped a leaf in his cup of hot coffee. There was no reaction.

Then he thought of an even stronger threat. He could burn a leaf with a lighted match. As soon as the idea came to him, he reported

"Back in two weeks,
sweetheart."

"Now
get growing."

later, the polygraph reacted wildly. It seemed as if the plant were actually reading his mind.

Since that first startling experience, the polygraph expert has conducted many more tests. He is now convinced that communication is possible between humans and plants. And he believes that it can take place not only by sound but simply by thought transference.

However, when other scientists try to duplicate such experiments in their own laboratories, they are less successful. As a result, they tend to dismiss this type of investigation as muddled pseudo science (false science) or even outright fraud. One plant physiologist at Colorado State University was asked to comment on the subject. His comment was short: "Pure garbage!" he said.

Was he right? You might try an experiment of your own. If you are only testing whether sound affects plants, you won't need a polygraph. But you will need to design two identical growing environments. If you work at school, perhaps your science teacher will help.

Either at school or at home, set up two flat, shallow containers. In each one, plant the same number of lima beans or radish seeds. Plant enough to make up for any bad seeds. Use the same type of soil for each container and exactly equal amounts of water.

Your containers must also be exposed to the same light, temperature, and air currents. Yet only one can be exposed to sound. This is the tricky part.

A lot depends on where you do the experiment. At home, you might have two rooms side by side, with similar windows. You could put a container on each windowsill.

Using a tape recorder or a radio, play music to one of the containers for at least two hours a day. Keep a record of when the seedlings sprout in each container, how many come up, and how fast they grow. When the time comes for transplanting, take a close look at the seedlings. Do you notice any marked difference between the two sets? If you want to be really sure of your results, repeat the same experiment several times.

If you want to test for thought transference, beam encouraging thoughts at one set of plants while ignoring the other.

What if there is no noticeable difference, no matter what you do? Does that prove that the whole idea is nonsense? Or does it just mean that the plants don't feel like co-operating? Or could it be that they would rather hear a ghost story?

CONSTANCE TABER COLBY
Author of children's books

Shuttle vehicles would be needed between the earth and its colonies in space. The model above is one design suggested as part of a space shuttle system.

A SPACE COLONY

Readers of science fiction are very familiar with the story of people leaving the earth to set up a colony in space. But the colonization of space may not remain science fiction. In May, 1974, a number of scientists and astronauts met at Princeton University in New Jersey to discuss their ideas on the subject.

Are space colonies possible? Six pairs of astronauts have landed and walked on the moon. Other astronauts spent several months working in Skylab, the U.S. space laboratory, as it orbited the earth. All these pioneers returned safely. The evidence is strong that human beings, properly protected, can live away from the earth for long periods of time.

Getting the colonists to their place in space presents many problems. Research is being done on space shuttles, re-usable space ships for carrying people and cargo. Unlike today's spacecraft, the shuttles would return to earth, landing horizontally like jet planes. Shuttles could cut out much of the huge expense of spacecraft that can be used only once.

A space colony could be placed at one of several points in space, where it would be equally attracted by the gravitation of the earth and of the moon. At such a place the colony would be stable—it would not fall toward either of these bodies.

One "housing" design suggested for the colony is a cylinder, about 300 feet (91 meters) long (about as long as a football field) with a diameter about twice as great.

The members of the colony, perhaps as many as 2,000 people, would live within the cylinder. It would spin several times a minute, to provide an artificial gravity for the inhabitants.

Where would the colonists get the food, water, and other materials needed for survival away from the earth? At first, some materials might have to be brought from the earth. After a colony was established, it might become self-sufficient. Large meteors in space might provide some of the materials needed for building. Meteors are rich in nickel and iron, two of the most useful metals we have on the earth. And scientists have evidence that some material in space contains water and hydrocarbons (compounds of hydrogen and carbon). As on earth, these compounds could be the raw materials for producing many complex useful substances.

The energy needed for making new materials, for running machines, for heating and cooling, and for growing food would be obtained from the sun. There is no night in space, so the sun's light is always available as a source of energy.

Some people believe that space colonies might be the only way to save the human race. If people pollute earth's atmosphere, fight a nuclear war, or permit uncontrolled population growth, leaving earth could be the only means of survival. However, others insist that people should try to solve their problems on earth first. But whatever point of view one has, there is no denying the great adventure involved in proving it is possible to live where no one has ever lived before.

DIAGNOSIS BY SATELLITE

Hundreds of satellites have been placed into orbit around the earth in recent years. So the launching of one more satellite—on May 30, 1974, by the United States—did not cause much stir. But this satellite, the ATS-6 (Applications Technology Satellite), promises something new—a special kind of close involvement of millions of people.

The ATS-6 differs from previous communications satellites mainly in the way it is being used. It is providing live, two-way television to remote, isolated villages in Alaska and the Appalachian and Rocky mountains. Such places are often cut off from television and radio reception by distance, mountains, or atmospheric conditions.

Television and radio signals travel in straight lines. They do not follow the earth's curvature, so they cannot be received well over long distances. Communications satellites like the ATS-6 are one solution to the problem of worldwide reception. The satellite is placed in orbit 22,300 miles (35,880 kilometers) above the equator. At that distance, it takes the satellite 24 hours to circle the earth. Since the earth also rotates on its axis once every 24 hours, the satellite seems to "stand still" over the same spot on the earth.

Television and radio waves are beamed from huge antennas to the satellite. The satellite receives the waves, amplifies (strengthens) them, and beams them back to the earth. In this way, instant communication by radio and television is made possible all over the earth. Many programs can be relayed at the same time without interference.

A nurse, a medical technician, or other public health worker in a village can make use of the ATS-6 to talk to a doctor hundreds of miles away. The doctor can see and talk with the public health worker and the patient on two-way television. The doctor can study the X-ray pictures and electrocardiograms made by the public health worker, and give advice for treating the patient. With the help of the satellite, doctors in small towns and villages can consult with experts in hospitals and medical schools. The satellite also enables doctors in remote areas to keep up with recent developments in medicine.

There are many other ways the ATS-6 can be used. Universities are planning graduate courses in which teachers in widely separated areas can participate as if they were all in the same room. Plans are even being made for adult-education courses.

Besides doing its medical and educational work, the ATS-6 will be used in various experiments. For example, it will be tried in air traffic control over the heavily traveled air lanes of the North Atlantic Ocean. It will also be used to relay information gathered by weather satellites.

After a year of service to the United States, the ATS-6 will be moved to a position in which it can serve another part of the world for one year.

Artist's conception of an ATS satellite. The ATS-6 communications satellite is being used in medicine, education, and in other fields.

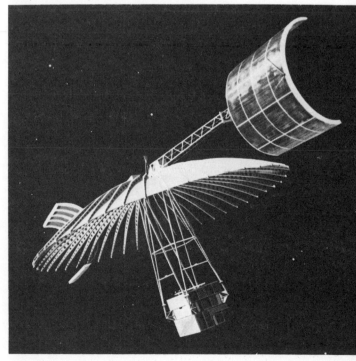

Two little Witkars are caught in a big traffic jam in Amsterdam.

THE WITKAR

It looks something like a golf cart or a white top hat on wheels. It's even been called "the flying bathtub." You can see it moving along, slowly but surely, at a top speed of 20 miles (32 kilometers) per hour. Just what is this odd vehicle? It's the Netherlands' Witkar, or "white car," a small electric two-seater. And it's becoming more and more popular every day.

Every large city in the world is aware of and concerned with the destructive effects of noise and air pollution. The automobile is a major source of this pollution. Recently, there have been many suggestions for a replacement for the standard car. But none of these ideas have been particularly convenient or practical, economically speaking. However, Amsterdam engineer Luud Schimmelpennink seems to have come up with an interesting and promising vehicle.

The Witkar is working very well in Amsterdam, a city with serious noise and air pollution. The Witkar is a battery-powered car, and therefore nonpolluting and quieter than most cars. Since it runs on batteries, it needs no gasoline. (The burning of gasoline is a cause of air pollution.) When necessary, the batteries can be recharged at any Witkar station, located 2.4 miles (3.9 km.) apart.

The Witkar is also perfect for the heavy traffic of downtown Amsterdam, where no one needs to drive any faster than the Witkar is able to go. And it is easier to find a parking place for this minicar—three Witkars fit into a spot that a standard-sized European sedan would take up.

The Witkar is not for sale. It can only be rented. Since an average trip in a Witkar costs less than half as much as a taxi ride, many people can afford the cost of the rental.

In order to drive this little car, one must subscribe to the Witkar Co-operative Union, which operates a fleet of Witkars. For a small annual fee, each member receives a special magnetic key. The key can be inserted into a computerized control box at any Witkar station. The computer makes a note of the transaction, and the member is supplied with a car. When the driver returns the car (to any Witkar station), the computer signs him in, makes a note of the mileage, and charges it to his account.

For a trial period, fifteen Witkar stations have been built. The first station was opened on March 21, 1974. And this may be just the beginning of many Witkars to come.

A RELIC
FROM THE SEA

In ancient times, when little was known of the true immensity of the earth, the Mediterranean Sea was the great highway of the Western world. Stretching from the shores of the Middle East to the Strait of Gibraltar, and from southern Europe to northern Africa, the Mediterranean was a natural route for ships carrying goods from one land to another. In fact the name "Mediterranean," which comes from Latin, means "in the midst of the land."

Some years ago, the remains of one such ship were found off the coast of Cyprus in the eastern Mediterranean. The ship, a merchant vessel trading among the islands of Greece, probably sank during a storm. The ship is believed to date from about 350 B.C., which would make it the oldest ship yet reclaimed from beneath the sea.

Scientists were first alerted to the possibility of such a discovery in 1967, when a Cypriot diver told archeologists he had found some large jars, called amphorae, buried in the sand. The contents of the amphorae—probably wine—had been part of the ship's cargo. Efforts to raise the sunken vessel, however, were complicated. First the necessary money had to be raised and a team of archeologists and other scientists gathered together. A total of $350,000 was finally obtained from various organizations, and the difficult work was started.

The recovery and restoration of the 45-foot-long (14-meter-long) ship took seven years of painstaking effort. The ship itself was lying in almost 100 feet (30 meters) of water and was buried under several feet of sand and mud. The sand had to be cleared away before the ship could be cut into sections and then raised to the surface. One of the greatest problems facing the recovery team was the possibility that the wood would disintegrate when it came into contact with the air. After 2,300 years under water, the cellulose, of which wood is partly composed, had disappeared, and the ship threatened to crumble into dust. To prevent this, each part of the vessel that was brought to the surface was kept bathed in water until a cellulose substitute could be absorbed by the wood. This process alone took more than a year for some of the larger pieces.

About 75 per cent of the original ship has been preserved. Substitutes for the missing parts have been added to give what scientists hope is an accurate picture of the vessel.

The ship is displayed in a room in an old castle in Kyrenia, Cyprus, near the spot where the ship sank and where it was at last discovered.

A diver works on the 2,300-year-old merchant ship. At left are the amphorae, which were pointed so they could be stood in the ground.

THE LANGUAGE OF FLOWERS

How do flowers get their common names? The gods and goddesses of the Greeks and Romans were the inspiration for the names of some flowers. The iris, for example, is named for the Greek goddess of the rainbow. Many flowers are named after people. Thus, fuchsias were named after Leonhard Fuchs, a German botanist. With still other flowers, such as bluebells, the appearance of the flower gave rise to its name.

▶ SCIENTISTS' NAMES FOR PLANTS

Most flowers have more than one common name. For example, there is a wildflower that is called *daisy* in English, *marguerite* in French, and *margarita* in Spanish. Many flowers are even called by different names in different parts of the same country. As an example, look at these names: whiteweed, ox-eye, white daisy. Are these three different flowers? No. They are three of the common names of a certain kind of daisy. You can see why using only the common names of flowers can lead to confusion. People cannot always be sure that they are all talking about the same kind of flower.

A Swedish botanist found a way to avoid the confusion more than 200 years ago. He was Carl von Linné, better known by the Latin form of his name, Carolus Linnaeus. He developed a scientific method for sorting out, or classifying, living things, both plants and animals. This science is called taxonomy.

The taxonomist classifies living things, or organisms, according to their structure—the way they are built. A plant or animal must be observed with great care when it is being classified. In addition to studying both the inner and the outer structure of the organism, the taxonomist must compare it with other living things that are somewhat like it.

After it has been classified, the organism is given a pair of Latin names. The first name gives the larger group, or *genus,* to which the plant belongs. The second name gives the smaller group, or *species,* within the genus. Thus any botanist, from any country, knows that when he or she reads about *Chrysanthe-mum leucanthemum,* a particular type of daisy is meant, and no other.

▶ PLANTS NAMED FOR SCIENTISTS

Some plants are named after people, including scientists. You should be able to guess these plant names from the names of the scientists.

1. Michel **Bégon** was a French lawyer, judge, and amateur botanist of the late 17th century. Returning to France from an assignment in the Caribbean, he brought back some plants whose brightly colored flowers made them favorite houseplants. What is the name of these plants?

Begonia

2. Alexander **Garden** was a physician who practiced in Charleston, South Carolina. His great interest in botany led him into a correspondence with Linnaeus and other plant scientists. The plant named after him has waxy flowers that are very fragrant.

Gardenia

3. Louis Antoine de **Bougainville** was a French navigator and explorer who circled the globe in a three-year voyage that began in 1766. He and his fellow explorers mapped unknown areas of the Pacific Ocean, and made many botanical observations. A naturalist who took part in the expedition named a showy tropical vine after Bougainville. What is its name?

Bougainvillea

4. George Kamel (or **Camellus** in Latin) was a missionary in the Philippines. He wrote a book about the plants native to those islands. Linnaeus named a plant in his honor. What is the name of the plant?

Camellia

5. Anders **Dahl** was a Swedish botanist. The plant that was named after him has showy, many-petaled flowers.

Dahlia

▶ THE TULIP

The name of a well-known garden plant, the tulip, is connected with Turkish history. By the 16th century, after several hundred

Begonia

Gardenia

Bougainvillea

Camellia

Dahlia

A garden full of tulips . . .

. . . and roses in bloom.

years of warfare, the Turkish sultans had conquered North Africa, the Middle East, and large parts of eastern and southern Europe. By 1554 they were fighting with Austria. Ferdinand I, the Austrian ruler, sent a special ambassador to the Sultan in the hope of arranging peace terms. The ambassador, Augier de Busbecq, carried out his mission successfully. He also found time to observe and admire the Turkish gardens. Flowers of a kind he had never seen grew there. Some of them were brilliant red. Others were yellow. The flowers looked rather like the turban, or *tuliband,* worn by Turkish men. Busbecq used the word *tulipan* in referring to the flowers, and this was later shortened to "tulip." Busbecq brought tulips back to Vienna, to be planted in the royal gardens.

Before long, tulips became very popular in European gardens, and especially in the gardens of Holland. Tulip bulbs were so cheap that even poor people could afford to buy a few. Then a strange thing happened. Some bulbs began to change, producing strange flowers. At that time, no one knew why this was happening. There were very few of the changed bulbs, and there was no way to tell whether a particular bulb had changed until it had grown and its flowers appeared.

Ordinary tulip bulbs grew into plants with solid-colored flowers. But the changed bulbs produced flowers of more than one color, and the colors appeared streaked. The rarity of the streaked flowers made them very valuable. People were ready to pay the equivalent of thousands of dollars for a bulb whose flowers were streaked, because the seeds from these flowers could often be grown to produce more plants with streaked flowers.

Today botanists know that the streaking is caused by a particular kind of virus. Not only does a plant infected by this virus produce streaked flowers, its flowers in turn produce seeds that carry the streaking into the next generation.

Although huge sums of money were paid for the rare bulbs, a person did not have to be rich to gamble with bulbs. Any ordinary cheap bulb might produce streaked flowers and make its owner rich overnight. A "tulip mania" developed in Holland. Speculators in bulbs made and lost great fortunes. The government finally put an end to the madness by prohibiting speculation in bulbs.

After things quieted down the Dutch settled into the business of growing tulip bulbs. The bulbs of Holland became famous. They were exported to the Americas, to the rest of Europe—and even to Turkey, where it all began. Today the Dutch bulb industry produces about 2,000,000,000 (billion) bulbs each year.

▶ THE ROSE

Roses are among the most popular garden flowers. They are also among the most ancient flowers known. Fossils of rose plants found in the western United States date back almost 40,000,000 years. But botanists believe that the plants may have appeared in Asia as long as 60,000,000 years ago.

The original rose plants had small, simple flowers with only five petals. Wall paintings of these roses, made about 3,500 years ago, have been found in Knossos, an ancient city on the Greek island of Crete. Today there are hundreds of varieties of roses, in all colors and sizes, developed over the centuries by plant breeders.

Like so many other words, "rose" comes to us from the Greek, by way of Latin. *Rhodon* was the name the ancient Greeks gave to the flower. Under the Romans, the word became *rosa*. The name of one of the major Greek islands, Rhodos (Rhodes in English), comes from the word *rhodon*. More than 100 types of coins from ancient Rhodes carry a rose as a symbol of the island.

The term *sub rosa,* meaning "secretly" or "in confidence," also comes to us from the Greek by way of Latin. One of the ancient Greek myths tells us that Eros, the god of love, once gave a rose to Harpocrates, the god of silence. He hoped in this way to persuade Harpocrates to hide the follies of some of the gods. Eros was especially concerned about the follies of his own mother, Aphrodite, the goddess of love.

The myth led the Romans to adopt the custom of hanging a rose from the ceiling of a council chamber. It reminded members who attended the council meetings that anything that was said *sub rosa* ("under the rose") was to be kept secret.

Roses have often served in various ways as symbols. In the church of the Middle Ages, the rose became associated with the Virgin Mary. The stamps and coins of many countries are decorated with roses. In 15th century England a long series of civil wars came to be known as the Wars of the Roses because one side had a red rose as its symbol, and the other side, a white rose.

The scent of roses has been used in perfumes for many centuries. The perfume maker begins with a greenish-yellow oil that is distilled from the petals of roses. It is called "attar of roses." ("Attar" is from a Persian word meaning "perfumed.") Today most attar is made in Bulgaria. Attar is among the world's most costly materials. The value of 1 pound is nearly $1,000 ($2,200 for 1 kilogram). If you wonder why, you should know that at least 2 tons of rose petals are needed to make 1 pound of attar (4½ tons for 1 kg.).

Aster

Chrysanthemum

Anemone

▶ THE ANEMONE

It is said that the ancient Greeks believed that anemones bloomed only when the wind blew. Therefore they called the flower *anemōnē,* meaning "daughter of the wind." But there is another, more complicated myth that involves Adonis, a handsome youth beloved by Aphrodite. We are told that Adonis, while on a hunt, was killed by a wild boar. A crimson-flowered plant sprang from his blood. In the Hebrew and Arabic languages, Adonis was referred to as *Naaman* ("the darling," or "the charming one"), and from this the word "anemone" may also have come.

▶ THE ASTER

The aster is one of those flowers whose name comes from its appearance. It has long petals that radiate from a buttonlike center. The raylike petals suggest stars (although rays exist only in the imagination, not in the stars). So the Greek word *astēr,* meaning "star," came into use as the name of the flower.

▶ THE CHRYSANTHEMUM

"Chrysanthemum" comes from two Greek words meaning "golden flower." There are indeed many golden-colored flowers among the more than 150 species (kinds) of chrysanthemums. But these flowers, called "mums" for short, come in a whole rainbow of other colors. They vary a great deal in size, from

Forget-me-not

Geranium

the tiny daisy-like flower called feverfew to large showy flowers over 6 inches (15 centimeters) in diameter.

THE FORGET-ME-NOT

Many tales are told to explain the origin of the name of the flower called forget-me-not. One of the best known of these tales is that of a German knight, who climbed down a riverbank to pick flowers for his beloved. The knight fell into the swift-flowing stream, and as he was swept away he managed to toss the flowers to the lady, crying out as he did so, "Forget me not!"

The scientific name of the plant is based on the way its leaves look. The name is *Myosotis,* and it comes from two Greek words that mean "mouse's ear."

THE GERANIUM

The name of this plant comes from the appearance of its seedpods, which few people ever see. The end of each pod has a beak-like twist that suggests the shape of a crane's bill, and that is exactly what the plant was once called—the cranesbill. The Greek for "crane" is *geranos,* and so the word "geranium" came to be used.

To be accurate, "geranium" should be used only for the wild varieties of the plant. The familiar houseplants with red, white, and pink flowers are pelargoniums. The name is taken from the Greek word for "stork," *pelargos.*

NEW EYES ON THE SKIES

People have been interested in knowing about the sky above them since the very beginning of recorded time. It is easy to imagine early man looking up with wonder at the night sky. For the last 350 years or so, studies of the heavens have been aided by telescopes—optical telescopes, made with lenses or mirrors. These optical instruments have grown larger and more powerful as technology has advanced. In the last ten years astronomers have been given finer new "eyes."

There are two basic types of new telescopes. First, there are the new and more powerful optical telescopes. These instruments take advantage of all the latest advances in technology while still using traditional lenses or mirrors. And then there are the more spectacular of the new tools—the radio telescopes and related devices. Basically, the antennas of radio telescopes pick up the radio waves given off by objects in space.

▶ **NEW OPTICAL TELESCOPES**

Until recently the largest optical telescopes were all in the Northern Hemisphere and were all of similar design. These older large telescopes include three famous reflecting telescopes in California. They are the Hale Telescope, whose huge mirror is 200 inches (5 meters) across; the 120-inch (3-m.) reflector at Lick Observatory; and the 100-inch (2.54-m.) reflector on Mount Wilson.

Many of the new large optical telescopes are also in the Northern Hemisphere. In the mountains of the Caucasus, in the Soviet Union, near the village of Zelenchukskaya, is the world's largest reflecting telescope. It went into operation in 1974. Its main mirror is 236 inches (6 m.) in diameter.

A more unusual telescope is now under construction in the United States. It is to be used on Mount Hopkins, in Arizona. It is not one simple instrument, but actually six telescopes designed to work as one. Each of the six telescopes is 72 inches (1.8 m.) in diameter. The light reaching the six mirrors comes to a focus at a single point. Known as the Multiple Mirror Telescope (MMT), this instrument will have a light-gathering power equal to that of a huge single mirror 176

The mirror (*left*) and housing (*right*) of the Zelenchukskaya telescope.

inches (4.47 m.) in diameter. It is easier and cheaper to make six mirrors that are each 72 inches in diameter than to make a single 176-inch mirror. The MMT will be the world's third largest reflecting telescope when it is completed.

Other new optical telescopes built recently in the Northern Hemisphere include a 158-inch (4-m.) reflector at the Kitt Peak National Observatory in Arizona, a 107-inch (2.7-m.) reflector at the McDonald Observatory in Texas, and a 98-inch (2.5-m.) reflector at the Royal Greenwich Observatory in England.

One of the best observing sites in the Northern Hemisphere is located on the cone of Mauna Kea, an extinct volcano in Hawaii. A reflecting telescope with an 88-inch (2.24-m.) mirror is already in operation there, along with some smaller telescopes. The French and Canadian governments are co-operating in building a 142-inch (3.6-m.) telescope at Mauna Kea.

One of the big changes in astronomy in the past ten years has been the building of a number of new, large telescopes in the Southern Hemisphere. Three of them are in Chile. There is a 158-inch (4-m.) reflector, identical to the one at Kitt Peak, Arizona, on Cerro Tololo. The European Southern Observatory, on Cerro La Silla, has a 142-inch (3.6-m.) reflector and a 39.4 inch (1-m.) Schmidt camera telescope. A Schmidt telescope is a special kind of reflector, used for making wide-angle photographs of the heavens. The Schmidt telescope on Cerro La Silla is one of the largest instruments of its kind in the world. Las Campañas Observatory has a 101-inch (2.57-m.) reflecting telescope under construction.

Australia is also involved in building large optical telescopes. A new 150-inch (3.8-m.) telescope is being built at the Siding Spring Observatory by the British and Australian governments. Siding Spring also has a 48-inch (1.2-m.) Schmidt telescope, similar to the one at Mount Palomar in California. The Schmidt telescope at Palomar has already been used to make a photographic atlas of all the sky visible from the Northern Hemisphere. Now the Schmidt telescopes at Siding Spring and Cerro La Silla will be used to

A model shows the complex structure of the Multiple Mirror Telescope on Mount Hopkins.

The new telescope at Cerro Tololo, in Chile.

Some of the antennas of the Culgoora telescope.

of electromagnetic radiation. However, it has wavelengths, or frequencies, that cannot be seen by the human eye. Radio waves are just one example of this other kind of radiation.

Australia is a leading center for radio astronomy. Among the newer Australian antennas used for the study of radio waves from space is the Molonglo cross-shaped radio telescope. This instrument has 1-mile-long (1.6-kilometers-long) adjustable arms. These antennas are used for studying pulsars, quasars, and other strange phenomena in space. Another new Australian instrument is the Culgoora radio-heliograph. This instrument consists of 96 antennas, each 45 feet (13.7 m.) in diameter, arranged in a circle nearly 2 miles (3 km.) across. This giant instrument is used for studying the radio waves emitted by the sun.

An enormous, dish-shaped radio telescope is located at Arecibo, Puerto Rico. The 1,000-foot (304-m.) antenna has just been resurfaced with highly reflective aluminum panels. And a new radar transmitter has been added, making the telescope 2,000 times more powerful. This will make it possible to view the skies over a whole new range of wavelengths.

In the deserts of New Mexico, in the United States, construction has recently begun on a giant complex of radio telescopes. This instrument—called the Very Large Array (VLA)—will consist of 27 antennas, each 85 feet (25.9 m.) across. The antennas will be capable of being moved along double railroad tracks laid out in the shape of a gigantic letter Y. Each of the three arms of the Y will be 13 miles (21 km.) long. The combined signals from the 27 antennas will be used to form a single image, or picture, of the source of the radio waves that are picked up.

In addition to developing these new instruments for observing light waves and radio waves, scientists have developed new techniques for analyzing images received by them. Such techniques have made it possible to correct light images and radio signals that have been distorted in passing through the atmosphere.

make a similar map of all the stars visible from the Southern Hemisphere.

There is also an unusual instrument at the Narrabri Observatory in Australia. It measures the size of stars. It consists of two large mirrors, each composed of many tiny mirrors. The large mirrors are mounted on railroad cars that move on a circular track. By comparing measurements made when the two large mirrors are in different positions, astronomers can estimate the diameter of a star millions of light-years away.

▶ **RADIO ASTRONOMY**

A whole new kind of astronomy has become very important to the astronomers of the space age: radio astronomy. Its importance was emphasized when two British radio astronomers were awarded the 1974 Nobel Prize in physics. Radio astronomy uses radio telescopes and other related instruments, all of which view kinds of "light" that are very different from the visible light we see when we look out the window or turn on an electric lamp. Like visible light, this "light" is a kind

▶ **BEYOND THE ATMOSPHERE**

Besides visible light and radio waves, there are other types of electromagnetic radiation.

The giant "dish," or antenna, of the radio telescope at Arecibo, Puerto Rico.

These kinds of radiation—which include infrared and ultraviolet radiation, X rays, and gamma rays—are absorbed or scattered by the earth's atmosphere, and cannot be accurately detected by instruments on the ground. Scientists who wish to study radiations of this kind emitted by objects in space must use instruments that are situated beyond the earth's atmosphere. This means that there is the additional problem of sending equipment into space by satellite and of getting the information that has been recorded there back to earth. Signals can be radioed back from satellites such as the Orbiting Astronomical Observatory (OAO) and the Orbiting Solar Observatory (OSO). Signals may also be recorded by rocket-borne instruments that are retrieved when the instruments are parachuted to earth. It is also possible for a scientist-astronaut who is himself in space to receive the signals. That was what happened during the U.S. Skylab project.

R. A. REINSTEIN
Co-director, ISAR
(Institute for Scientific and Artistic Research)

This is what the Very Large Array telescope in New Mexico will look like when it is completed.

The recently discovered Roman villa in Oplonti.

OPLONTI

The well-preserved remains of a 2,000-year-old Roman villa, or country mansion, have been discovered in southern Italy, not far from the city of Naples. The villa, part of the ancient Roman city of Oplonti, had evidently been buried for centuries. An old map gave archeologists their first clue to the existence of the previously unknown city, which is believed to have been closely linked with nearby Pompeii. So far, the most striking find has been the villa, but excavations are in progress to uncover the rest of Oplonti.

The luxurious villa was obviously the home of a wealthy and prominent man. Designed along majestic lines, the building is square in shape and measures 180 feet (55 meters) in each direction. It is constructed around a traditional Roman central court, called an *atrium*. The villa was decorated with wall paintings and sculpture, which are in remarkably good condition. Gardens were planted both inside and outside the building. Since the Romans were particularly fond of bathing, it is not surprising that two of the rooms that have been uncovered proved to be a bath and a steam room.

Who the actual inhabitants of the villa were and what happened to them remain in doubt. But it has been suggested that they may have fled their home following the earthquake that scientists know struck the region in A.D. 62. If so, they were probably saved from the fate that befell the people of Pompeii.

Pompeii, a thriving city of about 20,000 people, lay in the shadow of Mount Vesuvius, the only active volcano on the mainland of Europe. In A.D. 79, Vesuvius suddenly came alive, spewing ash, cinders, smoke, and poisonous gases over a wide area. The eruption killed many of the inhabitants and buried Pompeii under many feet of volcanic material.

Pompeii lay buried for almost 1,700 years until, in the 18th century, efforts to unearth the ancient city were begun. Archeologists were amazed at what they found. They had expected to find the ruins of a completely destroyed city. Instead, the volcanic material that covered the city had preserved it. Paved streets, restaurants, wineshops, homes, and temples can still be seen. Even the imprint of the bodies of the victims who were struck down suddenly by the poisonous gases can be made out.

The discovery of Pompeii opened a window on the past, giving the world a picture of an ancient way of life. Archeologists believe that the recent discoveries at Oplonti may be equally important.

From Leonardo's newly found notebooks: a chain drive (*left*). It inspired a pupil's design for a bicycle, found in another notebook.

Diagram showing how the wind makes sailboats move.

LEONARDO'S NOTEBOOKS

Leonardo da Vinci, born in Italy in 1452, was one of the greatest painters of all time. Most people think of him as the painter of the *Mona Lisa,* the woman with the mysterious smile. But Leonardo also kept notebooks that show him to have been a great inventor, engineer, and mechanical genius.

Leonardo wanted to know how everything worked and why. In his notebooks he posed questions to himself and worked out the answers in brilliant and ingenious ways—by drawing diagrams, plans, and intricate designs. From his notebooks, we learn about his famous plans—for a flying machine, a diving bell, a rocket, and a parachute, among other things. Although working models of Leonardo's revolutionary inventions were sometimes made, most of his ideas were too advanced to be recognized as useful in his own time.

After Leonardo's death in 1519, a number of his notebooks vanished. In 1965 two of the missing notebooks were found. The notebooks had been "lost" in Spain's National Library in Madrid through a cataloging error. These two notebooks are called the *Madrid Codices* ("codices" is the plural of "codex," which means "manuscript book").

The first notebook is a rough draft of a handbook on the science of mechanics. All but three of the 22 basic devices used in modern machines were drawn and explained here, long before their use in modern times. Among many other designs, Leonardo sketched the gyroscope, the chain drive, the worm gear, and even the pendulum, which is usually credited to Galileo.

In drawing after drawing in the second notebook, Leonardo answers such questions as "How do waves move?" and "How does the wind make sailboats go?" There is a plan for a canal to link Florence with the sea; and there are drawings showing how musical instruments can be made to fit the human hand better. Leonardo thought of everything, it seems. And if these latest notebooks had been found 400 years sooner, who knows how they might have changed our history?

A clock mechanism designed by Leonardo.

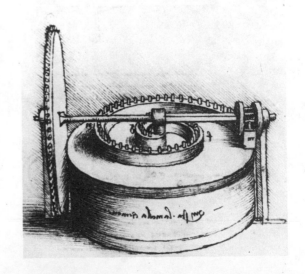

FUN TO MAKE AND DO

Go fly a kite!

PEANUT PETS

While shelling and crunching your way through a bag of peanuts, have you ever thought what strange, funny shapes some of the shells have? If you fiddle around with some shells one day, perhaps you can create these peanut pets. Here's what you will need to put them together: a bag of unshelled peanuts, pipe cleaners, all-purpose glue, poster paints, thin cardboard, and a pencil.

Whole peanut shells with the peanuts still inside are great for the body and head sections. Those with only one nut inside are just right for hands and feet. For the other parts of the body, you will have to split the shells apart before deciding what shape is best to use.

If you think you will have difficulty making some of them stand (like the caterpillar or octopus), glue the shells that make up the body onto a piece of thin cardboard. Then cut around the shape after the glue has dried.

To attach the pipe cleaners, punch holes in the shells with a dull pencil. You could also use a hairpin, nail, or the end of a paper clip to make the holes. Add a drop of glue to keep the legs, antennae, or arms securely in place.

You might want to paint the different parts before you put the creature together. Some parts will have to be painted or touched up after the animal is finished.

Have fun with your nutty zoo and enjoy the peanuts too.

MAKE A SNAKE

Snakes are fun to make and they can be created from all sorts of hodgepodge materials found around the house—from thread spools and soda straws to fancy beads, Ping-Pong balls, yarn, old stockings, and even macaroni. Look around your room. Maybe you will find something that would make a great snake!

Our nut and yarn snake is made from six strands of different-colored, medium-thick yarn 10 inches (25 centimeters) long. If you would like to make a fatter snake, use more strands.

Braid the strands. Put a small rubber band on each end. Gently pry open the shell of a peanut. Place one end of the braid inside one half peanut shell and glue in place. Glue the other half shell on top. Paint the eyes on and glue a piece of yarn on the peanut shell for the tongue.

Spool snake is one that even the youngest member of the family can make. String empty thread spools (any size will do) on colored pipe cleaner that is about 2 feet (½ meter) long. You may have to join two long pipe cleaners to get the length you want. Make a loop on one end of the pipe cleaner to hold the spools in place. Insert the other end of the pipe cleaner into the head, formed from crumbled aluminum foil. Use a small piece of pipe cleaner for the tongue. To make a rattlesnake, attach a bell to the tail end.

Following the same procedure you can use macaroni to create another fun snake. Tempera paints are great to use to paint the spools or macaroni.

The finished product: a baker's clay frame.

A BAKER'S CLAY FRAME

Did you ever bake cookies? It's fun to roll the dough and cut it out, or to make all kinds of different shapes with your hands. Sometimes the things you make seem to be too good to eat!

Baker's clay is a material you can make yourself. It lets you have all the fun of baking cookies, with the added pleasure of painting and decorating your creations and keeping them as long as you wish. With baker's clay, you can make small containers, jewelry, flowers, or wall hangings. You can shape funny animals or a set of tiny dishes, a flower holder to hang on the wall, or an ornament for the Christmas tree.

Sandy, who is thirteen, decided that she would like to use baker's clay to make something useful and decorative. She had an oval mirror that she thought would look very nice in a baker's clay frame.

WHAT SANDY USED

a large bowl
1 cup salt
1½ cups hot water
4 cups all-purpose flour
an oval mirror, 5 inches by 7 inches (13 centimeters by 18 centimeters)
a piece of thin cardboard, 8½ inches by 10½ inches (22 cm. by 27 cm.)
a piece of corrugated cardboard, 8 inches by 10 inches (20 cm. by 27 cm.)
a rolling pin
a foil-covered cookie sheet
evaporated milk
an old shoe box
self-adhering contact paper
white glue
acrylic spray
bottle caps, sticks, or other objects for making the designs
a picture hook

104

MAKE THE CLAY

Into a large bowl, pour 1½ cups of hot water and 1 cup of salt. Mix with a spoon until the salt dissolves. Add 4 cups of all-purpose flour to the water and mix until sticky. Now pour the mixture onto a floured surface and knead (press and push with your hands) until it becomes smooth—about ten minutes. If the dough becomes too dry, add a few drops of water. If it's too sticky, add a little more flour.

Once you have kneaded your baker's clay to the proper consistency, it can be kept in a tightly closed plastic bag in the refrigerator until you are ready to use it. If it seems to be too dry when you remove it from the refrigerator, a few drops of water and a little kneading will make it ready to use.

HOW SANDY MADE HER FRAME

Sandy decided to make a baker's clay frame that would be an 8-by-10-inch rectangle, with an opening for the mirror in the center. She started by making a pattern for her frame. Using an 8½-by-10½-inch piece of thin cardboard, Sandy drew and cut out the opening she wanted in the center of her frame. The pattern was slightly larger than the finished mirror would be because baker's clay shrinks a bit in the oven. She tried out her cardboard pattern by placing it over the mirror, making sure that the edges of the mirror didn't show at all.

Now Sandy was ready to cut out her baker's clay mirror frame. First she rolled out the baker's clay until it was ½ inch (1 cm.) thick. She placed her pattern over the baker's clay and cut around it with a knife. Next she cut out the hole for the mirror. The baker's clay that was cut away was put back in the plastic bag and returned to the refrigerator for use on another day.

Very carefully, using two spatulas and with an adult's help, Sandy lifted the baker's clay frame onto a foil-covered cookie sheet. (Smaller baker's clay objects are picked up with a spatula.)

A moderately hot oven was used. While it was heating, Sandy decorated the frame with lines and circles, using bottle caps and a nailhead to make circles, and a pointed stick for the lines. Sometimes the baker's clay seemed

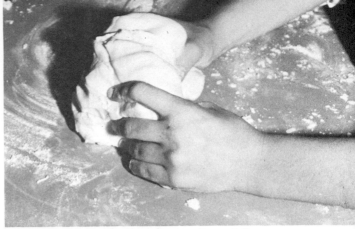

After mixing together the water, salt, and flour, knead the dough on a floured surface until it is smooth—about ten minutes.

Using a rolling pin, roll out the baker's clay dough until it is ½ inch (1 cm.) thick.

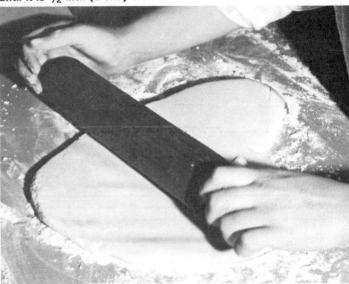

Using a cardboard pattern as a guide, cut out the baker's clay frame and the hole for the mirror to show through.

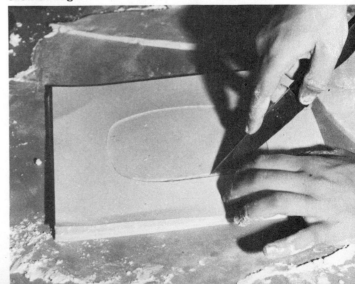

Place the frame on a foil-covered cookie sheet.

A nail is used to decorate the frame. Press the nailhead into the clay to make small circles.

The baker's clay frame is baked in a moderately hot oven for 1½ hours.

to dry out a little while she was decorating it. When that happened Sandy moistened it lightly with some water from a spray bottle.

After the decorations were completed, the cookie sheet was placed in the oven, and the frame was baked for 1½ hours. It smelled good! During the last half hour of baking, Sandy brushed some evaporated milk onto it to make it turn a shiny brown color. She had decided to do this instead of painting it after it was baked.

While the baker's clay was baking, Sandy glued the oval mirror onto an 8-by-10-inch corrugated cardboard backing. First she cut a piece of self-adhering contact paper exactly the same size as the mirror and attached it to the back of the mirror, because it is not a good idea to put glue directly on the back of a mirror. As soon as she had glued the mirror in place on the cardboard, she saw that she had a problem. The mirror was raised off the cardboard by about ⅛ inch (.3 cm.). Since the opening of the clay frame would be smaller than the mirror, the mirror would hold the frame away from the cardboard, and she would not be able to glue the frame to the cardboard.

Sandy had to build up ⅛ inch around the mirror. After looking around, she found an old shoe box made of cardboard almost the same thickness as the mirror. She opened the box out flat, cut out an 8-by-10-inch rectangle from it, and traced the oval mirror shape in the center. Next. Sandy cut some strips from the remainder of the box and glued these onto the backing. Then the piece of cardboard with the oval cut out was glued onto the strips. At last she had a surface to glue her frame to.

After baking for 1½ hours, the frame, now a rich brown color, was removed from the oven. Sandy allowed it to cool and then sprayed it with an acrylic spray. When this dried, only one step remained—to glue the baker's clay frame to the cardboard. This was easily done by applying plenty of glue. Sandy let the glue dry overnight before attaching a picture hook to the back and hanging her new mirror in her room.

SYBIL C. HARP
Editor
Creative Crafts magazine

Glue is applied to the extra piece of cardboard, which will then be glued to the built-up cardboard containing the mirror (below).

The mirror is glued onto a corrugated cardboard backing. The backing is then built up by gluing cardboard strips onto it. Another piece of cardboard is cut to exactly the same shape as the backing, with a hole for the mirror.

After the baker's clay frame is taken out of the oven, it is allowed to cool, and then it is sprayed with an acrylic finish. The final step is to glue the frame to the cardboard backing, and then it is ready to hang.

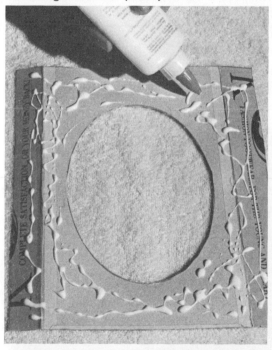

ODDS 'N' ENDS

MAKE A MARTIAN

Materials:
Small, round can
Plastic caps
Plastic stoppers
Paper squares
Circle of colored paper
Glue

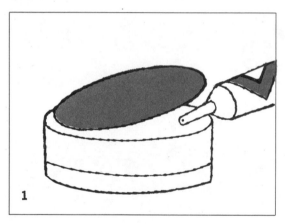

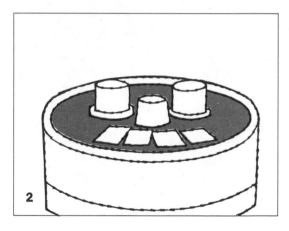

1 Glue the circle of colored paper to one end of the can to cover up any marks.

2 Glue on two plastic caps for the eyes, one for the nose, and the paper squares for the teeth.

3 Glue on two plastic stoppers at the sides of the can for ears. Use a large plastic cap for the base.

MAKE A BIRD

Materials:
Two small, round cans
Adhesive tape
Felt-tipped pen
White plastic cap
Lid from a glass jar
Glue

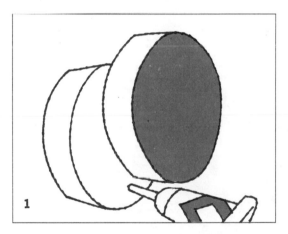

1

2

1 Glue together the flat surfaces of the two cans as shown in the drawing.

2 Stick on two circles cut from the adhesive tape to make eyes. Use the felt pen to color the pupils. Make a beak with the adhesive tape.

3 Glue the plastic cap on the glass-jar lid to form the base. Then glue the other end of the plastic cap to the can as shown in the picture.

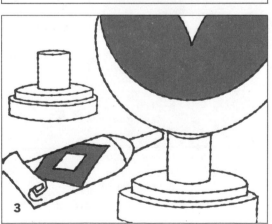

3

WORD PLAY

Pocket Money

Can you match each currency with its country?

Currency

1	balboa	11	lev
2	bolivar	12	lira
3	cedi	13	peseta
4	cruzeiro	14	piaster
5	deutsche mark	15	pound
6	dirham	16	quetzal
7	drachma	17	ruble
8	escudo	18	rupee
9	franc	19	yen
10	krona	20	zloty

Country

a	Morocco	k	South Vietnam
b	Britain	l	Poland
c	Italy	m	Panama
d	France	n	Venezuela
e	Soviet Union	o	Ghana
f	Sweden	p	West Germany
g	Bulgaria	q	Greece
h	Spain	r	Brazil
i	India	s	Portugal
j	Japan	t	Guatemala

Answers: 1,m; 2,n; 3,o; 4,r; 5,p; 6,a; 7,q; 8,s; 9,d; 10,f; 11,g; 12,c; 13,h; 14,k; 15,b; 16,t; 17,e; 18,i; 19,j; 20,l.

Great Ideas!

Can you match the great idea with the person or persons who invented or discovered it?

Great Idea

1 cotton gin
2 gyroscope
3 helicopter
4 phonograph
5 sewing machine
6 telephone
7 wireless telegraph
8 astronomical telescope
9 cellophane
10 polonium and radium

Inventor or Discoverer

A Thomas A. Edison
B Guglielmo Marconi
C Elias Howe
D Alexander Graham Bell
E Jean Bernard Léon Foucault
F Johannes Kepler
G Jacques Brandenberger
H Pierre and Marie Curie
I Igor Ivan Sikorsky
J Eli Whitney

Answers: 1,J; 2,E; 3,I; 4,A; 5,C; 6,D; 7,B; 8,F; 9,G; 10,H.

CORNCOB ZOO

Cut dry corncobs into sections. Glue them together in an animal shape. Make holes in the cob with a nail. Cut legs, antlers, and antennae from twigs. Insert and glue them in the holes. Color the cobs with tempera paint. Glue on big white paper eyes, and color the pupil with a black crayon.

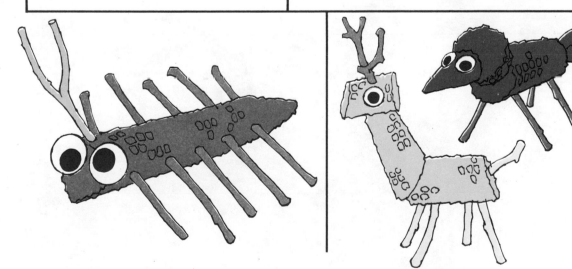

CREATURE KITES

If you look up one day and see a giant bee or a fantastically patterned Oriental butterfly hovering over your head—don't be alarmed! You are not about to be attacked by giant insects from outer space. The hovering creature may well be a kite.

The ancient Oriental sport of flying kites has always been popular with young people all over the world. But the young people of today are not satisfied with ordinary kites. They have discovered the beautiful insect and fish and bird kites first made by the Chinese and Japanese people centuries ago. These wonderful kites are still made to delight the children of the world, and they have become enormously popular. It's really very thrilling to feel a huge paper swallow or a fierce-looking Chinese centipede tugging at your kite string when a fresh breeze comes up. Why not try it?

A butterfly kite from China

112

A swallow kite from China

A bee kite from Japan

A centipede kite from China

A MIDDLE EAST SUPPER

Cacik
Kibbeh in pita bread
Salata
Dessert Couscous

The cuisine of the Middle East provides the inspiration for this meal, which has been adapted for ingredients that are generally available in most supermarkets. Although the names of the various dishes may be unfamiliar to you, you will recognize the flavors and ingredients in the recipes. These recipes will serve three or more.

Cacik (Yogurt Soup)

This is a refreshing cold soup with a zippy, tart flavor.

1   medium cucumber
1   teaspoon salt
2   8-ounce cups plain yogurt
Sprinkle of garlic powder
1   tablespoon chopped fresh mint
     or 1 teaspoon dried mint
White pepper
1   tablespoon white vinegar
     (optional)

Wash and peel cucumber and cut in half lengthwise. Using a teaspoon, scoop out the cucumber seeds and discard them. Grate the cucumber, using the fine teeth of the grater. Place the grated cucumber in a bowl and sprinkle with 1 teaspoon salt. Let rest for 25 minutes. During this time the salt will draw out the liquid from the cucumber.

Add the 2 cups of yogurt to the cucumber pulp in the bowl and mix well. Sprinkle with garlic powder and mix in chopped mint, saving a little to sprinkle over the soup when it is served. Add a dash or two of white pepper. You may add a tablespoon of white vinegar if you want the soup a bit more tart. Mix thoroughly, cover bowl, and place in refrigerator to chill. Serve very cold in small bowls, sprinkled with the remaining chopped mint.

Kibbeh in Pita Bread

Kibbeh is the hamburger of some of the Middle East countries. It is seasoned in various ways and can be fried, broiled, or baked, but the basis is always ground meat—generally lamb—and a grain, usually the cracked wheat product known as bulgur. Since chopped beef is more easily available than chopped lamb, you may substitute the beef.

Pita is the flat Arab bread that takes the place of forks and spoons in many Middle East countries. Pita can be split in two and filled with any kind of sandwich filling. It can be found in many supermarkets.

¾   pound lean ground meat
2   tablespoons instant
     minced onion
1½ tablespoons cold water
½   cup fine cracked wheat (bulgur)
1   teaspoon salt
Dash pepper
3–4 loaves of pita bread

In a medium-sized bowl, place chopped meat, minced onion, and water; and mix together. With a large wooden spoon, beat the mixture very well to make it light and fluffy.

Place the bulgur in a large wire strainer and rinse with cold water. Squeeze it to drain out all the water. Add the drained bulgur to the meat mixture, working it in thoroughly and beating the mixture to make it smooth and light. Add salt and pepper, and mix well.

Shape the meat into small, thin, round patties. The patties

may be fried in a skillet, with hot oil just covering the bottom of the pan, for 4 or 5 minutes on each side, or they may be broiled for 5 or 6 minutes on each side. Kibbeh is always cooked through and not rare in the middle.

Use a sharp-pointed knife around the outside edges of the pita to separate the top and bottom. Place the split pita in a warm oven for a few minutes to heat. To serve, place two or three meat patties on the bottom half of the pita, cover with the top half, and serve hot.

Salata (Mixed Salad)

2 cups salad greens (about ½ head of lettuce)
1 cucumber
1 large tomato (or 2 small ones)
4 or 5 scallions
1 green pepper
2 ounces feta cheese
8 pitted black olives
French (oil and vinegar) dressing

Wash all salad ingredients well and pat dry. As you prepare each of the salad ingredients, add it to the salad bowl. Use a bowl large enough to give you room to toss the salad easily.

Tear the washed and dried lettuce into bite-sized pieces. Peel cucumber, cut in half lengthwise. With a teaspoon, scoop out the seeds and discard. Slice cucumber crescents fairly thin and cut each slice in half. Cut tomato into small chunks. Trim scallions and slice thickly, including the green part. Cut green pepper in half, through the stem end. Remove core and seeds, and cut green pepper into small pieces. Crumble the feta cheese. Cut olives in half and add.

All this can be done in advance and refrigerated. To prevent a tired, soggy salad, add the dressing just before you serve the salad.

To toss the salad, use a large fork and spoon, and toss the ingredients gently so as not to bruise them. Add the dressing a little at a time, and toss between additions. You want to use just enough dressing to coat the ingredients and make them glisten; not enough to drown them. Serve salad on individual salad plates.

Dessert Couscous

Couscous, the national dish of North Africa, is a coarse-grained semolina, or cereal. But since it is not commonly available outside its country of origin, we have substituted farina, or Cream of Wheat, which is a fine-grained semolina.

Couscous is a popular accompaniment to the main course of meat or poultry, but Egyptian cooks often sprinkle it with confectioners' sugar and fruits and nuts, and serve couscous as a sweet. This is an adaptation of an Egyptian recipe.

2 cups milk
⅓ cup Cream of Wheat or farina
¼ cup sugar
½ cup raisins or dried currants
2 tablespoons chopped nuts

In a medium-sized saucepan, mix together the milk, farina, and sugar. Cook over a low flame for five minutes, stirring constantly. Add raisins or currants and mix thoroughly to distribute them. Serve in individual dessert bowls topped with the chopped nuts. The Egyptians use peanuts because those are the only nuts grown there, but you may substitute walnuts or pistachios. This dessert may be served warm or at room temperature.

STAMP COLLECTING

All over the world, prices rose higher and higher in 1974, and the hobby of stamp collecting was affected, along with almost everything else, by this worldwide inflation. Inflation affected stamps in two ways. Stamp collectors paid higher prices for the rarer stamps. A record price was paid for an American stamp—$47,000 for a 24-cent United States airmail of 1918. In addition, the postal administrations of the world found that they had to increase the prices of stamps, and many countries issued new stamps to meet new postal rates.

▶ 100 YEARS OF THE UPU

During the year the event most widely celebrated by the postal administrations of the world was the 100th anniversary of the Universal Postal Union (UPU). The organization, created in October, 1874, and since 1947 a specialized agency of the United Nations, has made possible the easy transportation and delivery of mail from one country to another. Before the UPU, international mail could be transferred only under treaties among the various nations of the world. International mail was sent by any one of several different routes to a faraway country, with each route involving a different price and period of delivery. The UPU ended all that. It is one international organization that has existed through wars and political upheavals, with all the members continuing to belong and to co-operate with each other.

In 1974, almost every nation of the world issued a stamp or a set of stamps to mark the centenary of the UPU. The United States released eight stamps showing famous works of art related to the writing or receiving of letters. On four of the stamps the words of the poet John Donne, "Letters mingle souls," appeared.

The Vatican's two UPU centenary stamps used themes from the Bible. One of the stamps showed Noah's ark with the dove arriving carrying the olive branch. The other showed a sheep drinking from a stream that flows from a mountain. On the mountain stand the Tables of the Law.

Two of the Swedish stamps had scenes of the Central Post Office in Stockholm, and a third pictured a postman on Sweden's northernmost postal route. Britain's set of four horizontal multicolor stamps showed steps in the development of mail transport by land, sea, and air. Nicaragua released nine stamps showing previous Nicaraguan stamps honoring the UPU.

▶ A THEME FOR "EUROPA" STAMPS

Each year the member nations of the Conference of European Postal and Telecommunications Administrations issue "Europa" stamps. In the past the stamps have had a common design, dedicated to the idea of European unity. In 1974, for the first time, the stamps had a common theme: sculpture. The theme allowed many of the European nations that belong to the CEPT to show examples of their great works of sculpture, from the past and the present.

Works of the sculptor Wilhelm Lehmbruck were reproduced on two stamps from West Germany, and figures by Auguste Rodin and Aristide Maillol appeared on two French stamps. Greece issued a set of three stamps, showing sculpture in three important styles of the ancient period of its art.

▶ WORLD CUP ISSUES

One of the most coveted cups in the world of sports is the Jules Rimet Cup, or World Cup, for football (or soccer, as it is called in the United States). West Germany, the host nation for the 1974 championship matches, won the cup. The competition takes place every four years.

Soccer is the favorite sport of millions of people, and nations all the way from Yugoslavia to Upper Volta issued stamps in honor of the competition. Among the Latin-American nations honoring soccer with new stamps were Chile, Uruguay, Paraguay, Nicaragua, and El Salvador. Brazil, the country of soccer immortal Pelé, issued a stamp showing a highly stylized green playing field with a player kicking a soccer ball.

Liberia, which did not compete, issued

UNIONE POSTALE UNIVERSALE

1874-1974

POSTE VATICANE L.50

IAS-ROMA-1974

1974 STAMPS FROM AROUND THE WORLD

7

Kokomo   Aceros plicatus

Papua New Guinea

Universal
Postal Union   Chardin
1874-1974   10c US

U.P.U.
1874-1974

UNITED NATIONS
1874 1974
10c UNIVERSAL POSTAL UNION

Copa do Mundo

CORREIO
Brasil 74   2,50

10 CENTS

Amethyst

UNITED STATES mineral heritage

10 CENTS

Petrified wood

UNITED STATES mineral heritage

10 CENTS

Rhodochrosite

UNITED STATES mineral heritage

10 CENTS

Tourmaline

UNITED STATES mineral heritage

ÍSLAND

EUROPA CEPT

20

1.00

中華民國郵票

REPUBLIC OF CHINA

Canada

World Cycling
Championships
Montréal 1974
Championnats
du monde
de cyclisme

8

ROMA HISPANIA

CORREOS
TEATRO DE MERIDA   **ESPAÑA**   5 PTAS
F.N.M.T.

10c
US

THE LEGEND OF SLEEPY HOLLOW

5½P Prizewinning fire engine 1863

1863

Indians of Les Indiens
the Pacific de la Côte
Coast   du Pacifique **Canada 8**

CANDIDO PORTINARI

UNITED NATIONS · 18c

Janthina janthina
KENYA

Nautilus pompilius
KENYA

A TOPICAL COLLECTION
OF SEASHELL STAMPS

45f STROMBUS BUBONIUS
REPUBLIQUE DE CÔTE D'IVOIRE
POSTES

POSTES 1972
5 UM
COQUILLAGE FOSSILE
REPUBLIQUE ISLAMIQUE DE MAURITANIE
C. SEGUIN   DELRIEU

POSTES 1972
15 UM
COQUILLAGE FOSSILE
REPUBLIQUE ISLAMIQUE DE MAURITANIE
C. SEGUIN   DELRIEU

1c
Cook Islands

1½c
Cook Islands

4c
Cook Islands

6c
Cook Islands

10c
Cook Islands

15c
Cook Islands

20c
Cook Islands

25c
Cook Islands

POSTES 10F
REPUBLIQUE TOGOLAISE

POSTES 20F
REPUBLIQUE TOGOLAISE

POSTES 30F
REPUBLIQUE TOGOLAISE

POSTES 40F
REPUBLIQUE TOGOLAISE

stamps reproducing photographs from early rounds of the 1974 competition. Yugoslavia's stamp pictured the Jules Rimet Cup itself. The Maldives issued a set of stamps showing players in action.

NEW STAMPS FROM MANY NATIONS

Among the stamps issued by the United States in 1974 was a set of four diamond-shaped 10-cent mineral heritage stamps, picturing polished stones—amethyst, rhodochrosite, tourmaline, and petrified wood cut and polished like a gem.

Other new issues included a block of four 10-cent stamps in the series celebrating the 200th birthday of the United States; a 10-cent stamp marking the first anniversary of the launching of the unmanned laboratory and space station Skylab 1; and a stamp illustrating an exciting moment in Washington Irving's tale *The Legend of Sleepy Hollow*. The stamp is part of the American folklore series.

A 10-cent envelope stamp picturing a tennis racket with a ball centered on it honored tennis. The popular graphic artist Peter Max designed a colorful semi-jumbo 10-cent stamp in honor of the Expo '74 World's Fair in Spokane, Washington, with its theme "Preserve the Environment."

The World Cycling Championships, usually held in Europe, were held in Montreal in 1974, and Canada issued a red, black, and silver 8-cent stamp to mark the occasion. The stamp, showing part of a bicycle wheel, carried text in English and French. Canada also issued stamps honoring the 100th anniversary of letter carrier service in Canada.

Canada, in preparation for its role as host of the 1976 Olympics, put out four more stamps. They showed people enjoying the winter sports Canada is known for: ice skating, snowshoeing, curling, and skiing.

Two other Canadian stamps issued in 1974 honored Indians of the Pacific Coast. One stamp showed the interior of a dwelling on Nootka Sound, and the other displayed a variety of artifacts.

Spain paid tribute to its Roman heritage with a new issue of eight stamps picturing ancient monuments, such as the Roman aqueduct at Segovia and the Roman theater in Mérida.

Surinam marked the 200th anniversary of its first newspaper with two stamps reproducing the first front page and the first editor's name. Britain issued a set of four attractive and interesting stamps showing fire-fighting equipment of the past 200 years. Two stamps in Nationalist China's folklore series showed a traditional juggler and magician practicing their arts.

Israel and Norway issued stamps featuring the work of their own artists. Papua New Guinea brought out a set of three stamps picturing lovely birds of the South Pacific: the kokomo, or wreathed hornbill; the muruk, or great cassowary; and the tarangau, or kapul eagle. The Cook Islands, also in the South Pacific, released a series of eighteen stamps, all picturing seashells.

YOUTH AND THE UN

The first International All-Junior Stamp and Literature Exhibition was held in New York City in July. The exhibition, sponsored by the United Nations, the American Philatelic Society, and the Club of United Nations Collectors, was open to juniors between the ages of nine and eighteen.

The participants showed exhibits relating to the United Nations, to a particular country, or to a theme. An awards banquet was part of the three-day event. An issue of four United Nations stamps paid tribute to the theme of peace. The stamps, part of an "Art at the UN" series, reproduced the Brazilian Peace Mural in the New York headquarters of the United Nations. The mural, by Cándido Portinari, pictures young people of many races.

TOPICAL COLLECTIONS

For anyone interested in starting a topical collection—a collection built around a theme—the stamps of 1974 offered a wide range of subjects to choose from. Sports, nature, sculpture, and painting were just a few of the topics to tempt the collector. Stamps showing seashells, of all kinds and from many countries, would make a particularly interesting and attractive collection.

CHARLESS HAHN
Stamp Editor
Chicago Sun-Times

MAKE A PRESENT

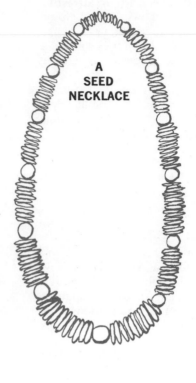

A
SEED
NECKLACE

What to Use:

Seeds from cantaloupe, honeydew melon, watermelon, or pumpkin

Odd beads or pearls from broken necklace

Strong thread, scissors, needle, tape measure, newspapers, paper toweling

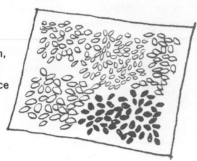

What to Do:

1. Collect seeds from the above fruits as your family eats them. Separate the seeds from the pulp of the fruits and wash them. Place the seeds on paper towels to dry overnight.

2. Thread your needle with a piece of very strong thread, about 80 inches (200 centimeters) long. Double the thread. Make knots on each end of the thread, leaving several inches of thread hanging below each knot. Remember that making a knot on each end of the thread is better than knotting them together, because they won't get tangled.

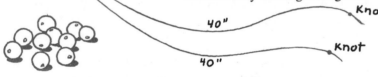

3. Push the needle and thread through the seeds to string them. String 12 or 14 cantaloupe seeds, then string a bead or pearl. Following the bead or pearl, string 12 or 14 seeds from a pumpkin, then bead or pearl again. You can also make the necklace from seeds alone, without beads or pearls, and string the seeds in a variety of sequences.

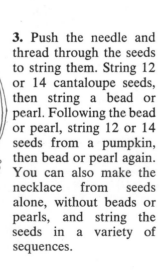

4. When all the seeds have been strung and your necklace measures about 36 inches (91 cm.), cut the thread, remove the needle, and tie the two loose strands together. Then tie both ends of the necklace together. Make several knots, so that the necklace does not break apart.

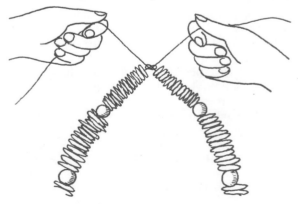

A PICTURE PUZZLE

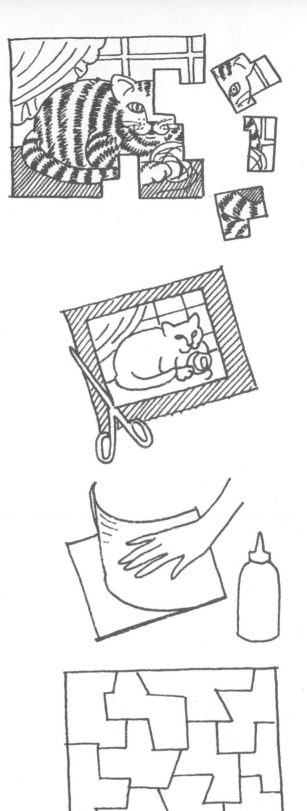

What to Use:

Picture from magazine, poster, or photograph

Cardboard of the same size as picture

Brown paper or self-adhesive paper such as Con-Tact or Marvalon

Glue, scissors, spray plastic sealer, pen or pencil, newspapers, tape measure

What to Do:

1. Spread newspapers on your working surface. Clip an interesting picture from a magazine, find an appealing old photograph of which there is a duplicate, or use a poster you may have on hand. Almost any picture will do, but you want to choose one that will interest the recipient of your gift.

2. Measure and cut the cardboard, if necessary, so that it fits the picture.

3. Glue a piece of strong brown paper, or press a piece of adhesive paper, onto one side of the cardboard. This is done to make the puzzle sturdier and easier to handle.

4. Glue your picture onto the other side of the cardboard. Spray the picture with spray plastic sealer. (Krylon is especially good.) Let it dry for about 15 minutes.

5. On the side of the puzzle which has the brown paper or adhesive paper, draw lines every which way. Bear in mind the age of the person to whom you will give the puzzle. If you are to give it to a child under six years of age, make just a few large pieces. If you are to give it to a teenager or an adult, you can draw many more lines to make many more pieces to the puzzle, which complicates the assembling. Adults are just as fond of puzzles as children. Cut the puzzle up according to the lines you have drawn on the back.

6. Reassemble the puzzle and put it in a box, if you have one. If you do not have a box, put the puzzle on a large piece of cardboard, and then wrap it in whatever paper you have decided to use.

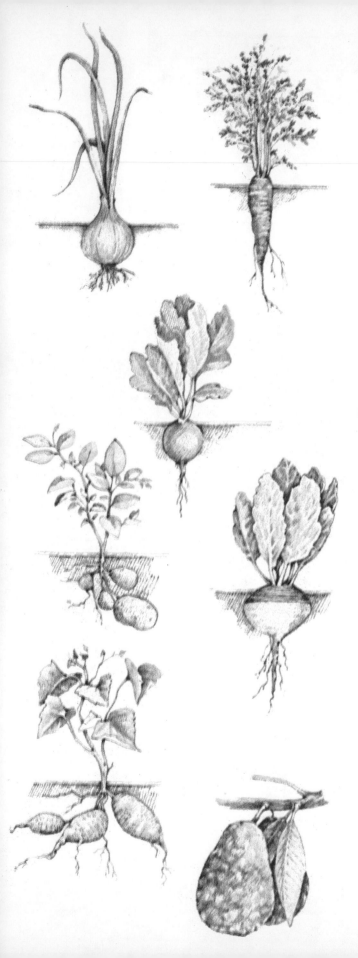

PLANTS FROM YOUR KITCHEN

Where can you get plants to decorate your room? You can buy them from a florist or a plant nursery—or you can look in the refrigerator in your kitchen. You will probably find onions, carrots, beets, potatoes, turnips, sweet potatoes, or an avocado. You can raise handsome plants from any of these vegetables.

Most of the vegetables mentioned can produce plants from their roots, stems, or leaves by a process called vegetative reproduction. However, the avocado is the one exception. It will produce a plant from the large nutlike seed at its center.

It's easy to grow plants this way, and it can be a lot of fun. You can also save on the cost of your plants.

▶ NEW PLANTS FROM ROOTS

Let's begin with a carrot. This familiar vegetable is actually the root of the carrot plant. While the plant is growing, its fernlike green leaves make sugar by a process called photosynthesis. The sugar passes down into the roots for storage. The roots grow longer and thicker as more of the sugary food reaches them. When the growing season ends, the plants are pulled up, and the bundles of golden orange roots are ready to be marketed, bought, and eaten.

All you need to start a new carrot plant is a good-sized firm carrot and a small bowl. Cut off the top inch of the carrot at its broad end. Set the cut-off part in the bowl. The rest of the carrot is yours for munching. Pour enough water into the bowl to cover about half of the carrot top. You will have to add water to replace water that evaporates.

Place the bowl in a window where the carrot top will get several hours of strong light every day. In a week or so you should see feathery leaves appear. As the carrot grows, more and more leaves will appear. Fine white roots may grow from the side of the carrot. You can use the same procedure with beet tops and turnip tops, and grow fine new plants from them.

There is another way to grow carrots, and you won't even need a bowl. The carrot acts as its own container. Cut across the middle of a large firm carrot. Keep the broad end of the carrot. Carefully scoop out the inside of the carrot almost to the bottom. With a toothpick, make two small holes in the sides of the carrot, through which you can pass wire or a nylon thread on which to hang the carrot. (Cotton thread may rot.) Fill the cavity of the carrot with water nearly to the top. Add water whenever it is needed to keep the carrot full. Beautiful feathery leaves will grow from the carrot after a week or two. You can keep your plant for many weeks if you remember to put water into it whenever necessary.

Another root that can grow into a pretty plant is the sweet potato. You will need a glass jar, some toothpicks, and a firm sweet potato. Stick several toothpicks into the sweet potato so it can be supported half in and half out of the water in the jar, with the pointed end down. Set the jar in a warm, shaded place. Check every few days, and add water to the jar when necessary. Change the water if it gets cloudy. When you can see roots and leaves growing, place the jar in a sunny window. Continue adding water whenever necessary. Your sweet potato vine will go on growing in the jar. Or you can set it into soil in a flowerpot, where it may live for years. Whichever way you grow it, the sweet potato plant will be lovely.

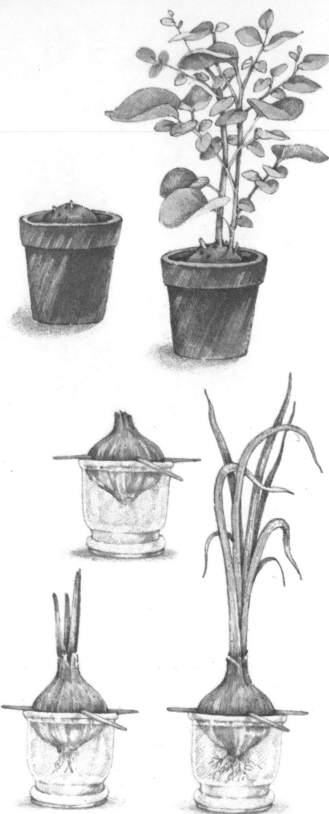

▶ NEW PLANTS FROM STEMS

You may not think that a white potato looks like a stem, but it is one. It's a special kind of thick underground stem called a tuber. The potato plant, like other green plants, makes its own food. This food, in the form of starch, is stored in the tuber.

Look at a potato closely and you can see little pits in its surface. These are called "eyes." Under the right conditions, an eye can develop into a plant bud. Potato farmers grow new plants by cutting potatoes into pieces. They make sure that each piece has one or two eyes. When the pieces are planted in the soil, the stems and roots of a new plant grow out from the eyes.

You can grow an attractive potato vine by setting up a white potato in the way that was described for sweet potatoes. Or if you would like to follow the potato farmer's method, cut the potato into pieces that all have eyes, and plant the pieces in soil in flowerpots.

▶ NEW PLANTS FROM LEAVES

An ordinary onion is a *bulb,* which can be used to start a new onion plant. Cut open an onion bulb from top to bottom. The thick, fleshy sections are leaves, although they do not look like leaves. When the onion plant is growing, it forms little bulbs beneath the soil. The food made by the plant passes down into the fleshy leaves of the bulbs, where it is stored. By the end of the growing season, the onion bulbs are large and filled with food.

Growing an onion plant in a jar of water is easy. Set the onion bulb in a jar, so that half the bulb is under water. Roots will grow down into the water, and green tubelike leaves will grow up out of the top of the bulb. The plant will grow in the jar for a long time, or you can transfer it into a pot with soil.

124

▶ NEW PLANTS FROM SEEDS

You have seen ways to grow new plants from roots, stems, and leaves. Now you should try to grow a plant from a seed. A really rewarding plant is the avocado. It is a handsome plant that can grow indoors to a height of 6 feet (2 meters) or more.

The avocado fruit usually has only one seed (pit). This seed is about 2 inches (5 centimeters) long. Scrape away any soft material that sticks to the seed, wash it, and let it dry. You can plant the seed in soil, but it is more fun to watch the start of growth in a jar of water. Push three toothpicks into the seed so it can be supported, broad side down, in the jar. Add water so that about half the seed is covered, and set the jar in a shaded place. Add water as needed every few days. You will have to be patient, for weeks may pass before you can see anything happening. When roots have begun to sprout from the seed, transfer it to a pot with soil. Leave about one fourth of the seed uncovered. A well cared for avocado tree can live indoors for years, but you should not expect to get any fruit from it.

Have fun planting!

COIN COLLECTING

The spotlight in coin collecting for the year 1974 was on gold and silver and on sharply higher prices for rare coins. An increased worldwide demand for gold had doubled the metal's value, and by April the open market price of gold had been pushed up to $180 an ounce. Silver prices rose too, going above the level of $5 per ounce.

The higher prices of bullion (uncoined gold and silver) led in turn to much higher market values for the gold and silver coins that are traded largely for investment purposes.

In the silver category most of the interest was focused on United States dimes, quarters, and half dollars of the period from World War II to 1964. The mushrooming interest in

British gold sovereign.

gold led British Treasury officials to decide in March to renew the minting of Britain's gold sovereign. Production of the sovereign had been halted in 1968.

Britain was not the only nation to reveal plans to launch gold coinages. Haiti announced it would issue a 1,000-gourde piece, and Israel announced it would issue a gold coin. The denomination was unspecified. Both coins were to be related to the observance of the bicentennial of the American Revolution.

It appeared highly unlikely that the United States would resume gold coinage. However, a law was passed lifting the ban on ownership of gold by United States citizens, effective January 1, 1975. Earlier in the year, a regulation had been issued, permitting ownership of all gold coin issues, from any country, dated before 1960. Before the two 1974 changes, only coins dated 1933 and earlier, and se-

lected issues of coins of the period 1934 to 1959, could be legally owned.

The long-range outlook for even higher silver prices led to an announcement by West Germany that the nation's silver 5-mark coin, an issue minted continuously since 1951, would be abandoned after 1974 in favor of a copper-nickel substitute. In France the 10-franc coin began appearing in nickel-brass, bringing to an end its ten-year life as a silver coin.

▶A POCKETFUL OF NEW COINS

Canada issued a commemorative dollar, honoring the centennial of the city of Winnipeg. The 1974 coin was struck in silver, for collectors, and in nickel, for regular use. It has been the practice in Canada to issue new dollar coins in the two metals.

Canada also continued its ambitious 1976 Olympic silver $5 and $10 coinage program. The coins introduced in 1974 brought the number of issues in the series to twelve. The profits from the Olympic coins are intended to help pay the costs of Canada's role as host of the Olympic Games to be held in Montreal in the summer of 1976.

Canadian silver Olympic $5 coin.

U.S. Bicentennial coin.

In the United States a nationwide competition was held to select designs to be used on a special Bicentennial quarter, half dollar, and dollar. The winning design for the reverse side of the quarter shows a colonial drummer. The design for the half dollar pictures Independence Hall, and the design for the dollar shows the Liberty Bell.

The first silver specimens of the coins were struck in August at the Philadelphia Mint. The silver strikes will be sold to collectors. The three coins will be produced for general release after July 4, 1975. They will be of cupronickel-clad copper.

In Peru a new coin the size of a silver dollar was released. The 200-sol piece commemorates two Peruvian aviation heroes. Venezuela released an interesting new coin —a special silver 10-bolivar commemorative

Venezuelan silver 10-bolivar coin.

marking the centennial of the first appearance of Simón Bolívar's likeness on Venezuela's coinage. Bolívar freed Venezuela from Spain in the early 19th century.

INTERNATIONAL COIN ISSUES

The first truly international coin issue was the 1968 "Grow More Food" coinage program of the United Nations Food and Agriculture Organization (FAO). A number of nations issued coins based on the common theme—Grow More Food. The coins were for circulation within the individual countries. The number of countries taking part in the program passed the 50 mark in 1974. A pair of special framed panels displaying 54 specimens of the more than 600,000,000 coins released since the start of the program were presented for permanent exhibit in the United States House and Senate agriculture committee rooms on Capitol Hill.

A second international coin issue was launched during the year under the auspices of the World Wildlife Fund and the International Union for the Conservation of Nature and Natural Resources. The issue is designed to draw public attention to endangered species

Indonesian wildlife coin.

of wildlife. Over a period of four years, each of 24 participating nations is to issue one gold coin and a pair of silver coins. The first three coins in the series were from Indonesia and depicted an orangutan, a Javan tiger, and a Komodo dragon.

RECORD PRICES FOR RARITIES

Price levels that were almost undreamed of in the 1960's became almost commonplace during 1974. The year opened with an 1804 United States silver dollar selling privately for $150,000. In September another specimen of the coin sold for $200,000. The figure tied the record price paid for a United States coin. The record had been set in May when an extremely high-relief example of the 1907 Saint-Gaudens double eagle ($20 gold coin) was sold at auction. The American sculptor Augustus Saint-Gaudens designed the coin during Theodore Roosevelt's presidency.

For a few days in May the Saint-Gaudens double eagle held the world record for a coin price, as well. But the title slipped from the

Greek dekadrachm, 483 B.C.

eagle's talons at a May 28 auction in Zurich, Switzerland, when the best specimen of a Greek dekadrachm known went for $314,000. The silver coin was struck in 483 B.C.

CLIFFORD MISHLER
Numismatic News Weekly

LIVING HISTORY

Tivoli Gardens—a dazzling fairy-tale world in Copenhagen.

Straw figures

Tin toys

Colorful clay pot

A straw band

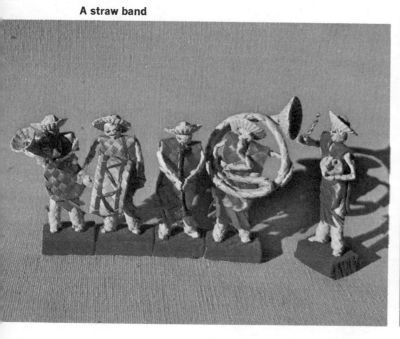

130

MEXICAN TOYS

The Mexicans, like most people everywhere, love toys. This makes the young people happy because their parents love buying toys for them. Every Mexican city and town has a market. There are always brightly colored, inexpensive toys for sale in the market. And Mexican toys are unlike any others in the world. Most of them are handmade. Some are made of gaily decorated clay. There are little clay animals and birds, kangaroos and mermaids. There are also clay figures that are really bells. They sound nice. There are straw toys—burros and bulls and dolls and bicycles. And there are brightly painted tin toys. The tin soldiers and horses are nice. And for special events there are huge paper-covered piñatas in fantastic animal shapes that are filled with small toys and candy.

Clay figures

Clay bells

WONDERFUL, WONDERFUL TIVOLI

Tivoli Gardens, the world-famous amusement park in Copenhagen, Denmark's capital city, has many wonderful attractions to delight the visitor. The sprawling, 20-acre (8-hectare) amusement center has beautiful buildings, flower-lined pathways, giant fountains, and a large artificial lake stocked with swans and ducks. Theaters, outdoor bandstands, and a spacious concert hall provide continuous entertainment to suit every taste. A playland area features games and rides. For the hungry visitor, Tivoli offers more than 20 restaurants and outdoor cafés.

Thousands of twinkling, colored lights illuminate the park and its buildings at night. Visitors feel they are in a fairy-tale world that might have been created by Hans Christian Andersen, the great Danish storyteller.

Tivoli is open from May to September. About 5,000,000 visitors pass through its gates each year. Once inside there is an almost endless array of dazzling sights to see and things to do. Not far from the main entrance stands one of Tivoli's best-loved attractions—the Pantomime Theater. In a pantomime the actors do not speak. The story is told through gestures, facial expressions, and dance steps. Each night, young and old alike are charmed by the performers and the accompanying music. The theater itself was built in 1874 and is the oldest building in Tivoli.

The most famous pantomime show in Tivoli is called *Pierrot's Rude Awakening*. The plot concerns Pierrot, a clownish character, who is the servant of a wealthy merchant. The merchant's daughter, Columbine, has fallen in love with a character named Harlequin. The merchant opposes the match and orders his servant Pierrot to keep the lovers apart. There are many twists and turns in the delightful tale as Harlequin and Columbine fool Pierrot by a series of clever tricks and the use of a magic wand. Against a backdrop of colorful street scenes and lavish balls, the story reaches a spectacular finale in which the two lovers are united at last.

The comedy technique of the pantomime performers captivates the audience. All the performers are familiar to regular visitors to Tivoli. But even a person watching the show for the first time will be entertained by the antics of Pierrot and the graceful dancing of the ballet corps. It is common for children in the audience to shout "Say something, Pierrot!" But Pierrot does not speak until the end, when he shouts "Long live Tivoli and the ancient pantomime tradition!"

Walking around the large artificial lake, the visitor passes a special area set aside for children. During the day it is a playground, with sandboxes, slides, circular stairways, and all sorts of things to climb on or play with. But in addition to being a playground for children, it is also a work of visual art for adults. Many of Denmark's most noted designers and artists gave of their talents to create this beautifully landscaped area.

At night, when Tivoli's more than 100,000 colored lights begin to glow, the gardens become a wonderful feast for the eyes. Standing near the lake, one can see the illuminated outline of the Chinese Pagoda, a Tivoli landmark erected in 1900. Actually, the Chinese Pagoda was inspired by Japanese temples. But the Tivoli guidebook notes, "We in Denmark are inclined to consider everything from the Far East as Chinese." Therefore the building, originally called the Illuminated Tower, is now officially known as the Chinese Pagoda. Appropriately enough, it houses a Chinese restaurant.

In one part of the gardens is a carnival-like amusement area. There are games and rides of every description. The visitor can practice his marksmanship with pellet-firing air rifles; or win a prize by knocking over some bottles. There is a "ghost train" that passes through a network of eerie tunnels. But for those who really want to be frightened out of their wits, a ride on the roller coaster is a must. The roller coaster, Tivoli's most popular ride, carries its shrieking passengers up and down a series of imitation mountains, swerving around sharp curves with heart-stopping suddenness.

In the center of Tivoli is the largest of the

Tivoli—a sparkling fantasy world.

At the Pantomime Theater the actors tell a story, but they do not speak.

133

The exotic Bazaar Building lights up Tivoli at night.

The Tivoli Boys' Guard prepares to march.

park's many fountains. It is in the shape of three linked circles, and is ringed by lights. Just behind it, stands the Tivoli Concert Hall. The present building was completed in 1956 to replace one burned down during World War II. The new concert hall is outlined with electric lights that flicker slightly like the gas lamps that adorned the earlier building. The hall is used all year round for concerts of classical and popular music and jazz. Many of the concerts during the Tivoli season are free to the public.

On the other side of the fountain, facing the concert hall, is the Lawn Stage. This popular outdoor theater presents variety shows. Here one may see jugglers, acrobats, high-wire performers, and a wide range of entertainers from all over the world. One may stand and watch the show without charge or pay a small fee for a seat.

On three nights a week, fireworks displays are put on just before the gardens close at midnight. The display includes spiraling rockets, and flares that burst open like blooming flowers or form interesting patterns against the dark sky. The fireworks display is very impressive, and there are ohs and ahs from onlookers as the flashing explosions take place.

TIVOLI BOYS' GUARD

Of all the wonderful things in Tivoli, none is more colorful or exciting than the Tivoli Boys' Guard on the march. Like an army of toy soldiers come to life, the young Danish guardsmen step off proudly. And what a splendid sight they are! A fife and drum corps leads the parade, followed by a 50-piece marching band and a color guard. Each boy wears a tall, black bearskin hat, a red tunic with a white belt, white trousers with a double stripe of blue braid, and a small dress sword. The uniform is modeled after the one worn by the Danish Royal Guard, which protects Denmark's royal family.

The weekend parades begin in front of the wooden cottage that serves as headquarters for the Boys' Guard. The band strikes up a march and the entire corps, led by an officer on a white horse, begins its parade around the park. To the rattle of drums, the shrill sound of fifes, and the brassy blare of trumpets and horns, the guardsmen march past crowds of Danish and foreign visitors. Some of the more enthusiastic onlookers fall in behind the guardsmen and march along with them.

The Tivoli Boys' Guard has been entertaining visitors to the amusement center for 130 years. The corps was organized by Georg Carstensen, the founder of Tivoli, on September 4, 1844. One year earlier, in 1843, Carstensen had obtained a royal permit from King Christian VIII to found an amusement area just outside the fortifications that then surrounded Copenhagen. Carstensen selected a site near the west gate of the city. (Since then, Copenhagen has grown beyond its original walls, so that Tivoli is now located right in the heart of the city.)

Carstensen thought it would be a good idea to have a corps of boys dressed in military uniforms—a sort of make-believe army—to add an extra dash of color to the fantastic world of the park. At first the guardsmen were used as sentries at the entrances to Tivoli. As their popularity grew, a fife and drum corps and a band were added.

All the boys in the corps are students who attend elementary and high schools in Copenhagen. The youngest is nine years old; the oldest is sixteen. Every year between ten and twenty new members are admitted to the Boys' Guard out of the hundreds who try out. It is a high honor to be a Tivoli Guard, and only those who have excellent school records are considered.

Candidates first have to prove they have musical talent by passing an entrance examination. Once over this hurdle, the new members must attend the Tivoli Guard music school for a period of one to three years, depending on their previous musical education. The youngest boys are put into the fife and drum corps, while the older ones serve in the color guard during their training period. After passing through the music school, the boys are promoted to the band.

Once in the corps, a boy must toe the mark. Discipline is strict, just as it is in a real army. Guardsmen attend music classes, rehearsals, and drill sessions all year round. Bandsmen have practice sessions three times a week, for three hours at a time. The fife and drum corps and the color guard rehearse twice weekly for a total of four hours.

When Tivoli is open the Boys' Guard holds parades every Saturday and Sunday evening. In addition to parades, the band gives weekly Sunday afternoon concerts, and holds an annual evening concert in Tivoli's concert hall. The Tivoli Guard is often called on to give special performances for visiting dignitaries and on Danish national holidays.

The guardsmen have traveled to many parts of the world to participate in foreign festivals. They have performed in most of the countries of Western Europe, including Sweden, Norway, Finland, Britain, France, Germany, Switzerland, Belgium, and Austria. Outside of Europe, they have been to the United States, Japan, Thailand, and Singapore.

It is easy to understand why Danes take such great pride in the Tivoli Boys' Guard— and indeed in the whole amusement park. No visit to Copenhagen would be complete without seeing Tivoli, which has been called "the capital of the Danish spirit."

HENRY I. KURTZ
Author, *John and Sebastian Cabot*

A Currier & Ives print of the famous battle between the *Monitor* and the *Merrimack*.

THE "MONITOR" REAPPEARS

In March, 1862, during the American Civil War, the Union warship *Monitor* and the Confederate warship *Merrimack* fought the first battle between ironclad ships—ships armored with iron plates to help them withstand cannon fire. Less than ten months later, the *Monitor* was struck by a savage storm and went down off Cape Hatteras, North Carolina. On the night of December 31, 1862, sixteen Union sailors were drowned as the most famous ship in the Union Navy plunged to its watery grave.

Efforts were later made to locate the sunken remains of the *Monitor*. But the Union warship remained lost among the more than 700 other shattered wrecks that litter the ocean floor off Cape Hatteras—often called "the graveyard of the Atlantic."

Then, in 1974, a research team from the Duke University Marine Laboratory at Beaufort, North Carolina, announced that they had located the wreck of the *Monitor*. The rusted hulk of the Union ironclad was discovered lying in 220 feet (67 meters) of water some 15 miles (24 kilometers) southeast of Cape Hatteras.

Two historical records played a large part in finding the *Monitor*. They were an 1857 coastal chart and the logbook of the U.S.S. *Rhode Island,* which was accompanying the *Monitor* on the night it went down. With these, the research team was able to limit the search area to a section of the Atlantic about 15 miles (24 km.) long and 5 miles (8 km.) wide. Equipped with newly designed underwater devices and other modern scientific instruments, the team put to sea in their research ship. They scoured the area for two weeks and found 22 wrecks. Examining the sunken ships with underwater cameras, they decided that only two of the wrecks had the familiar cheesebox-on-a-raft outline. (The *Monitor's* nickname came from its resemblance to the round wooden cheeseboxes common at the time.)

Closer observation showed that one of the wrecks was an old trawler (fishing boat) with a wheelhouse that looked a bit like the *Monitor's* turret (the round enclosure in which the ship's two guns were placed). The team then concentrated on the second wreck, and spent months examining it in detail. Mechanical scoops were used to bring up small pieces of the wreckage. Bits of pinewood and coal were found in the debris. Records showed that pine had been used in the construction of the *Monitor,* and that the ship had been powered by a coal-fired steam engine.

Underwater cameras then made films of the wreck, and a composite picture of the rear portion of the wreck was put together. After a careful study of the picture, the researchers were ready to make their findings public. On March 7, 1974—almost 112 years to the day after the *Monitor* and *Merrimack* had fought their historic battle—newsmen were told: "The wreck has to be the *Monitor* because the outline of the stern, the screw propeller, the keel, the turret, even the plating and riveting, though badly rusted now, matched the historical description we have of the ship."

▶ **THE FAMOUS *MONITOR***

When the *Monitor* was completed in 1862, it was 172 feet (52 m.) in length, with its armored deck only 1 foot (0.3 m.) above the water. A round turret, armored with wrought iron plates, was set in the middle of the ship. Two small, powerful cannon were mounted in the revolving turret.

On March 6, 1862, the *Monitor* left New York Harbor to join Union naval forces blockading the Virginia coast. Two days later the Confederate ironclad *Merrimack* sailed from its base at Norfolk, Virginia, to attack the Union fleet in Hampton Roads, at the mouth of the James River. Before the day was over, the *Merrimack* had badly mauled the Union fleet guarding Hampton Roads. The *Merrimack* suffered only light damage in the battle.

At dusk the *Merrimack* broke off the fight and steamed back to its anchorage. The plan was to bring the Confederate ironclad out the following morning to finish the job of destroying the Union fleet.

News of the *Merrimack's* victory sent shivers of terror throughout the North. In Washington, Lincoln's cabinet met in an atmosphere of despair. Some even feared that the Confederate ironclad might come steaming up the Potomac and shell the capital. But the Navy Secretary remained calm, and assured the others that their ironclad, the *Monitor,* was on its way to Hampton Roads.

In fact, the *Monitor* had already reached Hampton Roads.

On the morning of March 9, the *Merrimack* steamed out again, confident of an easy victory over the rest of the Union fleet. Suddenly the *Monitor* appeared from behind another Union ship. The first sight of the Union ironclad startled the Confederates, but they laughed at the tiny craft. It looked like David coming out to challenge Goliath. Then the fight started, and the laughter stopped.

The battle of the ironclads continued for more than four hours, but neither ship could do any serious damage to the other. Early in the afternoon the two ironclads broke off the battle. The *Merrimack* had sprung a leak and headed back to Norfolk. The *Monitor* did not pursue. Technically the battle was a draw; but the North gained more. The *Monitor* had fought the *Merrimack* to a standstill and had saved the Union fleet from complete and total destruction.

But what of the remains of the *Monitor?* The research team that discovered the wreck has recommended that it be left undisturbed. "There is no way to recover the remains in any useful form at this point. They would come apart, either down there or once fresh air hit them and a chemical reaction started." It was advised that the wreck be left alone until "we acquire the know-how" to recover it properly. It has also been suggested that the sunken warship and the area around it be declared a Marine Sanctuary.

HENRY I. KURTZ
Author, *John and Sebastian Cabot*

A mother takes her family for a walk at their Children's Village in France.

CHILDREN'S VILLAGES

When you hear the name "Children's Villages" it is hard to guess what they might be. But you will probably find the truth more fascinating than anything you guess. For the more than 100 Children's Villages located in 54 countries around the world have made a great many young people happy. And these are young people whose lives might not have been so happy if it weren't for Children's Villages.

Children's Villages are communities of young people who have lost their real mothers —and often their fathers as well. The villages provide these children with a new mother and a new home. However, Children's Villages have one unusual and important feature. The villages were set up, specifically, to provide new mothers and new homes for whole families of children. The villages are intended to keep together families of brothers and sisters when they are left without one or both parents.

Although many couples are able to adopt one or two children, there are few people who can afford to adopt a family of five or six children, for instance. And yet the best way to grow up is with your own brothers and sisters, if it is at all possible. Children's Villages have made this possible for many families of children all over the world.

The idea for Children's Villages had its origin in France during World War II. A social worker named Melle Masson opened her house on the outskirts of Paris to children who had lost their parents in the war. She worked first with a group of twelve boys between the ages of one and ten. As the original group of boys grew up, other children arrived. Melle Masson eventually founded an organization called Our House and kept in touch with other groups caring for children all over Europe. Another pioneer was Mother Himelda, a Dutch nun who specifically tried to re-unite families of brothers and sisters who had lost their parents and been separated as a result.

The creator of Children's Villages SOS ("SOS" is International Morse Code for "Help!") was an Austrian named Hermann Gmeimer. In 1949, when he was still a medical student in Innsbruck, Austria, Gmeimer founded the first real village of this kind.

Hermann Gmeimer had little idea in 1949 that his village would grow into a worldwide organization. The Children's Village system is supported, in part, by contributions from some 5,000,000 people around the world.

The children re-united in Children's Villages are brothers and sisters and must be under twelve years of age when they are admitted. The children go to live in their own special house. A "mother" takes over their upbringing completely until they are grown. Their house is always part of a community of ten houses or so. The groups of individual houses form a village. The village itself is placed under the direction of a man who is in charge of all the families.

The mothers in a Children's Village have 24-hour-a-day jobs. They must be unmarried and have no natural children of their own. Mothers for Children's Villages are chosen very carefully. They receive a salary from the organization as well as household allowances for their families. No one tells the mothers what to do with the family budget. Each woman runs her household just as mothers do everywhere in the world—according to the needs of the children.

The leader of the village has a demanding job, too. He keeps in touch with each of the families in his village and with the Children's Villages SOS organization. The leader of the village also works hard to keep the children who are under his care in touch with any remaining natural family they may have (married brothers and sisters, grandparents, aunts and uncles, and so forth.) The leader, or father, of a village has to look after the health and general welfare of all the children in all the houses in his village. He must truly be a father to everyone.

None of the Children's Villages are really isolated from the world around them. They are usually located near a town. The children are able to use the library, attend schools, and join clubs in the nearest town. They join local Boy Scout or Girl Scout–Girl Guide organizations, just as children do everywhere. When it is time for summer vacation from school, the children in a family do not all have to go on vacation together. One brother in a family might go off with his Boy Scout troup for a week or two of camping. His sister might take a bus trip with the Girl Scouts or Girl Guides.

In addition to the money raised all over the world for Children's Villages SOS, support for the villages is also contributed by the countries in which they are located. In France, for instance, the French government pays 88 per cent of the cost of running the French Children's Villages.

The International Federation of Children's Villages is divided into national SOS committees. These committees are based in countries around the world. There are even committees in countries that don't have Children's Villages of their own. In those countries, the committees raise funds for building villages in other countries. Canada and the Scandinavian countries have no Children's Villages of their own, but they are active in this kind of fund raising. UNICEF, the branch of the United Nations dedicated to helping children, is very active in helping Children's Village projects. UNICEF has been active in building villages in Africa, Asia, and South America.

The Children's Villages of the world have been a great success. They have been successful in the most important way of all—giving many families a happy life together. But Children's Villages have also accomplished another important thing. They have helped build some very good and useful world citizens. Many of the young people who have grown up in Children's Village homes have decided to devote their lives to helping other children in difficulties.

MACHU PICCHU

How would you like to visit one of the strangest and most fascinating areas in the world? It is called Machu Picchu and it is a fabulously beautiful ruined city perched high in the Andes of Peru. It is also called the Lost City of the Incas, because for centuries after it was built by the great Inca civilization, it disappeared—forgotten by men and history.

The journey to Machu Picchu begins at Cuzco. Cuzco was the high Andean capital of ancient Peru. Visitors headed for Machu Picchu board the tourist train at Cuzco at six in the morning. Their route takes them over 12,000-foot-high (3,650-meter) mountain passes guarded by snowcapped peaks, and through deep, tropical river gorges 6,000 feet (1,800 m.) lower. At Ollantaytambo, 45 miles (72 kilometers) north of Cuzco, the train passes the remote ruined fortress of the Inca emperor Manco. Manco fled there in the 16th century to escape the Spanish conquerors of the Inca empire. At Manco's fortress, walls built of stones as large as sofas look down on the passersby.

Beyond Ollantaytambo the train descends through dense jungle into the valley of the Vilcanota River (as the upper part of the Urubamba River is called). The river is a boiling torrent of muddy water that twists through the mountains like the coils of a snake. The jungle closes in. Tropical birds and monkeys chatter in the trees. The tracks end and the visitors leave their train and board a waiting bus. The bus takes them across a narrow bridge and up 2,000 feet (610 m.) in a series of hairpin turns to a saddle between two towering peaks. And there, in a setting of indescribable majesty, as shrouded in clouds as it is in mystery, stands Machu Picchu.

Except for the disappearance of its thatch roofs, which rotted away centuries ago, the city is almost unchanged from what it was more than four centuries ago, when 2,500 Incas lived there. Sun and mist play on the deserted plazas. Captured rainwater seeps into the terraced gardens that flank the white granite Temple of the Sun. Stairs carved out of solid rock lead from one plaza to another. Doorways open into the two-story palaces of the nobility and the convent of the Virgins of the Sun.

▶ **LOST AND FOUND**

Machu Picchu is the most perfectly preserved of the Inca ruins. The reason it is so well preserved is that it was unknown to the Europeans who plundered the rest of the Incas' vast empire. No mention of the city is found in any of the Spanish accounts of the conquest of Peru. It is not even mentioned in the history of the empire by Garcilaso de la Vega, who recorded the legends he had heard from his mother, an Inca princess, and his other Inca relatives. When the Spanish conquerors captured the last stronghold of the Incas, Manco's mountain retreat near Ollantaytambo, in 1572, Inca resistance to the Spanish collapsed. But apparently a tiny remnant of Inca civilization survived at Machu Picchu. Then it too disappeared. The jungle returned, and the city was hidden under a blanket of vines and ferns.

Legends about a hidden city of the Incas persisted, however. They were handed down from generation to generation by the Andean Indians, much as their Inca ancestors had transmitted the official history of the Inca empire. Spanish historians and missionaries reported the legends, but nothing was done about them. Finally even the legends themselves began to die out.

Then in the 1850's a French explorer, in an account of his travels in Peru, wrote that he had heard rumors of a lost city in the Andes. But again, nothing was done.

Finally, in the 20th century, Hiram Bingham, an archeologist from Yale University, found the French explorer's account. In 1911, Bingham explored the Urubamba River on muleback. He too heard rumors, and he followed them up. The Indians at first were reluctant to speak, but Bingham encouraged them with money. And at last, after systematic questioning throughout the area, he arrived at the astonishing ruins of the city that had been lost for so long.

The next year Bingham returned with an expedition. The gold that had once adorned the faces of the buildings had long since disappeared, but the party found pieces of gold jewelry, all of it women's jewelry. They unearthed scores of graves, and discovered that almost all of the skeletons were likewise women's. They found a watchtower, and a secret stairway leading down the mountain to a cliff, where the earth had been torn away, perhaps by an earthquake. The elaborate system of terraced gardens and irrigation canals suggested that the place had been designed to be self-sufficient. Machu Picchu had been a hidden world all to itself.

Bingham judged from his find that the city had been not a fortress but a last refuge from the Spanish conquerors for the sacred Inca Virgins of the Sun. Others, in a more romantic frame of mind, felt that it must have been the last capital of the empire itself. But to this day no one knows for sure what Machu Picchu was. However, the known history of pre-Columbian Peru tells the visitor to Machu Picchu a great deal about what life there must have been like. And at the height of their glory the Incas had an advanced way of life, by any standards.

▶ THE INCA WORLD

The mountain road leading to Machu Picchu, which Bingham's expedition also discovered under the jungle growth, still extends all the way from Colombia, the northernmost country of South America, to the middle of Argentina and Chile. The Incas' stone roads tied together an empire as extensive as that of ancient Rome. The roads brought to the capital at Cuzco as rich a variety of foods and arts and people as could be found anywhere on the entire continent at any time in history.

In a part of the world in which humans can barely subsist today, at elevations where the air is so thin that strangers often become ill, the remarkable Incas cut terraces out of the solid Andean rock. They covered the terraces with dirt, and brought fertilizer called guano (made, in part, of bird droppings) all the way from the Pacific Ocean to make their gardens grow. Their building blocks, which they split away from the granite outcroppings of the Andes by using fire and water, were so perfectly formed and skillfully fitted together

that even today it is impossible to pass a fingernail between the stones of some of their houses. Their mines produced gold and silver, both of which were used purely for decoration. Niches in the great halls of the Temple of the Sun at Machu Picchu once held life-size figures made of gold and silver and precious stones. Bands of decorative carvings, also made of gold and silver, were placed around the important buildings—just as bronze or stone ornaments decorate our buildings today. There was a great respect for the law in Inca society. The riches of the great public buildings were never touched. Of course, the penalty for theft in ancient Peru was death, and that just may have been one reason why the ornaments on public buildings went untouched.

▶ MODERN PROBLEMS

Machu Picchu, because it is such a perfect and beautiful example of an ancient city, bring visitors to Peru and the Andes from countries all over the world. Foreign visitors reach Cuzco by air, and then travel the additional miles to Machu Picchu.

The fame that has come to the lost city does present some problems. Archeologists are especially worried about modern hazards such as air pollution. If a modern city were to begin forming around the ruins of Machu Picchu, air polluted by automobile and industrial exhausts might well erode the ancient stone. Polluted air could do more damage in a relatively short length of time than wind, weather, and vines were able to do in centuries. And if every visitor to the ancient city took away a bit of stone as a souvenir, it would not take long at all for the sturdy walls to disappear.

As it is, Machu Picchu is one of the great treasures of the world. It tells the story of how a people lived and what their world looked like more vividly than any book can ever do. You somehow feel closer to a people when you can walk into their houses, go down the streets they walked every day, and enter the temples and public places where they went to celebrate the great events of their lives. Machu Picchu is a true time machine: it carries us into the past in a unique and fascinating way.

Modern Peruvian Indians try to keep alive their ancient Inca traditions.

Inca silver figures of llamas and a woman from the days of Machu Picchu.

In spring the ice begins to break at Dezadesh Lake in the Yukon Territory.

THE CANADIAN NORTH

For many hundreds of years North America was the continent of frontiers. People came to the New World to make a fresh start in a new land. By the middle of the 20th century, many people believed that North America had no further frontiers to offer. But nothing could be less true. The vast Canadian North—the lands lying north of the 60th parallel of latitude—is still an exciting challenge to human ingenuity and courage.

In Canada, most of the Arctic and sub-Arctic area is divided into two "territories," or regions administered by the federal government. The Yukon Territory borders Alaska. Its capital, Dawson, lies at the junction of the Klondike and Yukon rivers. East of the Yukon, the vast Northwest Territories extends eastward to Hudson Bay and north-

ward to include all of the islands of the Arctic Archipelago. Yellowknife, the territorial capital, stands on the northern shore of Great Slave Lake.

▶ THE LAND

Within the territories, the division between Arctic and sub-Arctic regions is usually the tree line. The tree line divides the Arctic tundra from the sub-Arctic taiga. The tundra is a barren, marshy desert. The taiga is evergreen forest. The tundra has thin earth, little precipitation, harsh winds, and, most of all, low temperatures, which prevent the growth of most trees.

The ground in the tundra is kept cold by long northern winters and by the frozen Arctic Ocean. Despite moderate to high

Two lively polar bears share an ice floe high in the Canadian Arctic.

temperatures in midsummer, the permafrost, or permanently frozen ground, never melts for more than a few inches below its surface. Shallowest on the seacoast and deepest inland, permafrost extends, at its deepest, 1,600 feet (490 meters) into the earth.

The northern climate swings from one seasonal extreme to another. Winter, lasting from October to May, has temperatures reaching 60–80 degrees below zero Farenheit (50–60 degrees below zero Celsius) inland and 40–60 degrees below zero F. (40–50 degrees below zero C.) near the sea. Inland temperatures can reach the 90's (the 30's C.) in July. Continental seacoast areas average about 50 degrees F. (10 degrees C.) in midsummer. Temperatures fall as you go northward through the Arctic Islands.

Throughout the North, rain and snow are light. As winter approaches, days shorten. In December there are 24 hours of darkness, though at times it is lightened to twilight by the moon and the northern lights. By con-

trast, the arrival of summer in June brings a brief period when there are 24 hours of sunlight.

Cold, dryness, and limited sunlight prevent farming in the Arctic. Indeed, these conditions make it difficult everywhere above the 60th parallel. The fact that the amount of available plant food is small limits the number of northern animals, birds, and fish.

Water plants, grasses, mosses, lichens, low berry bushes and about 900 species of flowering plants grow in the tundra. It is another world. A few trees manage to exist here, too. They include alders, birches, and willows. But they don't look like the trees in most of our backyards. They adapt themselves to the conditions of the area by growing low and hugging the ground. The taiga has a greater variety of trees and bushes.

Arctic creatures include musk-oxen, caribou, and several migrating species of seal, whale, salmon, duck, and goose. Falcons, ravens, owls, grouse, shellfish, and lemmings, and some seals, whales, bears, wolves, and foxes live there the year around. The sub-Arctic forest shelters mink, otter, marten, weasel, hare, muskrat, beaver, porcupine, caribou, moose, sheep, lynx, fox, wolf, bear, wolverine, and ptarmigan and other grouse. The rivers teem with salmon, whitefish, and grayling, and waterfowl as well.

▶ TRADITIONAL NORTHERN LIFE

The inhabitants of this harsh land are believed to have chosen to live here. Not surprisingly, the number of human inhabitants of the Canadian Far North is small. About 10,000 Eskimos live on the Arctic tundra, and about the same number of Indians live in the taiga.

"Eskimo" is an Indian word meaning "eater of raw flesh." The Eskimos refer to themselves as *Inuit* ("the people"). They are believed to be descended from Mongolian peoples who made their way some 5,000 years ago from central Asia northward across the Bering Strait to Alaska. About 4,000 years later, some Eskimos migrated to the Canadian Arctic from Alaska.

The Eskimos are a short, stocky people with straight black hair and brownish skin. Their eyes slant in Mongoloid fashion, and their cheekbones are high and broad, their noses small and flat or narrow.

Travelers have always found the Eskimos to be one of the world's nicest peoples. In good times or in bad they share food and shelter with friends or strangers. They also co-operate with each other to obtain the necessities of life. Yet there is great rivalry among Eskimos in the skills of storytelling, dancing, hunting, and fishing. Generosity, courage, and the ability to endure physical hardship are the qualities they admire most.

For centuries most Eskimo needs were supplied by fishing and hunting. Their clothing and footwear were made of skins. Their tents and boats were covered with animal skin. They also used animal hide, sinew, and bone in making snares, traps, fishhooks, spears, harpoons, bows and arrows, and even sleds. Soapstone lamps burning seal and whale oil were used for cooking, light, and heat.

Until very recently the Eskimos lived a nomadic life, moving camp as often as six times a year in search of game. In summer they pitched sealskin tents along the coast while they fished for salmon and harpooned seals. Sometimes they camped beside an inland lake or river where there were fish, berries, birds' eggs, and waterfowl. Inland, fall brought the year's biggest caribou hunt. The members of a family worked together to get meat for the winter and the best skins for clothing.

In early winter the Eskimos returned to the coast. They traveled on sleds pulled by half-tamed dogs. There they built themselves snowhouses, commonly called igloos, and passed the dark days by playing traditional games and by dancing and storytelling. Sometimes the men went out to hunt seals and other sea mammals through the animals' breathing holes in the ice.

In the longer days of March and April, the Eskimos spread out along the coast to hunt seal, walrus, and caribou. By June the hunters had taken to the sea in kayaks (one-man boats) or umiaks (larger cargo vessels) to pursue whales and other sea mammals.

Training in the skills of Eskimo life began early in childhood. Besides hunting and fishing, the men made tools, weapons, houses, and boats. The women gathered berries, roots, and grasses, cooked, and made clothing. Eskimo women were treated with respect and given a voice in decision making.

Harsh as it seems to us, life on the seacoast was easier for the Eskimos than forest living was for their Indian cousins. Inland, the Indians lacked the rich food resources of the sea and its moderating effect on the climate.

Most Indians living in the taiga are of the Athapaskan language group. It is thought that the Indians also migrated from Asia, but centuries before the Eskimos. Their appearance is also Mongoloid, although their cheekbones are not so high, their faces not so flat, and their skin not so brown as the Eskimo's. Their noses are larger and more pronounced, their bodies thinner and more supple.

Like the Eskimos, these Indians were a nomadic people. They spent their summers in the river valleys, fishing and gathering roots and berries. During the warm months, they lived in skin tents or bark lodges. But when the days turned cold at the end of August, they built themselves houses, often dug into the ground. These were insulated along the sides with moss or brush. The door was an animal hide and the fireplace a mound of earth.

In midwinter the Indians traveled into the mountains by snowshoe or on sleds. There they hunted caribou, moose, and smaller animals. They used snares, traps, bows and arrows, spears, clubs, and crude bone or copper knives in their hunting. While on the trail they lived in tents. In spring they returned in moose-hide boats or canoes to their campgrounds in the valleys.

The Indians shared many customs with the Eskimos. Indian families also co-operated to obtain food. They, too, made their clothing from skins and used hide, bone, and sinew in their tools and weapons. Both peoples loved competitive sports and storytelling. They played many of the same games. Wrestling was a favorite sport with Indians and Eskimos. Unlike the Eskimos, the northern Indian tribes had chiefs.

The two groups did some trading in surplus goods—small animal skins for salmon, carvings, and oil. Yet relations between the Indians and the Eskimos of the Far North were distrustful. There were bitter disputes and even fighting.

▶ CHANGING LIFE IN THE NORTH

Traditional life in the Far North was brought to an end by the coming of the white man. The Vikings were probably the first Europeans to enter the coastal waters of North America. They undoubtedly met the people of the North. On their heels came men of many nations, all hoping to discover a northwest passage to the rich lands of Cathay and the Indies. By the 17th century the British had claimed the frozen land and its treasure of animal pelts.

To exploit this source of wealth, the Company of Gentlemen Adventurers Trading Into Hudson's Bay was formed in 1668. It shortened its name, eventually, to "Hudson's Bay Company." By its fur trading, it brought about regular contact between Europeans and the Indian and Eskimo peoples of the Far North.

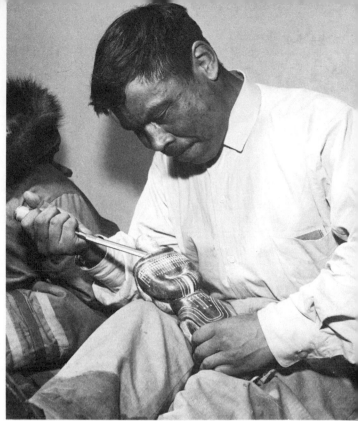

An Eskimo carver still knows the old skills.

The crops grow quickly in the Arctic summer at Aklavik, a settlement 120 miles (193 km.) above the Arctic Circle in the Northwest Territories.

In time, rivalry between the Hudson's Bay Company and other fur traders was to send brave men plunging farther and farther into both the tundra and the taiga to claim territory for their companies. Following explorers like Samuel Hearne, Sir Alexander Mackenzie, Thomas Simpson, and John Rae, trading posts sprang up along the northern rivers. At the same time, seagoing exploration continued to fill in the map of the Arctic islands and waters. More Eskimos came into contact with the traders.

Thus the fur trade brought the first real change the northern people had faced in centuries. Their life of hunting and fishing became one of fur trading and gathering food for the trading posts as well as for themselves. Through trade, they got tobacco, guns, ammunition, knives, kettles, and other implements. Never again would they be content to live only from the resources of the land and the sea.

About 1860, Christian missionaries began to arrive. The Indians and Eskimos soon adopted Christianity, mixing it with native beliefs. Indians and, to a lesser extent, Eskimos began to learn English. They adopted much of the white man's food and clothing, although the traditional Eskimo fur parka remains standard wear for all races in the North.

Over the years, traders, trappers, missionaries, prospectors, doctors, teachers, and members of the Royal Canadian Mounted Police settled north of the 60th parallel. They began hiring Indians and Eskimos to work in stores and on boats, and at hauling goods, building, guiding, and other service jobs. The diseases of civilization, to which the northern people had no immunity, were very harmful. Tuberculosis and pneumonia proved the most lethal.

Nonetheless, for most Indians and Eskimos the years from 1850 to 1945 provided a secure, contented life. Fur prices on the world market continued to rise, reaching an all-time peak in 1945–46. Then, in 1948–49, the fur market collapsed. About the same time, caribou became very scarce. By 1950 the Canadian Government knew that decisive action was needed to save its northernmost citizens from starvation.

Its first step was to put the northern people on government relief. Later, plans were tried to restore the self-sufficiency of the Indians and Eskimos. The development of resources, the creation of industry, and the improvement of education were the methods proposed.

As yet, success has been only partial. The Eskimos, who are quick to master machines and who have fewer whites competing for jobs in their territory, have adapted better than the Indians to the 20th century. Despite their poverty, many Indians would like to maintain their traditional way of life. Gradually, more young northerners are getting the education and training they need to be wage earners.

Transportation is vital to the Far North's development. There isn't enough of it yet. A few airstrips and roads, including the Alaska Highway, were built during World War II. Supply bases, weather stations, and a radar and communications network called the Distant Early Warning, or DEW, Line were also built during and after World War II.

The building of roads and airstrips, and all other construction in the North, are complicated by the northern land itself. Anything built must have a firm base that will hold up when summer melts the permafrost to spongy muskeg. Ski-planes and floatplanes don't need a concrete runway, but they're no good for carrying bulky or heavy goods. These goods must still be transported by water—and during warm weather.

Because of the high cost of transportation, the mineral wealth of the North has barely been tapped. Since 1970, some of the world's richest deposits of oil and natural gas have been found in the Mackenzie Delta and the Arctic Archipelago. To bring the petroleum to market economically, pipelines must be built.

The Canadian Government has insisted that the environment and the way of life of the northern people must be protected while the petroleum industry is developed. Much research has been done on ways of accomplishing this, but the Canadian Government's permission to proceed is not expected until spring of 1975 at the earliest. At present, small quantities of petroleum are shipped by pipeline or barge from the Yukon Territory

In the North seaplanes reach remote areas with mail and vital supplies.

and the southwestern portion of the Northwest Territory.

Besides petroleum, other important mineral resources of the Far North are zinc, lead, copper, silver, asbestos, cadmium, and pitchblende. Large-scale mining is done around Great Slave Lake and in the central Yukon in areas that have the necessary hydroelectric plants.

Although the North has plenty of waterpower, it has been harnessed only on the Snare, Taltson, Yukon, and Stewart rivers. Elsewhere, electricity is generated by diesel engines. The towns of Inuvik, Fort McPherson, and Frobisher Bay have each a utility plant providing electricity, heat, water, and sewage disposal for the whole community.

Alongside the technological advances, the traditional northern economy carries on, often with new ideas. The fur trade continues to this day and brings in several million dollars annually. Other natural products—Arctic char, salmon, brook trout, whale meat, blueberries—are finding markets in the outside world. With an eye to the future, the government is breeding reindeer for their meat, and the almost extinct musk-ox for its fine underwool. It is also experimenting with new varieties of wheat and other grains that will ripen in the short growing season.

Tourism is another government project that is just starting. However, an operation sponsoring and selling Eskimo carvings, lithographic prints, and other crafts today produces an annual income of $2,500,000.

It will be many years before the territories of the Far North can give citizens of every race the opportunities and benefits they need. In the meantime, bringing the North into an equal position with the rest of Canada challenges the skill and imagination of everyone who likes the great freedom of frontier life.

M. A. MACDONALD
Author, *The Royal Canadian Mounted Police*

Acadian villages looked like this before New France began to crumble.

THE ACADIANS

The people in this moving story are caught between two worlds—the world of the great French empire in North America called New France and the emerging world of a British-controlled Canada. The Beauchesne family is from Acadia, as Nova Scotia and parts of New Brunswick were once called. At the time of this story, Acadia has already been taken over by the British. The Beauchesnes have fled inland to French-controlled land near the St. Lawrence River. In a short time, this remaining part of New France will become the province of Quebec in British Canada.

It was 1755. The villagers were gathered around the fireplace of the Mathurin house in New France, in eastern Canada. Four strangers had just arrived from Acadia, and the neighbors were eager to hear the latest news from that troubled coastal region.

The four strangers were members of the Beauchesne family. A man with two small babies, the only ones left of his family of ten, and his sister Madeleine, who had lost all her children—these were the only members who had survived the flight from Acadia. One of the villagers welcomed them and gave them food and drink before questioning them. Then he turned to Beauchesne and asked, "Can you tell us what happened in Acadia?"

Madeleine was the first to speak.

"The English hunted us down and tried to capture us. We are among the few who were able to escape." Her eyes filled with tears and she could not go on.

Then Beauchesne continued the story.

Acadians, guarded by British troops, wait to be shipped into exile.

"We have always been a bone in the throat of the English. When they defeated the French, they took vast stretches of our land here in New France. They changed the name of our homeland to 'Nova Scotia,' and our capital, Port Royal, they renamed Annapolis Royal. Our captors tried to make us speak English and change from our Catholicism to their Protestantism.

"But many French colonists, we among them, refused to change. He who loses his language loses his faith, and he who loses his faith loses his soul. The French king may be able to hand over our prairies and our fields, but he cannot make us turn over our souls. We are French at heart, sons of New France.

"The worst moment of all came when the English tried to make us pledge allegiance to the British crown. Some of us did so, but only on condition that we would never be forced to bear arms against France, that we would be permitted to leave Acadia when we wished to, and that we would be allowed to practice our religion.

"For a while this was all the English asked. But in 1748, Edward Cornwallis, the English governor, once again tried to force us to swear an oath of absolute allegiance. Then, following the advice of our priests, thousands of us fled to Cape Breton Island off the coast or to other friendly French settlements.

"You can imagine how furious this made the English! They did everything in their power to prevent our going and declared that those who fled were rebels and traitors. In my own district they refused to allow people to leave, so my sister Madeleine and I had to stay on in the village with our families.

"The English were jealous of our fertile, well-cultivated fields, and they wanted to have them for their own. They envied our rich Acadian soil with its abundant harvests of good oats, barley, wheat, and feed for the animals.

"Our families had always prospered. Ten, twenty children grew up in our lovely wooden houses with their high thatched roofs. Orchards of fruit trees and productive vegetable gardens surrounded our houses, and we depended on no one for the necessities of life. The women wove cloth for our clothes from the wool of our sheep. Our linens came from the plants that grew in our fields. We made our harnesses and boots from our own leather, and our soap and candles from the fat of our animals. We gathered sap from the maple trees to make our sugar, and we made beer from the spruce trees. Woodcutting, cattle raising, hunting, fishing—all were profitable. We worked hard, and we were happy.

"The English realized that in spite of all their efforts, they could never make us join them. So they soon began to fill the land with their own Protestants. In 1749 they created a complete stronghold for themselves, called Halifax, on the eastern coast. A whole population of men, women, and children was transported from London to settle the area.

The oldest surviving Acadian house. It is in Meteghan, Nova Scotia.

"After the founding of Halifax and other, similar settlements, the English no longer needed us to protect them from the nomadic Indians who were friendly to us but not to the English. And they no longer needed us to make their colonies profitable.

"From then on they began to treat us more harshly. The lowliest English agent tried to make us obey his every wish; the courts made themselves hated by their violations of the law and their frequent denials of justice.

"Then this year our new English Governor ordered that our guns be taken from us. He seized our canoes and refused to allow us to use the rivers for commerce. And finally, with the help of 2,000 Massachusetts colonists, he laid siege to Fort Beauséjour, which was forced to surrender. French Acadia lost its last defense.

"It was shortly afterward that a proclamation was issued. We were ordered, on pain of the most severe punishment, to gather in the largest villages to hear an important message from the Governor. At Grand Pré all the male inhabitants, from the youngest to the oldest, were gathered into the church. Then Colonel Winslow, an English officer, stood before the altar and faced the men.

Calling them traitors and rebels, he told them that their lands were officially confiscated and now belonged to the British crown. Then came the hardest blow of all. Winslow added that the entire population was under arrest and that everyone would be deported to the thirteen British colonies in America.

"The men were the first to be shipped out. A heavy military guard led them to the mouth of the Gaspereau River where five ships out of Boston lay at anchor. The women and children followed their men from the church to the shore, weeping and praying and trying to embrace them one last time. Fathers, sons, and brothers were separated from one another and placed in five different groups, each group to be shipped to a different American colony. The men tried to protest the separation, but Colonel Winslow's troops, their bayonets fixed, forced them on board the waiting ships. The women cried out as their men were taken away. Their turn would come a little later, along with the children and sick old people.

"And that is how it was everywhere. Very few Acadians escaped forced deportation."

Beauchesne fell silent. For a long while he seemed lost in thought, unable to go on with the story. Then Mathurin said:

152

"And how was it with you, Beauchesne? Can you tell us what happened in your own village and how the four of you managed to escape?"

Beauchesne resumed his narrative.

"In my village," he said, "we were just able to reach the forest before the English troops could trap us. We hid on a hillside overlooking the village, and watched as they burned our houses, our barns, the mill, and the little church. My old mother, who had lived in that village all her life, died of sorrow at the sight.

"That was the first tragedy I myself had to face, but alas, not the last. But it's best that I do not dwell any longer on our personal sadness.

"Our flight was bitterly painful, for the winter was cold and the English soldiers had orders to shoot fugitives on sight. But our suffering was as a single drop of water in a vast sea compared with the suffering of many thousands of Acadians. Where are my countrymen now? Dispersed, robbed of their worldly goods? Cast up on inhospitable shores? Did they all die in a foreign land?"

Beauchesne's sad tale came to an end, and he fell silent at last. The listeners respected his silence and reflected for a long while on the tragedy of their Acadian brothers. Finally Mathurin poured another mug of beer for Beauchesne and said:

"In the name of all of us, I welcome you. There is no lack of work here for a strong fellow like you, and you may stay with us as long as you like. Your sister and your children—they, too, are welcome to stay."

Then Mathurin turned to the little children. "It's all right now, little ones," he said. "You are safe here with us on French soil. A new life is beginning, and our sons will love you as the brothers and sisters you lost once loved you. Once again you will sleep with a roof over your heads, and you will be able to eat your fill once more."

As Madeleine listened to the good man's words, her eyes shone with gratitude. Her thoughts turned to the life ahead, to days of hard work and happiness. All four of the newcomers, strangers no longer, gratefully accepted the warm hospitality offered to them. Acadia had become a thing of the past.

A statue of "Evangeline," heroine of Longfellow's poem about the Acadians.

MYSTERIOUS FOOTPRINTS

The majestic Himalayas in Central Asia form a picturesque natural barrier that separates northern India from Tibet. Located among the valleys, peaks, and ridges of this vast mountain chain are the states of Nepal, Bhutan, and Sikkim. At their highest level the mountains rise like giant, snowcapped spires to well over 20,000 feet (6,000 meters). Mount Everest, the highest of the many towering peaks in the Himalayas, soars nearly 5.5 miles (8.8 kilometers) into the sky.

The people of the Himalayas look upon their mountain homeland with reverence. They believe that gods, spirits, and strange beings live on the remote forested slopes. And perhaps the people are right. Since the late 1890's, stories of the abominable snowman—a strange apelike creature—have filtered through the mountain ranges to the outside world. Several explorers who have climbed the rocky heights of the Himalayas have sighted footprints of a large, unknown creature in the snow. But no animal or mysterious beast has ever been found—dead or alive. The peoples of Tibet call this strange beast *yeti*, which means "dweller among the rocks," and they claim to have seen him many times. He has been described as being half-man, half-ape, and covered with long, fine blond or reddish hair, except on his hands, his face, and the soles of his feet. He has very long arms that reach to his knees, and he walks on thick legs in an upright position.

However, there is no real evidence that the yeti, or abominable snowman, exists. Many of the stories about the creature are based on the large, unidentifiable footprints that have been found in the snow. But these footprints could belong to almost any of the wild animals that live in the Himalaya range. The tiger, leopard, yak, and bear are found in the higher altitudes of the mountains. At certain gaits, bears place the hind foot partly over the imprint of the forefoot. This makes a very large imprint that looks as if it might be the print of an immense human being—or

a monster. The Himalayan langur, a monkey with a long tail, bushy eyebrows, and a chin tuft, often leaves footprints that might also be mistaken for those of a large unknown animal. And sometimes the sun causes the tracks of an animal to melt into large footprints, thus giving the impression that a mysterious beast is roaming over the mountain slopes.

Explorers have also found that markings thought to be left by the abominable snowman could very well have been caused by lumps of snow or stones falling from higher regions and bouncing across the lower slopes of the Himalayas.

Whether or not the abominable snowman really exists is anybody's guess. But some people are convinced that it does. In the last several years many expeditions have trekked across the Himalayas in search of the creature. The explorers failed to discover anything except a few large footprints. They neither captured nor saw anything that resembled the snowman.

But strange beings resembling the abominable snowman have been sighted in other parts of the world. Bigfoot, a creature described as standing from 7 to 10 feet (2 to 3 m.) tall and weighing more than 500 pounds (220 kilograms), has been seen in the mountains of California, Oregon, and Washington, and in British Columbia in Canada. Hundreds of people have described the monster as apelike, with thick fur, long arms, powerful shoulders, and a short neck. He supposedly walks like a man and leaves huge footprints about 16 inches (41 centimeters) long and 6 inches (15 cm.) wide. That is why the Rocky Mountain Indians named the monster Bigfoot.

The Canadians think there might be a whole family of monsters roaming around. They call the creatures Sasquatch ("hairy men") after the legendary tribe of aboriginal giants in the folklore of the Indians of the Northwest Coast. The Chehalis Indians near Vancouver, British Columbia, believe that the monsters are the descendants of two bands of giants who were almost exterminated in battle many years ago.

In 1957 a Canadian lumberman claimed that 33 years earlier he had been kidnaped by a family of hairy apelike creatures while on a camping trip near Vancouver Island. He was held captive for about a week before he escaped. When the lumberman reached civilization, he decided to keep the story of his strange encounter to himself, for fear nobody would believe him. But when sightings of strange monsters began to occur in the northwestern United States and Canada in the 1950's, he decided to reveal his experience.

One strange creature was even captured—at least on movie film—by a startled monster hunter in the mountains of northern California in 1967. And although the film is jumpy and unfocused, it shows the image of a tall, long-legged, apelike animal covered with dark hair.

In 1973 stories of yeti-like monsters spread throughout the United States. Giant apelike creatures covered with white hair and uttering high-pitched screams were seen and heard in Florida, Pennsylvania, and Arkansas. The residents of Murphysboro, Illinois, a small town on the Big Muddy River, reported several monster sightings. In response to the calls of one frightened eyewitness, the police searched a desolate forested area near the river. They discovered a rough trail in the bush and peculiar footprints fast disappearing in the mud. Grass was crushed and covered with black slime. Broken branches dangled from large trees, and small bushes and trees were snapped in half. Suddenly a shrill, piercing scream broke the silence of the night, and neighbors, police, and police dogs raced for safety. The sound of the scream, after all the stories they had heard, was enough to convince the searchers, and later the whole neighborhood, that something strange was in the area. Several further sightings were reported in the following weeks. Then the sightings stopped and it seemed as if the monster had just disappeared.

In addition to the many sightings throughout the United States and Canada, several unusual footprints have been found and preserved in plaster. The footprints, like those of the abominable snowman, are human in

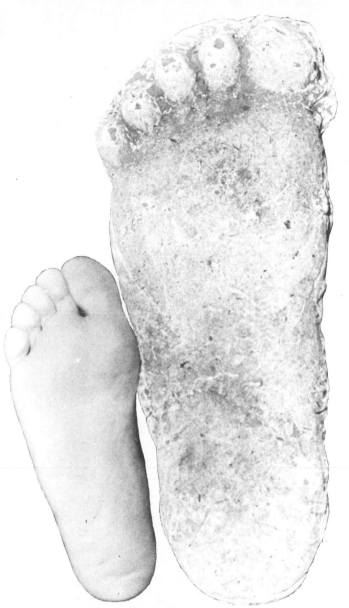

A cast of Bigfoot's footprint and a human foot.

appearance, but much larger than any man could possibly have made. Anthropologists and zoologists who have listened to eyewitness accounts, studied the film, and examined the plaster casts of the footprints have reached only one conclusion: Whatever it is called—abominable snowman, yeti, sasquatch, or Bigfoot—it's difficult to prove that it doesn't exist.

155

The old ways of gathering maple sap are still used in some places. When this man has made the rounds of his sugar maples, the big barrel will be full.

MAPLE LEAF INDUSTRY

Emblems or symbols have always played an important role in the lives of people and of nations. Representations of the maple leaf have been found throughout Canada from the country's earliest days. The maple leaf has been considered the Canadian national emblem since the 17th century. However, it did not gain full recognition until 1965, when a red maple leaf became the central part of the national flag of Canada.

For the people of the province of Quebec, the maple leaf is more than a national symbol. It symbolizes one of Quebec's major industries, the maple sugar industry.

And the maple sugar industry is no ordinary industry. There is nothing quite like the products made from the sap of the maple trees of Canada. You have to try maple syrup, maple sugar, or maple butter on a simple piece of bread or as part of an elegant dessert before you can fully understand how wonderful the maple tree is. Maple sugar and syrup can be used in making cakes, puddings, pastry, and ice cream, and to sweeten fruit; or it can simply be poured over ice cream. Maple syrup is used for glazing meats, especially ham; vegetables like carrots, parsnips, and sweet potatoes; and fruits such as apples, pears, peaches, pineapple, and cherries. They're all delicious!

In the province of Quebec, Canada's maple kingdom, it is hard to find a single person who doesn't eat his share of maple syrup, maple sugar, or maple butter during "sugaring-off time." For a citizen of Quebec, eating maple products is almost a civic duty. This tradition is reflected in the annual Maple Festival held at Plessisville, Quebec. Thousands of people gather here to sample the harvest of maple syrup, maple sugar, and maple butter.

THE INDUSTRY AROUND THE WORLD

Canada is not the only country where maple trees grow. In fact, you might be surprised to learn that in the Northern Hemisphere alone, there are 115 varieties of maple tree. Only 10 of these varieties are grown in Canada.

There are many maple trees in Europe, chiefly in France, and in Asia, principally in China and Japan and the countries of the Himalayas. Although all maple trees produce a sap that is more or less sweet, only a few species produces enough sap that is sufficiently sweet to be commercially profitable. Four of these species of maple thrive in the northeastern part of the United States and in southeastern Canada. Quebec's maples are the most beautiful in Canada and also the most productive. Quebec alone accounts for more than 85 per cent of Canada's total maple sugar and maple syrup production.

In the United States, the maple syrup and maple sugar industry is declining. For the past several years only about 4,500,000 of the 225,000,000 sugar maple trees in New England have been tapped. Ten states of the United States produce maple sugar and maple syrup in commercial quantities. They are Vermont, New York, Ohio, Michigan, Pennsylvania, Wisconsin, New Hampshire, Massachusetts, Maine, and Maryland. Their total production is less than two thirds that of Quebec.

HISTORY OF THE MAPLE INDUSTRY

Before the arrival of the Europeans in North America, the Indians knew about the value of maple sap as a sweetener. However, they did not develop any special way of harvesting it efficiently. If they wanted the sweet sap, they simply slashed the trunk of the nearest maple tree with a tomahawk or hatchet, dug into the tree trunk, and took out the accumulated sap. This crude harvesting method led to the destruction of many maple trees. In the early days of European colonization, the white man followed the Indians' method of slashing tree trunks, too.

Documents dating from the beginning of the 17th century indicate that the Indians in Canada drank both maple sap and birch water. They referred to both liquids as "healing waters." Unlike the sap of the maple, the sap of the birch is not sweet.

The Indians did not make maple syrup as it is now made. They gathered maple sap in great clay vats. Then they threw white-hot stones into the vats. The heat made some of the liquid evaporate and left a thicker liquid —but one that was not yet a true syrup.

For a long time, the early settlers in Canada left the collecting of maple sap to the Indians, though they helped them improve their methods. The European settlers used the maple products in their cooking and exported a small quantity to France. For almost 150 years, the production of maple syrup and maple sugar in New France remained a craft occupation, not a true industry.

Because the early settlers in Canada used maple products primarily for their own household needs, the methods they used in making them changed little through the 18th and 19th centuries. In fact, the people of Quebec did not wake up to the enormous possibilities of the maple sugar industry until around 1837, long after the English had taken over rule of Canada. In 1837, as a protest against being forced to buy cane sugar from British colonies in the West Indies, the French Canadians made a historic decision: They decided to increase maple sugar production.

Production of maple sugar increased enormously in the years following 1837. By 1851, according to official statistics, it reached 13,500,000 pounds (6,124,000 kilograms) of sugar.

MODERN METHODS

One of the first important advances in the maple sugar industry was the introduction of modern methods of boring into the trunk of the maple tree to tap it instead of slashing it. The traditional tap-hole is about $7/16$ inch (11.1 millimeters) in diameter. The first spouts for tapping were made of elder wood. These were eventually replaced by aluminum spouts. Originally the sap dripped from the tap-hole into wooden or birchbark containers. Then metal buckets came into use for collecting the sap. First they were made of tin, then copper, and finally aluminum.

Now history is catching up with the maple industry again, and aluminum buckets are be-

The man at right is boring a tap-hole. The other man is inserting a spout into a completed hole.

A full bucket of sap is emptied into a collecting bucket, and the steady drip continues.

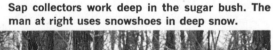

Sap collectors work deep in the sugar bush. The man at right uses snowshoes in deep snow.

Sugaring off is fun. Hot syrup is spilled into a snow-filled trough to harden. Then you eat it!

coming obsolete. In the past few years, two new methods have been adopted for gathering sap. The most practical and promising of these methods consists of channeling sap directly from the trees into a network of plastic tubes. The sap is carried from the trees into vats or storage containers near the sugarhouse. This system is gaining general popularity in Canada.

The other new method of gathering sap is potentially even better. It involves pumping the sap from the buckets on the trees into a vat or container that is moved through the maple grove by a tractor.

One thing that the Canadians don't like about the new methods of gathering sap is that they take the fun out of the whole thing. The traditional sugaring-off parties held at the sugarhouses deep in the forest were a lot of fun. In maple groves where the old methods are used, the sap is brought to the sugarhouse in a huge vat carried on a truck or even a horse-drawn sleigh. When the first sap is boiled in the sugarhouse, everyone gets to sample it poured over a fresh plate of snow.

The day may not be far off when the equipment may be perfected to the point where the sugarhouse will look like a miniature factory. Eventually, there may be nothing to see but shining metal containers, hermetically sealed vats, and a maze of pipes.

▶ PREPARING THE SAP

The sap of the maple tree is the basis of the whole maple industry. It is composed of more than 97 per cent water and an average of 2.5 per cent solids, primarily sucrose. Somewhere in the chemical makeup of maple sap is a mysterious ingredient that gives the sap its distinctive aroma—but no one knows what that ingredient is.

The quality and quantity of the sap a tree produces depend on a number of factors. They include the age, size, and health of the tree; the abundance of the tree's foliage; and the depth of its roots. The condition of the soil in which the tree grows is also important, as is the weather—especially the temperatures during the summer preceding the sap gathering and the temperatures at the time of the gathering. Cold nights, and days with temperatures of from 45 to 50 degrees Fahrenheit

(7 to 10 degrees Celsius), are ideal conditions for a harvest of delicately flavored sap.

Incidentally, maple trees are never tapped before they are 40 years old. At this point their trunks measure about 12 inches (30 centimeters) in diameter. The average height of sugar maples is from 80 to 90 feet (24 to 27 meters), with a diameter of from 2 to 3 feet (0.6 to 0.9 m.). The exception to this is found in the United States, in Ohio, where maples reach heights of up to 130 feet (almost 40 m.) and diameters of about 5 feet (1.5 m.).

To produce a gallon or a litre of maple syrup takes 20 to 40 times as much sap—depending on the percentage of sugar in the sap. Ideally, the sap should be processed on the day that it is gathered, so that the delicate aroma of the sap is retained.

In making maple sugar the sap is boiled at a higher temperature than it is in making maple syrup. After the sap is boiled, it is cooled and beaten vigorously until it is a dull yellow color. Then it is poured immediately into molds and cooled further.

Hard sugar is cooked at a temperature a few degrees higher than soft sugar, and it is cooled and beaten vigorously until it is a dull it is beaten thoroughly. When it becomes yellowish and has the consistency of a thick paste, it is poured into molds to harden.

Maple butter is obtained by boiling the sap at a lower temperature than is used for soft sugar, and allowing it to cool to room temperature. Before being placed in jars, the maple butter is beaten to a soft paste.

From the standpoint of quality, maple syrup is classified as: deluxe (a very clear amber color with a pure, sweet aroma); clear (a clear amber color with a sweet aroma); intermediate (a dark amber color with a strong aroma); dark (a dark amber color with a strong aroma and sometimes a trace of fermentation).

It is interesting to note that the maple trees that give the best syrup also have the best wood for furniture making. The wood of all maple trees makes excellent fuel.

Certainly, of all the natural wonders of North America, the maple tree has been one of the most useful. It has been an especial friend to the people of Quebec.

OLD SAN JUAN

There are really two San Juans in Puerto Rico. One is the modern city with its busy International Airport, high-rise buildings, white luxury hotels glittering in the sun, and rapidly expanding suburbs. The other is Old San Juan—a city of yesterday.

Old San Juan is only seven blocks square, but it has a special grace and beauty that make it unique in the Western Hemisphere. Some of the narrow streets are paved with small blue-gray blocks called *adoquines*, which were cast from iron slag in Spain and brought to Puerto Rico in the late 19th century. Two of the most charming streets are Callejón de las Monjas (Lane of the Nuns) and Caleta del Hospital (Little Street of the Hospital). They are actually stone stairways for pedestrian use and are the only remaining "step streets" in the old city. Many of the houses of Old San Juan have balconies with wooden or wrought-iron balustrades like those in the oldest sections of Spanish cities.

Everything in the little community of Old San Juan—the houses, the churches, and the fortifications—has a sense of time about it. The past casts long shadows here. Years ago a Spanish visitor to Puerto Rico wrote these words: "Walk through Old San Juan and you walk through the long and dim corridors of time. It is a pleasant walk and somewhere you will stop and find yourself standing in a small, sunlit plaza. Then you will look about and say with slow wonder, 'I am now standing in a quiet corner of Old Spain where all is serene and time flows on endlessly.'"

The report is still a true one.

The city of San Juan was founded over 450 years ago by Juan Ponce de León, the Spanish explorer. Most of the old walls of the city still stand. The massive fortress called El Morro guards the entrance to San Juan harbor as it has done for hundreds of years.

El Morro is probably the best place to begin a walking tour of Old San Juan. Construction of the fortress was started in 1539. It was completed more than 200 years later. El Morro juts into the ocean like the prow of a huge ship. At one time it was a key defense point in the vast series of fortresses Spain built to protect its empire in the New World. The old limestone fortress has six levels and rises to a height of 140 feet (43 meters) above the sea. On its land side is a vast field, which covers a system of underground tunnels. There is a nine-hole golf course in the grounds of El Morro. Three holes are played within the filled-in moats of the fortress.

El Morro has seen many attacks from the land and the sea during its long history. In 1595 Sir Francis Drake tried to enter the harbor to capture the cargo of a disabled Spanish galleon that had put in at San Juan. The guns of El Morro forced him to retreat and sail away. In 1625 a Dutch fleet entered the harbor and landed troops, who occupied the city. The Dutch set up cannon and trained them on El Morro. However, they could not penetrate the defenses. In despair, the Dutch troops boarded their ships and left Puerto Rico. They realized that they could not hold the island if they did not hold El Morro. Centuries later, in the Spanish-American War, Admiral William Sampson of the United States Navy attacked the Spanish-held city of San Juan but caused little damage to the thick walls of El Morro. Today the grand old fortress is part of the San Juan National Historic Site and is administered by the National Park Service.

It is a short and pleasant walk in the sun to the next place of interest in Old San Juan, the Church of San José. Founded in 1532, it is one of the oldest churches in continuous use in the Western Hemisphere. Some historians claim it is the oldest. The building is striking, with exceptionally beautiful vaulted ceilings. The Church of San José was built by Dominican friars, who designed the building to mirror the late-Gothic architectural style of Spain. The church was built on land that had been given to the Dominican friars by Ponce de León himself.

The sense of the past is especially strong when you come to the Casa de los Contrafuertes. This building, with its thick masonry buttresses, is said to be the oldest residence in San Juan. Recently restored, the building now houses a Pharmacy Museum, a Graphic

The massive fortress of El Morro juts into the ocean like the prow of a ship.

One of the two remaining "step streets" in Old San Juan.

161

Cristo Street, paved with the original blue-gray *adoquines*, leads to the Cristo Chapel.

Arts Museum, and a Santos Museum. The collection of *santos* is especially interesting. *Santos* are small religious figures carved from wood by artisans called *santeros*. There were once many *santeros* in the countries of the former Spanish empire. However, as the years pass, there are fewer and fewer men to carry on this tradition. The Santos Museum preserves the very best work of the Puerto Rican *santeros*.

The deep religious tradition of the Puerto Rican people runs through all phases of their lives. San Juan Cathedral represents the past and the present in Puerto Rican religious life. The cathedral is visible from almost all parts of the old city. The original building was built of wood and thatch in the 1520's. However, it was destroyed by a ferocious hurricane. The imposing building that you see today was, for the most part, built in the

The gift shops in Old San Juan sell a varied selection of goods from all over the world. This shop, with its charming interior courtyard, has the atmosphere of an old Spanish home.

162

early 19th century. The city's founder, Ponce de León, is buried in the cathedral. When you pause beside his marble tomb, you get the feeling of being close to a fabulous figure in colonial history. Ponce de León founded the Spanish colony of Puerto Rico and was its first governor. But he was also a wanderer who had an amazing vision. Ponce de León searched for the legendary Fountain of Youth. Although he never found it, there is something very impressive in his gallant attempt.

There are things of great beauty in San Juan Cathedral. A number of the paintings that hang there are attributed to José Campeche, one of the island's finest painters. Campeche was the son of a freed slave. It is said that the King of Spain asked Campeche to come to Spain as a court painter. However, Campeche preferred to remain in Puerto Rico among his own people.

Next you might like to take a walk down the Caleta San Juan. You will find yourself —once again—deep in Puerto Rico's colorful past. For here, at the end of the narrow street, is the huge city wall with its famed San Juan Gate. Completed in 1641, the gate at the edge of the sea was once the main entrance to the old city. When a new governor or bishop arrived from Spain, he was met at the San Juan Gate by a party of local officials and important citizens. After the official greetings were over, the group walked ceremoniously up Caleta San Juan to the cathedral. At the cathedral's high altar they offered prayers of thanksgiving for the safe completion of the voyage.

It is important to remember now, in an age of relatively safe travel, just how dangerous an ocean crossing was in the days of small sailing ships. Aside from the constant danger of storms and hurricanes, there was the ever-present danger of attack from pirates and other enemy ships. And San Juan was not, in the old days, a very safe place ashore either. In addition to El Morro, the Spanish were forced to build other fortresses to protect the city from raiders. As you walk along the city walls, you will see the two sentry towers of La Fortaleza. It was in these towers, in the old days, that sentries stood and peered out to sea, ready to give the alarm at the first sign of an enemy ship that was approaching.

La Fortaleza was, in fact, the first fortress built in San Juan. It was one of the first examples of a "modern" European fortification in the New World. La Fortaleza was twice occupied by invaders: once by the English in 1598 and again by the Dutch in 1625. During the 19th century the building was remodeled to look more like a palace than a fortification. La Fortaleza has, in fact, been the official residence of Puerto Rico's governors for hundreds of years.

Just a short distance from La Fortaleza is the tiny Cristo Chapel. This beautiful building commemorates a mysterious and exciting event in Puerto Rico's history. During the 18th century a highlight of the island's famous San Juan fiesta—held in honor of Puerto Rico's patron saint—was a horse race run through the streets of the city. The people would watch excitedly as the riders galloped through the narrow alleys and streets of the course. In the fiesta of 1753 a young racer named Baltasar Montañez rode his horse down the Cristo Street leg of the race at a furious pace. As he came to the end of the street, he could not check the horse's speed in time to make the necessary turn. Both horse and rider plunged over the low wall at the street's end and fell into the sea below. According to legend, Baltasar Montañez survived the fall. To commemorate the event, the Spanish governor of Puerto Rico ordered that a chapel be built on the exact spot where the spectacular fall took place.

Cristo Chapel looks much as it must have looked when it was first built, two centuries ago. It is one of the smallest religious buildings in the world. It seats no more than a dozen people.

These are just a few of the fascinating places you can visit in Old San Juan. A trip to the old city is truly a voyage back in time to the exciting days of the Spanish exploration of the New World. Perhaps the most important thing of all about Old San Juan, however, is the great pleasure it is to be there. Old San Juan forms the most charming possible bridge between the past and the present.

THE FLEA MARKET

In the town you live in, you may have seen signs that say "Flea Market Saturday!" If you went to see what a flea market was all about, you may have had quite a surprise. It was certainly not a place to buy fleas. What you probably saw were old books, pots and pans, dishes, glasses, stuffed moose heads, and a huge variety of other things all jumbled up together. But the odd term "flea market" has an interesting history. The flea market originated in Paris, and the Paris Flea Market is still the most famous. It was probably named "Flea Market" because many of the old things sold there were suspected of having fleas in them.

▶ A PARIS LANDMARK

The Flea Market of Paris has been imitated, but it has never been equaled. It is known all over the world. It attracts not only tourists, but a wide variety of antique dealers and collectors. In fact, it attracts anyone who is looking for an unusual experience.

An endless variety of things are sold in the Flea Market. Everything from the most ordinary household goods to fine works of art is displayed. If you want to buy an Egyptian mummy or a carriage (if you happen to have a horse to pull it) or a church pew, you may be able to find it at the Flea Market. You will certainly have to look through a great many piles of things to find what you want, but if you have patience your own special treasure will turn up. But even if you don't find what you're looking for at the Flea Market, going there is a valuable experience in itself. On a nice day an afternoon spent at the Flea Market is bound to leave you with many pleasant memories.

The Flea Market began about 1860. In 1860, France was at the height of its famous Second Empire period, and a wealth of goods from all over the world seemed to end up in Paris. But even more important, the city of Paris had begun to spread out. There was an obscure spot just outside the city in a neighborhood where very poor people lived and stray dogs seemed to end up when they had run away from home. Petty thieves and crooks of all sorts gathered there, at a spot near the Porte de Clignancourt, which had been one of the medieval gates of Paris. Here they bartered or sold their merchandise. The largest group of shady fellows who gathered to trade were called, in French, the "lock-pickers." The fast deals they made at Clignancourt required just as much skill as their trade of lock-picking. Soon the respectable people of Paris heard about the huge variety of goods being traded and went out to Clignancourt to see what they could find.

Now more than a century has passed since the Flea Market started. Today it is organized like a little city—with a lot of modern rules and regulations. And yet it is still a place where truly offbeat treasures are sold. You can find art objects of all kinds there, as well as used home furnishings of every description, old books, and "hippie" costume.

▶ A LITTLE BIT OF EVERYTHING

The Flea Market is actually made up of five distinct market areas. The oldest market is called Vernaison. It has been operating for 75 years. You can find the wildest mixture of things in the Vernaison that you have ever seen. There is old clothing and used household gadgets of every sort. You might find an old casserole (in more or less usable condition) or silver table knives that might have belonged to your grandmother. You might find cracked drinking glasses, patched trousers, and a set of old false teeth—all displayed together. Collectors of antique arms have found medieval swords, as well as German helmets from World War II.

In the Malik market (Malik, the story goes, was the name of an Albanian prince who settled in the area), you can find clothing of all sorts. There is an abundance of surplus clothing from American Army-Navy stores, which has been very popular with French young people recently.

The Jules Vallès market (named for a 19th-century French writer) is the smallest of the markets. It almost disappeared in 1946 after Paris had been liberated by the Allies. The legal document with which the authorities tried to close the Jules Vallès market referred to the "unhealthiness of the surround-

If you look hard enough, you can find just about anything at the flea market.

ings." Unhealthy or not, the Jules Vallès market is still there, selling a wide variety of merchandise.

The Paul-Bert market has "everything from a stuffed horse to Chinese pen holders." It is an especially colorful market, and many people consider it the most interesting section of the Flea Market. You will find odds and ends from all over the world that you would never see in any ordinary store.

The Biron market is unique in that it features new things. Sometimes items can be found here that would cost much more in the large department stores of Paris.

▶ TRICKS OF THE TRADE

Tradition says that you can find anything at the Flea Market if you look long enough. That may be true, although you often come away with something completely different from what you went for. Up to now there have been no reliable estimates of the number of people who visit the Flea Market every year. At the Paul-Bert market a white-bearded salesman estimated that about 10,000,000 tourists and other visitors come every year. Unfortunately there is no precise way to check the accuracy of his estimate. There is no price of admission to the market and therefore no precise way of keeping count.

Prices at the Flea Market are hard to keep track of. They seem to follow the ups and downs of the economy. In good times they are reasonably high; in hard times, low. The Flea Market was once famous for "good buys." The good buys of the old days have become rarer and rarer—but they are not impossible to find. The important thing to remember when you go to the Flea Market is that it is primarily the place to go for ordinary used things—household goods, furniture, clothing. Despite the markets that carry genuine antiques or new items, ordinary used goods predominate.

If you talk with the men and women who work in the Flea Market, you will get a good idea of what it's like. An elderly man who runs a used furniture stall in the Biron market volunteered some of his impressions of the Flea Market. He was a real expert because his father had worked there before him.

"Imagine," he began, "the huge piles of worthless stuff they used to bring here and sell, out in the open. My father was there—along with a lot of others—to try to sell what you really have to call junk. But remember how many works by painters who are now well known were sold for the price of a rusty saucepan or a blanket full of holes. Imagine what the competition in the old days was like! Men fighting for a little square of ground to show their wares. Imagine what sales pitches those old dealers gave their customers. But the people who come to buy today— what do I think of them? They're people looking for roots. They are searching for a past because they feel they have none. They feel they want beautiful old country furniture, for instance, but they don't like it unless it has a good wax finish on it and has been prettied up a bit. They also like to have picnics while listening to sentimental old tunes played on the accordion—but they can't be bothered with the ants who always come to a picnic. For more than 30 years, I found it a joy to discover a lovely, gracious object of some kind covered with dust and offered for sale at a miserably small price. I would restore it patiently to its full beauty! But the patience, the love—people lack the time for all that. Now one doesn't do anything but try to put something in working order before trying to sell it. And when we really fix things up, the price goes way up as a result and people aren't so happy about that. Things go full circle!"

A gloomy outlook? Or great honesty? Who can say. Buyers and sellers will never agree on this point. The Flea Market certainly isn't attracting any fewer people.

▶ MODERN TIMES

One thing is certain—you can tell what's going on in the world by watching the Flea Market. For instance, after Vatican Council II when many changes were made in the rites of the Roman Catholic Church, the Flea Market was flooded with religious objects of all kinds. There were statues, crucifixes, and elaborate vestments offered for sale. And in 1972 there was a new interest in France in everything to do with the 1920's. Books, plays, films, and fashions began to reflect that era. The Flea Market was suddenly filled with things from the 1920's.

Life in the Flea Market reaches a peak of activity on the weekend. Thousands of restorers, collectors, curiosity seekers, and people with nothing else to do pour in. Without doubt, in a good year, the Flea Market is quite profitable for the men who sell there. And it is now run along much more conventional business lines than it used to be. A group of businessmen own the land occupied by the market. The merchants rent their display space from the corporation. Now there is less selling from pushcarts. And there are rules and regulations too. For instance, it is illegal to sell used handkerchiefs or napkins in the Flea Market because of the danger of spreading germs. However, people selling these items illegally get around the law by pinning them to the underside of umbrellas. When they get word that a policeman is nearby, they quickly close the umbrella.

The future of the Flea Market? From time to time you read something in a Paris newspaper about a general closing. There's not much chance of that happening. The Flea Market has really become part of every tourist's visit to Paris. But there are trends that point to change. There will probably be more and more specialization in the various markets. Used household goods will become an even bigger category of sales. On the other hand, art objects of great interest will probably be seen less often. The "good old days," when you just might happen to find a genuine Cézanne painting in a pile of worthless junk, are probably over. As in many other areas, the picturesque and the poetic are giving way to the fast and profitable business deal—even at the Flea Market.

A Mohawk worker walks the high steel with traditional bravery and grace.

MOHAWK SKY WALKERS

There he was, about 1,500 feet (460 meters) above the huge, sprawling city. All about him was clear blue sky. Far below him lay the gleaming band of the Hudson River, and beyond it the shores and green meadows of New Jersey. The day was sunny and there was a gentle wind.

From the crowded and busy street below he looked no bigger than a toy man, a tiny figure clinging to a thin spire of steel. This man, standing on the very tip of the tower, was a high-steel worker. He had walked the narrow girders of the steel skeletons of many skyscrapers as they rose floor by floor, higher and higher into the New York City sky. From the time of his youth this man had worked on skyscrapers and bridges. It was his calling, his way of life. Every working day this man

dared the heights, he and others of his people. This was the way they made their living.

They were Mohawk Indians.

By tradition, Mohawk Indians work on bridges, skyscrapers, and other structures that reach high into the air. The Mohawks have made an impressive record for themselves in New York City. They helped build the twin-towered World Trade Center—a structure that rises to the almost incredible height of 110 stories. They worked on Rockefeller Center, the Chrysler Building, the United Nations buildings, the famed Verrazano-Narrows Bridge—in fact, Mohawks have worked on almost every skyscraper and on many of the high bridges that stand in and around New York City. They have also worked on bridges and skyscrapers in other parts of the United States and in Canada.

But it is the Mohawk high-steel men of New York City that we are concerned with. For their story is an especially fascinating one—a story that begins hundreds of miles away, near the St. Lawrence River. It was there, on the Caughnawaga reservation in Canada, that most of the Mohawk steel men were born.

"Yes, that is the place," Tom Bennett said. "Just over the border in Canada. That's where most of us grew up. And then we came down here to the big city."

He was sitting on a subway train, on his way to his job on a skyscraper that was going up on Fifty-fourth Street in Manhattan. Tom Bennett, Mohawk Indian, lives in Brooklyn, across the East River. Tom was sitting next to two other Mohawk steel men who live in the same neighborhood. When Mr. Bennett gets up in the morning he can look across the river and see some of the skyscrapers he has helped build. They stand majestically outlined against the gray morning sky.

"It's a good sight to face in the morning. It makes you feel that you have contributed something to the making of a great city. Over the years some of my fellow steel workers have lost their lives building skyscrapers and bridges. You can be careful and sure-footed and all that, but somehow or other you make a mistake, and then you fall."

He sighed.

"It's a long way to fall, I'll tell you that. By the way, as far as I know there's not one Mohawk steel man buried in the city. We have our dead carried back home to the reservation and they are buried there. And that's been going on for fifty years or so."

"Fifty?"

He nodded. "The Mohawks came down to New York in the 1920's during a building boom. You know, high-steel men come from all over. I've worked alongside Irish, Polish, Russian, Italian, and Swedish steel men. But lots of fellows think it strange that Indians from the forests should become high-steel men. Well, I guess, in a way, it is. I guess you're wondering how Mohawk Indians from a reservation in Canada have come to walk the high steel sixty, seventy, and eighty stories above the streets of a city."

"I am. But before you start, can you tell us this? I've heard that Mohawk Indians have absolutely no fear of heights. Is that true?"

Mr. Bennett glanced at his two neighbors, who were listening intently. He smiled at them and then he turned back and said: "Well, you'd have to take every Mohawk man, woman, and child and set them on a narrow girder sixty stories high and find out. See if they yell and want to get down on good solid ground again."

He chuckled and smoothed his dark hair with one of his strong hands. Then he began to speak again.

"But I can say that as far as I know, from my own experience, it is so. Mohawk Indians do not fear heights. Why it is so, I can't tell you. There are a lot of theories, and who knows which one is true? I've even heard that there have been studies made by scientists."

At this point, one of Mr. Bennett's companions touched him on the shoulder and then began to speak to him. He spoke in the Mohawk language and Tom Bennett listened with concentrated attention. Finally he nodded, and then he turned and said:

"This is Ed Martin. And he tells me that he was tested and questioned by a scientist up at Columbia or some other New York university. He's not sure anymore. When was it, Ed?"

Martin, who was a short and stocky man of about 50, shook his head.

"I'd say about twenty, twenty-five years ago. I can't really remember, Tom. But I do remember going there and spending maybe two to three hours with them."

"But they didn't tell you what they found out?"

Martin shook his head.

"I don't think they found out anything of any use, Tom," he said.

"Just that you don't fear height, eh?"

Martin nodded and smiled.

"Just that," he agreed.

Tom Bennett turned back to us and began speaking again:

"So you see, no one really knows if it is so with every Mohawk Indian or why it is so. But let me tell you this. It was because so many of my people did not fear heights that they first became high-steel men."

"How did it happen?"

"Well, this goes back to the 1880's. At that time a Canadian construction company began putting up a railroad bridge across an arm of the St. Lawrence River. One end of the bridge was being built on a section of the Mohawk reservation land. In those days most of the workers on high structures came from the old sailing ships. They were sailors who had spent years climbing the rigging of ships in all kinds of weather, so they were used to working up high. Well, the Indians of the reservation used to come and watch these sailors climbing about on the bridge. Before long the Mohawks themselves had accepted the challenge and were up on the bridge, climbing to its highest part. They just stood up there, outlined against the sky, and looked all about them. They were as pleased as they could be with the view, and they weren't in the least worried about how high they were or how far they would fall if they made a misstep."

"No fear of heights."

Bennett and his companions nodded.

"Also as surefooted as anyone could be. Well, the construction company people heard about this and they started to put two and two together, and because they could count they came up with four."

He laughed softly.

"Well, they figured out that here was a good source of high-iron workers. So they said to themselves, 'Why don't we train these Indians and teach them riveting and other skills?' And that's what happened. Soon the Mohawk Indians of the Caughnawaga reservation were working in different parts of the country on construction jobs."

"By 'country' you mean Canada, don't you?"

"Yes."

"How about the United States? When did the Mohawk high-steel men come to this country to work?"

Tom Bennett turned and spoke for a short while with his companions. Then he said:

"No one can say exactly when it happened. Better to put it this way: Over the years some of my people traveled across the border and worked in some of the cities and other places on the other side. Word sort of drifted up to them that a bridge or a building was being put up, so they made their way there. But not too many of them."

"So it was in the 1920's that Mohawk high-steel men came to New York City?"

"Yes. That's when we really came down in numbers. As I told you, there was a big building boom going on in New York City. Everything was expanding in those days. A lot of skyscrapers went up at that time. So we came down and settled in Brooklyn—the home of the Brooklyn Dodgers."

"Why Brooklyn?"

"Simple. It's just a short subway ride from Manhattan, where most of the jobs were. And the neighborhood we picked was a friendly one and pretty cheap to live in. At one time we had about 400 Mohawk Indians living in downtown Brooklyn. It was a very nice community, and we got along well with our neighbors. On weekends a lot of us would get into our cars and travel upstate, and then we'd go over the border and into Canada."

"Back to Caughnawaga?"

He nodded. "Yes. Back to our people. We've always kept strong ties with our family and friends up there. In fact, I just came back from a visit this past weekend. My daughter, who's just turned nineteen, likes her people so much that she's decided to go to college in Canada. Well, the college is not too far from the reservation. So whenever she gets free time, she drives over for a visit."

"What is she studying?"

"She wants to be a doctor. Our children out in Brooklyn go to the public schools and have the same games and sports the other youngsters do. They watch the same television programs, and follow and root for the same teams. The last World Series, between the Dodgers and Oakland, my two boys were so charged up that they almost drove me up the wall."

He nodded at his companions with a smile and continued.

"They have the same problem, too."

"You said that at one time there were over 400 Mohawk Indians living in the Brooklyn community. How is it today?"

"Not the way it used to be."

"Why? What happened?"

"I really don't know."

Tom Bennett paused for a while and

thought. A sad, almost brooding look had come into his dark and gentle eyes. Then he began to speak again.

"I don't know . . . and I do." He sighed. "What happened was that there came a big slump in construction. Also there were jobs elsewhere in the country. So the people took off and went looking for those jobs. Some even left construction work altogether. We still have our Mohawk community down there in Brooklyn, but it is not what it used to be. Maybe there will be a big lift in the construction field, maybe the whole economy will get better. Then things will change again. Or maybe we'll all have to go back to the reservation in Canada. One can only wait and see what will be."

He leaned forward and then said in an earnest voice:

"By the way, there are about 10,000 Indians living in New York City today. They've come here for many reasons. They are from many tribes and they have a great variety of jobs. A lot aren't working at all. So we Mohawks in high steel are but a small percentage of all the Indians in New York City. All in all, things are not good for the Indians today. Some of us, the young especially, feel that a lot more could be done to help the Indians find their place in this society. A lot of us are just not making it. And something should be done."

"Are the Mohawks part of the Iroquois people?"

"Well, many centuries ago there were five tribes living in what is now New York State. They all got together and formed a league which the early settlers called the Five Nations. Those were the Iroquois. The five tribes are the Seneca, the Cayuga, the Onondaga, the Oneida, and the Mohawk. We were a hunting and farming people."

"And now you walk the high steel."

Bennett smiled and then he and his two companions got up from their seats. The train had come to their station.

"Now we go to walk the high steel," he said again, and then he shook hands and got off the train and went up the steps and out into the city street. Soon the three Mohawk Indians were high above the city, their figures outlined against a clear, blue sky.

There is no hesitation in this steel worker's walk—even though he's several stories up.

GRASSE—CITY OF FLOWERS

When we speak of the Côte d'Azur ("azure coast") of the south of France, we think of a ring of towns gilded by the sun, with white houses, sheltered by palm trees, cypresses, and yews, meeting the blue waves of the Mediterranean. The picture is accurate—except that now skyscrapers have sprouted up along the Côte d'Azur and stand like fortresses of tourism.

We're apt to forget that back from the coast in this part of France there is a region with a long, rich history. Here, in the 8th century, people lived in walled cities and defended themselves, from the tops of their ramparts, against the raids of the Moors. In this region you can still see, in fragments of blackened walls, traces of the religious wars of the 16th century.

North of Cannes, the newcomer to the south of France will discover the rose and yellow ramparts of Grasse, France's flower and perfume capital, a city of 32,000 people. It is from here that the precious bottles with labels of the great perfume houses and the great designers go out into the world. Sometimes the finishing touch is given and the packaging done in Paris, and sometimes in Munich, Tokyo, or New York. But there would be no Chanel No. 5, no Calèche by Hermes without the precious floral essences extracted in Grasse by a long, secret process.

Grasse is surrounded by a group of towns that are equally picturesque and almost as well known. There is Saint-Paul-de-Vence, where painters, writers, and producers come to work and talk on the terrace of the famous inn, the Golden Dove, and there is Vallauris, the town of potters to which Picasso gave new life. Grasse itself is nestled in an immense garden where recently 280 tons of jasmine, 400 tons of roses, and 400 tons of violets were grown in one year.

One of the most famous sons of Grasse was the 18th-century painter Jean Honoré Fragonard. In his canvases, with their garlands and borders of flowers, you can see that the artist kept in his memory the flowers of his native city.

The climate and the soil of Grasse combine to produce ideal conditions for growing flowers. In the summer vast fields are ablaze with orderly rows of blossoms. Farmers on the outskirts of the city raise, along with other crops, orange trees, jasmine, and roses to supply the perfume industry.

▶ **THE SECRET OF GRASSE**

Perfume and perfume making, of course, go far back in history, all the way back into antiquity. The ancient Chinese used musk, a substance obtained from the male musk deer, as a perfume, and the ancient Egyptians used myrrh, the resin of certain trees. Cleopatra is said to have perfumed herself for Mark Antony.

The Bible contains references to fragrances such as musk, myrrh, frankincense, and spicy balm. Perfume was used as it is today, for its pleasing odor. Fragrant woods and spices were also burned as incense in religious ceremonies. (The word "perfume" comes from Latin words meaning "through smoke.")

It is believed that the first workshop for the manufacture of perfume in France was created by a Florentine who had come to France with Catherine de Médicis in the 16th century.

The mystery of the city of Grasse is the way all the thousands of tons of flowers grown in the region are concentrated into tiny bottles of sparkling clear perfume. Actually Grasse's secret is not new. A corporation of perfume makers of Grasse was founded in 1724.

From all the tons of flowers that are gathered, a precious product termed an "essential oil" must be obtained. The essential oil is the ingredient that gives a perfume its fragrance.

A material called a fixative makes a perfume last. Ambergris, a waxy substance formed in a whale's stomach and found floating in the ocean, is a fixative.

An essential oil is a highly concentrated product. You must start, for example, with 220 pounds (100 kilograms) of roses in order to obtain just about ⅕ ounce (5 grams) of essential oil. At one time all essential oils were obtained from natural materials: flowers, leaves, fruits, roots, and seeds. Today some are entirely made in the laboratory.

There are several methods by which natural essential oils may be obtained. The oldest method is one known as steam distillation. The flower petals are put into large tanks and slowly heated. The vapors that rise from the tanks are collected as they cool.

Another method is pressing out the oils, or the chemist may use a method called "enfleurage." In this process, the flower petals are placed on trays on which a layer of pure animal fat has been spread. The fat absorbs the fragrant oils. The first petals are removed, and fresh ones are placed on the layer of fat until the fat is saturated with the perfume oils. The fragrant fat produced in this way is called a pomade. The perfume oil is extracted from it with alcohol.

The most common method is extraction by solvents. The oils are dissolved out of the flowers by solvents, such as alcohol and benzene. After the flowers are treated a waxy substance known as a "concrete" is obtained. This is further treated to obtain the final product—the oil known as the "absolute."

▶ COMPOSING A PERFUME

It is with these base products that the chemist goes about creating a perfume the way a painter goes about creating a canvas. Chemists know whether they want to obtain a perfume that is light or heady, fresh or heavy, for daytime or evening, for the city or the country, for a blonde or a brunette.

Chemists are by no means limited to rose and jasmine for their palette of fragrances. Grasse brings in from other parts of France orange blossoms, lemons, tuberoses, mimosa, narcissus, lavender, and moss. Orrisroot and bergamot (a pear-shaped orange) are imported from Italy, vetiver (a grass with fragrant roots) from Java, vanilla from the Antilles or Tahiti, citronella (a fragrant grass) from China, and mint from Brazil.

In addition to all the natural essences, today there is the whole range of oils created in the laboratory. Among them are oils that smell like lemon verbena, orange blossom, rose, and gardenia. These synthetic oils may be used in combination with natural ones or by themselves.

In the laboratories of the great perfume houses of Grasse, the visitor can see all the precious essences that go into perfume and watch the 2,500 people who work in the perfume industry at their tasks. In this group are the chemists who blend, correct, sniff, and perfect the perfumes.

Trainees who have come from all over the world learn how to smell perfumes and to judge them expertly, and they cultivate their ability to remember fragrances. After 18 months the trainees receive the title of perfume creator.

▶ THE PERFUME INDUSTRY

The volume of business done by the perfumers of Grasse is modest in comparison with that done by some of the giants of the chemical industry. The modest annual figures are explained by the fact that the essences are sold in small quantities which can be increased almost indefinitely by the addition of other products, such as alcohol.

But even if the annual earnings are small, the perfume industry of Grasse has always fascinated the key figures in the international chemical business. And the old families of Grasse, in order to share in international competition, have become associated with businesses of international scope. Thus, Hoffman-La Roche, a Swiss group; Unilever, a Dutch group; and Pfizer, an American concern, all have interests in Grasse.

In return, Grasse has its most loyal customers in West Germany, in the United States (where it is predicted that in 1975 men will spend as much on cosmetic products as women will), in Belgium, and in Japan.

The industrialists of Grasse have kept up with the times and, in addition to perfumes, sell products for use in detergents and insecticides, as well as flavorings for foods.

Certain essential oils (such as ginger) are used mainly to flavor foods. Other oils (such as lemon oil) are used both as flavorings and in perfumes, and certain oils (such as rose) are used mainly for perfumes. So, although you may use lemon-scented soap and eat lemon-flavored cookies, you're not likely to spray on ginger perfume or drink rose cola.

At Fragonard, a perfumery established in the 19th century, freshly picked rose petals are aired before being distilled (*above*); and a perfume creator works in the laboratory (*below*).

YOUTH IN THE NEWS

Papillon, by Drew Peyronnin, 17: A 1974 Scholastic Photography Award winner.

An Outward Bound climbing team reaches its goal—the top of a mountain.

OUTWARD BOUND

> I went to the woods because I wished to live deliberately, to front only the essential facts of life, and see if I could not learn what it had to teach . . . .
> Henry David Thoreau, *Walden*

Outward Bound is a program that supplements traditional forms of education. It uses the challenges of the natural environment to help young people learn through self-discovery. Outward Bound is an educational experience of personal growth. The program teaches people to understand and cope with the forces of nature. It also teaches people to work by themselves and as a group. They learn, in fact, that success often requires the help of others.

The Outward Bound story began in 1941 at Aberdovey, Wales. There a German-born educator, Dr. Kurt Hahn, founded the first school. It was designed as a school for survival for young merchant seamen. From this school has grown a worldwide network of 32 Outward Bound schools or centers on 5 continents, serving 17 nations. Each national Outward Bound organization operates independently, but maintains informal contacts with Outward Bound groups in other countries through the Outward Bound Trust in London, England. Queen Elizabeth's husband, Prince Philip, is a patron of the organization.

The courses offered by Outward Bound schools are open to everyone over the age of 16½ who is in good health. There are a few additional summer courses specifically designed for those aged 14½ to 16½. Because the students come from differing social, economic, and ethnic backgrounds, they provide a variety of viewpoints that add to the learning experience.

Activities at an Outward Bound school

may include rock climbing, mountaineering, skiing, running, rope work, whitewater and flat-water canoeing, sailing, and navigation. The program varies somewhat from school to school, depending on the geographic location and the character of each school.

The standard course is 21 to 28 days long. During the first week everyone takes part in fitness training and conditioning through daily activities such as running and hiking.

All participants undergo extensive instruction in safety training to enable them to cope with the particular environment in which the course is taking place; the use of specialized equipment, such as snowshoes, canoes, or mountain-climbing gear; search, rescue, emergency evacuation, and first aid techniques; field food planning and preparation; map and compass use and route finding; traveling skills appropriate to the environment; expedition planning; and awareness and protection of the environment.

In addition to the courses offered at their own schools, Outward Bound has adapted its educational concepts for other institutions in an effort to reach more people. Hundreds of schools, colleges, and social agencies are now using variations of the Outward Bound wilderness theme.

For example, in the United States several colleges and universities have such programs for undergraduate and graduate students. A number of universities give credit either for attendance at an Outward Bound school or for involvement with some other Outward Bound programs. Many United States high schools also give credit for Outward Bound or run their own programs.

A number of the students attending Outward Bound courses receive some form of scholarship assistance. But the majority pay a tuition fee.

▶ **A PERSONAL ACCOUNT**

"Up! Up! Everybody up!" The instructor's voice leaves no doubt about what to do.

By pulling together, these young people conquer heavy seas off Maine.

Testing for agility.

Climbing a wall—with help from her friends.

Dawn filters through the maze of the forest and ends in a sunny patch on your dark blue sleeping bag. Crawl out . . . stand up . . . shiver into shorts and sneakers.

"Follow me!" The instructor's voice—self-assured and enthusiastic—rings out again. He's running, his feet are scarcely audible on the pine-needled forest floor. You and your ten companions follow, your chests heaving, moving so fast you feel warm in the cold air. Who are these strangers? How will you get along with them?

Abruptly the instructor stops at the edge of a stream. He yanks off his sneakers without untying the laces and plunges in.

You hesitate on the bank.

"Everybody in! Quick! Before you cool off!"

You wade, stumble on a rock, fall forward. Instinctively you plant your feet on the bottom, surface, and gasp. Your yell rings through the forest, and a shiver runs the length of your body.

You have begun your first day at Outward Bound.

Breakfast is over, and the gear has been divided among your group. Your pack weighs 40 pounds (18 kilograms) or more, and you wobble under it, up, up, up a steep and rocky trail. Mosquitoes ignore your generous coating of bug spray. Between swats, you sop the sweat from your forehead with a wadded red bandanna. There are three or four weeks of this ahead. You wonder for a moment whatever made you sign up for Outward Bound.

A few days go by: sun, rain, wind, bone-chilling cold, muggy heat, meadows of wildflowers, mud, sand, cinders, blisters, more bugs, sails, oars, paddles, life jackets, hardhats, climbing ropes. Wilderness life is becoming almost comfortable.

The days go on. Night hikes. Ecology. Bivouacs. Re-supply, service projects. For Final Expedition your group is divided for the first time since the course began. That means almost no supervision from your instructor.

Then Solo, the mystery that prompts more wondering than all the rest of Outward

Wanting to succeed is the way to pass this test.

Bound. It's not a survival experience in the physical sense. But for most people, Solo— with only clothing, rudimentary shelter, a minimum of food—is the first experience of absolute solitude.

Your instructor outlines your boundaries of a few hundred yards. "Don't wander. Build a shelter. I'll check on you daily and be back for you in about three days."

Suddenly he's gone. You feel you must do something. Build your shelter, explore your territory. It all takes maybe an hour, but you aren't sure. Your instructor has taken your watch.

A breeze makes the lake lap at the shore, and fat, black tadpoles wiggle in the shallows. At last the sun drops behind a hill, and you pull on your parka and try to sleep.

All night you doze, waking with cold and hunching down in your bag. Finally the stars and half-moon are gone. The sun isn't up, but morning is as good as here. The longest night of your life has ended.

The last few days of the course are full of details—equipment check-in, waiting for the bus. It occurs to you for the first time that it's all almost over.

You can make a long list of skills you have acquired. You can count new friends. You can feel new muscles.

But perhaps the greatest experience was to live closely with the natural world, with its beauty and harshness—to realize that you are related in subtle and complex ways to all the creatures of the earth.

Or the discovery that you can trust others —indeed, you must—must share, must risk opening yourself to others, must help others if the goal is to be reached.

And perhaps the physical challenges of Outward Bound taught you things you needed to know about yourself, stripped away masks and fears, gave you a new feeling of confidence.

As one Outward Bound student said: "We are better than we know. If we can be made to see it, perhaps for the rest of our lives we will be unwilling to settle for less."

HENRY W. TAFT
President, Outward Bound, Inc.

YOUNG HEADLINERS

Paul Zeitz, 15, of New York, received the highest score in the third U.S.A. Mathematical Olympiad. Paul was one of the U.S. representatives in the 1974 International Mathematical Olympiad. The Soviet Union placed first; the United States second.

Lena Zavaroni (*below*), one of 1974's new singing sensations. One of her records has already sold over 1,000,000 copies. The Scottish lass belts out her songs with such enthusiasm that you almost forget that she's only 10 years old.

At 13, Abla Khairi, of Cairo, Egypt, became the youngest person ever to swim the English Channel. Abla crossed the 21 miles (33.8 kilometers) of choppy water between Cape Gris-Nez, France, and Dover, England, in 12½ hours.

These girls are a few of the 48 young people from 12 countries who took part in the month-long 1974 Children's International Summer Village, in Tarrytown, New York. The program, begun in 1951, tries to promote world peace by gathering together people of different cultures.

Five-year-old Claude Brooks was the official greeter when Britain's Princess Margaret and Lord Snowden attended a performance at New York's Dance Theater of Harlem in 1974. The youngest dancer in the company, Claude brought down the house with his rousing stick dance.

When the revival of *Gypsy* opened on Broadway in 1974, 9-year-old English-born Bonnie Langford appeared as Baby June and became a star. Her singing, ballet dancing, and tricky baton twirling dazzled audiences.

The title "smartest kid on the block" may have belonged to 17-year-old Eric Lander (*left*) of New York in 1974. Eric won the $10,000 scholarship in the annual Westinghouse Science Talent Search for his work on an intriguing new concept in number theory.

The boys all wear naval uniforms and have rosy faces and angelic voices. They are in the Vienna Boys' Choir, which celebrated its 50th anniversary in 1974. There are actually 4 choirs of 24 boys each, bringing a bit of Austria to the rest of the world.

In March, 12-year-old Atha Mathieu became the youngest member of a U.S. parks commission when she was chosen to fill the youth seat on the San Anselmo, California, Parks and Recreation Commission. Atha feels parks are for kids, and they should help run them.

Larry Kokos, a 14-year-old from Pennsylvania, won 1974's national marbles championship. This was the first time in fourteen years that a boy and a girl had competed for the grand national championship. Larry beat his opponent, Susan Regan—but just barely.

Eight-year-old Asya Minasyan, an accomplished composer, lives in Soviet Armenia. She started playing the piano when she was 3 years old, and composed her first piece of music two years later. Since then she has written dozens of pieces of music.

In 1974, 12-year-old Becky Schroeder of Ohio patented an invention—probably the youngest person to do so. She found a way to write in the dark. Becky invented a luminescent backing sheet. The sheet has horizontal lines, drawn with phosphorescent paint (paint that glows in the dark). The sheet is placed under ordinary writing paper, and the phosphorescent lines show clearly through.

BJÖRN BÖRG: ON THE COURT

Just pick up the racket, toss the ball into the air, and give a good hard swing. Sounds simple, doesn't it? But it isn't. There's more to the sport of tennis than simply swinging a racket. It takes time, patience, perseverance, and practice to get the ball over the net and within the boundaries of the opposite court. Ask those who play tennis, and they're sure to tell you how difficult it is. But they'll also tell you that the result is worth the effort.

Take Sweden's teenage tennis star Björn Borg, for example. In one year he has swung his way into the top ranks of the world's professional tennis players. "Tennis is hard work, and I have a long road ahead of me," he has said. But he didn't mention the good distance he had already traveled.

Björn comes from Södertälje, a suburb of Stockholm, Sweden. Södertälje is famous for manufacturing parts that go into Volkswagen bodies, as well as for producing tennis and ice hockey players. But it took Björn Borg and his exploits on the tennis court to put his hometown on the map.

Björn's journey to tennis stardom began when he was just nine years old. His father won a tennis racket in a Ping-Pong tournament, and gave it to Björn. Björn practiced holding the racket, scurrying about the court, hitting the ball, and timing his serve. All this eventually paid off. In the next few years, Björn won junior tournaments in Berlin, Barcelona, Milan, and at the Orange Bowl in Miami, Florida. At the age of seventeen he joined the WCT—World Championship Tennis—circuit, and found himself pitted against such tennis pros as John Newcombe, Rod Laver, Stan Smith, Jimmy Connors, and Arthur Ashe.

After the WCT experience, Björn put together a winning streak of seventeen straight matches, ending with his victory at the Italian Open in June, 1974. This victory made Björn —at the age of seventeen—the youngest male player ever to win a major international tournament. He followed this triumph by capturing the men's singles at the French Open and the Swedish International Open—all in a matter of months.

Preparing for these tournaments is not an easy task, no matter how good you are. And no one knows this better than Björn. "Tennis is my fun," he says. "I have given up a lot of things for this. Ice cream, chocolates, close feelings for friends. Tennis is all I know, or want to know. It is my life."

TANYA TUCKER: COUNTRY'S TEEN QUEEN

Sixteen-year-old Tanya Tucker has burst upon the music scene with all the force, vitality, and excitement of an Elvis Presley. But she's not a carbon copy of Elvis. She's her own, special kind of singer. Tanya's phrasing of a song, and the sweet, emotional way she gets the message of the song across, are just part of her distinct style.

Tanya's father recognized the potential talent in his daughter several years ago. At the age of nine, when the Tucker family lived in Nashville, Tennessee—home of country music—Tanya climbed onto stages to sing with such country singers as Ernest Tubb, Mel Tillis, and Leroy Van Dyke. She entered talent contests and also entertained at beauty pageants and nightclubs. By the time she was thirteen years old, Tanya was known in Nashville as the "Cheatin' Heart Kid" after the well-known ballad "Your Cheatin' Heart" by Hank Williams.

Tanya's first real break came in 1971 when she was introduced to Billy Sherrill, a Columbia Records producer, in Las Vegas, Nevada. Sherrill flew her back to Nashville, where she recorded "Delta Dawn." It became a hit single and the title song of her first album. The album, too, was an instant best seller, sending Tanya on her way.

Other single records and albums followed. Three of the albums reached the magic top ten list. There were guest appearances on nationwide television programs, and eventually the grueling experience of cross-country tours. Tanya's tours, unlike those of other recording artists, are actually family excursions. Tanya's brother, Don, usually drives the touring bus. Her father, who also acts as Tanya's business manager, and her mother and sister ride along as company. Her brother says that they all "want to be with Tanya in case any problems arise."

Her mother and father try to supervise Tanya's schedule closely when she's on the road. Traveling from one town or city to another, and then doing two or three shows a day, leaves little time for sleep. When the schedule becomes too hectic, Tanya's father makes sure his daughter has a week off, just to catch up on rest and relaxation. These periods of comparative calm, although infrequent, give Tanya the opportunity to pursue some of her favorite pastimes, one of which is horseback riding.

Ambitious and energetic, Tanya plays about 200 one-nighters a year. But sleepless nights aside, she must be doing something right. She has enough self-confidence to say that in a joint appearance, she could "blow Helen Reddy off stage." That's quite a claim for a young girl from Seminole, Texas—where she was born on October 10, 1958—to make. But she may be right.

Seascape, by Peter
Schorse, Canada.

Amish Buggy, by
Bob Sacha, 16, U.S.

Autumn Leaves, by
Roy Jansen, 17, U.S.

188

YOUNG PHOTOGRAPHERS

Photography is rapidly becoming the favorite art form of the world's young people. Look around you when you go to a large gathering attended by young people. Half the young people there, or so it seems, will have cameras slung over their shoulders. Both Scholastic Magazines, Inc., in the United States and *The Canadian Magazine* in Canada sponsor annual photography contests in which thousands of young photographers participate. This selection of prize-winning photographs from the Scholastic Photography Awards of 1974 (sponsored by the Eastman Kodak Company) and the 1974 National Photo Contest in Canada will give some indication of what good photographers young people have become. These young photographers have tried to capture moods, textures, and feelings. In a way, they have stopped time.

Dog and Cat, by Paul Salmon, Canada.

Lily, by Jaye Bergquist, 17, U.S.

She Came On Like a Dream, by Terry Shafer, 15, U.S.

Untitled, by Dave Mattocks, 15, U.S.

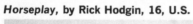

Reflections of the Past, by Milt Baldwin, 17, U.S.

Horseplay, by Rick Hodgin, 16, U.S.

190

YOUNG ARTISTS

Every two years, UNICEF (United Nations Children's Fund) sponsors an international drawing contest. The contest focuses the attention of people on the work that UNICEF does for the welfare of children around the world. It also gives young people an opportunity to show their talent.

In 1974, more than 230,000 children, from countries all over the world, submitted drawings. *The Little President,* a short story by Peter Ustinov written for UNICEF, and the theme "My Family" were the subjects that these drawings so charmingly illustrated.

Ivan Morua Castañeda, 8 years old, Peru.

Thao Viengxay Vichitvongsa, 15 years old, Laos.

Jude Tilbury, 12 years old, Guyana.

Joel Montúfar, 13 years old, Guatemala.

192

Nigar Haque, 14 years old, Pakistan.

Dale Terrence Russell, 15 years old, Jamaica.

Francisco José March Guerra, 12 years old, Nicaragua.

Rocio González Jiménez, 9 years old, Spain.

194

A visitor from Taiwan gets a Boy Scout jamboree in Idaho off to a good start.

BOY SCOUTS

Since their founding, the Boy Scouts have always had the ideal of world brotherhood as one of their chief goals. By the creation of opportunities for the youth of the world to learn more about each other, the chances for creating a more understanding adult world in the future become better.

The World Scout Conference was founded with the goal of world brotherhood specifically in mind. Scout leaders affiliated with the Conference are encouraged to help Boy Scouts participate in a number of programs aimed at promoting international friendship and understanding. One popular program sponsors correspondence between members of Scout units in different countries —a sort of Scouting "pen pals" plan. Other programs sponsor visits of Scout groups from one country to Scout groups in another country. There are also programs sponsoring participation in international Scouting events of all kinds. The World Scout Conference is also active in raising money for the World Friendship Fund.

In 1974 there was a great deal of international Scouting activity as well as the wide range of national events that is always a part of an active Scout's year in any country.

▶ **THE INTERAMERICAN CONFERENCE**

One of the major events in international Scouting in 1974 was the Interamerican Scout Conference. The Conference, which was attended by representatives from 24 countries of the Western Hemisphere, was held in Miami, Florida, in August. The purpose of the Conference is to strengthen the ties between the Scouting organizations and the Scouts of the Americas. It is held every other year. In 1974, as in previous years, the Conference was a forum for discussing new programs for the member nations.

In addition to the main conference, the Interamerican Regional Youth Forum also met in Miami. Fifty delegates from the member countries of the Interamerican Scout Conference discussed progress made in a number of international projects.

An exciting feature of the Miami meeting was the presentation of the Silver World Award. The Boy Scouts of America pre-

Two Canadian Boy Scouts plan a hike the right way —carefully, using a map and compass.

Program, the nationwide commemoration of the country's 200th anniversary.

The Cub Scouts participated in national and international programs. Nationally, they were involved in studies of the contribution of the American Indians to American life, and in the Keep America Beautiful program. This program was concerned both with ecological awareness and with preserving the country's natural beauty. Internationally, the Cub Scouts in the United States learned about the customs of other countries and of other peoples. This kind of program was very much in keeping with the Scouting principle of world understanding. The Cub Scouts were also active in 1974 in supporting the World Friendship Fund.

The Boy Scouts of America continued their involvement in Project SOAR (Save Our American Resources) in 1974. Over 4,000,000 Cub Scouts, Boy Scouts, and Explorer Scouts took part in SOAR-sponsored programs set up to collect paper, metal, and glass for recycling.

The Explorer program, designed for young men and women of high school and college age, is the fastest-growing program of the Boy Scouts of America. In 1974 some 2,500 young adult delegates attended the Fourth National Explorer Presidents' Congress. Delegates to the Congress—who represented 30,000 Explorer units throughout the United States—made history by electing Mary Van Lear Wright, a seventeen-year-old Massachusetts high school senior, as the first woman Explorer president.

In 1974 the Congress also drew up guidelines for the planning of new Explorer activities and group projects. A unique feature of the Congress meeting was a seminar in which delegates met and talked to experts from every major interest field. There were experts on a wide range of subjects, from aviation to the social sciences. As a young adult group, the Explorers are especially interested in vocational and career planning.

Both older Scouts and men and women members of Explorer groups have become more and more involved in more advanced kinds of outdoor activity. In 1974 more young people than ever before took advantage of the millions of acres of publicly and

sented this award to three distinguished Scouters in recognition of their service to the youth of the world. The recipients were Victor Steiner of El Salvador, and Gustavo Vollmer and L. Esteban Palacios, both of Venezuela.

▶ ADVENTURES IN SCOUTING

The Boy Scouts of the United States worked hard in 1974 to contribute to both national and international Scouting projects. Many of the American Scout activities were centered on America's National Bicentennial

The Boy Scouts have always been experts at camping out. The Scouts above are breaking out cooking equipment for preparing a meal. The Scouts below are building a drying rack where cooking utensils will dry after washing.

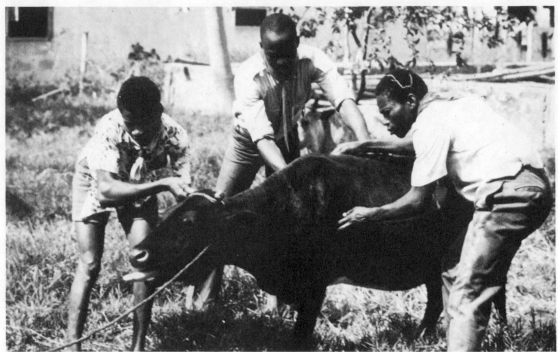
These young Kenyans start learning how to be farmers in the Boy Scouts.

privately owned wild land and waterways made available to Scouting groups. Mountain climbing, wildlife study, rugged trail hikes, canoe trips, and outdoor camping were all part of the program. The thousands of young men and women who took part in these wilderness adventures began to get a genuine idea of what the nation's natural heritage is like, and how important it is to preserve it. Their adventures also included a firsthand study of techniques of land management, conservation, wildlife management and preservation, and forestry.

▶ THIRD EXPLORER OLYMPICS

In August, 1974, the Third Explorer Olympics were held on the campus of Colorado State University in Fort Collins, Colorado. More than 2,000 young men and women competed in 28 Olympic sports for college scholarships and Olympic medals.

The Explorer Olympics are sanctioned by the United States Olympic Committee. In addition to competition in major Olympic sports, there were academic contests and competitions of various kinds. Outstanding sports figures and coaches conducted a number of sports clinics and seminars as well.

▶ AMERICAN INDIANS

Over 200 American Indian leaders and their families met at Philmont Scout Ranch in New Mexico for the Seventeenth American Indian Leaders Seminar on Scouting. Acting in cooperation with the Boy Scouts of America, representatives of 35 Indian tribes participated in seminars and conducted workshops aimed at adapting Scouting programs to the needs of the Indian community.

Other aims of the meetings included the developing of Indian youth leadership through Scout seminars, and increasing the support for Scout programs among Indians by increasing the involvement of local Indian councils in Scout affairs. Growing Indian participation in Scouting seemed particularly appropriate because of the contribution made by American Indian culture to the world of outdoor activities and to the appreciation of nature.

ALDEN G. BARBER
Chief Scout Executive, Boy Scouts of America

A Senior Scout from the United States (*right*) and an Israeli Ranger (*left*) meet at an international Girl Scout and Girl Guide gathering in Israel.

GIRL SCOUTS AND GIRL GUIDES

There are more than 6,500,000 people in more than 90 countries around the world who are active in Girl Scout or Girl Guide groups. The World Association of Girl Guides and Girl Scouts is the international body that helps the national groups work together toward their shared goals of peace and better understanding among the peoples of the world.

▶ **ACTIVITIES AROUND THE WORLD**

In the 1970's Girl Guide and Girl Scout organizations in many nations engaged in activities that contributed to the development of their countries. On their own, or with the help of private and government agencies, Guides and Scouts in both industrialized and developing countries are working in a number of worthwhile areas. There are programs in family life, the education and status of women, literacy, ecology, and other areas.

In Guyana, for instance, Girl Guides are taking part in a Grow More Food program. This program has as its goal a better standard of living for Guyana, to be achieved by the cultivation of the country's fertile land. The Girl Guides of Guyana are also interested in helping set up small co-operative industries of various kinds.

Girl Guides in the Caribbean nation of Jamaica have been waging a battle against illiteracy. They are working in special literacy camps, where children are taught to read. The Guides are also involved in running special classes for school dropouts. The older Jamaican Ranger Guides, for their part, are active in their government's National Family Planning Program.

In Peru the Guides have started a National Nutrition Project. Peruvian Guides try to help expectant mothers plan proper diets. They

American Cadettes learn all about the fine art of transplanting plants.

Japanese Senior Scouts visit the United States.

also help work out balanced diets for babies, preschool children, and school-age children.

The Girl Guides of Sri Lanka (Ceylon) have made a unique contribution with their Family Life Education Project. They have staged several plays and a puppet show as part of their campaign to make the people of their country more aware of the possibilities of population planning.

The Girl Scouts of the United States of America (more simply known as the Girl Scouts of the U.S.A.) had a full program of national and international activities in 1974. Because it is the largest voluntary organization for girls in the world (more than 3,500,000 girls and leaders), its activities are unusually varied.

Every year Girl Scouts of the U.S.A. provides opportunities for young and adult members to go overseas. It also co-ordinates programs for Girl Scouts and Girl Guides who wish to come to the United States. In 1973, a group of Senior Scouts went to Jamaica to participate in the campaign against illiteracy. They learned so much from the Jamaican Girl Guides that they were able to start a similar project for high school dropouts in the United States. Adult leaders took part in a Western Hemisphere conference in Peru.

Canadian Girl Guides atop the Pyramid of the Sun in Teotihuacán, Mexico.

Scouts in Micronesia learn to weave reed mats.

The purpose of the conference was to find ways for Girl Scouts and Girl Guides to help their countries solve domestic problems.

In another valuable international exchange, adults and girls from Girl Scouts of the U.S.A. went to Sangam, the World Association center in Poona, India. There they met with Indian girls and leaders to discuss many topics. Other American girls and leaders attended Girl Guide camps in Sweden, France, and Greece.

Girl Guides and Girl Scouts from many parts of the world came to the United States in the 1970's. The visitors took part in special events sponsored by local Girl Scout Councils. In many cases they visited the four large Girl Scout National Centers in the United States. Many of the visiting Scouts, Guides, and leaders stayed with American families.

The Girl Scouts of the U.S.A. has its own special international organization. The organization is called Troops on Foreign Soil (TOFS). This organization brings the Girl Scout movement to the children of American civilian and military families living overseas. More than 26,000 girls participate in TOFS. TOFS Scouts have become involved in programs all over the world. In Germany they have worked with handicapped children. In the Philippines they joined with Philippine Girl Scouts in creating a Fil-Am Camp, where activities included sharing handicraft skills. Other TOFS programs have been developed in Korea, Taiwan, and Norway.

The Girl Guides of Canada participated in a number of international activities in 1974. They sent representatives to Girl Guide and Girl Scout meetings around the world. They also welcomed visiting Girl Guides and Scouts from many other countries to Canada. Canadian Girl Guides represented their country in Mexico, India, Trinidad and Tobago, Norway, the United States, Finland, the Netherlands, and Guyana.

The event held at the International Camp of the Four Winds in Finland in the summer of 1974 was an especially interesting experience for the attending Canadians. Girls from many countries were introduced to Finnish culture in the most delightful ways. They enjoyed plentiful Finnish food, folk dancing, sailing with Finnish Sea Rangers, and historical tours. The visit to Guyana's Golden Jubilee Camp by a number of Canadian Guides was also an exciting experience—complete with a visit to the prime minister's house.

▶ WORLD ASSOCIATION ACTIVITIES

The World Association of Girl Guides and Girl Scouts was formed to bring girls from all over the world together to discuss their common problems and goals. This does not mean that Guiding and Scouting are the same in all countries. But each national organization tries to give its members opportunities for developing character and high standards of citizenship, and for providing many kinds of service to the community.

International friendship among Guides and Scouts has led to some very real co-operation on projects. For instance, after the World Conference in 1972, Mexican Girl Guides invited Belgian Girl Guides to join them in a project. The project was to teach basic health and hygiene practices to the people of a small village near Puebla, Mexico. The Belgian Girl Guides, aided by a travel grant from UNESCO, spent six weeks in the Mexican village, working with the Mexican Guides.

National Scouting and Guiding organizations apply for membership in the World Association. Every three years national delegates meet at a World Conference. They decide future policy for the organization and elect the World Committee.

The day-to-day work of the World Association is carried on by the World Bureau in London, England. Its staff comes from many countries. The working languages of the Bureau are English, French, and Spanish. The purpose of the Bureau is to help member organizations exchange ideas and information and to keep in touch with what sister organizations all over the world are thinking, saying, doing, and planning.

Four World Centers are used by girls and adults for training sessions, conferences, and vacations. They are Olave House in London; Our Chalet in Adelboden, Switzerland; Our Cabaña in Cuernavaca, Mexico; and Sangam in Poona, India.

The World Association has consultative status with the United Nations and its specialized agencies. At national and international levels, World Association members support various programs organized by UN agencies. Through UNESCO, the World Association has also received help for a number of its own projects. These projects include a vocational rehabilitation center for handicapped girls in Tanzania; centers for out-of-school education and vocational training in Egypt; and a literacy program in Mexico.

To aid member organizations in their own development, the World Association started the Mutual Aid program. Through this program one or more national organizations can help another national organization get started by providing money for essential supplies.

The great holiday for international Girl Scouts and Girl Guides is called Thinking Day. It is held every year on February 22. This day is the joint birthday of Lord and Lady Baden-Powell. Lord Baden-Powell founded the entire Boy Scout and Girl Scout and Girl Guide movement. Lady Baden-Powell is still World Chief Guide. Girl Guides and Girl Scouts make a special effort to meet in groups on Thinking Day to think of their sisters all over the world and to give a contribution to the Thinking Day Fund.

RICHARD G. KNOX
Girl Scouts of the U.S.A.

WHAT'S OUT THERE?

Who or what lives in outer space? Most adults would say there are probably beings who in one way or another are people like us. Science fiction writers have written countless stories with characters who are "people like us." The Museum of Science, in Boston, Massachusetts, wanted to find out what young people thought about the subject. The museum conducted an Alien Life Forms contest, asking young people to submit drawings or models of space creatures and to describe the planets on which they live. Most of the entries, like the ones on this page, showed creatures that bore little resemblance to human beings. Try to answer the question for yourself—what do you think is out there?

The Cleos, by Ellen Kosmer, is a silicon being from the solar system of the star Tau Ceti.

Nicolas Rasmussen's tiny Air-Quiverers, lifted by heavy winds, float above the surface of Mars.

Richard Shibley's alien creature swims through a liquid atmosphere on a planet like Jupiter.

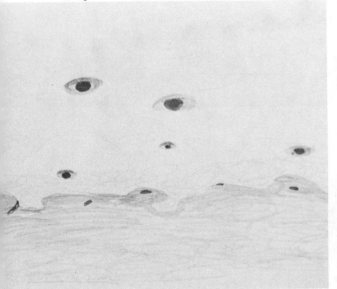

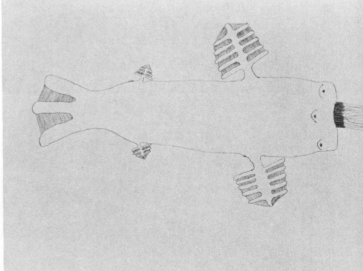

FUN TO READ

Convicted of witchcraft, this tragic young Salem woman awaits execution.

THE WITCHES OF SALEM

Forbidden Games: January, 1692

The Salem tragedy began with something that sounds very simple and innocent: girls gathered in a kitchen, listening as the cook told ghost stories and read fortunes.

Life was harsh in Puritan New England. It was made up of nothing but hard work and prayers. In Salem that winter, the kitchen of the minister, Samuel Parris, was the scene of the only fun in town. Naturally the girls of Salem came there every time they could slip away from their chores. Outside, bitter winds drove snow hissing against the windows. Inside, by the cozy hearth, the candle cast huge wavering shadows—a large turbaned head, encircled by smaller heads, some in Puritan caps. There was the sound of whispering and nervous giggles. Who will meet a handsome stranger? Who will marry a rich man from Boston?

Tituba, Parris' gaily turbaned West Indian cook, was a Christian now. But in this freezing wilderness, she recalled her sunny Caribbean childhood—dancing people, beating drums, Voodoo rites. Here she had a fascinated audience for tales of spirits and spells. Now she read nine-year-old Elizabeth Parris' fortune in her palm. From the shapes that egg white formed when poured into a glass, she prophesied a husband for Elizabeth's eleven-year-old cousin, Abigail Williams. Next, for Ann Putnam, who was twelve, . . .

"No!" Elizabeth whimpered, terrified. She had just realized that they were playing with the Devil. They mustn't let Tituba go on.

A fierce look from Ann silenced her. "Don't be such a baby!"

The others—they were all older, some even nineteen or twenty—looked at Elizabeth with scorn. Tituba knew charms that could help a girl catch any man she wanted. Would Baby Elizabeth spoil things? "If you tell . . . !" Ann threatened.

Elizabeth stopped crying. But her hand, the hand Tituba had read, was shaking. She couldn't make it stop. It felt as if it didn't belong to her. Was it bewitched? What they were doing was the most horrible kind of sin. Didn't the others know it?

The others knew it, but they didn't want to face it—yet. Tituba's fortune telling was no ordinary game that you might play today. For 1692 in Salem was a time and place where the Devil and sin were as real to everyone as germs are to us. And the games in the preacher's kitchen were dangerous games that would end with the deaths of twenty people.

Deadly Beliefs

To understand the Salem tragedy, you must understand the power of belief.

Suppose someone hypnotizes you. In the trance, you believe anything he says. He touches your arm with a pencil and tells you the pencil is a blazing torch. You jump back with a cry of pain. An ugly, red blister swells on your arm. He only had a pencil, but you are burned because you believed it was a torch. You have the blister to prove it.

No reputable hypnotist harms anyone. But laboratory experiments with willing subjects have proved the power of belief— even mistaken belief—to raise real blisters.

Anthropologists have studied tribes in which everyone believes in magic. There, if a man knows that a witch has cursed him, the man dies. This is called "the voodoo death." The victim can only be saved if a more powerful witch removes the curse.

In the 17th century, most people believed that some people really were witches. People thought God and the Devil battled for men's souls. Often the Devil bought souls. He paid for them with magic power. If you agreed to his bargain, you signed your name in blood in the Devil's book. Then you were a witch. The Devil owned you, and you did his evil work. You could also get even with your enemies by magic. If you even dreamed that you had made a pact with the Devil, you might truly believe you were a witch. If others believed you were too, and believed that you had cursed them, they might become quite ill.

Reading palms, predicting the future, casting spells—all these were magic. As such, they belonged to the Devil and his servants, the witches and wizards. So they were sins of the blackest kind to these children of the strict religious world of 17th-century New England. If you were caught engaging in this sin, the minister would tell you that you were going to suffer terrible punishments —here and hereafter—and you would believe him.

Now, imagine that you believe in witches. You have let a witch read your palm and cast spells for you. You would be as guilty as the witch, for you had shared in the sin. And furthermore, she might bewitch you. What a terrible choice—to be mixed up in witchcraft, or be a victim of bewitchment! You were afraid of the witch, afraid of awful punishment, and afraid your sin might be found out any minute. How healthy would you be feeling with all these fears?

Tituba tells her fascinated audience about spirits and spells.

The Sickness Begins: February-March, 1692

Elizabeth was not feeling healthy at all. She woke screaming at night, seeing terrible demons all around her. When her father picked her up to soothe her, she didn't recognize him. She shook and stared and laughed like a maniac. She ran in terror from things no one else saw.

Abigail was having fits too. All the girls who knew Tituba well were behaving strangely. One, Mary Warren, worked for John Proctor. John threatened to spank her if she didn't stop having fits. Mary stopped, as long as John was around, but when he went away she began twitching again.

But Samuel Parris loved his little daughter Elizabeth. He was frightened by her fits, rather than annoyed, and he called the doctor. The doctor could find nothing physically wrong. Yet Elizabeth was clearly very sick. There was only one answer—the girl had been bewitched.

The terrible news flashed through the village. Witchcraft was loose in Salem! All the girls were bewitched.

Samuel Parris and the other men got the girls together and prayed with them. They begged the girls to tell who had bewitched them. The witch must be found, so the source of the evil could be stamped out.

At first there was no answer. The girls rolled on the floor and twitched and screamed for help. Invisible shapes were tormenting them. But who?

Finally one of them murmured, "Tituba." They all took up the cry. Another girl whimpered, "She's not alone. I see Sarah Osborn." At once there was more screaming and writhing, and then another name was shouted above the noise, "And Sarah Goode!"

The girls had chosen well. Both Sarahs were strange women who were unpopular with their neighbors. Mrs. Goode had the reputation of muttering curses at people who crossed her. Sarah Osburn was sick (or said she was sick), so she seldom went to church. That alone was cause for suspicion. All the decent people of Salem spent a lot of time in church.

On March 1, the accused witches were examined. Sarah Goode's husband said Sarah must be a witch, because she treated him so badly. Her four-year-old daughter Dorcas said she had seen her mother's "familiar spirits." Familiar spirits—or familiars, for short—were a witch's helpers. They usually took the form of animals. Sarah Goode's familiars were supposed to be a black bird and a yellow bird, both of which Sarah would send to torment people. The girls accused Sarah to her face. Then they fell to the floor, shrieking that Sarah's ghost had come out of her body and was pinching and biting them in revenge for the accusation.

This performance—being tormented by the witch's "ghost" right in court—set a pattern for future hearings. Whenever an accused person looked at the "afflicted children," they had fits, and cried that the person's ghost was torturing them. If the accused bit her lip, the girls bit their lips and said she made them do it. The fits stopped if the accused touched the victim.

This kind of evidence was called "spectral evidence" (evidence of ghosts or spirits). Increase Mather and his son Cotton Mather, both famous Boston ministers, said no one should be convicted of witchcraft on spectral evidence alone. The Devil could take over the ghostly form of an innocent person, they said. But the cries and writhings of the girls were convincing, and it was mainly spectral evidence that sent the "witches" to the gallows.

Sarah Goode said she was not afflicting the children—but Goody Osburn was. Goody Osburn denied it, but the judges had caught her lying about other things. Then Tituba appeared. The whole drama changed abruptly. Tituba confessed that she was indeed a witch!

Look once and you see a pretty girl. Look twice and you see a witch!

She was not afflicting the girls, Tituba said, but the Devil had certainly come to her and asked her to serve him. In his book, she had seen the names of Goode and Osburn. They were witches. She had flown through the air with them—all riding on poles.

Then Tituba dropped a bombshell: she had seen nine names in the Devil's book! Who were the other witches? She didn't know. The people of Salem shook with terror. Everyone looked at his neighbor. Is it you? And the witch hunt was on.

The Witch Hunt: March-May, 1692

The three formally accused witches were put in jail. But the girls were more tormented than ever. In March, Ann Putnam cried out that Martha Corey's ghost was torturing her. The village was shocked. Martha was a highly respected church member. However, she was skeptical: she didn't think there were any witches in Salem, and she thought the girls were "distracted" (crazy). Martha joined the other accused witches in jail.

The next woman accused, Rebecca Nurse, was a saintly old lady. When the minister preached about Rebecca's being a betrayer of the faith, her sister Sarah Cloyse marched out and slammed the church door behind her. The afflicted girls promptly cried out that they had seen Mrs. Cloyse at a witches' meeting, along with Rebecca, Martha, and Mrs. Goode. Tituba's husband, John, said Sarah Cloyse and Elizabeth Proctor had both tried to force him to sign the Devil's book. The girls immediately screamed that Mrs. Proctor's ghost was perched on a beam of the courthouse, and the ghost of her husband, John, was beating them!

Mary Warren, the maid John Proctor had spanked for her fits, recovered briefly and admitted that all the accusations were false. She and her friends had been "seeing things," she said. But the girls shrieked that Mary, too, had signed the Devil's book. In danger of being called a witch herself if she continued her denials, Mary went back to having fits and accusing others. Opposing the "afflicted children" could put you in danger of your life.

By June, Salem's jails were jammed with about a hundred people. Sarah Osburn had died in prison. Tituba, little Dorcas Goode, and about fifty other people had confessed that they were witches. Their fantastic confession stories usually accused others of engaging in witchcraft with them, and so brought new witches to the jail.

It looked as though New England were threatened by a massive witchcraft conspiracy. The Governor of Massachusetts appointed a special court to try the Salem witches.

The Hangings: Summer, 1692

At the first session, June 2, the court tried only one witch: Bridget Bishop. Workmen taking down a wall of her cellar had found dolls with pins stuck in them. In almost all times and places, witches have used this method of cursing their victims. This was "hard evidence" of guilt. Although Bridget denied the charge, she was hanged on June 10.

The court had no hard evidence against the others. Nevertheless, in July five more women were executed, including saintly Rebecca Nurse and fierce Sarah Goode, who died cursing her judges. The trials went on all summer. By September 22, nineteen people, all protesting their innocence, had died on the gallows. Fourteen were women. Martha Corey was one of them. Five were men, among them skeptical John Proctor and George Burroughs, once minister of Salem. Burroughs had been married twice, and both of his wives had died under suspicious circumstances. Elizabeth Proctor escaped hanging because she was expecting a child.

None of those who confessed to being witches (and accused others) were put to death.

The state took the property of confessed witches, and that of those who were hanged, so that in either case their heirs got nothing. One man, Giles Corey, refused to plead either guilty or innocent. For "standing mute," he was pressed to death—killed by having heavy stones placed on his chest, one by one. He was the only man ever legally executed by torture in America. But his sons inherited his property.

Possibly Giles Corey's death shocked people back to sanity. Perhaps the fever had run its course. After that, no one was ever again hanged in America for being a witch. Accused people were acquitted. Others, though convicted, were not executed. The "afflicted children" continued to accuse people, but few believed them any more. By the following spring, the court released the remaining prisoners, about a hundred people, and the epidemic was over. For years afterward, the people of Salem prayed for forgiveness for their share in the witch hunt.

One of the girls falls to the floor during Sarah Goode's testimony.

The Mystery

The mystery of Salem remains. Were the "afflicted children" simply liars and frauds? Did they fake their bone-crushing convulsions and the marks on their arms? Why? To get attention? Did they send innocent people to the gallows to escape the minister's wrath if he should find out about their fortune-telling games?

Or did terror and guilt make them believe that they were in fact bewitched? Did they then suffer from hysteria—a mental illness that can cause fits, bleeding, blindness, paralysis?

Did those who told wild tales of witches' ceremonies actually believe that they themselves were witches? What kind of experience made a confessed witch swear she had flown through the air riding on a pole? Did Bridget Bishop, if indeed she stuck pins in her dolls, believe she was injuring an enemy by doing it? And if her enemy knew she was doing it, did he suffer?

Or were the confessed witches just confessing to save their lives, not believing a word they said? If so, what kept the other accused people from confessing and avoiding the gallows?

No one can now give a factual answer to these questions. But if you are curious, you can find some kind of answer by reading the records of the Salem court and deciding for yourself.

a historical story by ELISABETH MARGO

THE GUICCIOLI MINIATURE

It was past midnight, and the orchestra had stopped playing. He got up from his seat at the table in the café and walked across the huge Piazza San Marco. He turned and went past the facade of the cathedral, past the Doge's Palace, which gleamed white with all its tracery, and then down between the two high pillars to the water's edge. He stopped and looked out at the canals. With his eyes he followed the gliding of a gondola, and then he saw an empty *vaporetto,* ghost-like and fast moving, far out in the center of the channel. And he was looking out across St. Mark's Canal to the dim outlines of San Giorgio Island when a shadow fell across the pavement and he heard a man's voice.

"You American?"

Jerry nodded silently.

"Just come to Venice?"

The stranger was a tall, lean man with a haunted look in his eyes. Even though the night was damp and hot, he wore a coat and an old hat with the brim turned down. His hands trembled as if he had a fever.

Out in the channel the *vaporetto* vanished into the darkness.

"Been here a few days," Jerry said.

The sleeves of the man's long coat were frayed, and his lean face had a stubble of beard on it.

He's down and out in Venice, Jerry thought. And so he wasn't surprised when he heard the man say, "Maybe you can help a fellow American?"

Jerry waited.

Then he saw the man put his long hand into his coat pocket and draw out a small object that glistened in the half-darkness.

"Give me ten for it and it's yours, kid."

"What is it?"

"A miniature. I painted it myself. It's worth a good hundred. Two hundred. More. But give me ten dollars and you'll have something to take home to your girl."

He put the miniature into Jerry's hand, and it was cold, almost icy to the touch.

"Ten dollars. You're about eighteen, right? You have a girl, right? Bring her something from Venice." Then he asked, "How long are you going to be here, kid?"

"Till tomorrow afternoon."

"Then you're going home?"

"Yes."

"Home," the man said—and was silent.

And all the time they were talking the icy miniature lay between Jerry's closed fingers. Suddenly the man spoke again.

"Give me ten dollars. It'll be the best buy you'll ever make."

His hand grabbed Jerry and pulled him to a little pool of light. "Take a good look at it."

Jerry lifted the miniature into the spill of light. He saw that it was beautiful.

"The Guiccioli miniature," the man said in a hushed voice, "a copy of the Guiccioli miniature. The original is in the Pitti Palace in Florence. I stood there and copied it, day after day until they wanted to throw me out. The Guiccioli miniature."

It was the face of a very beautiful woman with brown, liquid eyes and auburn hair. Her features were small and perfectly shaped. But it was the eyes that haunted Jerry—the amazing eyes.

He looked up slowly.

And now the eyes of the man were glittering.

"I came here years ago to be a great painter. And I'll soon die and all I have to offer is a copy. My whole life is nothing but a copy. Nothing. Nothing. Give me ten bucks for the picture."

Jerry looked down again at the miniature and then, suddenly, with a shock, he remembered. Teresa Guiccioli . . . Lord Byron, the great romantic poet . . . the two of them had been in love. Byron must have had the miniature painted to carry with him when they were apart. And so this was Teresa Guiccioli, Byron's Countess Guiccioli.

"How about it?"

Jerry hesitated. "I've got very little money left myself," he said. "I came over here with only a little money. I'm a college student. So, you can see, I . . . ."

His voice trailed off into silence. The look in the man's eyes pierced him. The stranger seemed so desperate, so alone, so filled with dread. He began to plead.

"The original is priceless. Go to the Pitti and compare it with this copy. You won't be able to tell the difference. Byron had it painted by one of the great artists of the day. The original is worth a hundred grand—a hundred grand, kid. And I'm offering it to you for ten bucks. I'm broke. Nobody wants to buy it from me. I need money. I need it badly—anything I can get."

Out on the glimmering canal the lean form of a gondola wavered into view and then slowly faded into the darkness. The sound of a boat whistle came from a great distance. It was a haunting, mournful sound.

"All right," said Jerry. "I'll buy it."

They moved out of the pool of light, and Jerry gave the man the money. He dropped the miniature into his pocket.

"It's the best buy you ever made." The man's voice was now mocking and bitter.

"What are you going to do with the money?" Jerry asked.

"Eat. And then get a ticket out of here."

"Where to?"

"Where can a doomed man go?"

The man's eyes glittered and then faded into the darkness.

Jerry stood there a long time. Then he turned and made his way back, across the great square and past the empty tables of the cafés. He went into a long, gloomy arcade and from there along the quiet alleys and narrow streets. He passed over a narrow bridge and came at last to his *pensione,* the little boarding-house he was staying at. The whole time he walked he felt as if he were being followed. He felt as if a long, lean shadow were walking behind him. He turned to look over his shoulder a number of times on the way. No one was there. There was nothing behind him but the empty alleys and streets—and the night.

Jerry Moore went into the *pensione* with its peeling walls and climbed up the dark flight of stairs. He opened the door of his little room and went in. He turned on the light and looked again at the miniature. He thought of Byron and the lovely poetry he had written—"She walks in beauty, like the night . . . ." He could still remember that from English class. He looked at the terrifying beauty of the woman in the miniature. Subtly, the strange, glittering eyes of the man came into his consciousness. He heard the despairing words again, even though he tried not to:

"Where can a doomed man go?"

Suddenly, the miniature grew even icier to his touch. The beautiful face of the woman began to seem almost repellent to him. His hands became clammy.

Jerry got up and went to the old, streaked mirror that hung on the wall. It was his own face that looked back at him—but it had changed somehow. His face was now white and drawn with fear. His eyes had become two black pools.

Where can a doomed man go?

And now Jerry felt that for some strange, inexplicable reason, with the passing of the miniature to him, he, too, had become a doomed man. The painter had passed the curse to him.

Jerry turned out the light. He went over to the window and opened it wide. He stood there, looking down at the dark waters of the canal. He knew that these were the same dark Venetian waters that Lord Byron had looked into in 1819, when he had first seen the miniature of his beloved countess, Teresa Guiccioli.

Beloved?

No! Repellent. Terrifying.

Jerry's face was tight with fear. He looked as frightened as the poor painter had looked when they had made their bargain near the canal.

Then Jerry shivered slightly and turned away from the window.

His sleep that night was restless. He awoke several times. Once he was sure he heard something. He sprang right out of his bed. He stared straight ahead and broke out in a cold sweat. He knew he could not stay in this room any longer. He dressed in a panic.

He stood for an instant in the center of the room, stock-still.

His eyes fixed on the doorknob. He could have sworn that it was beginning to turn, slowly.

Then he screamed. And the knob stopped turning.

After a while, Jerry went to the door. He turned the lock very carefully and very slowly. He opened the door cautiously, an inch at a time. He peered out.

The hallway was dim but he could tell it was empty. There was no one outside.

Jerry closed the door. He went to the window of his room and stood there, looking down at the canal as he had earlier in the evening.

It was then that he made his decision.

He went to the bureau and picked up the miniature. He looked at it for the last time. Then he went over to the open window and threw the tiny painting down into the black water.

There was a splash and then a vast silence.

And in that silence Jerry felt—for the first time since he had met the mysterious painter—like himself again. He felt as if a great weight had been lifted from him.

He was free of the curse—if there was one.

Then he began to laugh silently, and said aloud, "Silly superstitious fool!"

He went back to bed. This time he slept soundly and didn't wake until the sun was streaming in through the open window.

Just before his plane took off that afternoon, the stewardess came around with a selection of magazines and newspapers for the passengers to read. Jerry took one of the Italian newspapers. He settled back in his seat and began to read it. It always gave him pleasure to speak and read Italian. That was one of the reasons he had come to Italy—to improve his Italian. There was a slight smile of pleasure on his face as he began to read. He slowly turned the first page. Then the smile slowly left his face.

He had come upon a picture of the man—the man he had met by the canal, the sad painter. The painter was lying on his back on a cobblestone street, his face turned up to the sky.

Jerry read further.

The "painter" had been one of three men who had stolen the Guiccioli miniature from the Pitti Palace. Then he had double-crossed his partners and had run off with the treasure. His partners had finally caught up with him in Venice, after chasing him all over Italy.

The police had captured the murderers and were now searching desperately for the priceless miniature.

Jerry slowly put down his newspaper.

"Is anything wrong?" the stewardess asked him.

Jerry did not answer.

a short story by JAY BENNETT

POETRY

IF SPRING

If spring
Should come
When we wished
For it,
It wouldn't
Matter.

The bud
Will get
Fatter,
The snow
Will shatter
At its own
Pace.

The lace
Of the spider
Takes time.
The face
Of the sun
Must be
Spun
By waiting.

ROSAMOND DAUER

MY OLDER SISTER

She's taller.
She's wider.
But I don't mind
Because I'm kind.

She's bossy.
She's rude.
And sometimes
Crude.
But I don't mind
Because I'm kind.

She was born
Before me.
And my parents
Prefer her,
She thinks.

Well,
If I didn't mind,
And if I weren't kind,
I'd give her a
Pinch
And not run an
Inch.

But,
Since I don't mind,
And
Since I am kind,
I'll just
Holler
And tell
On her.

ROSAMOND DAUER

CRAB MEADOW BEACH

Seagull flashes
His belly in morse code.

Sand licks
Her clay clean enough to fire.

While Moon reels in,
You and I toe and bucket clams.

MARY JANE MENUEZ

MARCH

Bird wit
Is a frozen mobile
Orbiting
Trees, like rain,
When the wind
Flaps her elbows,
Pivots and half
Whistles.

The sky
Outlines a white
Yard sale.
A flood is made;
Undaunted,
A snowman stands
On a pick-up truck,
Smoking.

A rainbow,
Straight as a ruler,
Pulls yellow
From a cloud
And flags down a sled;
Then circles brush
The salt road
In a dry run.

MARY JANE MENUEZ

PLEASE DON'T INTERRUPT

I'm George Washington
Crossing the British.

No! No!
The Delaware. The Delaware.

I'm a nervous dinosaur
And I'm alive right now.

No! No!
Once upon a time. Long ago.

That's what *you* say.
Cross *me*
And I'll eat you up!

ROSAMOND DAUER

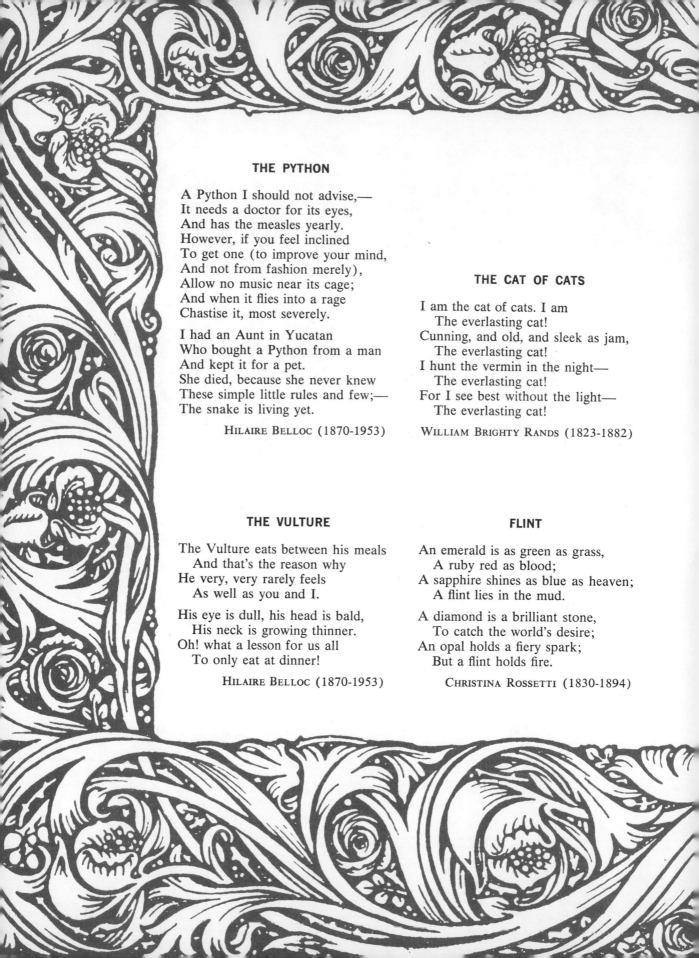

THE PYTHON

A Python I should not advise,—
It needs a doctor for its eyes,
And has the measles yearly.
However, if you feel inclined
To get one (to improve your mind,
And not from fashion merely),
Allow no music near its cage;
And when it flies into a rage
Chastise it, most severely.

I had an Aunt in Yucatan
Who bought a Python from a man
And kept it for a pet.
She died, because she never knew
These simple little rules and few;—
The snake is living yet.

HILAIRE BELLOC (1870-1953)

THE CAT OF CATS

I am the cat of cats. I am
    The everlasting cat!
Cunning, and old, and sleek as jam,
    The everlasting cat!
I hunt the vermin in the night—
    The everlasting cat!
For I see best without the light—
    The everlasting cat!

WILLIAM BRIGHTY RANDS (1823-1882)

THE VULTURE

The Vulture eats between his meals
    And that's the reason why
He very, very rarely feels
    As well as you and I.

His eye is dull, his head is bald,
    His neck is growing thinner.
Oh! what a lesson for us all
    To only eat at dinner!

HILAIRE BELLOC (1870-1953)

FLINT

An emerald is as green as grass,
    A ruby red as blood;
A sapphire shines as blue as heaven;
    A flint lies in the mud.

A diamond is a brilliant stone,
    To catch the world's desire;
An opal holds a fiery spark;
    But a flint holds fire.

CHRISTINA ROSSETTI (1830-1894)

TWO LITTLE KITTENS

Two little kittens, one stormy night,
Began to quarrel, and then to fight;
One had a mouse, the other had none,
And that's the way the quarrel begun.

"I'll have that mouse," said the biggest cat;
"You'll have that mouse? We'll see about that!"
"I *will* have that mouse," said the eldest son;
"You *shan't* have the mouse," said the little one.

I told you before 'twas a stormy night
When these two little kittens began to fight;
The old woman seized her sweeping broom,
And swept the two kittens right out of the room.

The ground was covered with frost and snow,
And the two little kittens had nowhere to go;
So they laid them down on the mat at the door,
While the old woman finished sweeping the floor.

Then they crept in, as quiet as mice,
All wet with the snow, and as cold as ice,
For they found it was better, that stormy night,
To lie down and sleep than to quarrel and fight.

ANONYMOUS (c. 1879)

WHAT ARE HEAVY?

What are heavy? Sea-sand and sorrow;
What are brief? Today and tomorrow;
What are frail? Spring blossoms and youth;
What are deep? The ocean and truth.

CHRISTINA ROSSETTI (1830-1894)

Louis Riel, the Métis hero, is shown in this old engraving wearing the traditional outfit of the 19th-century fur trapper. The moccasins and leggings are Indian. The jacket, rifle, and hat are distinctly European.

LOUIS RIEL: A PICTURE BIOGRAPHY

Louis Riel, the Canadian historical figure, was ahead of his time in many ways. Today we are not surprised to hear of political or social activists fighting for the rights of a minority. But to the people of 19th-century Canada, Louis Riel was a very surprising and even shocking figure. He found a cause he believed in—the cause of his own people, the Métis—and dedicated his life to it. Indeed, he lost his life because of it.

Louis Riel was himself a Métis. "Métis" is the term, in French, for a person who is partly North American Indian and partly European. Riel's mother was half French and half Indian. His father was Irish. Riel was born in 1844 in St. Boniface, now in the province of Manitoba. But in Riel's day, there was no Manitoba, and St. Boniface was in the Red River Settlement, in an area called Assiniboia.

The Métis had special problems. Canada was rapidly becoming a modern nation with increasing independence from Britain. A new province called Manitoba was planned for Canada. It would replace Assiniboia and enter the Canadian Confederation in 1869. The Métis were becoming increasingly nervous. Would their lands be taken from them and given to new settlers? Would they have a voice in the new Canadian government? The Indians had treaties with the government, and the whites had their basic rights guaranteed under English law. But the Métis belonged to neither ethnic group. They couldn't be sure what rights they would have. In 1868, Louis Riel became secretary of the National Committee of Métis. Riel was determined that the officials of the new province of Manitoba not be allowed to take office until the government guaranteed the rights of the Métis in the area. Riel and his followers took action—in fact, there was armed conflict between the Métis and government forces.

From then on, Riel dedicated his life to fighting for Métis rights. Eventually a bounty was offered for his capture, and he was forced to flee to the United States. He settled down in Montana and married a Métis woman. But in 1884 he was called back to Canada by the Métis of Saskatchewan. They too were feeling the impact of Canada's westward movement and were anxious to ensure their rights. Riel's return to Canada was the beginning of the end for him. He defied the national government, and in 1885 he was finally arrested, and charged with treason. He was tried and convicted. On November 16, 1885, he was executed. But Louis Riel has remained a powerful symbol for many Canadians. Today he is being re-discovered as a significant figure in Canadian history.

Louis Riel was a religious man who had never intended to become a soldier. But when he took up the cause of his own Métis people, Riel was forced to fight. The issues were explosive and led to two major armed conflicts—the Northwest Rebellion of 1869–70 and the Northwest Rebellion of 1885. The map (*right*) shows the Red River Settlement, where the Rebellion of 1869–70 took place, and the Saskatchewan River country, where the Rebellion of 1885 was fought. The Métis were fighting for a way of life. From the earliest days of European settlement in Canada, the Métis had been expert fur trappers and fur traders. They roamed the forests and rivers of western Canada in search of beavers, otters, and other fur-bearing animals. They traded the pelts to the fur companies for clothes, supplies, and pocket money. But the freedom of their way of life was far more important to the Métis than money or supplies. As Canada's western wilderness began to be divided politically into provinces, and settlers came to farm on the riverbanks where the Métis trapped, a basic conflict developed. Riel understood the love of his people for their way of life and tried desperately to save it. The Canadian Government took the Northwest Rebellions very seriously too. It was trying to build a modern nation. In the course of the Rebellion of 1885, Riel set up a provisional government at Batoche on the South Saskatchewan River. The Canadian Government in Ottawa sent 4,000 troops under Major-General Frederick Middleton to crush the rebellion. This photograph of General Middleton's troops (*below left*) was taken during his campaign against the Métis at Fish Creek. The Métis held the government troops for a while at Fish Creek, but General Middleton's forces soon pushed on to Batoche. Batoche fell and Métis resistance crumbled. This interesting old print (*below right*) shows the actual moment when Riel, bearded and exhausted, surrendered to General Middleton. The Métis' world was gone forever.

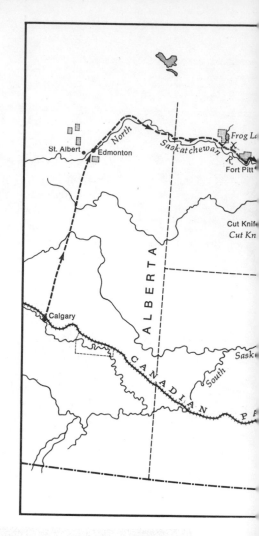

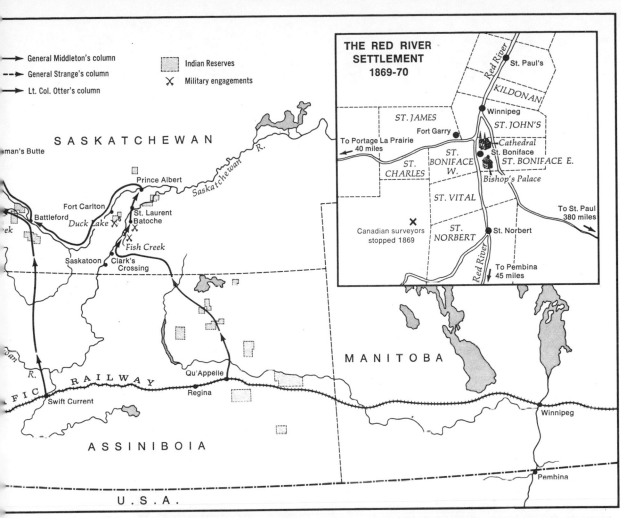

THE LITTLE PRESIDENT

"Have you finished with the bathroom?" asked his mother.

"Yes," called the Little President through the door, hardly thinking what he was saying.

"Your father and I have to go out to a big reception tonight," his mother went on, in a somewhat querulous voice, "and I haven't done my hair yet!"

Hair, hair, thought the Little President, grown-up women are always talking about doing their hair, and it looks exactly the same after they have done it as before. What a waste of time! The Little President was in his bath, supposed to be washing himself. But that he also deemed a waste of time, so instead he was propelling his small steamer on the surface of the bath, creating waves with his feet, and watching his proud vessel negotiate the hazards of nature.

"And I haven't shaved yet!" cried his father, the Big President, rattling the door handle.

"Nearly finished," called the Little President.

His father was a man of considerable importance who had to go to functions about twice a month wearing a lot of medals he had been given for some reason or other. The Little President had no inkling what his father was President of, and between you and me he didn't really care, not because he didn't love his father, but rather because he wasn't sure what a President was.

Just as he was creating a veritable tempest by agitating his feet up and down and, alas, spraying the walls with warm soapy water, his proud ship turned turtle, and sank without warning. He picked it out of the water, and turned it over to let the water run out. Then he kept quite still so the water would calm again, and re-floated his ship, which immediately sank again.

Just as the Little President was puzzling over this, he noticed that the bath taps were now covered in blue trousers, and he saw a jolly old man with a red face and white whiskers sitting between them.

"Who are you?" enquired the Little President.

"Me? I'm an Admiral. And I've just sunk your ship, twice."

"Sunk my ship? Why did you do such a dreadful thing?" asked the Little President.

"Dreadful? Not at all. At least, it depends how you look at it, I suppose. It may seem dreadful to you, but to me it seems glorious."

"Glorious to sink ships with men in them? How can it be?"

"How can it be? It's simple. Every time I sink a ship I get a medal. And I am particularly fond of medals, perhaps because I'm an admiral."

"My father has many medals, and he's never sunk a ship in his life," said the Little President, annoyed.

"People get medals for all sorts of reasons," replied the Admiral, "but Admirals only get them for sinking ships." And he sighed. "Times are hard," he went on. "Fewer and fewer little boys play with ships in their bath, and you can sink as many ducks as you like, you'll never get even a small medal."

"I'll give you a medal for not sinking ships," proposed the Little President.

The Admiral brightened.

"That's a splendid idea," he barked. "It's much easier not to sink them than to sink them. To sink a ship you need a ship. Not to sink one you only need an empty bath."

"So that's agreed," said the Little President, as he stepped out of his bath. He fetched one of his mother's hair curlers, and clamped it onto the Admiral's coat.

"Agreed," cried the Admiral, saluting, and disappeared clumsily down the overflow of the bath.

The Little President was just putting on his pajamas when he heard an odd scraping sound. His father, in spite of the fact that he always insisted on the Little President's tidiness, often left his own tube of shaving soap open, and it would ooze out over the glass bathroom shelf. Now a little old man with a spade was battling with it, trying to sweep it away.

"What *are* you doing, little old man?" asked the Little President.

"Me? Sweeping the snow off the skating rink, you silly child, can't you see that? The season begins at any moment, all the tourists will arrive, the orchestra will strike up the waltz, and no one will be able to skate because some careless giant has spilled all this snow on our rink."

"I'll help you," said the Little President, drawing his index finger along the surface of the shelf, and gathering the shaving soap on it.

"Where are you going to put it?" asked the old man in alarm.

"I'm going to throw it away."

"Don't waste all that good snow! Make us a snowman at the end of the rink. That will attract the customers."

The Little President squeezed more shaving cream onto the shelf, and made a snowman for the old fellow, using a couple of cough drops which he found in the medicine chest as eyes.

He had no time to finish his work to his satisfaction since his father began banging on the door.

"That's enough now, come out of there!"

"I'm coming."

Taking the precaution of shutting the light, the Little President unlocked the door, and rushed past his parents into his own room.

"Why d'you shut the light?" he heard his father ask. "You know perfectly well I'm going in there."

"I'm saving electricity," the Little President declared. "We all should, the Government says."

There was no arguing with his son, and yet the father felt a little suspicious, as he always did when the Little President came out with a really complicated answer.

From his bed, the Little President heard his father's voice far away.

"Oh, it's too bad, my dear. Look at this mess. Bath water all over the walls and ceiling, and—what's this? He doesn't shave yet, does he? At his age?"

When his parents came to say good night, the Little President prudently pretended to be asleep, although he was as wide awake as only someone pretending hard to be asleep could be.

"How innocent he looks," crooned his mother, glittering in all her finery.

"Yes, the little horror," laughed his father, and as he laughed, all the medals on his chest clinked. The Little President dared to peep through his almost closed eyelids, and was dazzled by the sight.

They turned out the light, and went their way. The Little President allowed a little time to elapse, then he carefully tiptoed out of bed, turned on the light again, and went to the bathroom to see what had happened to his snowman. His mother had swept it all away. Everything was spotless, and he was about to leave the room when he heard some feeble sobbing. Looking closely at the shelf, he perceived the little old man seated on his father's razor, weeping gently.

"Oh, please don't cry!" appealed the Little President.

"Can't help it," sobbed the old man. "We've had an avalanche . . . the whole season's ruined . . . the skaters all went home afraid . . . I'll have to sell the rink."

"Here," said the Little President. "This is your reward for the Best Snowman of the whole season."

And he gave the old man another of his mother's hair curlers.

"What is it?" asked the old man, struggling under its weight.

"It's a piece of modern sculpture which is presented every year for the Best Snowman. You are the deserving winner."

The old man made a long acceptance speech which none of the skaters applauded, since they had all gone home long ago.

The Little President was on his way back to his room when he thought he heard a noise in the kitchen. He was just in time to see a puff of smoke twist from the spout of the kettle, and a moment later a gas ring was in flames.

"What's going on here?" he cried, blowing the flames out and making *absolutely sure* the gas was turned off.

The lid of the kettle slowly rose, and a tank commander peeped out.

"Why did you blow out the fire?" he rasped.

"Who are you?" asked the Little President amazed.

"The Tank Commander," replied the aggressive little fellow. "I opened fire because I wish to destroy the stove."

"Destroy the stove? What a silly idea!" cried the Little President. "If you do, we won't be able to have any more hot food."

"I'm very sorry for you," said the Tank Commander. "But that is really not my business. I do what I am told."

"Told? By whom?"

"I'm not sure. I only know that every time I open fire with my spout, I get a medal."

The Little President brightened. He recognized that the Tank Commander must be a prey to the same demon of destruction who tried to get the Admiral to sink his ship and who tried to get him into trouble with the snowman.

"I'll give you a medal for not shooting at the stove," said the Little President, running to fetch another of his mother's hair curlers. He slipped it over the Tank Commander's head, so that he could no longer move.

"What's this?" asked the Tank Commander unhappily.

"It's a medal that's so big that it covers you entirely, so that there is no doubt in the mind of anybody who sees you that you have a very important medal indeed."

This made the Tank Commander very happy even though he couldn't move, and the Little President left the kitchen, determined now to find the evil spirit who was doing such dreadful things in the house.

He looked everywhere. In his father's study he found a small musician seated at the base of the radiator, playing the organ.

"You play very beautifully," said the Little President in admiration.

"If you knew anything about music, and especially the works of Johann Sebastian Bach, you'd realize this organ is dreadfully out of tune."

"It isn't an organ," said the Little President. "It's a radiator."

"Have you ever heard of the works of Johann Sebastian Bach played on a radiator?" asked the musician.

"No," agreed the Little President, who had never consciously heard of works of Johann Sebastian Bach played on anything.

"If you were a nice little boy," said the musician, "you'd tune the organ for me—all you've got to do is to take a spanner from your father's toolbox, and let the water out of the pipes. It's that what is making them out of tune."

"Oh no," cried the Little President. "I see your game. You want to get me into trouble by flooding the house!"

Instead of fetching his father's spanner he fetched another of his mother's hair curlers.

"There," he said to the organist.

"What's that?" asked the latter, stopping in the middle of a grand arpeggio.

"The first prize for organ playing."

"But what is it?"

"It is a spiral harp—listen." And the Little President plucked the metal wire with his fingernail.

"That is a beautiful sound!" cried the organist, grasping his new instrument as though he had played it all his life, and disappeared.

The Little President decided to be a good boy and go to bed, but on his way he heard a note of C sharp, repeated several times with increasing power, coming from the drawing-room.

Putting on the light, he saw that the keyboard of the piano was open and a tiny dentist was at work attacking the keys with a sharp instrument.

"What are you doing?" cried the Little President.

"Cleaning the teeth of this beast. Some of them are entirely black."

"They are supposed to be black, you silly man," said the Little President.

"I am not a silly man, I am an eminent dentist," yelled the tiny dentist with a tiny yell, and attacked the note of C sharp, just next to middle C.

"C sharp, C sharp, C sharp!" complained the piano.

"You are hurting it," said the Little President.

"It's its own stupid fault," muttered the dentist. "If you neglect your teeth, you see what happens!"

The Little President saw it was useless to argue, so he ran to fetch another of his mother's hair curlers. "I hope there aren't any more little men in the house," he reflected. "There are only two medals left."

Running back to the drawing-room he presented the hair curler to the dentist.

"What is that?" asked the dentist, intrigued.

"A medal, of sorts—but I think it could be made into something useful."

"I see it as a cotton-wool dispenser, or perhaps something to hold open the mouth of a rebellious patient," muttered the dentist. "Yes—that's it."

"Well you can only have it if you promise to leave the piano alone."

"You think I enjoy cleaning black notes?" asked the horrid tiny dentist.

"Don't you even say thank you?" enquired the Little President.

"What for?"

"The medal."

"Thank you," replied the dentist, with ill grace. Then he left, walking on the hair curler, which rolled obliging before him.

Darko Delalle, 13 years old, Yugoslavia.

"Ah!" he cried, delighted now, "that's even better! It's a most original form of transport!"

The Little President went into the hallway, and called out aloud.

"Who was responsible for all the little people who tried to make me do naughty things and who did naughty things to me?"

He fancied he saw a movement in the umbrella stand. Looking closer, he noticed that his parents' umbrellas weren't umbrellas at all, but a couple of gloomy vultures, their long wings drooping to the carpet, their thin and shiny necks curling into a handle.

Above: Marek Malanowski, 12 years old, Poland.
Below: Jean Davoigneau, 13 years old, France.

"Was it you?" gasped the Little President.

"We have to do something to express ourselves," groaned the larger vulture. "How would you like our life? Never go for a walk unless it's raining. Never see the sun. Most of our lives spent in a dark corridor."

"But where did all the tiny people come from?" asked the Little President.

"From the gloom of our thoughts," croaked the lady vulture.

"If you lived most of your life here, dry and dark, or outside, wet and cold, you'd have gloomy thoughts like us."

"How can I cheer you up?"

"You gave all the others medals, I believe," moaned the gentleman vulture. "I suppose we will be left out as usual."

"You can have the last medal, on condition you promise never to do anything naughty again, or make me do anything naughty again!" said the Little President.

"We agree," squawked the vultures in unison, shaking their feathers mildly.

The Little President dropped the last of his mother's hair curlers into the larger of the two umbrellas.

"Thank you," rasped the vultures politely.

Just then the Little President heard voices. Gracious, how time had flown! He just had time to turn out the lights and jump into bed before his parents returned.

"I'm so tired, I think I'll go straight to bed," he heard his mother say.

"What horrible weather, it's pelting with rain," his father added. "I'll just put my medals back in their boxes then I'll go and put the car in the garage."

"Don't forget to take your umbrella," his mother called from the bathroom.

There was a pause.

"I can't understand what's happened to all my hair curlers," his mother exclaimed. "There's not one left in the box, and yet I'm sure they were all there."

The Little President heard his father take his umbrella, and then his surprised voice:

"Here's one of your hair curlers—in my umbrella!"

"How on earth could it *possibly* have got there?" asked his mother.

"Oh dear," thought the Little President pretending hard to be asleep. "The vultures will be simply *furious* that their medal has been confiscated so soon after I gave it to them. Now, next time my parents go out, all that naughtiness is going to start all over again. If it's as difficult as this to run a house, how much more difficult must it be to run a country!"

by PETER USTINOV
story and pictures specially prepared for UNICEF

The Twin Sisters

Early one morning Klaus, a young merchant who was going to sail to the far ends of the earth in order to carry on trade, went down to his boat in the harbor of the town. Because the crew had not yet finished loading all the costly cargo, and he had time to spend, he took a walk along a country road. When he had gone some distance, he met two pretty young girls. Each carried a flower in her hand and sang a merry song.

They were as alike as two berries and Klaus could see at once that they were twins. As they came up to him they stopped and curtsied.

"Noble sir, would you show us the way to the city?" asked one.

"Gladly," answered Klaus, "I'm just out for a walk and ought to turn back now, so we can join company a way."

So they walked back together to the city. The more Klaus looked at the two girls the more they pleased him. Yes, they pleased him so much that he wanted to ask one of the two to be his wife and the mistress of his house. But he did not know which one he liked the better, for they were equally pretty; the only difference was that one had brown eyes and the other, blue.

He soon learned that the girl with the brown eyes was named Rosa, and the one with blue eyes was Lena. Their parents, country people, had many children and had a hard time getting along, so the girls were going to the city to look for work.

"What would you say if I should help you get work?" he asked, when they were about to part at the road to the harbor. "My mother is going to employ two maids to take the place of two who had to leave."

With that he took out a paper, wrote some words on it, and told the girls to give it to his mother.

"You can find her easily. All you have to do is to ask the way to Merchant Klaus' home. Anyone can show you the right way."

The girls curtsied and thanked him. The next day the merchant sailed out upon the wide sea, and Rosa and Lena went to his big house, which was in the middle of a large and beautiful garden.

When they knocked at the door, the old lady herself came to open it. After reading what her son had written, she asked them to come in and stay, for there was much work to do in the large house and she was glad to get help.

Next she showed them what work there was to do in the house.

"You will divide the duties between you," she explained.

Rosa, especially, was happy hearing this, for she knew very well how she would like the work divided. She took her sister aside, and showed her her soft white hands. At home she had always arranged to get the easiest work.

"You see what beautiful hands I have. They are more beautiful even than yours. It would be a pity if I should spoil them by scrubbing, sweeping, and weeding in the garden. You do the heavy work, since you are used to it. I'll dust, lay the table, and sit and sew."

Lena looked puzzled. She did not understand why the heavy and hard work should fall to her, and why Rosa should always get the lighter tasks.

Rosa put her arms around her sister and coaxed: "I'll tell you a secret. If I keep myself pretty and neat, in time I might become mistress of this house when Merchant Klaus comes home. Didn't you notice how he looked at me?"

"No," answered Lena. "I didn't notice he looked more at you than at me."

"Maybe not, but *I* noticed it," persisted Rosa. "Though we are alike in many ways, I have brown eyes and you have blue. Everyone says brown eyes are livelier and prettier than blue. And my white hands are pleasing too. Lena, surely you wouldn't be sorry if I married the master and became mistress of the house?"

Of course Lena wished her sister well, so they divided the duties as Rosa desired.

In the beginning everything went smoothly. After some months the old lady was so satisfied with the girls that she showed them a large wardrobe. In the wardrobe hung dresses that had belonged to her daughter. From among these dresses each sister was allowed to choose one. Most were plain, well-made, everyday dresses, but there were also two fancy ones for holidays. While Lena chose a plain dress, Rosa kept fingering the fancy ones.

The old lady patted Rosa kindly and said: "You ought not to choose one of those. You will have far more use from one of the plain dresses. See how the dampness has injured the delicate fabrics."

She spread out the holiday dresses and sure enough, there were a few dark spots on them.

But Rosa did not care about that, and chose the fancier of the two.

"These spots don't matter, if I can only get something to put over them," she said, greedily fingering a fringed and faded silk shawl.

"You may have that too," said the old lady a bit sadly.

Rosa thanked her, and at once put on the dress and shawl.

One afternoon, a year later, while the old lady was out, there came a knocking at the gate, and when Lena went to open it, before her stood a workman with a blond beard and with hair falling down to his eyes.

"Good-day, little damsel," said he. "Herr Klaus sent me here with greetings to the lady of the house, and has ordered me to look after the garden so it will be in good condition when he returns home."

Lena asked him to come into the kitchen. She set out food and chatted with him. Rosa heard them from the drawing-room where she was dusting, so she came to find out who was there. But when she learned the visitor was only a hired man whom Herr Klaus had sent, she drew herself up proudly and said: "Welcome, my good man, but I must remind you to stand up and bow when you meet your betters."

The hired man, staring at her, rose and bowed stiffly.

"Pardon me, lady, but I was so astonished that you and the maid are so alike, that I forgot to be polite."

"Better late than not at all!" returned Rosa haughtily. She turned on her heel and went back into the drawing-room.

After some time, the old lady returned. She looked in surprise at the man whom she had never seen before, but after reading the letter from her son, she nodded and declared the man could go into the garden and begin his work. This he did, and a splendid workman he proved to be. After a few weeks the garden blossomed as if it were a paradise.

Lena liked nothing better than to weed the garden and help the man bind up the plants.

Together they sang songs, chatted, and played while they worked. Rosa became jealous as she stared from the window of the drawing-room and listened.

"But he's only a hired man," she told herself. "When one is certain to be a fine lady some day, a dull time alone is better than amusement with a person like that."

One Saturday evening when their work was finished, Lena and the hired man were enjoying themselves more than usual. No matter how elegant Rosa wanted to be, she could not help going into the garden to see what was happening.

The young people were playing ball. The gardener threw the ball so high that Lena had to stare up at the sky a long time. When it finally did fall, Lena skipped as lightly as a linnet over the grass to catch it.

"Will you join us?" she called out when she saw Rosa.

Rosa did not answer. She thought it was not quite proper for her to play ball with a hired man. But she could not resist so she, too, began to run after the ball.

It was not so easy for her to run, for she got tangled in her long dress, and the large silk shawl made her so warm that she had to stop often. At last she could not endure it, so she unfastened the shawl and threw it on a bench.

"What does it matter if *that* man sees the spots? I needn't mind him, for he's only a hired man," she told herself.

Now the man stopped suddenly and stared at her.

"Look at those spots!" he cried. "And I thought you were elegant through and through!"

Rosa became so angry she found herself blushing to the roots of her hair.

"How dare you?" she scolded. "But that's what I get for lowering myself to play with a common laborer!" With that, she snatched up the silk shawl and ran into the house.

A few days later when the work in the garden was finished, the man went to the old lady for his wages. He explained he had to travel on his way. He received his money and the old lady's thanks. Then he bade a friendly farewell to the entire household.

With tears in her eyes, Lena walked with him through the garden. She was sad because he was leaving, and felt that all her life would be empty when they could no longer work and play together. Just before they reached the gate, he stopped, looked at her fondly, and said: "Do you know you are the sweetest girl I have ever known? Will you wait for me, and become my wife some day?"

Lena's face brightened: "Of course I'll wait for you, though it be for a hundred years!"

"No," he assured her, "it won't be as long as that." Finally he kissed her, nodded farewell, and went on his way.

At once the house seemed hushed and silent. Lena could not sing any more. She went around sadly, longing for the gardener to come back. "It may take a long time," she thought. "It's not easy for a poor man to work himself up in the world."

A couple of days later, the house again became lively, for Herr Klaus came sailing home and entered the door with boxes of goods. When he stood in the drawing-room in his rich attire, wishing everyone "Good-day," he seemed more handsome than before.

After he had embraced his mother, he greeted the two girls and asked if they were happy in his house. Rosa answered, "Yes." She curtsied, laughed, and tossed her head so that her curls danced about her face.

But Lena answered sadly, curtsied like a schoolgirl, and tried to leave the room quickly so as to go back to her duties.

Herr Klaus grasped her hand. "Perhaps you aren't happy? You don't look as cheerful and lively as you did when we met on the road."

"Oh, yes, Herr Klaus, of course I'm happy," Lena answered.

Herr Klaus shook his head and looked inquiringly at Rosa.

"The only thing the matter with her," explained Rosa, "is that she's lonesome for the hired man who did the gardening. They chatted together and got along fine."

"Then we'll see if we haven't something here that will chase away sorrow," said Herr Klaus.

At his bidding, two sailors carried in one of the chests he had

brought home with him, and after he had opened it with a small key, he took from it costly fabrics, silken shawls, gossamer scarves, embroidered shoes, painted parasols, and glittering bottles.

After he had presented his mother with the greater part of these gifts, he gave the rest to the two girls, who were smiling with pleasure. When they thought all the presents had been given out, Klaus took from the bottom of the chest a splendid necklace with stones set in gold. However, the stones shone but dimly.

"Here I have the best gift of all," declared Herr Klaus. "I bought this from a Persian. When I put it around the neck of a pretty girl I can see at once if her soul is as beautiful as her face. If her soul is pure, all the stones will shine like real diamonds."

"That's marvelous!" exclaimed his mother.

"Now I shall try it on each of you," announced Klaus.

While he was speaking, he looked at Lena and walked toward her with the necklace. But Lena withdrew in alarm.

"No, no, Herr Klaus!" she cried. "I am only a servant. Try it on my sister. She's much more refined and elegant than I."

Herr Klaus went to Rosa who laughed and stretched out her neck to receive the gift. But when the necklace encircled her throat, the stones shone no brighter than before.

"I know what's the matter," said the merchant, "the necklace does not show well on that faded silk shawl." With one jerk he snatched off the shawl. There stood Rosa in the spotted dress.

Herr Klaus looked very solemn. "The necklace is just as dim now as before," he said as he took it off.

Full of shame, Rosa threw her hands before her face and ran up the stairs into her own room. She pulled off the dress that had brought her this shame and fell on her bed and wept.

When Rosa had left the room Herr Klaus again went to Lena with the necklace in his hand.

"Let's try it, if only for fun," said he.

Though she tried to push him away, he snapped it around her neck. Instantly his mother uttered a cry: "See, see how it sparkles!" she cried in delight, for she loved Lena as a daughter.

Lena raised her hands and tried to take off the necklace, for she felt she could not accept such a valuable gift. She explained to her young master that she had promised to wait for the man she loved.

Herr Klaus took her hands and held them fast. "Let the necklace stay where it is," he exclaimed. "Consider it a wedding present when you marry the gardener."

"But that might take a long time. Who knows if he will ever come back?" said Lena mournfully.

"Close your eyes and turn around three times!" cried Herr Klaus, with a hearty laugh.

Surprised and doubtful, Lena did as she was told. When she opened her eyes again, she was struck dumb with astonishment. Before her stood the man whom she loved; yet he wore Herr Klaus' clothes and shoes!

To her shocked surprise, the gardener pulled off his hair and beard, and again Herr Klaus stood before her.

"I put on this disguise and returned to my own home as a laborer to find out for myself which girl had a pure soul beneath her pretty face. Now I know which girl I want to marry; and since you, Lena, have already promised to marry me disguised as a gardener, everything seems clear and simple. There is no need to delay any longer!"

Klaus put his arm around her waist and the two danced around the room, while the mother clapped her hands in joy.

A week later the wedding took place.

Never in the history of that town had such festivities been seen. All night long the guests and Klaus and Lena danced in the same garden where the "hired man" and the little maid had learned to know and to love each other.

After some time even Rosa learned to be happy, for she really loved her sister way down deep in her heart.

a Swedish story from Scandinavian Stories
by MARGARET SPERRY

WHERE HAVE WE MET?

Do you know these characters from books you have read? Try to match each character with the book in which he or she appears and the author of the book.

BOOK		AUTHOR		CHARACTER	
A	The Hobbit	1	Louisa May Alcott	n	Mole
B	Treasure Island	2	Laura Ingalls Wilder	o	Smaug
C	Little House in the Big Woods	3	E. B. White	p	Dorothy
D	Little Women	4	J. R. R. Tolkien	q	Buck
E	The Wind in the Willows	5	A. A. Milne	r	Fern
F	The Call of the Wild	6	J. M. Barrie	s	Paul Revere
G	Winnie-the-Pooh	7	Kenneth Grahame	t	Peter
H	Johnny Tremain	8	L. Frank Baum	u	The Red Queen
I	Through the Looking-Glass	9	Johanna Spyri	v	Long John Silver
J	Charlotte's Web	10	Robert Louis Stevenson	w	Laura
K	The Wonderful Wizard of Oz	11	Esther Forbes	x	Wendy
L	Peter Pan	12	Jack London	y	Jo
M	Heidi	13	Lewis Carroll	z	Christopher Robin

Answers: A,4,o; B,10,v; C,2,w; D,1,y; E,7,n; F,12,q; G,5,z; H,11,s; I,13,u; J,3,r; K,8,p; L,6,x; M,9,t.

WORLD OF ANIMALS

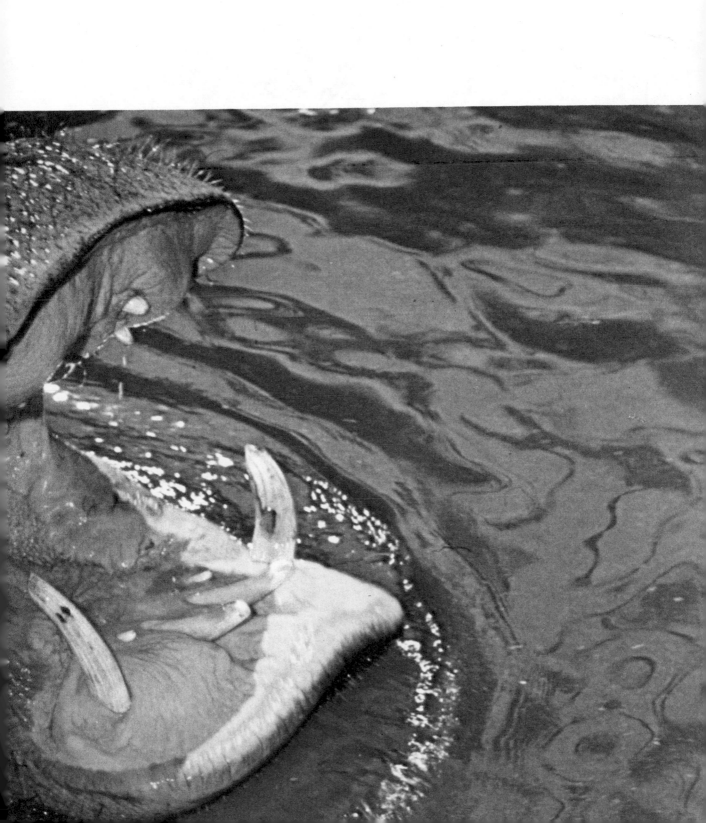

Ibexes frolic at Hai Bar South. The ibex is the wild goat mentioned in the Bible, and is the emblem of the Israel Nature Reserves Authority.

ANIMALS OF THE BIBLE

In the sandy scrublands south and east of the Negev desert is a nature reserve. Like nature reserves all over the world, it is a place where endangered species of animals are given a safe place to live. But this is a nature reserve with a difference. For it is in Israel, and many of the animals living there are animals mentioned in the Bible.

This reserve, Hai Bar South (*hai bar* means "wildlife" in Hebrew), is one of several reserves run by the Israel Nature Reserves Authority (NRA). Since 1963 this organization has been setting aside natural areas throughout Israel as wildlife reserves. It has also been collecting wild animals, both in Israel and in other countries.

The head of the Nature Reserves Authority is Major General Avraham Yoffe. This retired Israeli tank commander is profoundly concerned with wildlife preservation. And this concern, no less than his military exploits, has made him a living legend in Israel. The story

is told that in the midst of an artillery duel during the Sinai campaign of the Six Day War (1967), Yoffe ordered his tanks to hold their fire so that a rare bird could cross the battlefield in safety. On another occasion he ordered a military encampment moved to protect a field of wildflowers. And on the last day of the war he had his game wardens out, armed with metal signs with the emblem of the NRA on them. The wardens were instructed to locate any suitable areas in the newly captured territory and mark them off as nature reserves.

▶NOAH'S PARKS

The nature reserves in Israel are sometimes called "Noah's Parks," referring to the Bible story of Noah and his ark. Unlike Noah, the men who run the nature reserves are not putting all their beasts in one place. Israel has several nature reserves in various stages of development throughout the country.

Hai Bar South is the chief of these reserves. It is situated at the southern end of the Aravah, the great valley that runs from Lake Kinneret south to the Gulf of Aqaba. Here, a few miles north of the port of Eilat on about 10,000 acres (4,000 hectares) of grassland, small but promising herds of wild asses (two kinds), gazelles, addax antelope and ibex are being raised. The ibex is the wild goat of the Bible. The head of an ibex is also the emblem or symbol of the NRA. Hai Bar South provides a suitable environment for these animals to live the life they are accustomed to in the wild. The reserve also gives shelter to breeding stock of these and other rare animals. Their offspring, it is hoped, can one day be released in other reserves.

Another reserve, this one in northern Israel, has been set aside in the marshes of Hula. These marshes were once a resting-place for water birds. The marshes are located on the flyway—the route that northern birds follow on their winter migration to Africa and back again in the spring. Much of the marshland at Hula had been drained as part of a reclamation project. Now that scientists have begun to understand the environmental value of wetlands better, efforts to preserve the marshes' original character have begun. Besides being a resting-place for migrating birds, Hula is a home to water buffalo, wild boar, and the African wildcat.

Still another reserve, Hai Bar North, is being developed in Galilee. There the NRA hopes to raise roe deer, Syrian bear, more ibex, and even leopards and lions. Lions are now extinct in Israel. However, they were once well known and are frequently mentioned in the Bible. (The lion was the symbol of the tribe of Judah and the house of David in the Old Testament. In the New Testament the lion was used as a symbol for Christ.) There are still a few leopards left in the hill country of Israel. The NRA game wardens regularly leave goat carcasses for the big cats in certain selected places. When the hungry leopards come to know that they can find food in these places, they leave the area's domestic livestock alone.

Many of the animals mentioned in the Bible are extinct in Israel but can be found in other countries. They may be living in the wild or in zoos or nature reserves.

THE NAMING OF BEASTS

If in some ways the NRA is doing the work of Noah, in other ways it finds itself faced with a problem like Adam's. In the Book of Genesis (chapter 2, verses 19–20) we read that God brought all the animals to Adam "to see what he would call them: and whatsoever Adam called every living creature, that was the name thereof." But the NRA's problem is not giving names to creatures—it is finding out what creatures are meant by certain names. It wishes to preserve the animals mentioned in the Bible. But sometimes it is very difficult to know which animals they really are.

Part of the problem is a very common one. The everyday names of animals and plants are never exact. We talk about "deer" or "foxes" without bothering to say which kinds we mean. There is a science called taxonomy that gives a proper, two-word name to every known kind of animal and plant. These names, which are written in Latin, allow us to talk about an animal and know exactly which animal we mean.

When the NRA wants a certain kind of animal, it's no good asking for it by the Hebrew name it has in the Bible. They must find out what modern taxonomists call it. And that causes some interesting problems.

DEER, CONEYS, AND UNICORNS

In the First Book of Kings it says that among the meat served at King Solomon's table was that of "harts, and roebucks, and fallow deer" (I Kings 4:23). "Hart" is the old name in English for a male red deer. Taxonomists call the red deer *Cervus elaphas*. This large, handsome animal, with his magnificent head of antlers, is related to the American wapiti. The roe deer (roebuck is the male) is called *Capreolus capreolus* in scientific language. It is a cousin of the American white-tailed deer and looks a lot like it, too. There are several kinds of fallow deer. However, the one that was common in the Holy Land in Biblical times was the Persian fallow deer, *Dama mesopotamica*. Of all these kinds of deer, the Persian deer is the only one that is seriously endangered. In fact, it was thought to be extinct until a small herd was found in Iran. Efforts are now being made

The mysterious "unicorn" of the Bible may have resembled this scimitar-horned oryx.

The hyrax—"a rabbit without a tail, and with short legs and small ears."

The Persian fallow deer has been around since Biblical times, but is now seriously endangered.

to protect them, and the NRA hopes to acquire some for Israeli animal reserves.

Scientists know that all three of these deer lived in the Holy Land in Biblical times. However, there are no sure means of knowing which deer are meant in which Biblical passages. The names "hart" (or "hind" for the female), "roe," and "fallow deer" in the English Bible represent, respectively, the Hebrew words *ayal, tzebi,* and *yachmur.* But scholars disagree on the accuracy of the traditional translations. For instance, *tzebi,* according to some scholars, was not a true deer at all but a gazelle. It was either *Gazella dorcas* or *Gazella arabica.* As the dorcas gazelle had been badly overhunted, the NRA decided to protect it—whether it's the Biblical *tzebi* or not.

Another case of a translation presenting a puzzle is that of the animal called in the English Bible a "coney." Psalm 104, which mentions a lot of animals, speaks of the rocks as a refuge for the coneys. "Coney" is an old English word for "rabbit," but the Biblical coney isn't a rabbit at all. It was called *shafan* in Hebrew. The scientists now think it was the hyrax, *Heterohyrax syriacus.*

Hyraxes form an order of animal all to themselves. Their nearest relatives are the elephants and the manatees (or sea cows). Their feet are quite remarkable. They have nails like hooves and yet are able to climb rocky surfaces with great ease. The hyrax has been described as looking like "a rabbit without a tail, and with short legs and small ears" —if you can imagine all that. Since the hyrax is unknown in Europe, though common throughout Southwest Asia and North Africa, the translation "coney" for the Hebrew name *shafan* is understandable.

Perhaps the most fascinating animal question in the Bible is the identity of the strange creatures called "unicorns." Several times in the Old Testament, reference is made to creatures called, in Hebrew, *re-em.* The mysterious *re-em* appear in poetic passages referring to their strength, their ferocity, their untamability, and their leaping. The men who translated the Hebrew Bible into Greek called the *re-em monokeros* ("one-horn"). In Latin, for some reason, this name was changed to *rhinoceros* ("nose-horn") or, more logically, *unicornis* ("one-horn"). The English word is derived from Latin.

Ancient Greek and Latin authors had described the unicorn as a beast with the body of a horse, the head of a deer, the feet of an elephant, and the tail of a lion. This mysterious beast was said to have a single, black horn in the middle of its forehead. For many centuries it was commonly believed that there was such a beast. When scientists decided that the unicorn did not exist, scholars began to speculate that when the ancient authors were talking about unicorns, they really meant the Indian rhinoceros.

But what about the Biblical *re-em*? Had that creature really been a rhinoceros, too? It did not seem likely. Then a scholar remembered that another ancient people of the Middle East, the Assyrians, had known of animals they called *rimu*—and that name may have been pronounced a lot like *re-em.* The Assyrians had depicted the *rimu* in their famous relief carvings. Many scholars now agree that the Biblical *re-em* and the Assyrian *rimu* were names for the aurochs. And what was the aurochs? It was a huge wild ox, the ancestor, it is believed, of our modern domestic cattle. Unfortunately the aurochs is now extinct.

It seemed to many people that the Biblical *re-em* would never be found. But among the animals that conservationists are trying to save from the fate of the aurochs is the Arabian oryx, *Oryx leucoryx.* This graceful, white antelope of the Arabian desert has long straight horns, and a tassel on its tail, which do make it look a little like pictures of the mythical unicorn. And its Arabic name is *ri'm.* Arabic and Hebrew are closely related languages. Could this, at last, be the *re-em* of the Bible?

The Arabian oryx is so gravely endangered that the NRA has not yet been able to acquire any. However, it has acquired some members of a closely related species, the scimitar-horned oryx, *Oryx dammah.* This oryx has backward-curving horns (like the scimitar, the ancient, curved sword of the Middle East) and is now found in northern Africa. The NRA's oryxes are now in Hai Bar South.

If the NRA cannot be quite sure what Adam or the Biblical writers called the beasts, it is still doing its best at Noah's task—saving man's fellow creatures.

AND THEN THERE WERE NONE

Since the beginnings of life, some animals have successfully fought for survival. Those that were not strong enough, or could not adapt to their environment, did not survive.

Over the centuries, hundreds of animals died out and were replaced by others. But now, many, many animals are disappearing from the earth and they will not be replaced. And that means that in the near future people may never see a living elephant, tiger, or wolf.

Throughout the world, animals are disappearing at an alarming rate. Since 1600, about 120 species of mammals and 162 species of birds have become extinct. In the United States, between 1600 and 1850, only two mammal and three bird species were lost. Since then, however, 57 species of mammal, bird, and fish have been lost forever.

Today, there are about 400 animals in the world that are recognized as "endangered species." They face certain death if something is not done to protect them. In addition to these animals, there are thousands more whose numbers are dwindling. Each year the threatened-species list grows longer.

What is happening to these animals? Why are they disappearing in such great numbers? Hunting and killing is one of the answers. Thousands of years ago, as the human population increased, people swept across new lands in search of food and shelter. As these adventurous hunters and their tribes marched across continents, they killed many of the large mammals that lived in the strange new lands. Eventually the hunting became excessive. This is called overkill, and it means that people destroyed more animals than they needed for survival. Because of overkill, some 33 groups of species disappeared within a few centuries. Among them were the mastodon (an early relative of the elephant), long-necked camel, giant beaver, and saber-toothed tiger.

This was only the beginning. Today, technology has joined humans as a killer of animals. Animal survival in the 20th century depends largely on whether people can use their knowledge more constructively. In a short period of time, human beings have learned to change the environment to suit their own needs. In so doing, they have used too much of the earth's living natural resources. Many of the world's forests have been leveled in search of valuable timber. Wetlands have been drained, and superhighways have been constructed over miles of natural habitat. Spawning grounds have been damaged; oil and chemicals have been spilled into oceans, rivers, and lakes, and have polluted the air. Unspoiled wilderness has almost become a thing of the past.

Many experts believe that because the environment has been altered, thousands of animal species will soon disappear. They will either die because they cannot adapt to the changed environment, or they will move to remote areas that have not yet been touched by people.

The changing environment is not the animals' only enemy. Each year a growing number of hunters kill leopards, ocelots, cheetahs, and tigers for their precious furs. Whales, crocodiles, and turtles are hunted for their skins or shells, for food, or as trophies. Animal collectors are still another danger. Each year they snatch millions of wild animals and fish from their natural habitat, and ship them to zoos and pet dealers throughout the world. Many of the animals die during the long journey from their home in the wilds to the cages of the world's zoos.

In recent years, people concerned with the environment and animal experts have become more and more aware of the dangers to wild animals. Several organizations and governmental agencies, such as the World Wildlife Fund and the International Society for the Protection of Animals, have been established to find ways to protect animal life. With the help of these groups, many of the animals now on the endangered species list are protected by laws.

Unfortunately, the new laws and the wildlife refuges that are being built will come too late for many animals.

THE BLUE WHALE

Modern technology is helping to destroy one of the oldest creatures on earth—the whale. As far back as 2000 B.C., hungry men were killing a few whales with crude harpoons. Because these encounters were usually difficult and dangerous, not more than two whales were killed in a year's time. But eventually large oceangoing ships, with iron harpoons and strong towropes, were being built. Whalers took to the seas in search of giant whales and caught them by the thousands. By 1880, the huge population of whales was greatly reduced.

Today, one of the most threatened whales is the mighty blue whale—the largest creature ever to inhabit the earth. This gigantic mammal, found in all the oceans of the world, is larger than 30 elephants. Between 1930 and 1940 there were over 100,000 of these enormous creatures swimming the oceans. Now only a few thousand remain. The International Whaling Commission has forbidden the killing of the blue whale, but some nations have refused to go along with the ruling.

THE WHITE, OR SQUARE–MOUTHED, RHINOCEROS

Like the lion, antelope, and hippopotamus, the white rhinoceros was once found almost everywhere in Africa. The huge white rhino was regarded by hunters as one of the most dangerous and unpredictable animals in the world. It would often charge from ambush or dash frantically through a campsite, trampling and killing those who were unfortunate enough to be in its way. This danger, however, did not stop the hunters from tracking down and killing the animal. By the end of the 19th century, only about a dozen white rhinos were sheltered in game reserves in what is now the Republic of South Africa. These rhinos were thought to be the last of their kind. But because of people's concern, the white rhinoceros multiplied in such numbers that today a surplus has been exported to Mozambique and Rhodesia, where the animal had been extinct for more than 74 years. But the white rhino is still not completely out of danger. To make sure of its survival, the huge white, or square-mouthed, rhinoceros is currently protected by law.

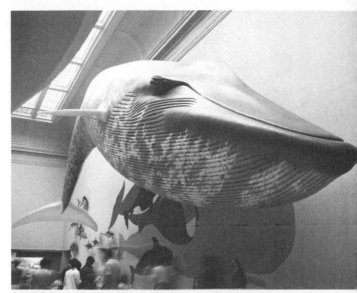

A model of the great blue whale, one of the giants of the world's oceans.

A white rhinoceros and her calf on a game reserve in Africa.

The stork, which often builds nests in chimney tops, is a threatened species in Western Europe.

For hundreds of years timber wolves have been hunted and killed by man.

THE STORK

The stork, Europe's most popular bird, may soon vanish from the skies of Western Europe. During 1934–35, there were nearly 10,300 nesting pairs (male and female) of storks in Sweden, Denmark, Germany, the Netherlands, Switzerland, and Austria. By 1958 the number of birds had dropped to just over 5,000 pairs, and they had disappeared completely from Switzerland and Sweden.

More than one hundred years ago, people helped the stork by clearing the forests to build farms. The thatched roofs and the chimneys of the farmers' cottages served as nesting places for the busy storks. The birds, in turn, aided the farmer by eating the mice, grasshoppers, and caterpillars that destroyed the farmer's crops.

But now the few thousand storks that are left in Western Europe are threatened. Marshlands, which provide the stork with frogs and other food, are being drained. Hard roofs have replaced the thatch that provided the storks with nesting sites. And storks gobble up polluted dead fish or insects poisoned by insecticides.

The greatest threat to the storks, however, is the hunter. Although the bird is protected by law in Western Europe, hunters still hide along the migratory routes and kill many of the birds as they make their yearly flights.

GRAY, OR TIMBER, WOLF AND THE RED WOLF

Gray wolves were once found throughout much of the Northern Hemisphere. But from the moment the Europeans came to America, they have continually destroyed the wolf. And the wolves seldom, if ever, fought back. Now, although the gray wolf is still found over large areas of Canada and northern Asia, and in parts of Europe and northern Mexico, fewer than 100 gray wolves remain in the United States outside Alaska and Minnesota. And though Minnesota has several hundred timber wolves, they are seriously threatened by hunters, trappers, livestock ranchers, and the fur industry. The red wolf, of which only 300 are left in Texas and Louisiana, faces a major problem because it lives almost entirely on private land and feeds on livestock owned by ranchers. So, to preserve the red wolf, the wolves are being "livetrapped" and either taken into captivity or put in an area where there is no private livestock.

The wolves must be saved because they are important in helping to maintain the balance of nature. Not only does the wolf help keep herds of deer, elk, moose, and caribou at desirable population levels, but it also feeds on the potentially harmful rodent and rabbit.

▶ASIAN LIONS

The Asian lion, which once roamed from southern Europe to India, is another animal in serious danger of disappearing from the face of the earth. The 200 or so Asian lions that remain now live in the Gir forest in the Kathiawar peninsula, north of Bombay, India. Plans have been made to build a second refuge near the Gir forest in the hope of increasing the number of lions.

At one time the Asian lion, which differs from its African cousin in its grayer tint and sparser mane, roamed through parts of Iran and Iraq, but it has disappeared from there in recent years. Since the lion's habitat is open grasslands and scrub country, the animal was an easy target for hunters. Now, with open land being taken over for agriculture, the lion's home has been greatly reduced. Domestic livestock are now grazing in areas where wild antelope, deer, and pigs once roamed. And these wild animals were the natural prey of the lions.

▶WILD HORSES

Two million wild horses roamed the American West a century ago. Now, there are fewer than 25,000 mustangs, and these animals are threatened by rustlers, poachers, poor range conditions, and the desire of ranchers to protect grazing land for their cattle.

Each year thousands of wild horses are gathered in roundups. Some are illegally shot, while others are sent to ranches or shipped off to slaughterhouses. For many years airplanes and helicopters have been used to gather the wild herds. In the process, the mustangs are driven for up to 600 miles (966 km.) in temperatures far below the freezing mark. Many of the horses hurtle over cliffs during the long journey, or are shot outright. Several organizations have been formed to stop the capture and slaughter of wild horses.

The few remaining Asian lions can be found only in the Gir forest, in India.

One day soon, wild horses may vanish from the prairies of the American West.

Its valuable skin makes the American crocodile the prey of hunters.

▶ AMERICAN CROCODILE

The American crocodile, which lives in Florida's streams, lakes, and swamps, is an endangered species in the United States, but not elsewhere. The crocodile can still be found in large numbers in Jamaica, Cuba, the Pacific Coast from the mouth of the Gulf of California to Ecuador, and the Atlantic Coast from Yucatán to Colombia.

But the United States is another story. The American crocodile found in southern Florida has been a victim of hunters for many years. Manufacturers were paying high prices for the crocodile skin. The tough skin makes a high-grade leather that is used to make luggage, pocketbooks, belts, and shoes. Also, crocodile musk glands are used in the manufacture of perfume. In many countries of the world, laws have been passed to protect the crocodile. But in the United States the laws have not always been obeyed. So further steps were taken. In some states, the sale of products made from the crocodile has been forbidden.

Because the crocodile is such a valuable creature, hunters shot and killed all they could find. Now, only about 500 crocodiles are left in southern Florida. Although the population is slowly declining, some scientists believe that because it can breed in captivity, the American crocodile will survive.

▶ WHOOPING CRANE

A century ago the whooping crane could be found throughout much of the North American continent. But as people began to build homes in once desolate areas, the cranes began to disappear. Many of the prairie marshes where they once nested in great numbers have been drained, and the crane has had to find a new home.

But the birds faced other difficulties as well. Each spring, whooping cranes migrated from their home on the Gulf coast of Texas to the region of the Great Slave Lake in Alberta, Canada, where they breed. During this flight, many of the cranes were shot. They usually fly high, often out of sight, but sometimes they came within gun range. And even though there were laws to protect the cranes, some hunters mistook them for other fowl.

Today, there are barely more than 50 of the birds left. Although this number is small, it is also encouraging. Just 25 years ago, there were fewer than a dozen whooping cranes. The directors of the Patuxent Wildlife Research Center in Laurel, Maryland, were convinced that the only way to make sure the whooping cranes survived was to take them captive. The center now has seventeen thriving whooping cranes, all of which were hatched in captivity.

The whooping crane has become a symbol of the save-the-wildlife movement.

▶ CHEETAH

At the end of the 19th century, the cheetah roamed from central India through the grasslands of Asia, Arabia, and Africa. Today the cheetah is rarely seen or has disappeared completely in all these areas except for east, central, and south Africa. There are about 15,000 left.

Unlike many other animals, the cheetah has a difficult time getting used to new surroundings. It feeds on small antelopes, like gazelles and impalas. New African cities are claiming a great part of the once wild grasslands, where herds of antelopes grazed. So the cheetah is losing not only a home, but an important food source as well.

Cheetahs, unlike many of their cat cousins, are not secretive in their daily habits. They hunt by day and in open plains. So they are easily spotted by hunters who kill them for their fur, or take them captive. But the cheetah is not the only animal that hunts or roams in open country. And all those that do are running a grave risk.

The list of rare and endangered animal species keeps growing, and in a short time, may well number over 1,000. Almost no animal or bird is safe. People and the environment are threatening them all—from the Asian lion to the Zanzibar red colobus.

Like many other animals, the cheetah has been added to the list of endangered species.

WHAT IS IT?

A long-armed starfish larva. When grown, it will have five arms and be 25 times as large.

An overhead view of a giant clam surrounded by strange underwater formations.

A rear view of a peacock, with his tail feathers elegantly fanned out.

Watch out for the back of this porcupine, or you'll be hit by a tail full of quills.

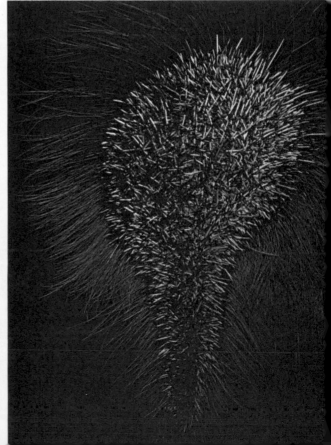

This strange object is a discarded caribou antler that was found in the Arctic. After a period of time it became covered with lichen and took on this odd texture.

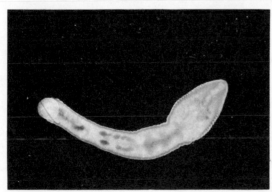

A pond leech.

A leafhopper.

A white jumping spider.

An enlarged view of part of a polychaete worm.

LOVING IS . . .

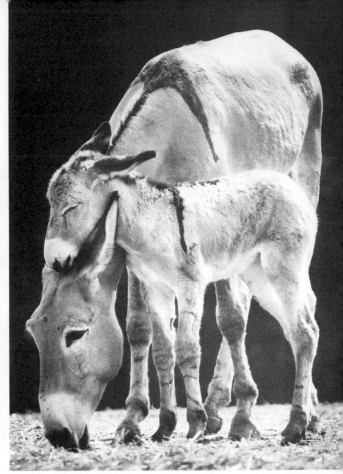

CATS HAVE A NOISY SMILE

Dr. Paul Layhausen of the Max Planck Institute, in West Germany, has been trying to find out what makes cats tick. Or rather purr, for it's through the purr that we really get to know a cat.

He has studied all types of cats, analyzing the purring noises they make and trying to discover the reasons for them. These are not always as obvious as they may seem.

It appears that a cat's purr is rather like a person's smile: It usually means they are happy, friendly, relaxed—though there can be other, less attractive meanings.

An oddly irregular purr can be the sign of what Dr. Layhausen calls a "crazy, mixed-up cat." An older cat, wise and resigned, may be simply playing at being a kitten when he purrs. "That's a sure sign of regression," says Dr. Layhausen.

Some cats purr solely to gain advantage from a human being (usually food or some special privilege) or even from another cat. (It seems there are cats, low down on the feline scale, that will curry favor with a higher-class cat by employing a "snob" or "diplomatic" purr. In fact, there is quite a lot of status seeking in the catty scheme of things.)

A real aristocrat among cats often owns a purr that's different, marking him out from the common herd. Yet at times he will use an ordinary purr to show other cats he's not really stuck-up at all.

If you can't interpret your cat's purr, however, don't worry. According to Dr. Layhausen, many of the variations are put on for special occasions. Most of the time an ordinary, well-fed, well-balanced cat purrs simply out of a lovable mixture of contentment, friendliness, and affection.

These African antelopes are right at home with a pair of African comb ducks.

TORONTO'S NEW ZOO

On August 15, 1974, the people of Toronto were finally able to see what their city's most exciting new attraction was like. It had been planned for and dreamed of for over ten years. The first visitors were not disappointed. For when the gates of the Metro Toronto Zoo opened for the first time, visitors knew at once that they were seeing one of the world's most unusual zoos. Although the formal opening of the zoo was not scheduled until June 1975—and some of the exhibits were still incomplete in 1974—visiting the Metro Toronto Zoo was already an exciting experience.

For a number of years the people responsible for planning zoos have tried to place animals in homelike settings or environments whenever possible. It has been proved that animals in captivity are happier and healthier, and are more likely to reproduce, if they live in something approaching their natural en-

vironment. In many ways the Metro Toronto Zoo has carried that idea further than any other modern zoo. Animals that live close to each other in nature are grouped together at the zoo in surroundings as much like those they would have at home as possible. There are even familiar leaves and plants for the animals to nibble—or trample—if the spirit so moves them. The zoo environments are actually planted with trees and plants from the part of the world that is being reproduced. In fact, Metro Toronto Zoo is almost as interesting to botanists as it is to animal lovers. During the winter months some of the animals must be moved indoors. But even the indoor environments suggest the part of the world the animals come from—they are not at all like ordinary cages. The whole purpose of Metro Toronto Zoo is to bring the visitors and the animals into as close a relationship to

White-tailed gnus outside the African Pavilion.

Boy meets crocodile in the Indo-Malayan Pavilion.

South African fur seals take an afternoon nap.

261

The zebras graze peacefully in an area just outside the African Pavilion.

The Indo-Malayan Pavilion has lush jungle plants.

These wisents are kept in by a water barrier.

Polar bears perform underwater for visitors.   **Congo buffaloes lounge toward their shady pool.**

each other as possible without harming either group.

Because Metro Toronto Zoo has been planned so carefully and is so complex in design, it has taken a long time to build. The first plans for the zoo were begun in 1963. It is, as it nears completion, one of the four largest public zoos in the world, covering some 710 acres (285 hectares). When the zoo is finally completed, it will have animals and plants grouped in several major regional areas: Eurasia, the Americas, Africa, Indo-Malaya, and Australia.

To take a single exhibit area as an example of how the new zoo plan works, let's take a look at the African area. For the animals from the equatorial rain forests of Africa, there is the giant African Pavilion. In addition to all the appropriate plants and greenery, the pavilion has among its animal occupants two young gorillas named Barney and Caroline, mandrills, two kinds of antelopes, pygmy hippos with their own private jungle swimming pool, Congo buffalo, various kinds of monkeys, the marsh mongoose, and bush babies. Various kinds of African fish and aquatic reptiles also inhabit the pavilion—including the monitor lizard, dwarf crocodiles, lungfish, electric catfish, African frogs, and many other strange creatures.

In the outdoor African Paddocks there are penguins, fur seals, baboons, lions, elephants,

and hyraxes. In the African Savannah section there are zebras, white and black rhinos, giraffes, gemsbok, springbok, gnu, hippos, bat-eared foxes, and various kinds of African cranes. All these African animals have heated indoor homes, too—when they need them. And in every other geographical exhibit area, the groupings will be just as rich, exciting, and varied.

Metro Toronto Zoo has been everyone's favorite cause around Toronto. Individuals and organizations have contributed to its building, including business and civic groups of all kinds. And Toronto's young people made a unique contribution to the zoo. School children in and around Toronto contributed to the zoo through Project Noah. This project was named after Noah's famous ark of animals in the Bible. It allowed young people to raise money and then use it to purchase specific animals for the zoo. You can be sure that the young people of Toronto will be making frequent visits to the zoo to see if their own animals are doing well in their fascinating and handsome new homes.

From the time when the very first plans were made for Metro Toronto Zoo, it was everyone's intention that it be a special and unique place. There is every indication, from the response of delighted visitors, that the new zoo is living up to those expectations and will continue to do so as more exhibits open.

COMPUTER CHIMPS

If you have a pet dog, you have probably managed to teach him some tricks. "Beg," you may say, and your dog will sit up and hold out his paws as if begging for food. "Sit" and "Fetch" are other simple commands that the dog has learned to obey.

Beyond getting him to understand these few commands, though, there is not much you can do to get your pet to understand you. Have you ever tried to talk to your dog? He may seem to understand your mood from the tone of your voice, but he certainly doesn't seem to understand the meaning of the words themselves. Language seems far too complicated for him. All he knows are a few commands, a tiny fraction of the many hundreds of words you know. Moreover, you use the words in all sorts of combinations with many different shades of meaning. This is far too complicated for your dog. Talk to him and he only looks at you with a puzzled expression.

Until recently it was generally believed that what is true for your dog is true for all animals. No animal, it was thought, possessed man's ability to communicate through language. Now this view is being challenged.

During the past few years scientists have had surprising success in teaching language to chimpanzees. The animals have actually proved capable of engaging in simple conversations with humans. Since chimps can't talk, the conversations are carried on by means of hand gestures similar to those used by deaf people, or by means of keyboards connected to computers. The chimpanzees have proved themselves so adept at communicating by these means that some scientists wonder whether man can claim to be the only animal that uses language.

▶ WASHOE LEARNS SIGN LANGUAGE

The first success in teaching language to chimpanzees occurred in the late 1960's. Two psychologists at the University of Nevada began to teach the sign language used by deaf people to a chimpanzee named Washoe. Washoe's training began when she was one year old, about the same age at which a human child may utter his or her first words. At first the learning process went slowly, and during the first seven months of training Washoe learned only four signs. Then she began to learn faster. During the next seven months of work she learned nine new words. In a third seven-month period she picked up 21 new signs. By the end of three years of training, Washoe could understand and make the signs for 85 words, and during the following year her vocabulary jumped all the way up to 160 words.

Not only did Washoe learn a lot of words, she also learned how to combine them into sentences. She also was able to make new words out of words she already knew. For example, when she saw a swan for the first time, Washoe invented the term "water-bird." She also proved able to apply words learned in one situation to other situations. Thus, she learned the word "open" in connection with a house door but extended it not only to the doors of refrigerators, cars, and cupboards, but also to the tops of jars. An even more remarkable extension of meaning occurred with the word "dirty." Washoe learned the word originally in reference to soiled objects. But when she came into contact with a nasty rhesus monkey, she began to refer to it as "dirty monkey." Now she uses "dirty" as a kind of swearword, repeating the gesture "dirty, dirty," whenever somebody annoys her.

▶ LANA AND THE COMPUTER

As word of Washoe's success spread, other scientists began to teach languages to chimpanzees. Today this work involves a half dozen or more chimps in various research centers around the United States. In 1974, one of them, Lucy, became the first chimpanzee ever to grant an interview. During her interview Lucy handed a comb to the reporter and asked him to comb her. Later the reporter asked Lucy if she wanted to go outside. Lucy's answer, in sign language, was, "Outside, no. Want food, apple."

In addition to teaching sign language, scientists are also training chimpanzees to communicate by means of a computer. Using a computer forces the animal to be more precise in its use of language than it has to be in order to communicate through sign language.

Lana at the computer.

At the Yerkes Primate Research Center in Atlanta, Georgia, a chimp named Lana sits in front of a computer keyboard and punches the plastic keys. Each key has a symbol on it, and each symbol stands for a word. Rules of grammar and usage are programed into the computer, and Lana has to follow them in order to get the computer to accept her messages. For example, suppose Lana wants milk. If she pushes the buttons that say, "Please, machine, give milk," the computer will fill up a container with milk. But if Lana says, "Please, machine, make milk," the com-

puter will reject the message. Lana has even learned to use punctuation. When making a statement, she uses a period at the end. When asking a question, she uses a question mark.

Where will all this lead? Some scientists think that methods used with chimpanzees can be applied to children with severe learning problems. Another possibility is that intelligent chimps like Lana can actually work with scientists to help them understand the behavior of other chimps.

BENJAMIN HAIMOWITZ
Science writer

The llama, a relative of the camel, is thought to have migrated from North America to South America. It is a beast of burden and is raised for its fleece.

ANIMALS OF SOUTH AMERICA

South America has the most varied animal population of any continent. It also has some of the most unusual animals on earth. For—like Australia, which also has odd animals but fewer of them—South America was an island when the Age of Mammals began. Cut off from the interconnected continents of Europe, Africa, Asia, and North America for some 60,000,000 years, it existed as a world apart. When a land bridge to North America was established, South America encountered the animals of the outside world for the first time. Over the centuries, many of South America's native species have died out. But a few survived. And it can truly be said that they are unlike any other creatures on earth.

This little, wide-eyed opossum is no bigger than your fist. Opossums are the only marsupials that live outside of Australia.

The alpaca, like the llama, is found only in the Andes. Both animals were used by South American Indians even before the Spaniards came.

The sloth, inching its way up a tree, seems so lazy that its name is a synonym for laziness. Sloths, which originated in South America, like the Amazon rain forests.

This jaguar is not too far from the Amazon River. Invaders from the north, jaguars crossed the land bridge of Panama millions of years ago.

The armor-plated armadillo curls up inside its armor when attacked. The armadillo originated in South America, but now inhabits the warmer parts of both Americas.

This peculiar-looking animal is a manatee, or sea cow. Manatees are mammals that came from the north and now live in the coastal waters of tropical regions.

The glant anteater has a snout as long as its tail, the better to eat ants with. It has always lived in the dry South American grasslands where there are lots of anthills.

ANIMALS
IN THE NEWS

Right: These Mongolian wild horses are among the rarest animals in the world. They made their debut at the Bronx Zoo, in New York, when the zoo opened its Rare Animal Range Exhibits in June. Known as *Equus Przewalskii* to experts, the Mongolian wild horse is the only true wild horse in existence. Far Right: A chestnut colt gets to know his mother shortly after being born in November. But this is no ordinary little colt. He has a very famous father—Secretariat, 1973's Triple Crown winner—and is Secretariat's first offspring.

No, it's not a bum steer—it's a beefalo. At least that's what this extraordinary cross between a cow and a buffalo is called. The meat of this hybrid, the result of 17 years of experimentation, tastes like beef but is higher in protein and lower in fat.

A baby Cape hartebeest and its mother. Born on Mother's Day in Georgia, it is one of the few of these rare African antelopes to have been born in captivity.

A Sinai, or Palestinian, leopard was photographed for the first time ever in November, 1974. It had long been feared that the animal was extinct. Then a photographer, Giyora Ilany, took pictures of one in the Israeli hills near the Dead Sea—proof positive that the big cats still exist.

WORLD OF SPORTS

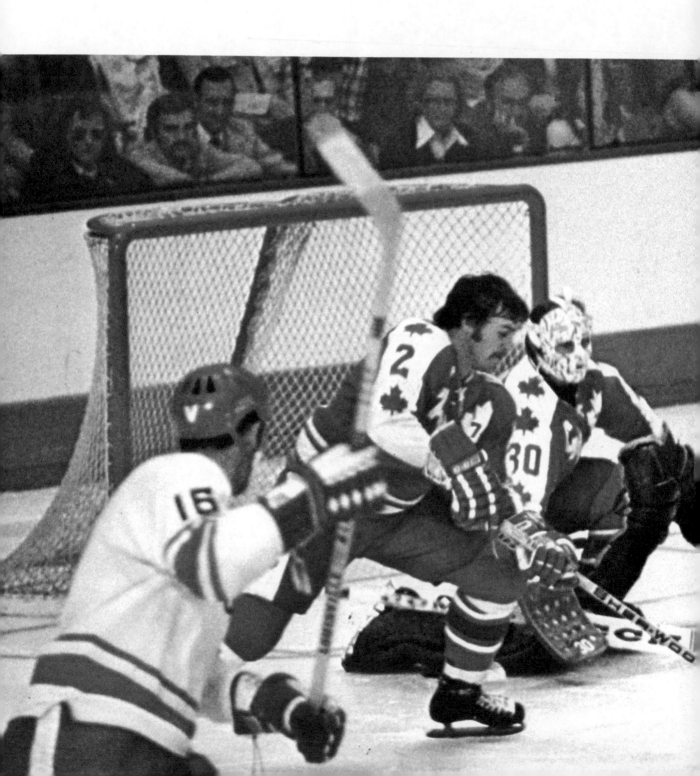

Team Canada and the Soviet Union battle for the puck.

"Safe!" yells the umpire as Steve Yeager of the Los Angeles Dodgers slides into second during a World Series game against the Oakland Athletics.

BASEBALL

Baseball glory was shared by Hank Aaron and the Oakland Athletics in the 1974 baseball season.

The 40-year-old Aaron, in his 21st year in baseball, remained typically calm and cool as he approached a baseball record that most people once thought beyond reach—Babe Ruth's 714 career home runs. On April 4, in Cincinnati's Riverfront Stadium, on his first swing, Aaron homered, tying Ruth's record. A few days later, on April 8, in the Atlanta Braves' first home game, Aaron surpassed the record with his 715th home run. By the end of the season the right-handed slugger had hit a total of 733 home runs. Despite a previously announced intention to retire, Aaron signed a two-year contract with the Milwaukee Brewers of the American League, thereby returning to the city where he had begun his major-league career. Aaron's powerful bat is expected to be used in the designated hitter's position.

The Oakland Athletics, in the first all-California World Series, won four out of five games from the Los Angeles Dodgers to achieve their third straight baseball championship. They thus became the sport's dominant team, inviting comparison with the old New York Yankees, who had won championships with machine-like regularity. The A's were outhit in the World Series as they gained three of their four wins by narrow 3–2 margins. But spectacular defense and pitching stopped the strong-hitting Dodgers. Oakland's star relief pitcher, Rollie Fingers, who appeared in four games, was voted the most valuable performer of the series.

In the regular season Oakland led the Western Division of the American League for the entire route. But in the Eastern Division the New York Yankees and the Baltimore Orioles fought it out right down to the last days of the campaign. The Orioles won with a spectacular finish, winning their last eight games, and 27 games out of 33, ending two games ahead of the Yankees.

In the playoff for the pennant, the Orioles defeated Oakland in the opening game; then the A's won three games in a row. The last game was an unusual contest in which the winners had eleven walks and only one hit.

In the National League, the Dodgers led the Western Division by a secure margin until the last stages of the race, then held off the Cincinnati Reds to win by four games. In the Eastern Division, the battle went down to the wire, the Pittsburgh Pirates emerging with a one-and-a-half game edge over the St. Louis Cardinals. In the playoff, the Dodgers duplicated the performance of the Oakland Athletics by winning three out of four games from Pittsburgh.

Hank Aaron's pursuit of Babe Ruth's record almost overshadowed another spectacular record-breaking effort in the 1974 season. Lou Brock, 36-year-old outfielder for the St. Louis Cardinals, stole 118 bases to break Maury Wills's twelve-year-old record of 104.

When honors were awarded after the season had ended, Jim "Catfish" Hunter of the Oakland Athletics and Mike Marshall of the Los Angeles Dodgers were voted the Cy Young awards for the best pitchers. Marshall, who appeared in a record-breaking 106 games, was the first relief pitcher to win the award. Most Valuable Player awards went to Steve Garvey of the Dodgers and Jeff Burroughs of the Texas Rangers.

Batting honors were won by Rod Carew in the American League and Ralph Garr in the National League. Carew, of the Minnesota Twins, captured his third consecutive batting crown with a .364 average. Garr, of the Atlanta Braves, won with a .353 mark.

Hank Aaron hits No. 715, breaking Babe Ruth's career home-run record.
Date: April 8, 1974
Site: Atlanta Stadium
Inning: Fourth
Opposing pitcher: Al Downing, L.A. Dodgers
Distance: about 400 feet (120 meters)
Type of pitch: Fastball

1974 WORLD SERIES RESULTS

		R	H	E	Winning/Losing Pitcher
1	Oakland	3	6	2	Fingers
	Los Angeles	2	11	1	Messersmith
2	Los Angeles	3	6	1	Sutton
	Oakland	2	6	0	Blue
3	Oakland	3	5	2	Hunter
	Los Angeles	2	7	2	Downing
4	Oakland	5	7	0	Holtzman
	Los Angeles	2	7	1	Messersmith
5	Oakland	3	6	1	Odom
	Los Angeles	2	5	1	Marshall

FINAL MAJOR LEAGUE STANDINGS

AMERICAN LEAGUE

Eastern Division

	W	L	Pct.	GB
Baltimore	91	71	.562	—
New York	89	73	.549	2
Boston	84	78	.519	7
Cleveland	77	85	.475	14
Milwaukee	76	86	.469	15
Detroit	72	90	.444	19

Western Division

	W	L	Pct.	GB
*Oakland	90	72	.556	—
Texas	84	76	.525	5
Minnesota	82	80	.506	8
Chicago	80	80	.500	9
Kansas City	77	85	.475	13
California	68	94	.420	22

*pennant winners

NATIONAL LEAGUE

Eastern Division

	W	L	Pct.	GB
Pittsburgh	88	74	.543	—
St. Louis	86	75	.534	1½
Philadelphia	80	82	.494	8
Montreal	79	82	.491	8½
New York	71	91	.438	17
Chicago	66	96	.407	22

Western Division

	W	L	Pct.	GB
*Los Angeles	102	60	.630	—
Cincinnati	98	64	.605	4
Atlanta	88	74	.543	14
Houston	81	81	.500	21
San Francisco	72	90	.444	30
San Diego	60	102	.370	42

MAJOR LEAGUE LEADERS

BATTING
(415 or more at bats)

AMERICAN LEAGUE

	G	AB	H	Pct.
Carew, Minnesota	153	599	218	.364
Hargrove, Texas	131	415	134	.323
Orta, Chicago	139	525	166	.316
McRae, Kansas City	148	539	166	.308
Piniella, New York	140	518	158	.305
Maddox, New York	137	466	141	.303
Burroughs, Texas	152	554	167	.301
Randle, Texas	151	521	157	.301
Yastrzemski, Boston	148	515	155	.301
Allen, Chicago	128	462	139	.301

NATIONAL LEAGUE

	G	AB	H	Pct.
Garr, Atlanta	143	606	214	.353
Oliver, Pittsburgh	147	617	198	.321
Gross, Houston	156	589	185	.314
Buckner, Los Angeles	145	580	182	.314
Madlock, Chicago	128	453	142	.313
Zisk, Pittsburgh	149	536	168	.313
Garvey, Los Angeles	156	642	200	.312
Smith, St. Louis	143	517	160	.309
McBride, St. Louis	150	559	173	.309
Brock, St. Louis	153	635	194	.306

PITCHING

	W	L	ERA
Hunter, Oakland, AL	25	12	2.49
Jenkins, Texas, AL	25	12	2.82
Ryan, California, AL	22	16	2.87
Tiant, Boston, AL	22	13	2.92
Cuellar, Baltimore, AL	22	10	3.11
Busby, Kansas City, AL	22	14	3.39
Perry, G., Cleveland, AL	21	13	2.51
Kaat, Chicago, AL	21	13	2.95
Niekro, Atlanta, NL	20	13	2.38
Messersmith, Los Angeles, NL	20	6	2.59
Wood, Chicago, AL	20	19	3.59

HOME RUNS

	HR
Schmidt, Philadelphia, NL	36
Bench, Cincinnati, NL	33
Wynn, Los Angeles, NL	32
Allen, Chicago, AL	32
Jackson, Oakland, AL	29
Perez, Cincinnati, NL	28
Cedeno, Houston, NL	26
Tenace, Oakland, AL	26
Darwin, Minnesota, AL	25
Burroughs, Texas, AL	25

East (Kaohiung, Taiwan) takes on West (Red Bluff, California) in the Little League World Series.

LITTLE LEAGUE BASEBALL

For the fourth consecutive year, and for the fifth time in six years, the Little League World Series was won by a team from Taiwan. The team, from the city of Kaohiung, swept the tournament at Williamsport, Pennsylvania, with three overwhelming triumphs. The championship final resulted in a 12-1 victory for Taiwan over Red Bluff, California. In reaching the final, Taiwan had achieved easy success over Tallmadge, Ohio (11-0) and New Haven, Connecticut (16-0).

In the fifth inning of the final game Red Bluff scored the only run of the series against Taiwan. This ended Taiwan's string of 45 innings without giving up a run, over a three-year period of world series play. Twelve-year-old Lin Wen-hsiung, the Taiwanese pitcher, was the most valuable player. In addition to pitching a one-hit shutout in the opening series contest, and a two-hitter in the last game, he walloped two home runs in the last game. This brought Taiwan's home run total to five during the series, tying a Little League World Series record.

Little League baseball underwent major changes during the year. Early in the summer officials of Little League Baseball, Inc., regulating the play of 2,500,000 boys in 32 countries, announced that they would permit girls to play. The decision ended a two-year controversy that had begun in Hoboken, New Jersey, when Little League officials declared that twelve-year-old Maria Pepe could not play on the local team. The threat of court action eventually ended the sex discrimination. This was made official in December when President Gerald Ford signed legislation to admit girls into Little League.

The most unexpected change occurred in November. Little League Baseball, Inc., announced that the World Series would be limited in the future to U.S. teams. Foreign teams would not be permitted to play. No official reason was given for the decision.

John Havlicek wheels with the ball past Kareem Abdul-Jabbar in an NBA championship game.

BASKETBALL

Professional basketball produced two major surprises during the 1973–74 season. The first was that the Boston Celtics won the National Basketball Association (NBA) championship, and the second was that the New York Nets achieved success in the American Basketball Association (ABA).

Boston won four out of seven games from the Milwaukee Bucks in the NBA tournament. The seventh and decisive game, played in the Milwaukee arena, was won by a 102–87 score. For the Celtics, coached by Tom Heinsohn and led by John Havlicek and Dave Cowens, it was a return to the days when Bill Russell had been their star performer and they had been perennial champions. Russell had retired after the 1968–69 season, and in the thirteen years before that, the Celtics had won 11 titles.

It was thought that the New York Nets were too young and too inexperienced a team to take the ABA championship. But with the help of Julius Erving the Nets beat the Utah Stars in four of the five games in the final series to gain the championship. Erving also was the leading scorer in the league during the regular season, as he led New York to its division title.

College basketball provided still more surprises. The first occurred in regular season play, when Notre Dame snapped UCLA's 88-game winning streak. Then, after having won the National Collegiate Athletic Association (NCAA) title seven consecutive times, and nine times in the last ten years, UCLA was dethroned by North Carolina State University. The team that is known as the Wolfpack eliminated UCLA, 80–77, in double overtime in the semifinal. It then went on to defeat Marquette, 76–64, in the NCAA championship final. North Carolina State's David Thompson was named the outstanding player in the NCAA tournament.

Bill Walton, UCLA's All-American center, ended a brilliant three-year collegiate career. He joined the professional ranks by signing a contract for several million dollars with Portland, Oregon, of the NBA.

In the National Invitation Tournament (NIT), second in prestige to the NCAA competition, Purdue University defeated Utah in the final, 87–81. Utah had reached the final round of the NIT by walloping Boston College, 117–93. At the same time, Purdue had defeated Jacksonville, 78–63. The Purdue-Utah contest was a classic confrontation between a fine defensive team—Purdue—and a high-scoring team—the Utes. Mike Sojourner, a sophomore from Utah, was selected as the most valuable player of the tournament.

FINAL NBA STANDINGS

EASTERN CONFERENCE
Atlantic Division

	W	L	Pct.
Boston	56	26	.683
New York	49	33	.598
Buffalo	42	40	.512
Philadelphia	25	57	.305

Central Division

	W	L	Pct.
Capital	47	35	.573
Atlanta	35	47	.427
Houston	32	50	.390
Cleveland	29	53	.354

WESTERN CONFERENCE
Midwest Division

	W	L	Pct.
Milwaukee	59	23	.720
Chicago	54	28	.659
Detroit	52	30	.634
K.C.-Omaha	33	49	.402

Pacific Division

	W	L	Pct.
Los Angeles	47	35	.573
Golden State	44	38	.537
Seattle	36	46	.439
Phoenix	30	52	.366
Portland	27	55	.329

NBA Championship: Boston

FINAL ABA STANDINGS

East Division

	W	L	Pct.
New York	55	29	.655
Kentucky	53	31	.631
Carolina	47	37	.560
Virginia	28	56	.333
Memphis	21	63	.250

West Division

	W	L	Pct.
Utah	51	32	.607
Indiana	46	38	.548
San Antonio	45	39	.536
San Diego	38	47	.447
Denver	37	48	.435

ABA Championship: New York

COLLEGE BASKETBALL

Conference	Winner
Atlantic Coast	North Carolina State
Big Eight	Kansas
Big Ten	Michigan
Ivy League	Pennsylvania
Mid-American	Ohio
Missouri Valley	Louisville
Pacific Eight	UCLA
Southeastern	Vanderbilt
Southern	Furman
Southwest	Texas
West Coast Athletic	San Francisco
Western Athletic	New Mexico
Yankee	Massachusetts

NCAA: North Carolina State

National Invitation Tournament: Purdue

North Carolina State's David Thompson grabs a rebound in the NCAA semifinals against UCLA.

279

"Touchdown!" signals the umpire as the Pittsburgh Steelers score against Oakland to take the AFC championship.

FOOTBALL

Events in the National Football League (NFL) followed a familiar pattern in 1974. The Miami Dolphins, who had won the two preceding Super Bowl games, made a sputtering start, but completed the regular season with an 11–3 record to capture their fifth consecutive Eastern Division title in the American Conference. The other division winners in the same conference were Pittsburgh (Central) with a 10–3–1 total, and Oakland (Western) with a 12–2 season, the best in the entire league. The Buffalo Bills, led by the great O. J. Simpson, gained the playoffs with the best record among runner-up clubs, 9–5. When the dust of the playoffs had settled, Pittsburgh emerged as the winner, defeating Oakland, 24–13, for the American Conference title.

In the National Conference, there was one surprising result. The St. Louis Cardinals captured the Eastern Division championship, for the first time ever, with a 10–4 record that was equaled by the Washington Redskins. The Cardinals earned first place in the divisional competition but both teams advanced to the post-season play, where they were joined by Minnesota (Central) and Los Angeles (Western), each with a 10–4 record. For the Vikings, it was the sixth time they had won their divisional title in the last seven seasons. In the National Conference championship game, Minnesota defeated Los Angeles, 14–10.

In Super Bowl IX, the Pittsburgh Steelers lived up to their billing as the favored team by defeating the Minnesota Vikings, 16–6.

A new professional circuit, the World Football League (WFL), was launched during the year, and made inroads in the talent of the establishment by signing star players, notably Larry Csonka, Jim Kiick, and Paul Warfield of the Miami Dolphins. Csonka, Kiick, and

Warfield were scheduled to join the new league in 1975. The WFL had financial troubles throughout the season, and its future seems bleak, but the new league staged a championship game in which the Birmingham Americans defeated the Florida Blazers, 22–21.

Among the colleges, the universities of Oklahoma and Alabama were the nation's leaders with identical 11–0 records. Alabama went to the Orange Bowl for a New Year's engagement with Notre Dame. The result was an upset victory for Notre Dame over Alabama, 13–11. It was the final contest as head coach of the Irish for Ara Parseghian, who resigned after eleven years. In his final campaign, Parseghian coached the team to a 9–2 record. During his stay at South Bend the overall tally was 94–17–4, figures that were in the tradition of Knute Rockne and Frank Leahy, legendary Notre Dame coaches.

Ohio State (10–1) edged Michigan, 12–10, in their battle for the Big Ten title, and the Buckeyes were matched in the Rose Bowl with Southern California (9–1–1). The outcome was close, with USC defeating Ohio State, 18–17. Baylor (8–3) became the Southwest Conference champion for the first time and was paired in the Cotton Bowl with Penn State (9–2). Baylor was overwhelmed by Penn State, 41–20. In the Sugar Bowl, Nebraska beat Florida, 13–10.

L. A.'s Jim Bertelsen is pounced on by the Vikings in the NFC championship game.

The play that won the Rose Bowl game for USC— a 2-point conversion pass against Ohio State.

COLLEGE FOOTBALL

Conference	Winner
Atlantic Coast	Maryland
Big Eight	Oklahoma
Big Ten	Ohio State; Michigan (tied)
Ivy League	Harvard; Yale (tied)
Mid-American	Miami
Pacific Eight	Southern California
Southeastern	Alabama
Southern	Virginia Military
Southwest	Baylor
Western Athletic	Brigham Young
Yankee	Maine; Massachusetts (tied)

Heisman Trophy: Archie Griffin, Ohio State

Archie Griffin, Ohio State's Heisman Trophy winner, in action against Indiana.

FINAL NFL STANDINGS

AMERICAN CONFERENCE

Eastern Division

	W	L	T	Pct.	PF	PA
Miami	11	3	0	.786	327	216
Buffalo	9	5	0	.643	264	244
N.Y. Jets	7	7	0	.500	279	300
New England	7	7	0	.500	348	289
Baltimore	2	12	0	.143	190	329

Central Division

	W	L	T	Pct.	PF	PA
Pittsburgh	10	3	1	.750	305	189
Cincinnati	7	7	0	.500	283	259
Houston	7	7	0	.500	236	282
Cleveland	4	10	0	.286	251	344

Western Division

	W	L	T	Pct.	PF	PA
Oakland	12	2	0	.857	355	228
Denver	7	6	1	.536	302	294
Kansas City	5	9	0	.357	233	293
San Diego	5	9	0	.357	212	285

Conference Champion: Pittsburgh

NATIONAL CONFERENCE

Eastern Division

	W	L	T	Pct.	PF	PA
St. Louis	10	4	0	.714	285	218
Washington	10	4	0	.714	320	196
Dallas	8	6	0	.571	297	235
Philadelphia	7	7	0	.500	242	217
N.Y. Giants	2	12	0	.143	195	299

Central Division

	W	L	T	Pct.	PF	PA
Minnesota	10	4	0	.714	310	195
Detroit	7	7	0	.500	256	270
Green Bay	6	8	0	.429	210	206
Chicago	4	10	0	.286	152	279

Western Division

	W	L	T	Pct.	PF	PA
Los Angeles	10	4	0	.714	263	181
San Francisco	6	8	0	.429	226	236
New Orleans	5	9	0	.357	166	263
Atlanta	3	11	0	.214	111	271

Conference Champion: Minnesota

1975 Super Bowl Winner: Pittsburgh

The first goal of the World Cup final between the Netherlands and West Germany is scored by the Netherlands in the first minute of play.

SOCCER

To the dismay of a favored team from the Netherlands, and to the delight of 80,000 roaring spectators in Munich's Olympic Stadium, West Germany won the World Cup in soccer in 1974. The result was especially gratifying because the West German squad had fallen short of the honor in its two preceding bids for the cup—it had been beaten by England in the 1966 final, and by Italy in the 1970 semifinal.

In defeating the Dutch, 2-1, for the World Cup, the West Germans topped a number of recent successes in international competition. In 1972 they captured the European Nations Cup, and before the World Cup play in 1974 they defeated Atlético de Madrid for the European Champions Cup.

In the matches leading up to the final at Munich, the Dutch were a powerful attacking force. They had beaten the Argentine entry, 4-0, and had eliminated a Brazilian team that played with tremendous violence. Since West Germany reached the final by only a 1-0 margin over Poland, the Netherlands was the strong favorite to take the trophy home.

A Dutch triumph appeared even more likely when they gained a 1-0 lead on a penalty kick after only one minute of play. A penalty kick by the West Germans evened the match at 1-1, and then the veteran Gerd Müller hooked the ball into the net, which put the home team ahead 2-1. Throughout the second half, the West Germans mounted a spectacular defense. By the end of the game, the Dutch had not scored since that first minute of play.

That important goal made by Müller may have been the last he will score for West Germany, for he indicated that he would soon retire. He will definitely be on the sidelines when the West Germans defend the championship in 1978, when World Cup soccer will be played in Buenos Aires, Argentina.

GOLF

Gary Player, capturing the 1974 British Open.

Gary Player of South Africa captured two of the four major golf tournaments in 1974, the Masters and the British Open. It was his second victory in the Masters and his third in the British Open.

The other two major tournaments, the U.S. Open and the Professional Golfers' Association (PGA) championship, were won by Hale Irwin and Lee Trevino, respectively. For Irwin, a former University of Colorado football player, the U.S. Open was his first major triumph.

The most spectacular performer of the year was Johnny Miller, a 27-year-old Californian. By October, Miller had finished first in eight tournaments on the professional tour. At that point, he had accumulated $346,933 in prize money, surpassing the single-season record of $320,542 established by Jack Nicklaus in 1972.

In women's golf, Sandra Haynie won the U.S. Open and, for the second time, the Ladies PGA championship.

PROFESSIONAL

	Individual
Masters	Gary Player, South Africa
U.S. Open	Hale Irwin, U.S.
Canadian Open	Bobby Nichols, U.S.
British Open	Gary Player, South Africa
PGA	Lee Trevino, U.S.
World Series of Golf	Lee Trevino, U.S.
U.S. Women's Open	Sandra Haynie, U.S.
Ladies PGA	Sandra Haynie, U.S.
	Team
World Cup	South Africa

AMATEUR

	Individual
U.S. Amateur	Jerry Pate, U.S.
U.S. Women's Amateur	Cynthia Hill, U.S.
British Amateur	Trevor Homer, Great Britain
Canadian Amateur	Doug Roxburgh, Canada
	Team
Curtis Cup	United States

The Soviet Union versus Team Canada: The Russians took the series of games by winning four, losing one, and tying three.

HOCKEY

With two major leagues in existence—the National Hockey League (NHL) and the World Hockey Association (WHA)—the 1973–74 hockey season resulted in two spectacular climaxes. The Philadelphia Flyers captured the historic Stanley Cup, the symbol of supremacy in the National Hockey League. Philadelphia had not had a winner in a major team competition for many years. Philadelphia also became the first expansion team (a new team) to win in a league dominated by the established clubs—mainly the Montreal Canadiens and the Boston Bruins. The Flyers, coached by Fred Shero, had the satisfaction of winning the final series from the Bruins, four games to two. The winning game for the Philadelphians was a 1–0 decision in which the lone goal was made by Rick MacLeish in the first period.

Bernie Parent, the goalie whose superb performance prevented the high-powered Bruins from scoring, was chosen most valuable player in Stanley Cup play. Ironically, Parent and MacLeish had once been members of the Boston club and had been traded away.

During the regular season Boston and Philadelphia had led their divisions—the Bruins in the East, with Phil Esposito and the celebrated Bobby Orr as the league's top scorers, and the Flyers in the West, with Bobby Clarke and MacLeish as their pacemakers. In the preliminary playoffs, Philadelphia survived a difficult semifinal struggle, defeating the New York Rangers, four games to three. Boston eliminated the Chicago Black Hawks, four games to two.

In the recently organized World Hockey Association, 46-year-old Gordie Howe came out of retirement to help the Houston Aeros in their successful bid for the Avco World Trophy. The Avco trophy is the new circuit's equivalent of the Stanley Cup. The Aeros reached the WHA championship series after finishing first in the West Division. But their opponents in the finals, the Chicago Cougars, had come through the playoffs after a fourth-place finish in the East. The series for the title resulted in a four-game sweep for Houston, in which only the opening game was close (3–2).

Gordie Howe had last won a championship in 1955 when he was with the Detroit Red Wings of the NHL. He came out of retirement primarily to play with his sons Mark and Marty—a situation that was unique in the history of professional sports.

The most exciting event in international hockey in 1974 was the series of games played between Team Canada and the Soviet Union hockey team. The Russians defeated the Canadian team, composed of players from the World Hockey Association, winning four games, losing one, and tying three. It was the second meeting between the two teams, Team Canada having won the first series in 1972. During that series, Team Canada had won four games, lost two, and tied one.

FINAL WHA STANDINGS

East Division

	W	L	T	Pts.
New England	43	31	4	90
Toronto	41	33	4	86
Cleveland	37	32	9	83
Chicago	38	35	5	81
Quebec	38	36	4	80
New Jersey	32	42	4	68

West Division

	W	L	T	Pts.
Houston	48	25	5	101
Minnesota	44	32	2	90
Edmonton	38	37	3	79
Winnipeg	34	39	5	73
Vancouver	27	50	1	55
Los Angeles	25	53	0	50

Avco World Trophy: Houston

OUTSTANDING PLAYERS

Scorer	Mike Walton, Minnesota
Rookie	Mark Howe, Houston
Goalie	Don McLeod, Houston
Most Valuable Player	Gordie Howe, Houston
Sportsmanship	Ralph Backstrom, Chicago
Defenseman	Pat Stapleton, Chicago

Gordie Howe (left) and his son Marty (no. 3) helped the Aeros beat the Cougars.

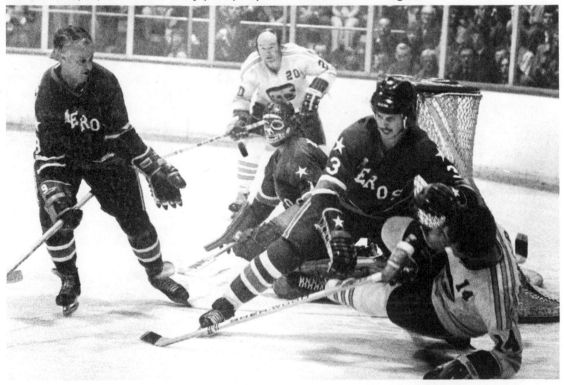

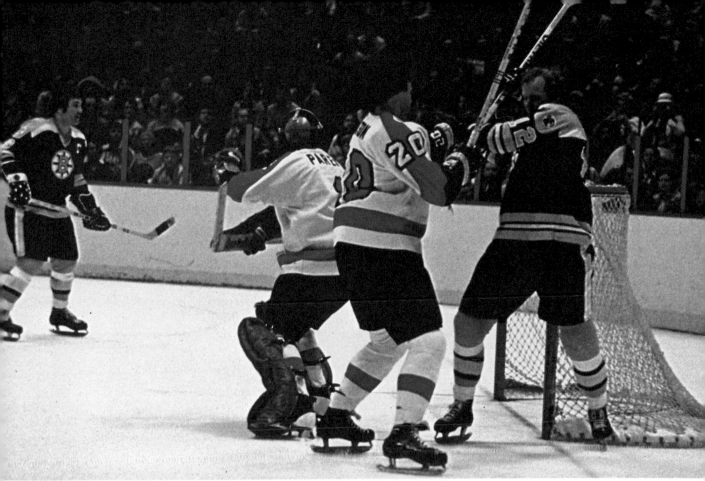

The Boston Bruins battle it out with the Philadelphia Flyers during a Stanley Cup game. The Flyers took the series four games to two.

FINAL NHL STANDINGS

East Division

	W	L	T	Pts.
Boston	52	17	9	113
Montreal	45	24	9	99
N.Y. Rangers	40	24	14	94
Toronto	35	27	16	86
Buffalo	32	34	12	76
Detroit	29	39	10	68
Vancouver	24	44	11	59
N.Y. Islanders	19	41	18	56

West Division

	W	L	T	Pts.
Philadelphia	50	16	12	112
Chicago	41	14	23	105
Los Angeles	33	33	12	78
Atlanta	30	34	14	74
Pittsburgh	28	41	9	65
St. Louis	26	40	12	64
Minnesota	23	38	17	63
California	13	54	10	36

Stanley Cup: Philadelphia

OUTSTANDING PLAYERS

Ross Trophy (scorer)	Phil Esposito, Boston
Calder Trophy (rookie)	Denis Potvin, N.Y. Islanders
Vezina Trophy (goalie)	Tony Esposito, Chicago and Bernie Parent, Philadelphia
Hart Trophy (most valuable player)	Phil Esposito, Boston
Lady Byng Trophy (sportsmanship)	Johnny Bucyk, Boston
Norris Trophy (defenseman)	Bobby Orr, Boston
Conn Smythe Trophy (Stanley Cup play)	Bernie Parent, Philadelphia

Irina Rodnina and Alexander Zaitsev—Russian figure skating champions.

Gustavo Thoeni (*rear*) skied to victory in the first Nations' World Series of Skiing.

ICE SKATING

FIGURE SKATING

World Championships

Men	Jan Hoffmann, East Germany
Women	Christine Errath, East Germany
Pairs	Irina Rodnina/Alexander Zaitsev, U.S.S.R.
Dance	Ludmila Pakhomova/Alexander Gorshkov, U.S.S.R.

United States Championships

Men	Gordon McKellen
Women	Dorothy Hamill
Pairs	Melissa Militano/Johnny Johns
Dance	Colleen O'Connor/Jim Millns

SPEED SKATING

World Championships

Men	Sten Stensen, Norway
Women	Atje Keulen-Deelstra, Netherlands

SKIING

WORLD CUP CHAMPIONSHIPS

Men	Piero Gros, Italy
Women	Annemarie Proell, Austria

NATIONS' WORLD SERIES OF SKIING

Men's Individual	Gustavo Thoeni, Italy
Women's Individual	Annemarie Proell, Austria
Over-all Team	Austria

U.S. ALPINE CHAMPIONSHIPS

Men

Giant Slalom	Bob Cochran, U.S.
Slalom	Cary Adgate, U.S.

Women

Giant Slalom	Marilyn Cochran, U.S.
Slalom	Susie Patterson, U.S.

East Germany's Ulrike Tauber set world records in the 200- and 400-meter individual medleys.

SWIMMING

WORLD SWIMMING RECORDS SET IN 1974		
EVENT	**HOLDER**	**TIME**
	Men	
200-meter freestyle	Tim Shaw, U.S.	1:51.66
400-meter freestyle	Tim Shaw, U.S.	3:54.69
800-meter freestyle	Steve Holland, Australia	8:15.88
1,500-meter freestyle	Tim Shaw, U.S.	15:31.75
100-meter breaststroke	John Hencken, U.S.	1:03.88
200-meter breaststroke	John Hencken, U.S.	2:18.21
200-meter individual medley	David Wilkie, Scotland	2:06.32
	Steve Furness, U.S.	2:06.32
400-meter individual medley	Andras Hargitay, Hungary	4:28.89
	Women	
100-meter freestyle	Kornelia Ender, E. Germany	0:56.96
200-meter freestyle	Shirley Babashoff, U.S.	2:02.94
400-meter freestyle	Shirley Babashoff, U.S.	4:15.77
800-meter freestyle	Jo Harshbarger, U.S.	8:47.50
1,500-meter freestyle	Jenny Turrall, Australia	16:33.95
100-meter breaststroke	Renate Vogel, E. Germany	1:12.28
200-meter breaststroke	Carla Linke, E. Germany	2:34.99
100-meter butterfly	Rosemarie Kother, E. Germany	1:01.88
100-meter backstroke	Ulrike Richter, E. Germany	1:02.98
200-meter backstroke	Ulrike Richter, E. Germany	2:17.35
200-meter individual medley	Ulrike Tauber, E. Germany	2:18.97
400-meter individual medley	Ulrike Tauber, E. Germany	4:52.42

Jimmy and Chris—champs at Wimbledon.

TENNIS

Tennis in 1974 was primarily a love story. It involved 21-year-old Jimmy Connors and his 19-year-old fiancée, Chris Evert, and their fabulous successes on the tennis courts of the United States and Europe.

The couple's major triumph during the year was achieved in the world's most prestigious tennis competition, at Wimbledon, England, in June. Jimmy and Chris captured the men's and women's singles, respectively. In their final matches they beat their foes in straight sets. Connors defeated the 39-year-old Australian Ken Rosewall, and Evert beat Olga Morozova. Morozova was the first Soviet woman player ever to reach the Wimbledon final. In a quarterfinal match, Morozova had eliminated Billie Jean King, winner of five previous Wimbledon titles.

By the time Chris and Jimmy reached the U.S. Open at Forest Hills, Long Island, in September, Chris had won 56 straight matches and ten consecutive tournaments, including the South African, French, and Italian championships, as well as Wimbledon. Together, they had earned more than $300,000 in purses. But Chris's chain of victories was broken in the semifinal by the Australian Evonne Goolagong. She, in turn, was beaten for the championship by Billie Jean King in an exciting three-set contest, 2–6, 6–3, 7–5.

Connors, however, added to his success at the U.S. Open. He defeated Rosewall, the same finalist he had faced at Wimbledon. The scores, 6–1, 6–0, 6–1, represented the most one-sided final in the long history of the Forest Hills tournament.

TOURNAMENT TENNIS

	Australian Open	French Open	Wimbledon	U.S. Open
Men's Singles	Jimmy Connors, U.S.	Björn Borg, Sweden	Jimmy Connors, U.S.	Jimmy Connors, U.S.
Women's Singles	Evonne Goolagong, Australia	Chris Evert, U.S.	Chris Evert, U.S.	Billie Jean King, U.S.
Men's Doubles	Ross Case/ Geoff Masters, Australia	Dick Crealy, Australia/ Onny Parun, New Zealand	John Newcombe/ Tony Roche, Australia	Bob Lutz/ Stan Smith, U.S.
Women's Doubles	Evonne Goolagong, Australia/ Peggy Michel, U.S.	Chris Evert, U.S./ Olga Morozova, U.S.S.R.	Evonne Goolagong, Australia/ Peggy Michel, U.S.	Billie Jean King/ Rosemary Casals, U.S.

Davis Cup Winner: South Africa

Rick Wohlhuter races to a world record in the 1,000-meter run.

TRACK AND FIELD

WORLD TRACK AND FIELD RECORDS SET IN 1974		
Event	**Holder**	**Time or Distance**
	Men	
100-yard run	Ivory Crockett, U.S.	0:9.0
880-yard run	Rick Wohlhuter, U.S.	1:44.1
1,000-meter run	Rick Wohlhuter, U.S.	2:13.9
1,500-meter run	Filbert Bayi, Tanzania	3:32.2
3,000-meter run	Brendan Foster, Britain	7:35.2
440-yard hurdles	Jim Bolding, U.S.	0:48.7
Shot Put	George Woods, U.S.	72′ 2¾″
Hammer Throw	Aleksei Spiridonov, U.S.S.R.	251′ 6″
	Women	
200-meter run	Irena Szewinska, Poland	0:22.0
400-meter run	Irena Szewinska, Poland	0:49.9
3,000-meter run	Lyudmila Bragina, U.S.S.R.	8:52.7
High Jump	Rosemarie Witschas, E. Germany	6′ 4¾″
Shot Put	Helena Fibingerova, Czechoslovakia	70′ 8¼″
Discus	Faina Melnik, U.S.S.R.	229′ 4″
Javelin	Ruth Fuchs, E. Germany	220′ 6″

Two Quebec Pee-wee teams battle it out. The goalie is ready for anything.

QUEBEC'S YOUNG PLAYERS

When you turn on your television set to watch a hockey game, you have probably noticed that many of the players, even on American teams, are Canadians. And many of them come from the province of Quebec. Most of the Canadian hockey players that you see began playing when they were very young. Hockey is the favorite sport of a great many Canadians. Most of the Canadian players belonged to minor hockey teams or to school teams when they began to learn the fundamentals of hockey. In Canada, "minor hockey teams" are generally teams for young people from 6 to 18.

In Quebec during the annual Winter Carnival there is an exciting international "Pee-wee" hockey tournament. This tournament

and the excitement that surrounds it give some indication of the great interest in minor hockey in Canada.

▶A NEW DEVELOPMENT

After World War II everyone in Canada and the United States became more involved with leisure sports—as either participants or spectators. In Canada, as part of this trend, interest in minor hockey began to grow. Parents and teachers and even national leaders began to encourage its growth. However, minor hockey still had no national organization. But in the little village of Chomedey (now part of Laval, Quebec) one man was becoming very impatient with the condition of minor hockey in Canada. In the end, it was

292

this man, Arthur Lessard, who became the father of minor hockey in Quebec. It was Lessard who led the battle that ended in the founding of the Association of Minor Hockey in Quebec (called AMQH for short) in 1968.

Before 1968 there was some inconsistency in the rules governing minor hockey in Canada. The recognized amateur sports groups had taken no great interest in it. The Canadian Amateur Hockey Association and the Amateur Hockey Association in Quebec placed much emphasis on recruiting the most talented young players for their teams. These young players were often slated for eventual competition in professional hockey. Professional hockey is a big business in Canada, just as it is in the United States. The young players were usually trained by playing in the junior or senior amateur circuits, where each team of the National Hockey League (NHL) had an interest in a minor league team.

Arthur Lessard was angered by what he considered a lack of true concern for the young players on the part of the leaders of professional and amateur hockey. Eventually he was able to gather a group of people who shared his ideas about the reform of minor hockey. As a result of their combined action, AMQH was born. The goal of the new organization was to make minor hockey a means for young people to enjoy themselves and learn something. They did not want it to be a convenience for professional hockey scouts.

Lessard and others agreed that hockey should not be a game that is restricted to future professional stars. "Every healthy child can play hockey," they added, "if anyone bothers to teach him the fundamentals of the game."

These beliefs and events were the real turning point for minor hockey throughout the province of Quebec.

▶ AMQH—WHAT IT HAS DONE

Let's take a look at what AMQH has accomplished since it was founded. During the first year of its existence, the organization set up more than 2,000 minor teams at various age levels. Last year, during the 1973–74 season, the association put together four times as many teams—over 8,000. These teams had about 130,000 young players from

Even a coach can find a hockey game exciting.

6 to 18 years of age. Depending on their ages, these players were ranked as follows: Atoms, Mosquitoes, Pee-wees, Bantams, Midgets, and Juveniles.

The AMQH has 17,000 instructors and 7,000 referees to run their minor league programs. The players and teams in the AMQH constitute a substantial percentage of all minor hockey in Canada. Even Ontario, the Canadian province with the greatest total population, is behind Quebec in minor hockey participation.

The work of the AMQH has been amazing. The association now has 130,000 young hockey players in well-organized leagues in 13 specified regions subdivided into 130 zones. The association maintains an up-to-date classification of its members ranked according to category and class. It manages to present a growing number of regional tournaments and provincial championship matches every year. And it manages to do it on a budget that barely exceeds $200,000.

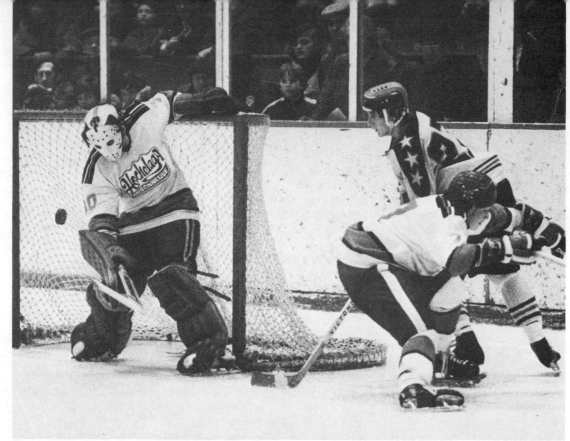

A puck from the rival team comes straight at the Maisonneuve goalie.

A tense moment in play: two Quebec Mosquito teams fight for the puck.

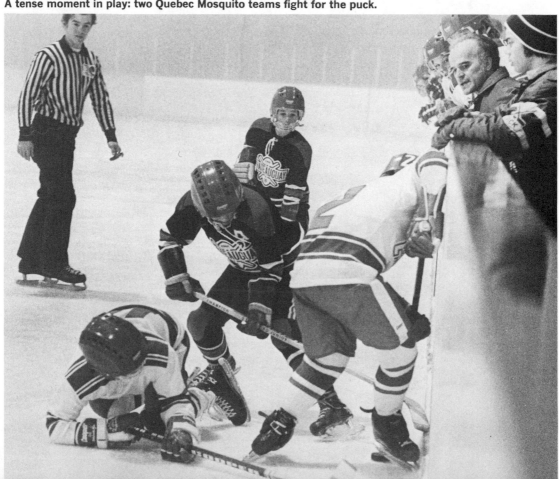

These totals do not include the young people who play on school, college, or other teams. It is estimated that at present more than 85,000 young people in Quebec play minor hockey outside the regular AMQH structure.

You can better appreciate this success when you realize that in Quebec in 1974 there were only 212 hockey arenas that could be used by minor league teams. (Ontario is better equipped, with almost twice that number of facilities.) Therefore, the AMQH must juggle the use of the few facilities it has. In any event, the future seems more promising. New arenas are being built throughout Quebec, with the assistance of government subsidies.

Elsewhere in Canada, the value of AMQH methods and practices has been recognized. The system of standards worked out in Quebec for the selection of minor hockey instructors and referees has served as a model for some systems in other parts of Canada and in the United States.

▶ RULES OF THE GAME

On the national level, Quebec has joined with other provinces in trying to make minor hockey rules as uniform as possible. Until very recently they had varied considerably from province to province. One ideal is to insist that every minor team be affiliated with a league in its own region before it can be affiliated with the Canadian Amateur Hockey Association.

The entire AMQH organization is voluntary. None of the elected directors is paid in any way for his services. The only people who are paid are a few of the administrative employees. All the other people involved with AMQH—directors of zones or regions, instructors, managers—volunteer their services to the young people who are the true amateurs of the hockey world.

The AMQH has been proud to contribute to the growing success of the international Pee-wee hockey tournament held during Carnival. This has become an important international competition for young people. In the past, teams of young people from the United States, France, Sweden, and Finland have come to take part in the competition. Czecho-slovakia will join the visiting teams in the 1975 competition.

Of course, there are still problems in the world of minor hockey. Because professional hockey is such a powerful force in Canada, it is important to protect minor hockey from "raids" by professional scouts looking for potential players.

In a real sense, the future of minor hockey in Quebec depends on two things: first, on the ability of the AMQH to resist attacks and pressures from outside; secondly, on the ability of the organization to pass along its spirit and know-how. The AMQH is developing fans in the United States as well as in other parts of Canada. Coaches and organizers of minor hockey in the New England states, where young people's hockey is increasing in popularity, are now coming to Quebec to see how the AMQH operates.

In eight short years, and with very limited means, the AMQH has brought new life to one of Canada's famous nurseries of future hockey greats.

The game is over and the two rival teams congratulate each other on how well they played.

These spelunkers examine rocks deep beneath the earth's surface.

ADVENTURE UNDERGROUND

People have always been fascinated by caves. Early man learned that caves could provide shelter from bad weather and fierce animals. When people began to build shelters above ground, caves became special, mysterious places. Sometimes religious rites were performed in caves, and legends grew up about mysterious underground grottoes.

Just the sound of the word "cave" brings exciting and mysterious adventures to mind. The word may make you think of beautiful caverns decorated by nature with elaborate carvings. Or you might be reminded of Tom Sawyer's cave in Mark Twain's great classic *The Adventures of Tom Sawyer* or the treasure cave of Edmond Dantès in Alexandre Dumas's *Count of Monte Cristo*. You might even think of bottomless pits of mysterious blackness in which bats and milk white, eyeless cave creatures live. Exciting cave stories fill the folklore of many nations. Some of the stories are based on true adventures. However, the entire world of cave-dwelling dragons, dwarfs, and demons vanished with the

coming of modern cave exploration. But throughout the ages fugitive slaves, noblemen, outlaws, herdsmen with their flocks, and just plain people have taken shelter in caves. Some people still choose to live in caves. Each major cave around the world has its own legend—almost its own personality.

In the past 25 years new techniques and equipment have advanced cave exploration very rapidly. There was an important discovery by cavers at Mammoth Cave, Kentucky, in 1972. Mammoth Cave has long been one of the world's major known caves. Where Indians once mined cave minerals by torchlight, modern cavers found passages that linked Mammoth Cave with four other caves in the area. Cave explorers had been looking for these passages for 100 years. The find was made after 18 years of intensive effort and hundreds of journeys of exploration lasting 18 to 24 hours and made under the most difficult conditions possible. Mammoth Cave explorers have now mapped more than 160 miles (250 kilometers) of passageways. More information is being discovered in Mammoth Cave and in thousands of other caves around the world every year. In many parts of the world, cave exploration—which is also known as caving or spelunking—has suddenly become a very popular sport.

▶ A WEALTH OF CAVES

Caves vary remarkably in size, pattern, and the type of rock in which they have been formed. Each type of cave has its own special features, but exploring is done in surprisingly the same way in the different types of caves.

The most common, most important, and most beautiful type of cave is the *limestone cave*. Limestone caves are "solution caves." This means that they develop in rock that can be dissolved or worn away easily by water from seepage and underground streams. Limestone is the chief rock of this type. There are also *lava tubes* and other types of lava caverns. These are common in areas like the western United States where there has been a great deal of volcanic activity. There are also lava caves in central Africa, in some parts of Australia, and on various volcanic islands. Iceland is a good example of a volcanic island. Lava tubes were formed as natural "sewers," or passages through which molten lava once flowed during volcanic activity. Some lava tubes are as much as 100 feet (30 meters) wide, and many of them are more than a mile (about a kilometer and a half) long. The third basic type of cave is the *glacier cave*. These are the most dangerous of all caves. They are found in glaciers and in snowfields. They are particularly dangerous because of the risk that the ice will shift and trap a caver, or that an avalanche will seal a cave shut.

Among these three major types of cave, each type contains some caves that consist largely of level, spacious corridors. Others in each class are just large enough to crawl through. And some are vertical, isolated pits with little or no cave area at the bottom of them. Some of each type have floor plans varying from long, single passageways to extremely complicated networks of passages. Some caves have two or more different levels. Some also have remarkably uniform features for distances of hundreds of yards. Others change maddeningly from crawlways to rooms and back again repeatedly, almost from foot to foot.

Limestone caves often sparkle with glistening stalactites (stone "icicles" on the roofs of caves; they are formed by dripping water that interacts with the stone over the centuries). Their halls may be gracefully hung with flowstone cascades and other beautiful speleothems, as scientists call stone formations in caves. Some other types of cave have these formations, too. A few caves have marvelous crystalline "flowers," mineral "ropes," and similar natural formations, which can be indescribably beautiful. The variety of shapes and colors and sizes is bewildering.

To the expert, the features of a cave are clear and direct clues that he can read. These clues help to make his explorations more interesting to the expert spelunker, or caver, and help him to learn more, too. Many a young spelunker has become so interested in this silent language of the caves that he has found his life's work in one of the many professions that can be used underground. These professions include archeology, geography, history, geology, hydrology, mineralogy, glaciology, paleontology, ecology, zoology, and medicine and public health (doctors dealing with men who work in mines and other underground areas have developed a specialized form of "underground" medicine and health care).

The techniques and equipment needed for safe cave exploration depend more on the location and individual features of a cave than on its type.

Limestone caves, like Mammoth Cave, are usually the longest and deepest. But there is one glacier cave that has more than 10 miles (16 km.) of mapped passages and many other passages that have yet to be mapped.

Glacier caves are especially complex, cold, windy, slippery, and subject to collapse and sudden flooding. Their exploration requires expert mountaineering skills as well as caving skills. However, you can meet the same problems in limestone caves.

Lava-tube caves are usually jagged and dark walled, lack beautiful stone formations, and are simple in pattern. And yet Dead Horse Cave, a lava-tube system in Washington State in the United States, is one of the continent's most complex and interesting caves.

The exploration of many minor types of caves differs little from that of the standard varieties.

▶ **A WORD OF CAUTION**

Spelunkers like undeveloped, "wild" caves best for many reasons. Some adventurers like the challenge of the unknown. Other cavers go underground in search of beauty and peace of mind. Some people are looking for scientific information, and others are just curious. But it is important to remember that you cannot just run into the nearest cave entrance or jump into the nearest hole in the ground on your own. You must have expert training and supervision in order to get anything worthwhile out of your spelunking experiences. Furthermore, without them you may easily get lost or injure yourself. Except for Injun Joe's treasure, which Twain made up, Tom Sawyer's underground adventure was very close to an incident that really happened. In what is now Mark Twain Cave in Missouri, Samuel Clemens ("Mark Twain" was his pen name) and a young girl friend actually did get lost. Even now, their cave seems to branch out in every direction. It takes excellent training and a good guide to avoid getting lost.

The other major problem caused by cave exploration is the destruction of the beauty and scientific interest of many magnificent caves by careless and inexperienced spelunkers. Several kinds of rare blind fish, helpless little bats, and incredibly fragile salamanders with legs like stubby toothpicks now face extinction. Fortunately, many caves and the creatures that live in them are safe for a while because of the difficulty of reaching them—but only for a while. The slogan of every thinking caver should be this: take nothing but pictures; leave nothing but footprints (and leave those only where they don't show); and kill nothing but time.

▶ **HOW TO BE A CAVER**

Caves differ greatly in their formations, the ease of entering and exploring them, and the degree of interest they offer the explorer. In many cases, beginners are not likely to recognize subtle dangers until they find themselves in serious trouble. Because of this, the best beginning for a spelunker is a guided tour of a well-illuminated commercial cave or cavern. The cave should be one where the guide turns off the artificial lighting for a while, too. Learning what a cave looks like in light and in darkness is a valuable lesson.

If possible, the second step in cave exploration should be to join a special spelunking tour at one of the commercially run caves. They often have these tours in addition to their regular sight-seeing tours. Spelunking tours are led by competent guides for small groups of properly prepared beginners. They take their groups into undeveloped, unlighted parts of the cave for an appetizing taste of real spelunking. These "wild" cave tours are comparatively new. When they are not available, the next best step is visiting caves that are officially listed as tourist attractions but are without lights or guides. If you remain in approved parts of these caves and wear warm, rugged clothing and shoes or boots with slip-resistant soles you will be able to make rapid progress in the fine art of spelunking with very little risk. Almost any reliable, smoke-free light is all right to use in caves like this. The important thing is that each person should have his own light and an equally reliable spare light in case a light is lost or broken.

In some caves, the beginner becomes a real spelunker quite rapidly. A talented beginner will start peering into mysterious squeezeways and guessing how the various cave features were formed. He may even begin to wonder what lies beyond the marked trail. People who want to go on with spelunking should prepare for it properly.

In the United States and Canada, preparing to be a spelunker is usually done through the National Speleological Society in Huntsville, Alabama. This organization has more than 100 chapters in the United States and Canada, and several thousand members of all ages. The staff of the organization is glad to direct people to the nearest group of experts with whom they can learn the basic techniques of spelunking. They'll have to learn about crawling through deep mud and cold water, chimneying and other climbing techniques, belaying (proper handling of a safety rope), and so forth.

In Spanish-speaking countries, you will find your local spelunking instructors by getting

Nature's wildly beautiful architecture at Meramec Caverns in Missouri.

in touch with the Sociedad Venezolana de Espeleología in Caracas, Venezuela. In France, you can contact the Société Spéléologique de France, in Paris.

A novice spelunker can save money if he checks with an expert before buying his equipment. You should not buy more than the clothing and gear you need at each stage of your progress. Experts will also know the best current models of each of the Twelve Essentials of Caving. These essentials are a helmet with a lamp bracket and a chin strap, a headlamp; two other dependable sources of light (plus waterproof matches); extra supplies (batteries and so forth) for each light source; a headlamp-repair and spare-parts kit; a compass; a first aid kit; a pocket-knife; reserve food, water, and halazone (water-purifying) tablets; a canteen; a survival kit; and a pack to carry all the other supplies and any more you may take.

The Boy Scouts of America also have a special training program for caving Scouts of high school age. Each group is led by a responsible adult, qualified by training and actual experience in caves.

In the United States alone, there will probably be a million cavers underground within ten years. With such hordes of cavers, good rules of cave safety and cave manners will become increasingly important. Each new cave explorer must be concerned not only with his own safety but with preserving each cave he enters. He must also conduct himself and his exploration in such a way that he and other cavers will be welcome back.

The international fellowship of cavers is a warm and fraternal group of men, women, and young people. And the joys of caving are endless. There is always the drive to discover new marvels. If you become a caver you will find that you are searching for underground halls of even more sparkling beauty, long-lost cave paintings, ever-longer passageways, ever-deeper pits, and ever-stranger animals—and even increasingly stickier mud!

WILLIAM R. HALLIDAY,
Author, *American Caves and Caving*

299

THE CREATIVE WORLD

These unusual, hand-painted wooden dolls from Japan were part of the crafts exhibition "In Praise of Hands."

A scrimshander decorated this whale's tooth with a scene of an exciting naval battle.

THE STORY OF SCRIMSHAW

Scrimshaw is a strange and fascinating word. If you know what it means, it will make you think of the days of great sailing ships when you hear it. If you don't know what it means, it still has an interesting sound to it. When the word scrimshaw is used today, it refers to objects of all kinds made from whalebone and whale ivory, and sometimes from walrus tusks. True scrimshaw must also be defined as that made by sailors aboard sailing ships.

Most of the scrimshaw found today in museums, private collections, and antique shops was made by sailors who served aboard the ships of the whaling fleets that sailed around the world in the early 19th century. The most famous whaling fleets were based in the ports of northeastern North America.

Today scrimshaw offers two exciting hobbies. It is still possible to buy small pieces of scrimshaw for a collection of your own. But it is also possible to learn how to make scrimshaw yourself—even if you don't meet the qualification of being a sailor serving on a sailing ship. Although the hunting of many kinds of whales has been limited and the sale of many products made from the whale has been banned, scrimshaw techniques can be used on other kinds of bone and on synthetic materials as well.

Part of the mystery surrounding scrimshaw has been created by a language problem. No one is sure where the word came from or what it might have meant originally. Some people say it is derived from a Dutch word. Other people believe scrimshaw is derived from a word in the language of the Indians of Nantucket Island off the coast of Massachusetts. (Nantucket had a famous whaling fleet in the 19th century.) The sea captains and sailors who kept logs, journals, and diaries had many variations on the word. It was *scrimschon, scrimshorn, scrimshandy, skrimshontering*. In *Moby Dick*, Herman Melville's famous novel of the great days of whaling, the word *skrimshander* is used. The modern form of that word—scrimshander—is used to mean a person who makes scrimshaw.

▶ GIFTS FROM THE SEA

Sailors made an amazing variety of scrimshaw objects in the 19th century. They usually made them while they were at sea, as gifts for their children, wives, mothers, sweethearts, and friends. They made everything from toys to useful and well-designed household tools. Many a New England housewife was able to hang out her wash with scrimshaw clothespins. Another favorite gadget made by sailors was the "jagging wheel." A jagging wheel, or pie crimper, was a kitchen utensil used for crimping the rim of a piecrust to seal the pie shut before sliding it into the oven to bake. Often the actual crimping wheel had an elaborately carved handle too. The handles of some jagging wheels had two- or three-tined forks that were used to prick holes in the piecrust to let the steam escape and keep the pie from boiling over. Jagging wheels sometimes became true art objects, with five or six intricately carved wheels in varying designs and sizes on one handle. These objects, it is believed, were actually made for scrimshaw design contests and were never really intended for kitchen use.

Another prized scrimshaw household gadget was the "swift." The swift was an intricately constructed reel used for winding yarn. A center pole, sometimes made of wood, held a set of whalebone arms that formed the reel for holding wool. The arms were jointed so that the reel could be collapsed easily and stored away when not in use. The arms were constructed very much like the "ribs" of an umbrella.

Sailors made a great many scrimshaw boxes of various kinds. Some were made entirely of whale ivory, which could be heated and pressed into a desired shape. Other scrimshaw boxes were made of wood and inlaid with whale ivory. There were also scrimshaw doorknobs, fans, cane handles, chessmen, dominoes, rings, bracelets, knitting needles, umbrellas with whalebone ribs, and cups, knives, forks, and spoons.

The most popular gift made by sailors for their sweethearts was a "busk." A busk was a long, flat piece of whalebone about 10 to 12 inches (20 to 22 centimeters) long. The top and bottom edges of the busk were rounded or scalloped. It was the fashion for young women in the early 19th century to insert a carved busk into a special slit pocket cut in the front of their bodice. The busks were sometimes inscribed with rhymes or with romantic sayings. They were often decorated with scenes—framed in hearts—of sailors and young women walking arm in arm. A lonely sailor inscribed on one busk "When this you see, remember me."

When most people today talk about scrimshaw, they usually have one special form of it in mind—the decorated whale's tooth. The

Three classic pieces of the sailor's art: a busk (*top*), an elaborate pie crimper (*right*), and a toy pigeon (*left*) that can really peck.

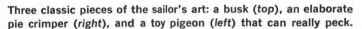
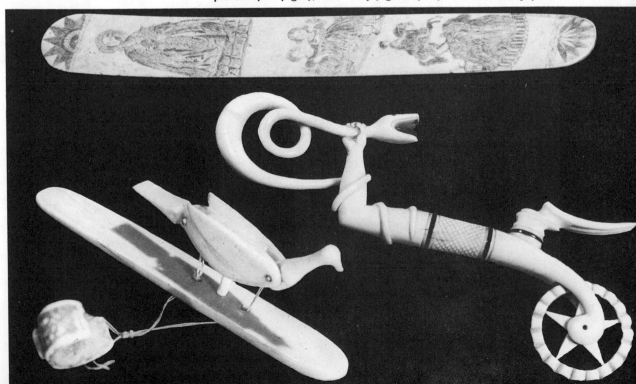

decorations on these big teeth range from patriotic scenes displaying the American flag to family groups sitting in their parlors, to pictures of ships under full sail and illustrations of life aboard whalers. Some teeth carry pictures of whaling boats being rammed by whales. Religious scenes are also found on 19th-century whales' teeth. Some of these pictures, it is believed, were made by Portuguese sailors who came from the Azores to sail with the Yankee whalers of New Bedford, Massachusetts.

▶ A SCRIMSHANDER AT WORK

Before a skilled scrimshander chose a whale's tooth to carve, there were preparations to make. To make whales' teeth suitable for carving, they were first soaked in brine (salt water). Then they were sanded to remove stains and rough spots. Sharkskin was often used aboard ship instead of sandpaper. The teeth were then polished with powdered pumice. At that point the scrimshander could decide which shape and color tooth would suit the carving he wished to do.

Essentially, there were two ways to carve a picture or a design on a whale's tooth. The scrimshander could draw the design freehand with a sharp tool directly on the tooth, or he could prepare a design on paper and transfer it to the surface of the tooth. The transfer was done in a very inventive way. The scrimshander placed the paper with the design drawn on it directly on the tooth. Then he took a sharp pin and pricked through the paper and into the tooth's surface. In this way he transferred all the important lines in the design onto the tooth. Then he could go to work with his cutting tools. Traces of the original pinpricks can still be seen on some pieces of 19th-century scrimshaw.

Once the design or scene was cut into a whale's tooth or a piece of whalebone, the scrimshander filled in the lines with lampblack or, in rare cases, with colored inks. Darkening the lines of the drawing made them stand out strikingly against the ivory-colored tooth or bone. There are also a few examples of whales' teeth with relief carving (carving in which the design is raised off the surface).

Since some of the designs executed by scrimshanders were very detailed and complex, a variety of tools were used in their execution. Aside from his trusty jackknife, the scrimshander might have used sail needles (inset in bone handles) for cutting in the design, and chisels, saws, and files.

▶ A PRACTICAL ART

Since whaling voyages lasted a very long time—sometimes stretching out to three or four years when the ships went to the Arctic or round Cape Horn to the Pacific—shipboard craftsmen had time to make more than gifts for their families. They also made tools and implements that were used aboard ship. These shipboard items included knife handles, mallets, rulers, straightedges, needles and thimbles (for the sailmaker), as well as replacement parts of various kinds for broken gear and tackle. Another tool that was often made of whalebone was the "fid," or "pricker." This tool, which looks like a giant needle, was used to prick apart, or separate, the strands of a rope being prepared for splicing.

▶ THE WHALING INDUSTRY

Although men on many kinds of sailing ships could make scrimshaw, it was aboard whalers that the art of the scrimshander flourished. A whaler could provide a steady supply of whalebone and whale's teeth, and whalers were at sea for the longest stretches of time. An expert scrimshander could devote many hours to his craft and still get his regular duties done. But the whaling industry did not exist for the sake of scrimshaw. It was a big business—especially in the United States.

Before the commercial uses of petroleum were developed, it was whale oil that was burned in lamps, and whale oil that was used to lubricate machinery. (The oil was obtained by boiling down the thick layer of fat, or blubber, that padded the whale's huge body.) Aside from its use by the scrimshander, whalebone was an important commercial product. The fashion industry needed it in the days when women wanted narrow waists and wide hoopskirts. The corsets that were used to make women's waists narrower were re-inforced with whalebone. And the hoops that made a woman's skirts balloon out were also constructed of whalebone.

The American whaling industry reached its peak by the middle of the 19th century. Nantucket was originally the most important whaling port, followed by Salem. Both towns were eventually surpassed by New Bedford, Massachusetts, which became the center of the American whaling industry.

The two types of whales most frequently captured by the Americans were the baleen and the sperm whale. The oil obtained from the sperm whale was called "sperm oil." Spermaceti, a waxy substance that was separated from the sperm oil, was used in candle-making. The baleen whale was nicknamed the "right" whale because its oil yield was so high. In place of teeth, the baleen whale has rows of baleen, long plates edged with hairy fibers. These plates—some 7 feet (more than 2 meters) long—hang from the whale's upper jaw and act as strainers to separate its food from the seawater. Baleen is composed of a substance called keratin—the same substance that forms fingernails, horns, and feathers. Although baleen is not bone, it is often called "whalebone." However, scrimshanders often call the real bones of whales "whalebone." They made scrimshaw of baleen, too. It is usually dark gray, with some yellow tones and occasional black streaks.

Two events brought about the decline of the prosperous American whaling industry. The first was the successful drilling for petroleum in Pennsylvania in 1859. By 1860 kerosene (which is made from petroleum) was being burned in lamps instead of whale oil. The second momentous event was the Civil War, which began in 1861. Many unarmed whaling ships were captured or destroyed by Confederate privateers. By the end of the Civil War the American whaling industry had been overtaken and surpassed by the Norwegian whaling interests. The Norwegians built ships that were true whaling "factories" with the most modern equipment for processing the captured whales. The Norwegians had also developed an efficient and deadly harpoon gun. The gradual extinction of some species of whales led to the signing, in 1931, of an international agreement regulating whaling. The agreement limited the number of whales that could be taken in any given year. The International Whaling Commission, established in 1946, now regulates whaling.

▶ SCRIMSHAW TODAY

The interest in scrimshaw has grown enormously in recent years as the interest in crafts has grown. Scrimshaw is the one craft that cay lay claim to being American in origin. Museums and private collectors have long been interested in scrimshaw. However, the personal interest of the late President John F. Kennedy in scrimshaw and his own superb collection of it increased general enthusiasm for the craft. Unfortunately the increased interest in scrimshaw has also made it more expensive to collect. But it is still available, and not all of it is expensive.

There is also a whole new generation of scrimshanders both creating new designs in scrimshaw and recapturing old designs. You might well want to try your hand at collecting new scrimshaw. But better still—why not become a scrimshander yourself? There are now kits available for making scrimshaw. You will also find that many craft centers have begun to give instruction in scrimshaw.

If you are about to become a scrimshander, you will certainly have many ideas of your own about designs for your work. But it would be interesting to take a look at the handiwork of the seamen who invented the craft so long ago. There are interesting collections of scrimshaw in many of the former whaling ports of the northeastern United States. But the most interesting place of all for the future scrimshander is Mystic Seaport in Mystic, Connecticut.

There is an excellent maritime museum in Mystic with many relics of the whaling era—including some fine scrimshaw. But the best exhibit of all is a real whaling ship. The *Charles W. Morgan,* the last American sailing ship built for the whaling trade, lies permanently at dock in Mystic. She was built in 1841 and made her last voyage in 1921. When you step aboard the *Charles W. Morgan,* you enter the world of the 19th-century seaman—the world in which the uniquely American craft of scrimshaw was born.

MARION B. WILSON
Artist and Collector

SONGS TO SING

THREE BLIND MICE with FRÈRE JACQUES

Voice 1: Three blind mice, three blind mice, See how they run, see how they run,— They all run af-ter the far-mer's wife, Who cut off their tails with a carv-ing knife, Did ev-er you see such a sight in your life As three blind mice!

Voice 2: Frè-re Jac-ques, Frè-re Jac-ques, dor-mez vous, dor-mez vous? Son-nez les ma-ti-nes, son-nez les ma-ti-nes: Din din don, din din don!

LA PALOMITA (Little Dove)

Allegretto – Tempo di habanera

Folk Song from
Paraguay

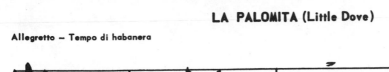

Ya sa- len las pa- lo- mi- tas, Per- fu- ma- das de re-
Now lit- tle doves are step- ping out, Each scen- ted with the mig-

se- da De ba- jo de la en- ra- ma- da Ca- da
non- ette Un- der the twi- ning ar- bor Each one

u- na con su ga- lán. Que bo- ni- ta es la
with her hand- some ca- va- lier. How love- ly is the dus-

tri- gueña Y que co- que- ta ella es- tá, Que gra-
ky one And what a lit- tle flirt she is, The dark-

cio- sa la mo- rena y la ru- bi- ta sin par —
haired one is grace- ful, And the blonde with- out a peer.

Just to prove that music has been around for a long time, MGM released "That's Entertainment," a film of scenes from old-time musicals. Esther Williams swam in "Million Dollar Mermaid," Gene Kelly danced in "Singin' in the Rain," and Judy Garland and friends sang in "The Wizard of Oz."

THE MUSIC SCENE

There were no huge musical gatherings in 1974, no Woodstocks, no Summer Jams at Watkins Glen, New York, to brighten up the popular music scene. The mammoth rock celebrations of years past, with their excitement and symbolic significance, have disappeared. The economic problems that have plagued the entire world may have contributed to the decline of the rock festivals.

These same problems were reflected in the moods, fads, and buying habits of the record-buying public. They reverted to the past—to happier, more carefree and untroubled times.

▶ MORE NOSTALGIA

Nostalgia, which first appeared on the scene several years ago, was still the craze. The movies and the theater contributed to the promotion of the sights and sounds of yesteryear. One of the year's most popular films, *The Sting*, starring Paul Newman and Robert Redford, ignited interest in Scott Joplin, a pioneer ragtime composer, who was born in Texarkana, Texas, in 1868. The sound track of the film was adapted by Marvin Hamlisch from Joplin's music. Hamlisch won an Academy Award for his adaptation, and the LP album based on the sound track of the film became the number one best-selling album.

With interest in Joplin's music soaring, no fewer than six different LP's of his ragtime music were listed on *Billboard*'s chart of best-selling albums. Five of the albums held the top five slots on the chart. The success and popularity of Joplin's music, however, came too late for the composer. Scott Joplin had died in 1917, his talents not widely appreciated in the music world. It took the nostalgia craze and the movie and record industries to bring well-deserved recognition to the man and his talent.

Another best-selling album was the sound track of *That's Entertainment*, a blockbuster movie of 1974. The film was a compilation of clips from MGM musicals from 1929 to 1958. Nostalgia buffs rushed to see such actors as Clark Gable, Jean Harlow, and Joan Crawford sing and dance for the first—and in some cases the last—time. The film was such an enormous success that the album was released almost immediately, equaling the popularity of the film.

Broadway also jumped on the nostalgia bandwagon with the musical hit *Over Here!* The show reached back to the 1940's and World War II for its story—and its stars. The singing Andrews Sisters—Maxine and Patty (the third sister, LaVerne, died a few years ago)—headed the cast. And everything about the production had the 40's sound. There was the eight-to-the-bar boogie-woogie, the close harmony vocalizing, and the big-band swing sound—all heard in the show or on the original cast album.

Good News, which first delighted theater audiences in 1927, reappeared for a brief run on Broadway in 1974 after touring the United States for a year. The show, starring Alice Faye, a popular motion-picture star of the 1930's and 1940's, featured such oldtime favorites as "You're the Cream in My Coffee," "Keep Your Sunny Side Up," and "Button Up Your Overcoat." The music brought back memories to a large part of the audiences, and introduced something new to the under-30 crowd.

Many recording artists of the 1950's and 1960's added their sounds to the nostalgia chorus. Country singer Brenda Lee, who had been on the inactive list for several years, returned to the recording studio. Pat Boone (of "white bucks" fame) signed on with a new recording company. The Beach Boys, who spent the 60's making "surfing" music, have returned to the charts with new sounds. Their *Endless Summer,* a two-record set of Beach Boys winners, met with great success. Two important rhythm and blues artists, Etta James and Esther Phillips (who used to be known as Little Esther), came out with new albums. Even Paul Anka appeared on the charts with his hit single, "You're Having My Baby."

Other comeback artists of the 1960's included the reunited Righteous Brothers—Bill Medley and Bobby Hatfield. Their first release in six years is *Give It to the People.* Martha Reeves left the Vandellas and made her debut during the year. Connie Francis, another famous performer from yesteryear,

Paul Anka recorded hit records while . . .

Bob Dylan performed in concert.

There are few ways popular recording artists can reach their public. Records, of course, are one way. But person-to-person, live audience contact is also important to the performer. There are, however, several stars who often refuse to play for mass audiences. They value their privacy too much. And for that reason, 1974 was a significant step forward for two of the world's best-known and seldom-seen singers: Bob Dylan and Frank Sinatra.

After an absence of nearly ten years, Bob Dylan returned to his legion of fans by way of a personal appearance tour. A sellout, 21-city cross-country tour drew star-studded crowds and great critical acclaim. *Rolling Stone,* the rock music newspaper, said, "Dylan opened the minds of American audiences to the possibilities of poetry and music, and freed the whole of American pop music from the restraints of the music hall, Broadway shows, and Tin Pan Alley."

The return of Sinatra was another newsworthy event. In 1972, Frank Sinatra announced his retirement and left the entertainment business. He stopped all recording and nightclub dates and cancelled personal appearances. But 1974 brought a mellowing mood to the "singers' singer." In October he appeared in concert before a sellout crowd of approximately 20,000 people at Madison Square Garden in New York City. The show was entitled "Sinatra—The Main Event," and it was exactly that. The concert was telecast live throughout the United States, and just to ensure that Sinatra's magic reached millions more, the event was recorded and sold as an LP album. This new burst of enthusiasm on Sinatra's part resulted in the recording of two more new albums, *Ol' Blue Eyes Is Back* and *Some Nice Things I Missed,* and more personal appearances—but this time with some additions. He appeared for the first time with his daughter Nancy and his son, Frank. The billing read "Sinatra—The Father, The Daughter, The Son."

▶ A NEW SOUND

Every year many new voices are heard in the recording industry, but few ever achieve stardom. One of 1974's exciting new sounds

also hit the comeback trail in 1974, but on the night club circuit rather than in the recording studio. One of the year's biggest hits was *You Smile—The Song Begins,* by Herb Alpert and the Tijuana Brass. To promote this album, their first recording in several years, the Tijuana Brass ensemble hit the road with a cross-country tour. The fans let them know they had not been forgotten.

Multi-award winner Stevie Wonder.

Johnny Rodriguez, a new star on the horizon.

The DeFranco Family, featuring young Tony DeFranco.

belongs to Johnny Rodriguez, from Texas. His "Ridin' My Thumb to Mexico" and "That's the Way Love Goes" made him the first Chicano to become a country music star.

Another new sound belongs to René Simard, a 13-year-old boy soprano from Quebec, Canada. Although unfamiliar to United States audiences, René has become one of the largest-selling recording artists in Canada. In the past two years, the people of Quebec have bought several million dollars worth of his records. René doesn't belong to the hard-rock school of music. He prefers to sing gentle ballads about growing up. His most recent hits include "My Mother Is an Angel" and "Sunday Afternoons."

Barry White, another newcomer, recorded a soul single, "Can't Get Enough of Your Love," and made a name for himself on the charts. The DeFranco Family, featuring 14-year-old Tony DeFranco, became the latest family to make good in the music industry. One of the most popular records of the year was their "Abra-Ca-Dabra" from the hit album *Heartbeat, It's a Lovebeat*.

▶ AND THE BEAT GOES ON

Stevie Wonder, called "the most creative and popular pop musician of his generation," was the subject of a *Newsweek* cover story. At 24, Stevie, who received the first Gold Record when he was 12, hit the charts with "Living for the City," and a number one album, *Fulfillingness' First Finale*. When

Success means Gladys Knight and the Pips.

Anne Murray, Canada's gift to the music scene.

"Stevie, the Wonder Man" wasn't writing and recording songs, he was busy collecting awards. Stevie was honored with the 1974 Grammy awards for Album of the Year (*Innervisions*), Pop Vocal Performance by a Male ("You Are the Sunshine of My Life"), and Rhythm and Blues Male Vocal Performance ("Superstition"). To *Newsweek,* his success symbolized "the vaulting new prestige and popularity of black musicians in America"

and the "almost complete erasure of the color line in pop music."

While Stevie Wonder was writing hits as well as singing them, other artists were also busy recording best sellers. Grammy Award-winner Roberta Flack sang "Killing Me Softly with His Song," and "Feel Like Making Love." Ann Peebles hit the charts with "I Can't Stand the Rain," and Al Wilson delivered the million-seller "Show and Tell."

After performing for years, Gladys Knight and the Pips scored the greatest success of their career in 1974. They had a series of number one soul songs that crossed over into the pop mainstream. Besides the hit singles "Midnight Train to Georgia," and "Imagination," Gladys and the Pips gained a gold record for selling more than a million copies of "You're the Best Thing That Ever Happened to Me."

Among the established stars, Helen Reddy was again listed on the charts, this time with "You and Me Against the World." Dionne Warwicke, The Carpenters, and Paul Simon all recorded hit songs. John Denver's "Sunshine on My Shoulders," and Elton John's "Goodbye Yellow Bird," proved to be popular with the record-buying public. And to no one's surprise, two ex-Beatles showed up on the charts. Paul McCartney's *Band on the Run* album and Ringo Starr's singles "Phonograph," and "You're Sixteen," proved what everyone knew all along—the two performers are loaded with talent. Peggy Lee's *Let's Love* (the title song was written by Paul McCartney) and Neil Diamond's *Serenade* were also hit albums.

Canadian songbird Anne Murray (who recently won her fourth Canadian female vocalist of the year award) went on a 60-city U.S. tour, promoting her current hit album *Love Song.* Anne's hot single "You Won't See Me," also featured in the album, climbed the charts.

One of the year's most popular songs was recorded by a group who had been around for several years, but suddenly found themselves an overnight sensation. "Tie a Yellow Ribbon 'Round the Old Oak Tree," sung by Tony Orlando and Dawn, was a pseudo-Dixieland novelty that really caught on. An import from Spain (with Spanish lyrics),

"Eres Tu" (translated as "Touch the Wind"), was a surprise hit for the Mocedades.

▶THE COUNTRY MESSAGE

One of the biggest success stories to emerge this year had nothing to do with a singer or a song. The place was Nashville, Tennessee—home of country music—and the object of all the attention and excitement was a building. After decades in the rickety old Ryman Auditorium, Nashville's Grand Ole Opry, the mecca of country singers, moved to a brand-new $15,000,000 home. It was such a momentous move that the opening night festivities were televised across the nation. Many of the stars who have performed with the Opry through the years returned for the festivities.

And some of the Opry artists had brand-new hits under their belts. The only strange things about the sound coming from the new home was that many of the songs had a slight rock flavor to them. The relation between country and pop music seemed to take a new turn in 1974. Pop-rock artists were recording country tunes, and country singers picked up the beat of rock music. Among those who participated in this new development were Charlie Rich, with "The Most Beautiful Girl in the World," Donna Fargo and "You Can't Be a Beacon," and Conway Twitty with "Honky Tonk Angel." Loretta Lynn's "As Soon As I Hang Up the Phone," Olivia Newton-John's "I Love You, I Honestly Love You," and Merle Haggard's recording of "If We Make It Through December" were three very popular songs that contributed to the new country-rock phenomenon.

▶BUT THE MELODY LINGERS ON

Popular music suffered some tragic losses in the past year and a half. Bobby Darin died in December, 1973. The great Duke Ellington, whose music had won worldwide acclaim, died in May, and Cass Elliot, who had come into her own after the breakup of the Mamas and the Papas, died suddenly in July.

Jim Croce, whose career as a songwriter-singer was just beginning to soar when he was killed in a plane accident in 1973, became a super-seller and a legend a year after his death. Jim had been in and out of the music business for years before he hit the big time. His smash single "Bad, Bad Leroy Brown," and the equally popular album *You Don't Mess Around With Jim,* sent him on his way. One best-selling record followed another. Several of the recordings he made just prior to his death appeared on the market in 1974, and Jim Croce became a hit all over again. There were three smash singles, including the poetic "Time in a Bottle," and two best-selling albums. *I Got a Name* was completed just eight days before his death. The melody of Jim Croce—like that of Cass Elliot, Bobby Darin, and Duke Ellington—lingers on for future generations to hear and enjoy.

ARNOLD SHAW
Author, *The Rockin' 50's; Honkers and Shouters: The Rhythm and Blues Years*

1974 GRAMMY AWARDS

Record of the Year	*Killing Me Softly with His Song*	Roberta Flack, artist
Album of the Year	*Innervisions*	Stevie Wonder, artist
Song of the Year	*Killing Me Softly with His Song*	Norman Gimbel, Charles Fox, songwriters
New Artist of the Year		Bette Midler
Pop Vocal Performance—female	*Killing Me Softly with His Song*	Roberta Flack, artist
Pop Vocal Performance—male	*You are the Sunshine of My Life*	Stevie Wonder, artist
Rhythm and Blues Vocal Performance—female	*Master of Eyes*	Aretha Franklin, artist
Rhythm and Blues Vocal Performance—male	*Superstition*	Stevie Wonder, artist
Country Vocal Performance—female	*Let Me Be There*	Olivia Newton-John, artist
Country Vocal Performance—male	*Behind Closed Doors*	Charlie Rich, artist
Original Score for a Motion Picture	*Jonathan Livingston Seagull*	Neil Diamond, composer
Score from an Original Cast Show Album	*A Little Night Music*	Stephen Sondheim, composer
Classical Album	*Bartok: Concerto for Orchestra*	Pierre Boulez conducting the New York Philharmonic Orchestra
Recording for Children	*Sesame Street Live*	Sesame Street cast

A flamenco dancer moves to the throbbing music of the guitar.

FABULOUS FLAMENCO

To many people flamenco music is the same thing as Spanish music. The influence of flamenco on Spanish music has been great. However, the unique, passionate, rhythmic music called flamenco is traditional only in the region of Andalusia, in southern Spain. It was in Andalusia, many centuries ago, probably in the days when southern Spain was ruled by the Moors, that the unique sounds and dramatic dances of flamenco developed.

Even the name "flamenco" has a fascinating story behind it. The word, in modern Spanish, means at least two things. It describes the particular style of song and dance from Andalusia; and it means, literally, "Flemish." "Flemish" is the name of the peo-

ple of Flanders, a region of Belgium. Spain once ruled large portions of Belgium and the Netherlands—including Flanders. When Spanish soldiers came back to Spain on leave from duty in Flanders and saw the bright skirts of southern Spain's singers and dancers, they remembered that the peasant women of Flanders also wore brightly colored, ruffled skirts. The soldiers began to call the singers and dancers of southern Spain "flamenco," or Flemish. Eventually, the ancient songs and dances these people performed were called "flamenco," too—even though they had nothing to do with the songs or dances of Flanders.

Of all of the folk music of Europe, Spain's is one of the richest. And the music of

Andalusia is the most influential and living. Throughout this region of snowcapped mountains and sun-scorched ravines, you can hear the mournful, vaguely Oriental chants of the *cante hondo,* the traditional flamenco vocal music, and the violent rhythms of the fandango, the traditional flamenco dance.

In *cante hondo* the singer tries to express *duende*—a deep, restrained, but intense emotion. In the fandango the dancer explodes in a frenzy of movement. When the dancer is a woman, the movement is made more exciting by the bright colors of her swirling, ruffled skirts. And whenever the dancers perform really well, the audience encourages them and expresses its admiration by yelling *"Olé!"*

Although most people agree that the origins of flamenco are Moorish (North African), the music was developed by Spanish Gypsies. Gypsies are still supposed to be the best flamenco performers. Legend says that only a Gypsy has the voice and emotion to sing the "deep song," the *cante hondo.*

The rules of the art of flamenco seem simple at first. The song itself follows a set pattern. The basic steps of the dance are set, too. The entire song often has a range of no more than six notes. The rhythms of the song and the dance are also established. But within the narrow limits of the form, a performer may employ fantastic skill and technique. Vocal decoration, the musical "ornaments" of grace notes and semitones, are used freely. The basic body movements can be ornamented or decorated too. Within the set movements of the upheld arms, the dancer twists his hands and moves his fingers. These gestures are called *filigrana,* and are a kind of physical decoration.

Originally, it is believed, flamenco was performed without instruments. The performer set the rhythm and the tempo by finger snaps (*pitas*) and handclaps (*palmadas*), both of which are still used. Then—as now—the performer would begin hesitantly, trying to capture exactly the right mood. Then, as the spirit moved him, the singer would move, then sing, "Ay . . . ," the shrill note growing in intensity until it broke into a vocal flourish.

The pure form of unaccompanied song was probably the part of flamenco that was inherited directly from the Moors. About 1,000 years ago the Gypsies, it is believed, began to use instruments when singing the traditional melodies. Gradually the flamenco musician—especially the guitarist—became just as important to the art as the singer and dancer.

Although the tradition of Islamic music from North Africa was widespread in Europe in the Middle Ages, its influence was strongest in Spain. There was much sadness and despair in Islamic music. The poor, hardworking people of southern Spain understood that sorrow very well. Flamenco first became popular with the poorest people. By the 19th century the music was connected with the men who worked in mines, with prisoners, and with poor people forced to live in workhouses. The only other people who liked flamenco, it seemed, were "serious," or classical, composers and musicians. They loved the melodies and rhythms of flamenco and came from all over Europe to sit in Spanish cafés and hear it played and sung. They wanted to use the sound of flamenco in their own music. Georges Bizet, a French composer, was probably the person who made flamenco popular all over the world. He wrote an opera called *Carmen,* about the adventures of a Spanish Gypsy girl. He filled the opera with songs and dances that were written in the flamenco style. When *Carmen* appeared in 1875 it was enormously popular, and suddenly people everywhere wanted to know more about Spanish music—especially flamenco.

Once flamenco became popular it began to change—even in Andalusia. Castanets and tambourines, which real flamenco performers disapproved of, were added. Many performers began to try to make the music sound even more Oriental and "strange" than it really did. Individual flamenco artists began to see how important it was to keep their performances as pure and accurate as possible, so that the real flamenco style would not be lost.

Today you can see performances of flamenco in many cities around the world. But the people who truly love flamenco still tell you that you ought to go to Andalusia to hear and see it as it should be. Flamenco fans believe that a small café in Andalusia—where the performers still pass a hat for contributions after their performances—is the very best place to learn what flamenco is all about.

THE PAINTER'S MAGIC EYE

The men who painted these three pictures lived in different countries and at different times in history. Francisco Goya, who painted the wonderful portrait of the boy in the red suit, was born in Spain in the 18th century. Paolo Uccello, who painted the fairy-tale battle of San Romano, was born in Italy toward the end of the 14th century. And Vincent van Gogh, who painted—in a special and amazing way—his own small bedroom, was born in the Netherlands in the 19th century. But these three very different men had one important quality in common. That quality is called genius. Genius makes Goya, Uccello, and Van Gogh citizens of a magic country where anything can happen.

▶ **THE BOY IN RED**

Have you ever had a cat as a pet? Have you watched him as he looks out of the window and follows every movement of a bird or even a butterfly outside? Have you watched him as his muscles grow tense, he freezes in place, and his wide eyes follow a fly buzzing about the room? He crouches, not quite lying, not quite standing, ready for anything. If you have noticed these things about cats, you will be able to understand the expressions on the faces of the three handsome animals in this painting.

The calico, the tabby, and the black cat in this painting are not in the least interested in how elegantly their young master, Manuel, has dressed to have his portrait painted. (In fact the real name of the painting is Manuel's full Spanish name. It is called *Don Manuel Osorio de Zúñiga*.) Nor are the cats interested in the famous painter Francisco Goya, who is standing at his easel, just beyond the frame of the painting, capturing them, as well as their master, for all time. They are not even interested in the green cage of finches that Manuel has been so careless as to leave on the floor. What these three cats care about more than anything in the world is Manuel's tame magpie, who is standing unconcerned, right beyond their noses—and within easy reach of their paws.

If you look carefully, you will see that Manuel has some control over the situation. He is holding a string that has been looped loosely around one of the magpie's legs. But the magpie seems totally relaxed and unconcerned about the cats. He is holding a card proudly in his bill. The card bears the signature of Francisco Goya and the painter's "trademark"—a palette, brushes, and a canvas. The magpie's complete lack of concern is obviously making the cats even more agitated. And they are probably a little annoyed, too. There is something in their look that says, "The nerve of that magpie!"

And what do you think of Manuel? He doesn't seem to be thinking about the drama his pets are involved in—right at his feet. He is probably looking over at the great painter and remembering that his mother told him to stand very still. I am sure that you have had your photograph taken, either by a photographer or by your father or mother. And I am sure you did not like being told to stand absolutely still. But when you think of it, Manuel would really have had to be very patient indeed. Although the shutter of a camera takes only a second to blink open and closed, a fine portrait like this one would have required Manuel to pose for Señor Goya for many hours, and always in the same position. History doesn't tell us how co-operative the cats were.

Why is this a great painting? It is great partly because Goya painted Manuel and the cats and the birds so beautifully. But more important, the painting is great because it captures perfectly for people of every age a very special moment in the life of a boy, his three cats, and his pet birds.

You have probably never seen a battle between opposing forces of mounted knights in full armor—except in the movies. It is unlikely that you ever will. But if you could have been an invisible spectator at any of the famous battles of the Middle Ages, it is certain that you would never have seen a battle quite like *The Battle of San Romano*.

The painting you are looking at seems to depict a moment in a kind of fairy-tale battle. You probably know that the knights of the Middle Ages rode into battle in elaborate and often beautiful suits of armor. And you probably know that the horses that carried their masters into battle were equally well dressed. But the painter has made this the most beautifully dressed group of knights and horses in history.

The odd thing is that this painting, despite the look of fantasy about it, depicts a real event in history. The painting is one of a series of panels created by the great Italian master of the 14th century Paolo Uccello. The full title of the panel you are looking at is *Niccolò Torrentino at the Battle of San Romano*. The battle occurred in northern Italy in 1342. It was one of a series of successful battles fought by the forces of the powerful Medici family of Florence. Niccolò Torrentino was one of their generals.

No matter what he painted, Uccello found visual patterns. He found patterns in great historic events and in quiet landscapes. The patterns he saw were unique.

The Battle of San Romano is not just a painting of a historic event. It is a painting about visual patterns. Uccello is dealing with the patterns of figures—of horses and men—in motion. The next time you watch a basketball game, see what happens in the instant after the referee blows his whistle. The players who have been madly running about the court freeze suddenly. For an instant, you will be able to see that the players are frozen in a kind of visual pattern. It is that kind of pattern that Uccello has shown us.

And there are patterns within the patterns. The colors the painter uses make a visual pattern. Everything in this painting seems to be red, black, white, and yellow—and an unusual light blue. Niccolò Torrentino, riding

a white horse, is at the center. Torrentino is wearing a beautiful turban and mantle of red and gold. His squire, the boy who rides behind him, is dressed in similar colors and has gold-colored hair. Even the lances of the charging knights echo the pattern.

Look at the ground beneath the horses' hooves. Even the broken lances are arranged in patterns. The odd helmets and stray pieces of armor that have fallen off and the breastplates that have fallen to the ground have fallen in interesting patterns. In fact, the whole scene looks like a chess game in progress.

The men and horses look like the pieces of a handsome chess set put out on a chessboard.

However, Uccello also knew that a few realistic details would make his fantasy picture all the more fascinating. The background of this painting is an entirely different world. In it you can see ordinary soldiers in a real Italian landscape. The small background figure at the far right carries a crossbow over his shoulder like a farmer with a hoe on his way to the fields. The small figure at the center is fixing his crossbow—just as you might adjust a tool you were going to use in the garden. The only thing in the background that is strange is that everything seems so relaxed—even the landscape. Uccello knew the value of contrast of mood as well as contrast of shape and color.

It is quite likely that Paolo Uccello could have painted a very realistic battle. But this view of the Medici victory at San Romano was painted more than a century after the event. The Medici wanted to be reminded of one of the great victories in the history of their family. But they wanted to be reminded in a beautiful and colorful way.

▶ VINCENT'S ROOM

This small, cozy bedroom in an ordinary house in the city of Arles in southern France is one of the most famous rooms in the history of European painting. It is hard to believe that such a plain—and, in some ways, quite ordinary—room could be so important, but it is. This is the room that Vincent van Gogh, the great 19th-century Dutch painter, lived in while he was painting some of his most famous pictures. It was this simple room that gave the painter some of the few hours of peace and rest he ever enjoyed in his short, hard life. As a kind of tribute to his little room, Van Gogh painted and sketched it

many times. This famous study of it is called simply *Vincent's Room at Arles.*

Despite many attempts, Vincent van Gogh was never popular with the great art dealers and collectors of his day. He accepted the fact that if he remained a painter he would probably have to lead a life of great simplicity and even poverty. But Van Gogh had already come to have a deep love of simple things and of simple people. He never truly resented the fact that he was poor. He did resent the blindness of those people who could not find beauty in his work.

You probably have a bedroom, either a room of your own or one you share with a brother or sister. There is probably no detail of your room that you do not know well. You can probably walk about it in the dark without bumping into the furniture. It is where you stay when you're sick. It may also be the place where you play when it rains and you can't go outside. It is certainly the place you go when you've gotten into trouble and your mother or father says, "Go to your room!" In other words, your room is your own special place, no matter what happens. That is the way Vincent van Gogh, in a life filled with serious problems, felt about his room in Arles.

Because he was a very good painter with a great deal of insight into things and people, Vincent (and Van Gogh liked to be called just Vincent) was able to communicate his own feelings about his room quite easily. It wasn't just his ability to show us what was literally in the room that makes Vincent speak to us so directly. He was able to let us see what he felt about the room and to make us feel it, too.

Vincent painted his room at the happiest time of day for most people—morning, with the early sunlight coming through the window. This is the way the room probably looked to Vincent when he went back upstairs after breakfast to get a book—or a paintbrush—he had left behind. The quality of light as he has captured it helps us to understand why Vincent liked his room so much.

The colors of the room and of everything in it help create the happy, warm feeling of the painting. White and blue are often happy colors. The walls of the room are light blue and the doors are a cheerful darker blue. Vincent's washstand has a dark blue wash-bowl and pitcher on it. There is a light, greenish blue water carafe and a clear drinking glass on the washstand, too. The white towel that hangs from a nail on the wall is beautifully drawn and painted. The sheets and pillowcases on the bed are white. The floor of the room is painted in light shades of purple.

Even the color of Vincent's plain furniture plays an important role in the painting. Although the chairs, table, and bed are tan, the tan is touched and brightened with patches of sunny yellow. Vincent's bed has a bright red blanket on it. The red is truly cheerful and reflects Vincent's love of bright colors. One of the joys of his life in the south of France was his discovery of its rich, bright colors, made dazzling by the sun. He had begun painting the darker, wetter colors of his native Netherlands. But once he found out what the colors of the south were like, he filled all of his paintings with them.

In this painting Van Gogh has allowed us to see the personal, intimate things he touched or looked at every day. Behind the head of his bed are the pegs on which he hung his painting smocks and his now-famous straw hat. Since he loved to paint outdoors in full sunlight, Vincent wore a floppy straw hat to protect his head from the sun and to shield his eyes from the blinding light. There are also pictures on the wall. Most of them are quite likely his own, although one of them might have been by his painter friend Paul Gauguin, who once lived with him in Arles. Because Vincent's touch is so honest, you probably enjoy looking into this very private corner of his life. Vincent wanted people to know him well and to like him.

There is another quality in this painting that is even harder to describe. It is a quality of great emotion. Vincent was a very emotional man and a very emotional painter. He had a unique way of making his viewers feel his emotions when looking at his paintings. The emotion is found in the lines that make up the objects in the room and the room itself. Nothing is drawn in a neat, orderly way. Vincent's lines are curved, and everything looks a little out of focus, a little off-center. There is something in the lines and curves of this painting that draws you into it and, in a mysterious way, into Vincent's actual mood. When you enter this painting—and many of the artist's other works as well—you are meeting Vincent himself, face to face. Vincent was quite capable of drawing neat, straight lines, but he knew the power of curved ones and used them well.

Vincent van Gogh is now recognized as a great painter. Although that recognition would have pleased him, another development would have pleased him even more. People have come to love his paintings. Vincent would consider this affection the most important recognition an artist can receive.

THE MAGIC SHOW

Presto chango! Hocus-pocus! Now you see it, now you don't. Or maybe it's the other way around. Well, no matter. Whatever it is, it's magic. And magic has taken the globe by storm. An elephant disappears here, pigeons and rabbits suddenly appear from a hat there, and people are sawed in half! But magic itself is not just an act that suddenly disappears and reappears at a snap of the fingers. It's been around for thousands of years, and if the current craze is any indication, sleight of hand will remain with us for years to come.

The mysterious world of magic and magicians began many centuries ago. In fact, it's quite possible that the round white pebbles found by archeologists in prehistoric caves were part of the equipment early entertainers used to beguile their fellow cavemen.

Early Greek and Roman writings tell of a number of famous magicians and jugglers. Their magical tricks included turning a wax model of a crocodile into a real one, juggling a dozen balls at one time, and cutting off the head of a goose and suddenly restoring it to its proper place moments later. Ancient conjurers and magicians of India and the Orient mystified audiences with incredible feats of magic. Goldfish bowls were plucked out of the air, and sticks of wood were turned into snakes.

But, presto . . . abracadabra, magic has come a long way in the last 3,500 years. And as if to prove that point, Doug Henning, a 27-year-old Canadian-born magician, is amazing Broadway audiences in the hit rock musical *The Magic Show*. Doug Henning doesn't keep his audiences entranced with small-time magic tricks. He doesn't wave a wand and pull a rabbit out of a top hat—although he does turn a dove into a rabbit. Doug does his conjuring on a grand scale. He doesn't refer to himself as a trickster. He bills himself as a master illusionist. What's the difference between magic tricks and illusions? "Show a small box empty and produce a bowl of goldfish—that's a trick," Henning explains. "Show a huge box empty and produce an elephant—that's an illusion."

And produce them he does! Well, maybe not elephants, but he does conjure up a real live cougar. This isn't just any cougar—it used to be a girl. But once Doug Henning exercises his magical powers, the girl turns into a cougar right before your very eyes! It's magic!

Henning's sorcery doesn't stop there. He goes the great Houdini one better by performing the famous "metamorphosis" in a record one third of a second. In this illusion, a girl is handcuffed and put in a sack, which is then put in a chest. The chest is locked and covered with a cloth. The cloth is removed, and before you can blink an eye, Henning has changed places with the girl—handcuffed inside the sack, inside the chest!

That's not all. He floats people in midair, makes people appear and disappear at the wave of a hand, takes them apart and puts them back together again. He causes various objects to soar across the stage. And just when you think you've seen everything, Henning takes a newspaper, tears it into shreds, and stands there holding the pieces before him. Without the help of a long-sleeved coat or a suspicious-looking long black cape, and with no hands behind his back, he proceeds to open his hands, revealing the newspaper restored without so much as a tear or a piece of tape! Have your eyes deceived you?

Henning is indeed a true master of illusion. He is a serious student of magic, but the talent was not acquired with the wave of a wand. It all began in Winnipeg, Canada, when he was ten years old. Doug started with a beginner's magic set, coin tricks, and a pet rabbit. As a teenager he took his highly polished magic act to coffeehouses and rock festivals. After graduating from college, Doug studied with master magicians all over the world. He also studied pantomime and acting because his ambition was to combine magic with theater. And presto! Before you could say "shazam," *The Magic Show* opened to rave reviews, and Doug Henning cast his spell on Broadway audiences.

Do you believe in magic? Well, if you do, just snap your fingers, say "abracadabra," and before your very eyes, amazing magic pictures will appear on the following pages. Presto! Chango! Abracadabra!

Doug Henning has sawed a woman in half in the hit Broadway musical *The Magic Show.*

Doug Henning and his magical linking rings.

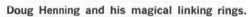

Presto! After performing a few quick moves, Doug presents the zigzag lady.

Will Doug escape from the "Bed of Horrors"?

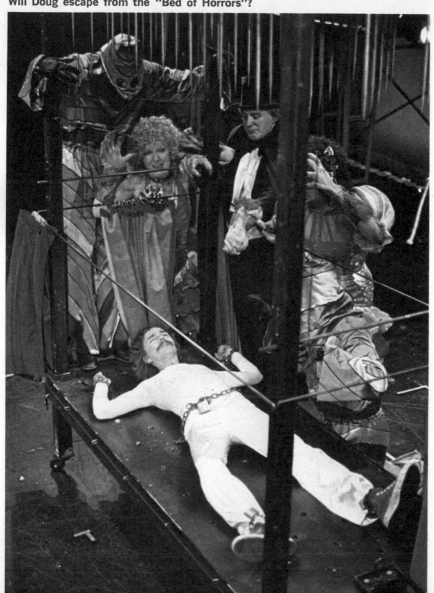

Dale Soules is balanced by one sword . . . and magic.

There are different ways to produce illusions. The Floating Woman: a rod supporting a narrow platform, is attached to a hydraulic lift hidden below the stage. The woman lies on the platform. As the rod rises, concealed from view in the magician's clothes, the woman appears to be levitating. Because of the way the rod and platform are connected (see diagram), a hoop can be moved from her head to toe, giving the impression that she is suspended in midair. The Severed Body: two women are used to create this illusion.

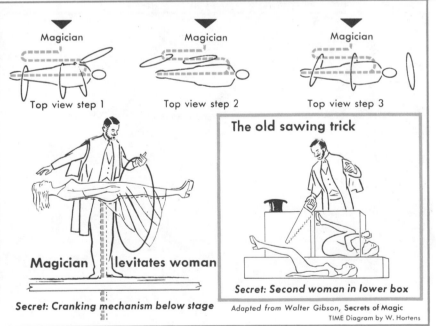

Magician

Top view step 1

Magician

Top view step 2

Magician

Top view step 3

Magician levitates woman

Secret: Cranking mechanism below stage

The old sawing trick

Secret: Second woman in lower box

Adapted from Walter Gibson, Secrets of Magic
TIME Diagram by W. Hortens

IN PRAISE OF HANDS

There are many differences between a hand-woven, hand-printed Indian cotton fabric and a machine-woven, machine-printed copy of an Indian cotton fabric. The handworked piece is more interesting in texture, more subtle in color, and more distinctive in detail.

For many years craftsmen and their friends have worked together to save the traditional crafts and stimulate new ones. In 1964, delegates from 46 countries met in New York and founded the World Crafts Council to further the interests of craftsmen. By 1974 the council had grown to an organization of 79 member countries, associated with the United Nations Educational, Scientific and Cultural Organization (UNESCO). Many of the countries belonging to the council had also set up national councils of their own.

The World Crafts Council holds a conference of craftsmen every two years. In 1974, in celebration of the tenth anniversary of the founding of the Council, the first World Crafts Exhibition was held, in Toronto, Canada.

More than 1,000 objects were selected for the impressive exhibition. They were chosen from work done since 1970. The exhibits were on view throughout the summer at Toronto's vast Ontario Science Centre. About 1,000,000 people flocked to see the show.

What attracted such unusual attention was the festival's extraordinary variety. The traditional crafts were magnificently represented. The ingenuity of modern craftsmen was shown in a great array of forms, materials, and designs.

Subtitled "In Praise of Hands," the exhibition was also a celebration of craftsmen themselves. Some of the craftsmen set up shop in the center and invited spectators to work with them. Others told or sang of the folklore of their crafts while they worked.

Many of the most beautiful and unusual objects were made from textiles. They were knit, woven, knotted, stitched, quilted, and crocheted. Some works showed the complex

A Canadian Eskimo crafted this charming wall hanging of appliquéd wool.

techniques of the Andean Indians, of South America. Their ancestors' handwoven ceremonial cloths had become an art form centuries before Christ. Other works drew on the European tapestry tradition. Also included in the exhibit were examples of an unusual method of painting called yarn painting. In this Mexican art form, yarns of various colors are carefully pressed into a layer of beeswax on a canvas. In this way a vivid picture or abstract design can be created.

Many visitors were interested in the ceramic displays. These ranged from useful pottery of primitive design to a pop art "wrapped parcel" made of stoneware. In between was a spectacular array of earthenware pieces—colorful Spanish and Latin American bowls, a beautiful dinner platter of classical Japanese design, modern dinnerware of Scandinavian design, and varied examples of African folk-craft.

Other exhibits contained glassware, jewelry, baskets, hammocks, hats, even boats—almost anything that expressed the individuality of its creator.

Notable among the exhibits were a beaded stool with a crocodile base, from Cameroon; a folk-art altar from Mexico; a traditional straw rain cape from Spain; and a porcupine-quill breastplate of Sioux Indian design. A feathered headdress from the South Pacific represented pure folk art—and plumed tiaras and evening bags from California were stunning commercial adaptations of it.

But of all the features of the show none involved the public so directly as the workshops. These were devoted to such crafts as quilting, weaving, baking, glassblowing, boat-building, and pottery making. Lessons were offered in how to make rope, dolls, masks, puppets, paper constructions, toys, and games. The center hired many craftsmen for the purpose. Spectators were invited to watch the demonstrations and to participate in them if they wished. Thousands did so. They threw pots on pottery wheels, sewed patches into giant quilts, wove fabrics on a handloom, even learned how to make their own simple looms.

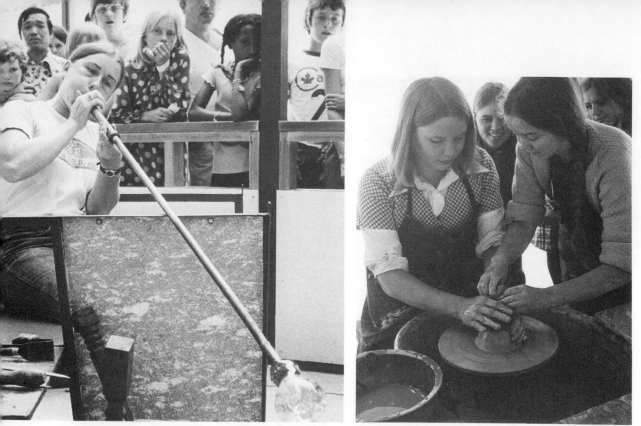

In addition to showing a great number of beautiful craft objects, the exhibition included craft workshops. Crafters demonstrated glassblowing (*above left*), pottery throwing (*above right*), and yarn painting (*below*).

Masks (*left*) and containers (*right*) from around the world.

How to make a psaltery—a musical instrument of ancient and medieval times.

Creating with rope.

Other shops offered instruction in making musical instruments, shearing sheep, silversmithing, and yarn painting.

In addition to the workshops there were performances of folk song and dance. Musicians and dancers came from as far away as Scotland, Africa, India, and Mexico. Of particular interest were the Australian aborigines, who combined demonstrations of folk art with folk music and dance. Audiences were enchanted by the traditional patterns in which the aborigines paint their bodies and by the exuberance of their native spear dances.

As perhaps never before the audiences saw the richness of folk culture. In particular, they saw the important connection between the mind and the hands, both in primitive people and in the artists of today. And, in fact, that was the whole point of the show—to make each visitor aware of creative craftsmanship and to awaken in each a desire to participate.

A study commissioned by the World Crafts Council indicates that the market for handcraft objects is enormous. If the objects are "well-conceived, well-made, well-packed, well-shipped and well-traded," the study shows, the market for them will not be satisfied in the foreseeable future.

The council has found no lack of those who practice creative crafts. A delegate from Mexico, for instance, reported that more than 5,000,000 Mexicans, nearly one sixth of that country's population, already support themselves wholly or in part by handcrafts.

This head of Ravana, a figure from Hindu myth, is made of bamboo strips covered with paper.

A papier-mâché tiger from Japan.

Steven Warner, as the little prince, meets the snake, played by Bob Fosse.

THE LITTLE PRINCE

Once upon a time, not very long ago, a French author wrote a charming book about a little prince who lived all alone on a tiny planet somewhere in the vast universe. The book was called *The Little Prince,* and the author was Antoine de Saint-Exupéry. Children and adults read and re-read Saint-Exupéry's fable. Its popularity became so widespread that the book was translated into many languages and went through countless printings. In no time at all, *The Little Prince* became recognized as a classic.

Because the book traveled to many lands throughout the world, people had the opportunity to read about the adventures of the little prince who leaves his home on Asteroid B-612—that's the name of his planet—and journeys to Earth in search of true happiness. The book introduced readers to a lovely flower who worried about her beauty—and catching a cold—and to a sly fox who wasn't really so

sly after all. In fact, his one ambition in life was to be tamed. And for those who like reptiles, there's a friendly snake who spends his day giving good advice.

Usually the combination of a tame fox, a proud rose, a friendly snake, a distant planet no larger than a house, and a little prince would make a fascinating fairy tale. And it does. But *The Little Prince* is more than just a fairy tale.

Saint-Exupéry may very well have written himself into the story. In addition to all the unusual creatures in the book, one of the main characters is an aviator whose plane has crashed in the middle of the Sahara, the enormous desert that covers most of North Africa. It is this pilot who eventually meets the little prince and relates to the reader the prince's story.

Some people feel that this part of the book is based on a dramatic episode in the author's life. Many years ago Saint-Exupéry crash-landed in the North African desert while attempting to set a flight record. He nearly died of thirst before a wandering nomad

The little prince, ruler of Asteroid B-612, waters his favorite rose.

rescued him. Perhaps Saint-Exupéry did meet some strange person from another planet, who was roaming through the Sahara. Well, whatever did or didn't happen is not really important. What is important is that Saint-Exupéry wrote a touching and beautiful story —a story meant for the whole world to read and enjoy. So if you'd like to find out more about the adventures of the little prince— and he has quite a few of them—you can visit your neighborhood library. There, among all the books on the shelves, you'll find *The Little Prince,* complete with watercolor illustrations by the author himself.

Paramount Pictures, however, had another idea. They've brought *The Little Prince,* based on the story by Antoine de Saint-Exupéry, to the motion-picture screen. And it's one of the most charming films of the year. Not only does the little prince appear in beautiful color, but you'll be able to meet the snake, the fox, and the lovely rose—all alive, and singing and dancing.

Now, it isn't an easy task to bring a fox, a reptile, and a flower to life as movie stars, but the film does just that. Bob Fosse, an actor-dancer-choreographer-director, plays the snake in this musical version of *The Little Prince.* And just in case you think it's easy to be a snake, think again. Mimi, an eight-year-old, 8-foot-long (2.4-meter-long) boa constrictor, who also has a part in the film, showed Mr. Fosse how to behave like a snake. This is probably the first time a snake has trained an actor to slither gracefully along the branches of a tree.

Character actor Gene Wilder plays the lonely fox who longs for someone to tame him. And Donna McKechnie makes her film debut as the lovely flower on Asteroid B-612.

Motion-picture and Broadway-stage actor Richard Kiley stars as the pilot who crashlands in the desert and is befriended by the little prince. And of course you can't have a prince without the help of a young man to play the title role. Over 700 actors were auditioned before 6½-year-old Steven Warner of London, England, was chosen to be the little prince who comes to Earth to learn the secret of what is really important in life.

Once the cast is assembled there's not much more to do . . . except, of course, to make the film. And to do that, it's usually necessary to travel, particularly if the locations are Asteroid B-612 and the great Sahara. The producer-director of the film, Stanley Donen, chose Tozeur, a small oasis town at the very tip of the Sahara in western Tunisia, as the location for the film. But the Sahara was just not quite right. A few changes had to be made before the desert was ready to be filmed. A shallow little lake with a small waterfall was conjured up in true movie fashion. A monster fish skeleton and a tree large enough to support two snakes—one human and one real—were also built.

After six weeks of filming in wind and rainstorms, and in the heat and sudden freezing cold of the desert, the film company moved to a movie studio near London, and that's where the film was completed. So what you see on the motion-picture screen is a combination of real desert and man-made desert. But you won't be able to tell the difference. Even Asteroid B-612 looks authentic, and Paramount Pictures won't say where those scenes were filmed. Maybe the film crew and young Steven Warner went on an interplanetary flight to find a planet no bigger than a house. When you make a movie, anything is possible.

There you have it. One of the most popular children's (and adults') books of all time is transferred to the screen. Oh, but wait just a moment. One important ingredient has been added. The producer decided that Antoine de Saint-Exupéry's beautiful story should have music.

Alan Jay Lerner and Frederick Loewe, who had teamed up to write the lyrics and the music for several hit Broadway shows, wrote the screenplay and lyrics and the music for *The Little Prince.* There are dances for the snake and the fox, as well as songs for the pilot and the prince. Everyone, in fact, sings and dances. It's a happy and touching film.

The Little Prince will probably always hold a special place in people's hearts. Antoine de Saint-Exupéry once wrote that "all grown-ups were once children—although few of them remember it." The film of *The Little Prince* is a reminder to both adults and children of what growing up is all about. The story is for everyone with the imagination to dream.

On Earth, the little prince meets many characters. A not-so-sly fox, Gene Wilder, gives the prince some friendly advice (*above*). Richard Kiley is the aviator (*below*), whose life takes on a new meaning after he meets the prince.

Glenn Gould is at ease in his recording studio—his private "concert hall."

CANADA'S UNIQUE MUSICIAN

One of the busiest and most popular pianists in the world is actually retired. At least that's what he says. But if you're Glenn Gould, Toronto-born pianist and composer, being retired is not that easy. In fact, it's a lot harder than working.

In 1964, at the height of his career, Glenn Gould abandoned the concert stage in search of something better. He grew weary of hotel living, hotel food, travel, applause, and concerts in general. So he officially declared that concert halls were dead, and he headed for greener pastures.

Many people predicted that this strange behavior would lead Gould to instant oblivion rather than greener pastures. But it was his fans who had trouble making the adjustment. They found it difficult to adjust to concerts without Gould and the eccentricities that were part of his performances: his ever-present glass of water; the sound of his squeaking piano stool; the piano propped up on blocks; and the muffler, sweater, and heavy jacket he always wore as a protection from drafts. They also most certainly missed the sound of Gould's humming and singing while he played Beethoven's piano sonatas, and the way he conducted the orchestra whenever he had a free hand.

But Gould is not one to disappoint his fans—or music lovers in general. In fact, he has been pleasantly surprising just about everyone since he began to play the piano when he was three years old. His mother, an amateur pianist herself, taught Glenn to read music. That was the beginning.

From 1943 to 1952 he attended the Royal Conservatory of Music of Toronto, where he studied piano, organ, and composition. At twelve, Gould became the youngest musician to receive a degree from the Conservatory.

Gould made his professional debut at the age of fourteen, with the Toronto Symphony Orchestra. He began concert tours when he was nineteen. He won international fame in his appearances with the Berlin Philharmonic, the New York Philharmonic, and the symphony orchestras of Detroit, Pittsburgh, Montreal, Dallas, Vancouver, and San Francisco.

In 1957, Glenn Gould became the first North American pianist to be invited by the Soviet Government to perform in Russia. He gave concerts in Moscow and Leningrad and earned the praise of Soviet audiences and critics. His performance of *The Goldberg Variations* in Moscow's Tchaikovsky Hall prompted one critic to assert that Gould was actually a 200-year-old man who had studied under Johann Sebastian Bach!

Gould returned to Canada in triumph and became the host of an hour-long weekly radio show, "The Art of Glenn Gould." In addition, he became the first concert pianist to appear before the Canadian Broadcasting Corporation (CBC) television cameras.

Then came the famous concert in Chicago's Orchestra Hall, in March, 1964: Gould walked off the stage and declared that his career as a concert pianist was over. "The habit of concert going and concert giving, both as a social institution and as chief symbol of musical mercantilism will be . . . dormant in the 21st century," he declared as he announced his retirement. And besides that, Gould felt that his concert performances were not as perfect as those he had recorded.

So there it is. Retirement at 32. Nothing but the good, lazy life—no traveling, no airplanes, no hotels, and no bad food. But for someone who has been busy learning, playing the piano, and entertaining since the age of three, retirement is not the real answer.

The photographs at right capture a recording session. Gould hears a passage played back (*top*) and then tries it again (*center*) in his precise but sensitive way. He still props up his piano so he can sit low when performing (*bottom*).

Gould found that after he had left the public stage, his influence on music grew. So he returned to the one medium that allowed him to play the piano whenever he wanted, to indulge in his passion for experimentation, and at the same time to avoid all the unpleasant moments that always seem to occur on the concert circuit. He took his talents into the recording studio.

▶ RECORDING AND EXPERIMENTING

Many serious artists sit before the microphones and record an overly rehearsed, perfectly arranged piano selection. But not Gould. He experiments. He may play the same passage over and over again before he selects the interpretation to be recorded for release. His reason is simple. If a pianist is going to play a selection that has been recorded many times, by every major artist, he should try to do it differently. The piece should stimulate and interest the listener, not remind him of some other pianist.

But Gould isn't different just for the sake of being different. There's a well-planned method in his madness. He feels that in order to make the musical score live, the artist may have to change some of the directions included in the score—even if they are the composer's own, and no matter who the composer was. Beethoven, Bach, Mozart—all leave room for fresh interpretation.

Sometimes he takes great liberties with the score. Gould's interpretation might cause a slow, moderate movement to be magically transformed into one with a brisk, lively tempo. The composer, if he is still alive, may cringe and shake his head in amazement. The music critics may also harshly disagree with the new sound, but the public seems to approve. Gould's recordings are best sellers more often than not.

In the beginning, Gould's records were dominated by his performances of the keyboard music of Bach. But since his "retirement," he has taken on many other composers. Gould has recorded a good deal of Beethoven, and most of Arnold Schoenberg's piano music. He has also made a series of recordings in which his selection of pieces has often been as unusual as his interpretations. He has recorded an album of a piano sonata by Sergei Prokofiev and one by Alexander Scriabin, and works by the 16th-century English composers William Byrd and Orlando Gibbons. Handel's Suites for Harpsichord, a Grieg sonata, and Bizet's *Variations Chromatiques* are other popular recordings.

▶ ANOTHER MEDIUM—TELEVISION

"Retirement" and those greener pastures turned out to be more than just the recording studio. Television has also played an enormous part in Gould's life of leisure. The success of his earlier television ventures spurred him onward. In 1966 and 1967 he televised a series of four "Conversations with Humphry Burton." In these programs, Gould played and discussed the music of Bach, Beethoven, Schoenberg, and Richard Strauss. Then, in 1974, he filmed an hour-long presentation of "Music in Our Time," in which he demonstrated the music of the 20th century's first decade.

▶ A VERY PRIVATE LIFE

Pianists, whether "retired" or not, have private lives, and Glenn Gould is no exception. He sometimes values his privacy more than anything else. When he's not in the recording studio, Gould is busy writing music criticism, articles and essays, and notes for his album covers. Radio also continues to hold a fascination for him. He wrote an hour-long dramatic program called "The Idea of the North." The show is about life in the isolation of Canada's vast northland, a region that Gould knows very well.

Gould reads a lot and often composes music. But one thing you won't find him doing is practicing the piano. He can't stand scales and exercises, and feels they are all part of a conspiracy perpetuated by music teachers everywhere. That's not to say that he refuses to practice at all. During a recent recording session, he had 38 minutes of music to record, but his total practicing time was a mere 7 hours and 50 minutes. Now to the beginner, this might sound like a very long time. But to almost every other professional pianist, it's shockingly inadequate. It goes against almost every important rule in the pianists' book. But then, Glenn Gould has been known to break quite a few rules in his career.

1974 AT A GLANCE

JANUARY

2   President Richard M. Nixon signed into law a bill requiring states to set a maximum highway speed limit of 55 miles (89 kilometers) an hour for cars, buses, trucks, and other vehicles. The action was taken to ease the energy crisis. Driving at lower speeds uses less fuel.

2   Carlos Arias Navarro was sworn in as Spain's premier. He succeeded Luis Carrero Blanco, who had been assassinated in December, 1973.

4   William B. Saxbe, a United States senator from Ohio, succeeded Elliot L. Richardson as U.S. attorney general.

6   The United States began year-round daylight saving time in a test to see if an extra hour of daylight in the afternoon would result in a saving of fuel. A few parts of the country, notably Arizona, Hawaii, and most of Indiana, were exempted from turning their clocks ahead one hour, because of special circumstances.

Year-round daylight saving time meant that many young Americans had to leave for school in the dark.

Comet Kohoutek streaks across the sky.

12 Comet Kohoutek, named for its discoverer, Czech-born Luboš Kohoutek, made its closest approach to the earth, a distance of about 75,000,000 miles (120,000,000 kilometers), in January. The Hale Observatories in California photographed the comet and its 13,000,000-mile-long (20,800,000-km.-long) tail.

14 Jules Léger became Canada's 21st governor-general. He succeeded Roland Michener, who retired after serving for almost seven years.

14 In Canada a bill to limit government wiretapping and other electronic eavesdropping became law. The new law also forbids all private bugging.

18 Egypt and Israel signed agreements to separate their military forces along the Suez Canal, and to limit their troops and arms in that area. The troops had been situated on the Suez front since the October, 1973, war.

19 Mrs. Ella T. Grasso, member of the U.S. House of Representatives, formally started a campaign for the office of governor of Connecticut. She was the first woman to run for that office in Connecticut.

25 Bülent Ecevit became premier of Turkey, heading a new 25-member coalition cabinet. The new premier was leader of the Republican People's Party.

FEBRUARY

3   Daniel Oduber Quirós was elected president of Costa Rica for a four-year term.

3   A new Cultural Revolution was under way in Communist China, led by Party Chairman Mao Tse-tung. Many young people had been involved in the previous Cultural Revolution, which lasted from 1966 to 1969 and led to a severe disruption of China's political and economic systems.

4   Patricia Hearst, the nineteen-year-old daughter of publisher Randolph A. Hearst, was kidnapped from her apartment in Berkeley, California, by a radical organization called the Symbionese Liberation Army.

5   After a three-month journey Mariner 10, an unmanned U.S. spacecraft, flew within 3,600 miles (5,800 kilometers) of Venus and began sending back to earth the first closeup pictures of that planet.

7   Grenada, the most southerly of the Windward Islands in the Caribbean, became independent.

The island-nation of Grenada became independent.

The Skylab space station will remain in earth orbit for about eight years. Future astronauts are to visit Skylab and direct the station's fall out of orbit into an uninhabited area.

8 The third and last Skylab crew returned to earth, ending the longest manned space flight—84 days, 1 hour, and 17 minutes in orbit around the earth.

13 Aleksandr I. Solzhenitsyn, the controversial Russian writer and Nobel Prize winner, was deported from the Soviet Union and stripped of his citizenship.

21 Pakistan officially recognized Bangladesh (formerly East Pakistan) as a separate nation. In 1971 the countries had fought a bloody civil war.

28 Egypt and the United States announced that they were resuming diplomatic relations, which had been broken off since the 1967 Middle East war.

28 Parliamentary elections were held in Britain. Neither the governing Conservative Party nor the Labour Party won an overall majority of seats. The last time neither main party won an overall majority was in 1929.

28 By the end of the month, gas rationing plans were in effect in certain parts of the United States. The plans were mandatory in Hawaii and New Jersey and voluntary in Oregon, Washington, Massachusetts, Maryland, New York, and the District of Columbia.

MARCH

1   A federal grand jury indicted seven men, including several of President Richard M. Nixon's closest aides, on charges of conspiracy to obstruct justice by covering up the Watergate scandal. All the men had served President Nixon either in his administration or with the Committee for the Re-election of the President.

4   In Britain, Harold Wilson, the Labour Party leader, became prime minister. He succeeded Edward Heath, the leader of the Conservatives, who had held the position since 1970. Heath resigned after the Conservatives had lost their majority in the February elections for the 635-seat House of Commons and after an unsuccessful attempt to form a coalition with the Liberal Party.

12   Carlos Andrés Pérez was inaugurated as president of Venezuela. In his inaugural address he said that Venezuela would seek to take possession of the oil industry, which was now largely owned by U.S. companies.

12   An eerie photograph that brought to mind Alfred Hitchcock's movie *The Birds* startled many people. It showed some 10,000,000 blackbirds and starlings swarming over the tiny community of Graceham, Maryland. The birds had been frightening livestock and raiding gardens for months.

Does this photo remind you of Alfred Hitchcock's movie *The Birds*?

The first public appearance of Princess Anne and Captain Mark Phillips since the attempted kidnaping.

12 Lieutenant Hiroo Onoda of the Imperial Japanese Army returned to Tokyo after hiding out in a Philippine jungle for almost 30 years. He was greeted by his 86-year-old father, his 88-year-old mother, and a crowd of cheering spectators. When he had learned of the Japanese defeat of 29 years before, Onoda had said, "Defeat or victory, I have done my best."

15 General Ernesto Geisel was sworn in as president of Brazil, for a five-year term of office.

18 The oil embargo against the United States, which had been imposed by the Arab oil countries during the 1973 Middle East war, was officially lifted by most of the countries.

18 It was announced that the course of Pioneer 11, the U.S. spacecraft bound for Jupiter, would be shifted for exploration of Saturn as well.

20 Queen Elizabeth's daughter, Princess Anne, and Anne's husband, Captain Mark Phillips, escaped unharmed when a gunman fired several shots into their car while attempting to kidnap the Princess in London.

23 Kenya lifted a five-month ban on elephant hunting after a study indicated that the elephant was no longer in danger of extinction. A permit is necessary to hunt one of the approximately 150,000 elephants in Kenya.

29 Mariner 10 sent the first closeup pictures of the planet Mercury back to earth. The television photographs revealed a surface marked by deep craters and crossed by valleys of unknown origin. There are indications that Mercury has an unexpected although very weak magnetic field. Tiny traces of gas, and something like an "atmosphere," were detected.

APRIL

2 President Georges Pompidou of France died at the age of 62. Elected in 1969, Pompidou was the second president of the Fifth Republic, succeeding Charles de Gaulle.

3 President Richard M. Nixon announced that he would pay more than $400,000 in back taxes plus interest. The Internal Revenue Service and a congressional investigating committee had concluded that the President had underpaid his taxes during his first four years in the White House.

3 The worst tornado disaster in almost 50 years struck the United States and Canada, causing a toll of over 300 people dead and over $1,000,000,000 worth of property damage.

8 A bill increasing the minimum wage from $1.60 to $2.30 an hour was signed into law by President Richard M. Nixon. The increase will occur in stages, from May, 1974, to January, 1976. Over 36,000,000 workers are covered by the provisions of minimum-wage legislation.

10 In Israel, Premier Golda Meir announced her resignation because of divisions in both her own Labor Party and the coalition cabinet that had been formed in March. Mrs. Meir's government would remain in office until new national elections were held.

A devastating tornado bears down on Cincinnati, Ohio.

A well-protected policeman is ready for anything during Colombia's elections.

13   Westar 1, the first U.S. domestic-communications satellite, was launched from Cape Canaveral, Florida. More satellites were to follow, and the new networks were expected to reduce communication costs within the United States.

17   William E. Simon was named secretary of the treasury by President Richard M. Nixon. He was to succeed George P. Shultz.

21   The first free elections in more than twenty years were held in Colombia. A 60-year-old law professor, Alfonso López Michelsen, was elected president.

25   In Portugal a seven-man military junta seized control of the country from Premier Marcello Caetano. The take-over ended over 40 years of authoritarian rule in Portugal, and the junta expressed a desire to bring democracy to Portugal, and peace to Portugal's African colonies.

26   A two-week strike by Canadian postal workers ended although pay negotiations were still in progress. Canadian airport fire fighters, who had also been on strike for higher wages, also returned to their jobs.

MAY

4   Expo '74 opened in Spokane, Washington. Ecology was the theme of this world's fair. Participating nations included the United States, Canada, Japan, and the Soviet Union.

6   West German Chancellor Willy Brandt resigned because of a scandal resulting from the discovery that a member of his staff was a spy for East Germany. On the following day, Finance Minister Helmut Schmidt was named as Brandt's successor.

8   In Ottawa, Canadian Prime Minister Elliott Trudeau's minority government fell when it lost a vote of "no confidence" in its budget policies. The House of Commons voted 137–123 to defeat Trudeau's Liberal Party. New national elections were to be held in July.

9   For only the second time in the history of the United States, the Congress began hearings for the impeachment of a president. The House Judiciary Committee began examining evidence that could lead to a recommendation of impeachment to the House of Representatives.

14   Dr. Donald Coggan was named by Queen Elizabeth II as the next archbishop of Canterbury. The archbishop of Canterbury is the spiritual leader of the Church of England.

As soon as it was announced that new elections were to be held in Canada, Prime Minister Trudeau began campaigning.

Francine I. Neff practices her signature, which will appear on all U.S. paper currency issued during her term as treasurer of the United States.

15 A report issued by researchers at the University of California at San Diego indicated that human beings may have lived on the North American continent as long as 48,000 years ago. Using new techniques, the researchers had tested skull fragments that had been found in Southern California.

17 A new weather satellite was launched from Cape Canaveral, Florida. From a point above the equator off the coast of Brazil, the weather station was to transmit pictures to earth every 30 minutes. The steady stream of photographs was expected to make it possible to give early warning of tornadoes, hurricanes, and other storms.

19 Valéry Giscard d'Estaing was elected president of France, defeating Socialist François Mitterrand, who had Communist backing. The 48-year-old Giscard d'Estaing became the third president of the Fifth Republic.

29 Francine I. Neff was named by President Richard M. Nixon as the treasurer of the United States. Mrs. Neff became the seventh consecutive woman to hold the position.

31 Israel and Syria signed a ceasefire agreement in Geneva, Switzerland, following an intensive 32-day effort by U.S. Secretary of State Henry Kissinger to bring about a settlement. The agreement called for a separation of armed forces on the Golan Heights by a United Nations buffer zone, and for an exchange of prisoners taken in the 1973 war.

JUNE

2 Eighteen-year-old Jigme Singye Wangchuk was crowned as the fourth hereditary king of the small Asian country of Bhutan. The coronation took place in the capital city of Thimphu. The new king became the world's youngest reigning monarch.

3 The U.S. Supreme Court upheld a ten-year-old act of Congress that requires employers to pay equal wages for equal work to women and men.

3 Yitzhak Rabin became Israel's fifth premier, succeeding Mrs. Golda Meir, who had resigned.

8 Ballet dancers Valery Panov and his wife, Galina Ragozina, were informed by officials of the Soviet Union that they had permission to emigrate.

15 Scientists from about 70 nations began a survey of the South Atlantic. Men and equipment, including planes, satellites, and research ships, were to observe weather and sea conditions for 100 days in one of the largest international scientific experiments ever conducted. Among the subjects to be studied were the origin and development of tropical storms, and global climate trends.

17 The British-French supersonic jetliner, the Concorde, landed at the Logan International Airport in Boston, Massachusetts, completing its first transatlantic round trip. The trip from Boston to Paris took 3 hours and 10 minutes, and the flight from Paris to Boston took 3 hours and 7 minutes.

The Concorde, a supersonic jetliner, lands in Boston, completing its first transatlantic round trip.

Jigme Singye Wangchuk was crowned king of Bhutan and became, at 18, the world's youngest reigning monarch.

17 In London, England, the historic, 875-year-old Westminster Hall, the oldest part of the Houses of Parliament, was damaged by a bomb explosion. There was no damage to the House of Commons or the House of Lords.

17 China and France conducted atmospheric nuclear tests. The Chinese blast occurred at a test range in northwestern China. The French test, one of a series, was conducted in the South Pacific.

23 Nine American astronauts arrived in Moscow to begin a three-week joint training program with Soviet cosmonauts. The training was for a space linkup between the U.S. Apollo and Soviet Soyuz spacecrafts scheduled for 1975.

25 An orbital research station, Salyut 3, was launched by the Soviet Union.

27 A ten-year development agreement was signed by France and Iran. Included in the pact were provisions for the sale of five nuclear reactors to Iran.

28 President Richard M. Nixon and Soviet leader Leonid Brezhnev, meeting for their third summit conference, signed a ten-year economic agreement designed to promote Soviet-American trade.

JULY

Isabel Perón, president of Argentina.

1   Argentina's president, Juan Domingo Perón, died at the age of 78. He was succeeded by his widow, Isabel Perón, Argentina's vice-president. Mrs. Perón became the first woman chief of state in the Americas.

8   In Canada, Prime Minister Pierre Elliott Trudeau and his Liberal Party won a majority in the House of Commons in parliamentary elections.

9   Earl Warren, former chief justice of the United States, died at the age of 83. As chief justice he had presided over the Supreme Court from 1953 until his retirement in 1969.

14   In Lagos, Nigeria, United Nations officials announced that more than 1,000,000 tons of food were being distributed to seven North African nations stricken by drought. The food was to help the people of Chad, Mali, Mauritania, Gambia, Niger, Upper Volta, and Senegal.

15   The government of Archbishop Makarios III, president of Cyprus, was overthrown. Cypriot troops led by Greek officers carried out the military coup. The majority of the population of Cyprus is of Greek descent, but there is a large minority of Turkish Cypriots.

16 Fifteen women were admitted to the U.S. Merchant Marine Academy as cadets. They became the first women cadets in a federal service academy.

17 President Valéry Giscard d'Estaing of France appointed journalist Françoise Giroud to the new post of Secretary of State for the Status of Women. The new cabinet member is a leading feminist.

22 A UN-sponsored ceasefire ended fighting between Greek Cypriots and Turkish forces on the island of Cyprus. Turkish troops had invaded Cyprus on July 20. Greece and Turkey agreed to meet in Geneva, Switzerland, for discussions on the Cyprus problem.

23 Greece's military junta resigned because of its failure to take over the island of Cyprus, and under threat of a war with Turkey. The next day, former premier Constantine Caramanlis, who had governed from 1955 to 1963, was sworn in as the head of a new civilian government.

30 The U.S. House Judiciary Committee recessed after having adopted three articles of impeachment against President Richard M. Nixon. The President was charged with obstruction of justice, unconstitutional use of his powers, and failure to obey subpoenas issued by the committee.

31 The Lieutenant Governor of the Canadian province of Quebec signed into law a bill making French the only official language of Quebec. The bill had been opposed by English-speaking Canadians and Quebec nationalists.

Athenians were jubilant after Greece's military government resigned.

AUGUST

9   Richard Milhous Nixon, 37th president of the United States, resigned. It was the first time in the history of the United States that a president had resigned. Vice-President Gerald R. Ford was immediately sworn in as the 38th president by Chief Justice Warren E. Burger.

14   A 40-year-old ban on private ownership of gold bullion (uncoined gold) in the United States ended, effective December 31, 1974, when President Gerald R. Ford signed legislation passed by Congress.

17   In India, Fakhruddin Ali Ahmed, a member of Prime Minister Indira Gandhi's Congress Party, was elected president. Ahmed replaced V. V. Giri, who had served a five-year term.

20   Nelson A. Rockefeller, former governor of New York, was nominated by President Gerald R. Ford to be the 41st vice-president of the United States. The nomination was subject to confirmation by the Congress.

26   Soyuz 15, a manned Soviet spacecraft, was launched, but it did not achieve its intended docking with the Salyut 3 space station, which had been launched earlier. On August 28 the two-man crew of Soyuz 15 made the first night landing of a spacecraft.

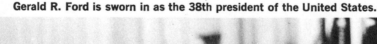
Gerald R. Ford is sworn in as the 38th president of the United States.

Tourists gaze at the *Spirit of St. Louis* in the Smithsonian Institution shortly after it became known that Charles A. Lindbergh had died.

26 Charles A. Lindbergh, the first man to fly solo across the Atlantic, died at the age of 72 in Hawaii. Lindbergh's nonstop flight from New York to Paris in 1927 made him a world hero. The flight, in a small plane named *Spirit of St. Louis,* took 33½ hours.

26 The 54th anniversary of U.S. woman suffrage was observed when President Gerald R. Ford proclaimed August 26 as Women's Equality Day.

30 In Bucharest, Rumania, the United Nations World Population Conference ended after meeting for two weeks. Over 1,200 delegates from 135 nations approved a Plan of Action intended to reduce the present annual population growth rate of 2 percent.

31 In Wellington, New Zealand, Norman E. Kirk, the 51-year-old prime minister, died. He was temporarily succeeded by the deputy prime minister, Hugh Watt, who was to head the government until the Labor Party elected a new prime minister.

SEPTEMBER

1   A U.S. reconnaissance jet, the SR-71 Blackbird, flew from New York to London in 1 hour, 55 minutes, and 42 seconds, setting a transatlantic speed record.

2   President Gerald R. Ford signed into law the Employee Benefit Security Act of 1974. The new law is a pension reform law to protect the retirement benefits of millions of workers.

6   Finance Minister William E. Rowling was named prime minister of New Zealand, succeeding the late Norman E. Kirk.

8   Former president Richard M. Nixon was granted a "full, free, and absolute pardon" for all offenses against the United States that he had committed or may have committed or may have taken part in during the period of his presidency. President Gerald R. Ford granted the pardon covering the period of January 20, 1969, through August 9, 1974.

9   Soviet cosmonauts and U.S. astronauts met at the Johnson Space Center in Houston, Texas, to train for the U.S.-Soviet space flight scheduled for 1975.

10   The West African territory of Portuguese Guinea became an independent country. The territory became the Republic of Guinea-Bissau after 500 years of Portuguese rule.

U.S. astronauts and Soviet cosmonauts share ideas at the Johnson Space Center.

Courageous (right) defeated *Southern Cross (left)* to win the America's Cup.

12 Emperor Haile Selassie of Ethiopia was deposed after having ruled for 58 years. A military committee had taken gradual control of the country after an army mutiny had occurred in February.

16 President Gerald R. Ford signed a proclamation that offered conditional clemency to Vietnam War draft evaders and military deserters. An oath of allegiance to the United States and up to 24 months of alternative public service were among the requirements for the approximately 28,000 men affected.

17 Three new countries were admitted to membership in the United Nations. They were Bangladesh, Guinea-Bissau, and Grenada.

17 The American yacht *Courageous* defeated the Australian challenger, *Southern Cross,* to win the America's Cup race series off Newport, Rhode Island.

20 It was announced that a thirteenth moon of the planet Jupiter had been discovered. Charles T. Kowal, a research assistant at the Hale Observatories on Mount Palomar, California, had photographed the thirteenth moon on three successive nights.

OCTOBER

1 Five men indicted in March by a federal grand jury went on trial in Washington, D.C., on charges of conspiracy to obstruct justice by covering up the Watergate scandal. The five included former president Richard M. Nixon's closest aides, H. R. Haldeman and John Ehrlichman, as well as former attorney general John N. Mitchell.

10 In Britain the Labour Party won a majority in Parliament in the second general election of 1974. Prime Minister Harold Wilson became the first British prime minister to win four general elections in the 20th century.

12 The Mexican Government confirmed reports of the discovery of large oil deposits in southeastern Mexico. The deposits are in the Mexican states of Tabasco and Chiapas. Although exact quantities were unknown, the find was being compared to petroleum deposits in the Persian Gulf and the Alaska North Slope.

Muhammad Ali sends George Foreman to the canvas in the eighth round, winning the world heavyweight boxing championship.

17 President Gerald R. Ford made an appearance before a House Judiciary subcommittee to explain his pardon of former president Nixon. Ford's appearance was historic in that it was almost unprecedented for a president to appear formally before a congressional committee.

22 The Canadian Government announced stricter regulations governing immigration. The new rules were made in an attempt to stop the rising unemployment rate in Canada.

23 The International Olympic Committee announced that the 1980 Summer Games would be held in Moscow and that the Winter Games would be held at Lake Placid, New York. (The 1976 games are to be held in Montreal, Canada, and Innsbruck, Austria.)

25 Human fossils found in central Ethiopia appeared to be about 4,000,000 years old, according to members of a joint American-French-Ethiopian anthropological expedition. It was believed that the fossils were 1,000,000 years older than the previously oldest known fossil, found in Kenya.

28 Arab heads of state recognized the Palestine Liberation Organization as the "sole legitimate representative of the Palestinian people."

30 Muhammad Ali regained the world heavyweight boxing championship by knocking out heavily favored George Foreman in the eighth round of their bout in Kinshasa, Zaïre.

THE 1974 NOBEL PRIZES

Chemistry: Paul J. Flory of the United States, for studies in macromolecules.

Economics: Gunnar Myrdal of Sweden and Friedrich von Hayek of Austria, for analysis of the interdependence of economic, social, and institutional phenomena.

Literature: Harry Edmund Martinson of Sweden, for his novels and poetry, and Eyvind Johnson of Sweden, for his novels.

Peace: Eisaku Sato of Japan, for attempts to stop the proliferation of nuclear weapons; Seán MacBride of Ireland, for work in behalf of human rights.

Physics: Sir Martin Ryle and Antony Hewish of Britain, for pioneering work in radio astrophysics.

Physiology or Medicine: Albert Claude and Christian René de Duve of Belgium, and George Emil Palade of the United States, for research in cell biology.

NOVEMBER

5 Voters' concern over the Watergate scandals and bad economic conditions swept many Republicans out of office in congressional, state, and local elections in the United States. The Democrats increased their majorities in the Senate and the House of Representatives, and won the crucial governorships of New York and California.

12 The General Assembly of the United Nations voted to suspend the Republic of South Africa from participation in its 1974 session. South Africa retained its membership, but its representatives were not permitted to speak or vote.

13 Yasir Arafat, leader of the Palestine Liberation Organization, spoke at the United Nations on "the Question of Palestine." The General Assembly had recognized the P.L.O. on October 14 as the only representative of the Palestinian people and had invited the organization to participate in the Palestine debate.

Delegates to the World Food Conference were asked to weigh themselves on the "Scale of Justice" and pay a tax on any excess weight.

Lampposts on the Ginza in Tokyo bear signs welcoming U.S. President Gerald R. Ford to Japan. The Japanese and U.S. flags hang side by side.

16 A UN-sponsored World Food Conference, devoted to the problem of hunger and malnutrition in the world, ended a two-week meeting in Rome, Italy. The conference recommended the establishment of a new UN agency, the World Food Council, which would guide food programs.

17 In the first Greek general election since 1964, the New Democracy Party of Premier Constantine Caramanlis won a majority of parliamentary seats.

18 President Gerald R. Ford flew to Japan, beginning an eight-day tour of Asia that included visits to South Korea and the Soviet Union. Ford was the first U.S. president to visit Japan. The state visits included meetings with Emperor Hirohito and Prime Minister Kakuei Tanaka of Japan, and President Chung Hee Park of South Korea.

24 Leonid Brezhnev of the Soviet Union and President Gerald R. Ford met in Vladivostok and reached tentative agreement regarding the limitation of nuclear armaments.

25 U Thant, the third secretary-general of the United Nations, died at the age of 65. U Thant, from Burma, had served for ten years before retiring in December, 1971.

DECEMBER

3   Pioneer 11, an unmanned American spacecraft, came within 26,600 miles (42,800 kilometers) of Jupiter, the largest planet in the solar system. Pioneer 11 sent information and pictures of the planet and its environment back to earth. The craft continued its flight through the outer parts of the solar system and was scheduled to fly by Saturn in 1979.

4   Prime Minister Pierre Elliott Trudeau of Canada and President Gerald R. Ford of the United States met in Washington for talks on oil, energy resources, and environmental matters.

7   Archbishop Makarios III returned to Cyprus as president. He had been in exile for almost five months after a coup forced him to leave the island in mid-July.

Pioneer 11 photographs of Jupiter—at left, from 660,000 miles (1,100,000 km.) and, at right, from 26,600 miles (42,800 km.).

 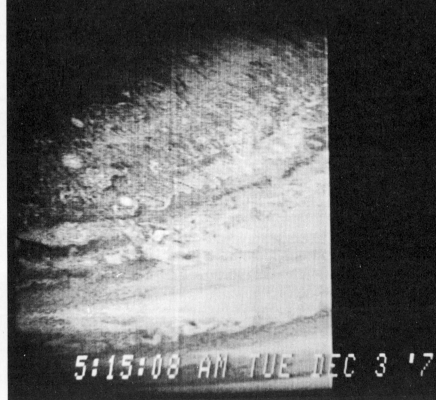

Nelson A. Rockefeller is sworn in as vice-president of the United States by Chief Justice Warren Burger.

8 In a national referendum, the citizens of Greece voted that Greece would become a republic, or, as it was called on the ballot, an "uncrowned democracy." As a result of the vote, King Constantine, who had been living in exile for seven years, was stripped of his title.

9 Takeo Miki was formally elected premier by the Japanese parliament. He succeeded Kakuei Tanaka. Tanaka had resigned, following accusations that he had used political office to acquire a personal fortune.

13 Malta, a Mediterranean island group, became a republic. The governor-general, Sir Anthony Mamo, was sworn in as the first president. Although it will no longer recognize the British monarch as its head of state, Malta will remain within the Commonwealth of Nations.

19 Nelson Aldrich Rockefeller was sworn in as the 41st vice-president of the United States after having been confirmed by both houses of Congress.

25 A cyclone struck the city of Darwin in northern Australia. Ninety percent of the buildings in Darwin were destroyed, and more than 20,000 people were left homeless. The cyclone injured hundreds and left about 50 people dead.

29 Northern Pakistan was struck by an earthquake that shook nine towns. Over 5,000 people were killed and 15,000 injured. The quake continued intermittently for 24 hours.

INTERNATIONAL STATISTICAL SUPPLEMENT
(as of December 31, 1974)

NATION	CAPITAL	AREA (in sq. mi.)	POPULATION (estimate)	GOVERNMENT
Afghanistan	Kabul	250,000	18,300,000	Mohammed Daud Khan—president
Albania	Tirana	11,100	2,400,000	Enver Hoxha—communist party secretary Mehmet Shehu—premier
Algeria	Algiers	919,593	15,800,000	Houari Boumédienne—president
Argentina	Buenos Aires	1,072,158	24,300,000	Isabel Perón—president
Australia	Canberra	2,967,900	13,200,000	Gough Whitlam—president
Austria	Vienna	32,374	7,600,000	Rudolf Kirchschläger—president Bruno Kreisky—chancellor
Bahamas	Nassau	5,380	193,000	Lynden O. Pindling—prime minister
Bahrain	Manama	240	230,000	Isa bin Sulman al-Khalifa—head of government
Bangladesh	Dacca	55,126	71,700,000	Mohammed Ullah—president Mujibur Rahman—prime minister
Barbados	Bridgetown	166	243,000	Errol W. Barrow—prime minister
Belgium	Brussels	11,781	9,800,000	Baudouin I—king Leo Tindemans—premier
Bhutan	Thimbu	18,147	900,000	Jigme Singye Wangchuk—king
Bolivia	La Paz	424,163	5,400,000	Hugo Banzer Suárez—president
Botswana	Gaborone	231,804	650,000	Sir Seretse Khama—president
Brazil	Brasília	3,286,478	101,700,000	Ernesto Geisel—president
Bulgaria	Sofia	42,823	8,700,000	Todor Zhivkov—communist party secretary Stanko Todorov—premier
Burma	Rangoon	261,789	29,600,000	U Ne Win—president U Sein Win—prime minister
Burundi	Bujumbura	10,747	3,600,000	Michel Micombero—president
Cambodia (Khmer Republic)	Pnompenh	69,898	7,700,000	Lon Nol—president Long Boret—premier
Cameroon	Yaoundé	183,569	6,200,000	Ahmadou Ahidjo—president
Canada	Ottawa	3,851,809	22,400,000	Pierre Elliott Trudeau—prime minister
Central African Republic	Bangui	240,535	1,800,000	Jean Bedel Bokassa—president
Ceylon (Sri Lanka)	Colombo	25,332	13,300,000	William Gopallawa—president Sirimavo Bandaranaike—premier
Chad	N'Djemena	495,754	3,900,000	Ngarta Tombalbaye—president
Chile	Santiago	292,257	10,300,000	Augusto Pinochet Ugarte—president

NATION	CAPITAL	AREA (in sq. mi.)	POPULATION (estimate)	GOVERNMENT
China	Peking	3,705,396	814,300,000	Mao Tse-tung—communist party chairman Chou En-lai—premier
China (Taiwan)	Taipei	13,885	15,000,000	Chiang Kai-shek—president Chiang Ching-kuo—premier
Colombia	Bogotá	439,736	23,200,000	Alfonso López Michelsen—president
Congo	Brazzaville	132,047	1,000,000	Marien Ngouabi—president Henri Lopès—prime minister
Costa Rica	San José	19,575	1,900,000	Daniel Oduber Quirós—president
Cuba	Havana	44,218	8,900,000	Osvaldo Dorticós Torrado—president Fidel Castro—premier
Cyprus	Nicosia	3,572	660,000	Archbishop Makarios III—president
Czechoslovakia	Prague	49,370	14,600,000	Gustáv Husák—communist party secretary Ludvík Svoboda—president Lubomír Štrougal—premier
Dahomey	Porto-Novo	43,483	2,900,000	Mathieu Kerekou—president
Denmark	Copenhagen	16,629	5,100,000	Margrethe II—queen Poul Hartling—premier
Dominican Republic	Santo Domingo	18,816	4,500,000	Joaquín Balaguer—president
Ecuador	Quito	109,483	6,800,000	Guillermo Rodríguez Lara—president
Egypt	Cairo	386,660	35,700,000	Anwar el-Sadat—president Abdul Aziz Hegazi—prime minister
El Salvador	San Salvador	8,260	3,900,000	Arturo Armando Molina—president
Equatorial Guinea	Malabo	10,830	300,000	Francisco Macías Nguema—president
Ethiopia	Addis Ababa	471,777	26,100,000	military government
Fiji	Suva	7,055	550,000	Ratu Sir Kamisese Mara—prime minister
Finland	Helsinki	130,120	4,700,000	Urho K. Kekkonen—president Kalevi Sorsa—premier
France	Paris	211,207	52,200,000	Valéry Giscard d'Estaing—president Jacques Chirac—premier
Gabon	Libreville	103,346	520,000	Albert B. Bongo—president
Gambia	Banjul	4,361	500,000	Sir Dauda K. Jawara—president
Germany (East)	East Berlin	41,768	17,000,000	Erich Honecker—communist party secretary Horst Sindermann—premier
Germany (West)	Bonn	95,976	62,000,000	Walter Scheel—president Helmut Schmidt—chancellor
Ghana	Accra	92,099	9,400,000	Ignatius K. Acheampong—head of government

NATION	CAPITAL	AREA (in sq. mi.)	POPULATION (estimate)	GOVERNMENT
Greece	Athens	50,944	9,100,000	Phaidon Gizikis—president Constantine Caramanlis—premier
Grenada	St. George's	133	100,000	Eric M. Gairy—prime minister
Guatemala	Guatemala City	42,042	5,600,000	Kjell Laugerud García—president
Guinea	Conakry	94,926	4,200,000	Sékou Touré—president Lansana Beavogui—premier
Guinea-Bissau	Bissau	13,948	510,000	Luiz de Almeida Cabral—president
Guyana	Georgetown	83,000	800,000	Arthur Chung—president Forbes Burnham—prime minister
Haiti	Port-au-Prince	10,714	5,200,000	Jean-Claude Duvalier—president
Honduras	Tegucigalpa	43,277	2,800,000	Oswaldo López Arellano—president
Hungary	Budapest	35,919	10,500,000	János Kádár—communist party secretary Jenő Fock—Premier
Iceland	Reykjavik	39,768	210,000	Kristján Eldjárn—president Geir Hallgrimsson—prime minister
India	New Delhi	1,266,598	575,000,000	Fakhruddin Ali Ahmed—president Indira Gandhi—prime minister
Indonesia	Jakarta	735,269	126,000,000	Suharto—president
Iran	Teheran	636,294	31,300,000	Mohammed Reza Pahlavi—shah Amir Abbas Hoveida—premier
Iraq	Baghdad	167,925	10,400,000	Ahmed Hassan al-Bakr—president
Ireland	Dublin	27,136	3,000,000	Cearbhall O Dalaigh—president Liam Cosgrave—prime minister
Israel	Jerusalem	7,992	3,200,000	Ephraim Katzir—president Yitzhak Rabin—prime minister
Italy	Rome	116,303	54,900,000	Giovanni Leone—president Aldo Moro—premier
Ivory Coast	Abidjan	124,503	4,700,000	Félix Houphouët-Boigny—president
Jamaica	Kingston	4,232	2,000,000	Michael N. Manley—prime minister
Japan	Tokyo	143,689	108,400,000	Hirohito—emperor Takeo Miki—prime minister
Jordan	Amman	37,738	2,600,000	Hussein I—king Zaid al-Rifai—premier
Kenya	Nairobi	224,959	12,500,000	Jomo Kenyatta—president
Korea (North)	Pyongyang	46,540	15,100,000	Kim II Sung—president Kim II—premier
Korea (South)	Seoul	38,022	33,000,000	Chung Hee Park—president Kim Jong Pil—premier
Kuwait	Kuwait	6,880	900,000	Sabah al-Salim al-Sabah—head of state Jabir al-Ahmad al-Jabir—prime minister

NATION	CAPITAL	AREA (in sq. mi.)	POPULATION (estimate)	GOVERNMENT
Laos	Vientiane	91,429	3,200,000	Savang Vatthana—king Souvanna Phouma—premier
Lebanon	Beirut	4,015	3,100,000	Suleiman Franjieh—president Rashid Solh—premier
Lesotho	Maseru	11,720	1,000,000	Moshoeshoe II—king Leabua Jonathan—prime minister
Liberia	Monrovia	43,000	1,700,000	William R. Tolbert—president
Libya	Tripoli	679,360	2,200,000	Muammar el-Qaddafi—president Abdul Salam Jallud—premier
Liechtenstein	Vaduz	61	21,000	Francis Joseph II—prince
Luxembourg	Luxembourg	999	350,000	Jean—grand duke Gaston Thorn—premier
Malagasy Republic	Tananarive	226,657	7,500,000	Gabriel Ramanantsoa—head of government
Malawi	Zomba	45,747	4,800,000	H. Kamuzu Banda—president
Malaysia	Kuala Lumpur	127,316	11,600,000	Abdul Halim Muazzam—paramount ruler Tun Abdul Razak—prime minister
Maldives	Male	115	120,000	Ibrahim Nasir—president
Mali	Bamako	478,765	5,400,000	Moussa Traoré—president
Malta	Valletta	122	325,000	Sir Anthony Mamo—president Dom Mintoff—prime minister
Mauritania	Nouakchott	397,954	1,300,000	Moktar O. Daddah—president
Mauritius	Port Louis	720	870,000	Sir Seewoosagur Ramgoolam—prime minister
Mexico	Mexico City	761,602	54,300,000	Luis Echeverría Álvarez—president
Monaco	Monaco-Ville	0.4	25,000	Rainier III—prince
Mongolia	Ulan Bator	604,248	1,400,000	Yumzhagiyn Tsedenbal—communist party secretary
Morocco	Rabat	172,413	16,400,000	Hassan II—king Ahmed Osman—premier
Nauru		8	7,000	Hammer DeRoburt—president
Nepal	Katmandu	54,362	12,000,000	Birendra Bir Bikram Shah Deva—king Nagendra Prashad Rijal—prime minister
Netherlands	Amsterdam	15,770	13,500,000	Juliana—queen Joop den Uyl—premier
New Zealand	Wellington	103,736	3,000,000	Wallace E. Rowling—prime minister
Nicaragua	Managua	50,193	2,000,000	Anastasio Somoza Debayle—president
Niger	Niamey	489,190	4,300,000	Seyni Kountche—head of government
Nigeria	Lagos	356,668	79,000,000	Yakubu Gowon—head of government

NATION	CAPITAL	AREA (in sq. mi.)	POPULATION (estimate)	GOVERNMENT
Norway	Oslo	125,181	4,000,000	Olav V—king Trygve Bratteli—prime minister
Oman	Muscat	82,030	700,000	Qabus ibn Said—sultan
Pakistan	Islamabad	310,403	66,800,000	Chaudri Fazal Elahi—president Zulfikar Ali Bhutto—prime minister
Panama	Panama City	29,209	1,600,000	Omar Torrijos Herrera—head of government
Paraguay	Asunción	157,047	2,700,000	Alfredo Stroessner—president
Peru	Lima	496,223	14,900,000	Juan Velasco Alvarado—president
Philippines	Quezon City	115,830	40,300,000	Ferdinand E. Marcos—president
Poland	Warsaw	120,724	33,400,000	Edward Gierek—communist party secretary Piotr Jaroszewicz—premier
Portugal	Lisbon	35,553	8,600,000	Francisco da Costa Gomes—president Vasco dos Santos Gonçalves—premier
Qatar	Doha	4,000	150,000	Khalifa bin Hamad al-Thani—head of government
Rhodesia	Salisbury	150,803	5,900,000	Clifford Dupont—president Ian D. Smith—prime minister
Rumania	Bucharest	91,700	20,900,000	Nicolae Ceauşescu—communist party secretary Manea Manescu—premier
Rwanda	Kigali	10,169	4,000,000	Juvénal Habyalimana—president
Saudi Arabia	Riyadh	829,997	8,500,000	Faisal ibn Abdul Aziz—king
Senegal	Dakar	75,750	4,300,000	Léopold Senghor—president Abdou Diouf—prime minister
Sierra Leone	Freetown	27,700	2,900,000	Siaka P. Stevens—president Sorie I. Koroma—prime minister
Singapore	Singapore	224	2,200,000	Benjamin H. Sheares—president Lee Kuan Yew—prime minister
Somalia	Mogadishu	246,200	3,000,000	Mohammed Siad Barre—head of government
South Africa	Pretoria Cape Town	471,444	23,800,000	J. J. Fouché—president Balthazar J. Vorster—prime minister
Spain	Madrid	194,897	34,900,000	Francisco Franco—head of state Carlos Arias Navarro—premier
Sudan	Khartoum	967,497	16,900,000	Gaafar al-Numeiry—president
Swaziland	Mbabane	6,704	500,000	Sobhuza II—king
Sweden	Stockholm	173,732	8,200,000	Carl XVI Gustaf—king Olof Palme—prime minister
Switzerland	Bern	15,941	6,500,000	Pierre Graber—president

NATION	CAPITAL	AREA (in sq. mi.)	POPULATION (estimate)	GOVERNMENT
Syria	Damascus	71,586	6,900,000	Hafez al-Assad—president Mahmoud al-Ayubi—premier
Tanzania	Dar es Salaam	364,898	14,400,000	Julius K. Nyerere—president
Thailand	Bangkok	198,456	39,800,000	Bhumibol Adulyadej—king Sanya Dharmasakti—premier
Togo	Lomé	21,622	2,200,000	Étienne Eyadema—president
Tonga	Nuku'alofa	270	90,000	Taufa'ahau Tupou IV—king Prince Tu'ipelehake—prime minister
Trinidad & Tobago	Port of Spain	1,980	1,100,000	Eric Williams—prime minister
Tunisia	Tunis	63,170	5,500,000	Habib Bourguiba—president
Turkey	Ankara	301,381	38,000,000	Fahri Korutürk—president Sadi Irmak—premier
Uganda	Kampala	91,134	10,800,000	Idi Amin—president
U.S.S.R.	Moscow	8,649,512	249,800,000	Leonid I. Brezhnev—communist party secretary Aleksei N. Kosygin—premier Nikolai V. Podgorny—president of presidium
United Arab Emirates	Abu Dhabi	32,278	300,000	Zayd bin Sultan—president
United Kingdom	London	94,226	56,000,000	Elizabeth II—queen Harold Wilson—prime minister
United States	Washington, D.C.	3,615,123	212,900,000	Gerald R. Ford—president Nelson A. Rockefeller—vice-president
Upper Volta	Ouagadougou	105,869	5,800,000	Sangoulé Lamizana—president
Uruguay	Montevideo	68,536	3,000,000	Juan M. Bordaberry—president
Venezuela	Caracas	352,143	11,300,000	Carlos Andrés Pérez—president
Vietnam (North)	Hanoi	61,294	22,500,000	Le Duan—communist party secretary Ton Duc Thang—president Pham Van Dong—premier
Vietnam (South)	Saigon	67,108	19,400,000	Nguyen Van Thieu—president Tran Thien Khiem—premier
Western Samoa	Apia	1,097	150,000	Malietoa Tanumafili II—head of state Tupua Tamasese Lealofi IV—prime minister
Yemen (Aden)	Madinat al-Shaab	112,000	1,600,000	Salem Ali Rubaya—head of state Ali Nasir Mohammed—prime minister
Yemen (Sana)	Sana	75,290	6,200,000	Ibrahim al-Hamidi—head of government
Yugoslavia	Belgrade	98,766	21,000,000	Josip Broz Tito—president Dzemal Bijedić—premier
Zaïre	Kinshasa	905,565	23,600,000	Mobutu Sese Seko—president
Zambia	Lusaka	290,585	4,700,000	Kenneth D. Kaunda—president

DICTIONARY INDEX

A

Au pair. A French phrase meaning "on even terms." It is currently used to describe an arrangement by which a person performs services in exchange for something other than a salary. An au pair girl, for example, is one who works for a family as a domestic or a nursemaid in return for board and lodging. Frequently such a girl is a foreigner, who teaches her language to her employers or their children and learns their language in return.

Auto-train. A special train that carries passengers and their automobiles. Such a train enables railroad passengers to take their autos with them. Some of the train cars are passenger cars, and the others carry only automobiles and luggage. When the train arrives at its destination, the automobiles are unloaded and made ready for their owners.

B

Backpack. A pack carried on the back of a camper or a hiker. It consists of a frame of lightweight metal covered by cloth or plastic, with compartments fitted to hold the person's spare clothing and other belongings in a compact bundle. As a verb, "to backpack" means to carry belongings in such a pack or to travel while carrying a pack.

Biker. A young person who likes to ride a motorcycle or motorbike, often with a group.

C

Cablevision. Cable television, or community antenna television (CATV). This is a form of television in which broadcast signals do not travel in the usual manner, directly from the transmitter to the viewer's receiving set. Instead the signals are picked up by a large master antenna, strengthened, and then carried by special cable to the homes of people who pay a regular fee for the service. Cablevision provides a better television picture than that usually received on regular, broadcast television. This is especially true in areas distant from television transmitters or those where mountains or tall buildings obstruct television signals.

Cityscape. A view of a city or part of a city, as seen by the eye or as pictured in a photograph or drawing.

D

E

Ego trip. An act performed by a person in order to satisfy his or her conceit or to impose his or her own will in a given matter. As a verb, to ego-trip means to act in accordance with conceit or self-interest.

Ehrlichman, John, U.S. public official 358
Electromagnetic radiation 96
Elephant, picture 258
   hunting in Kenya 345
Ellington, Duke, American composer and musician 313
Elliot, Cass, American singer 313
El Salvador 365
Employee Benefit Security Act of 1974, U.S. pension reform law 356
Endangered species of animals 250–55
   animals of the Bible 246–49
   cave animals 298
   coins 127
   Expo '74 exhibit 59
Energy
   shortage 340
   space colonies 84
England see Great Britain
Environment
   endangered species of animals 250–55
   Expo '74 59, 60
Equatorial Guinea 365
Erving, Julius, American athlete 278
Eskimos, people 146, 147, 148, 149
   carver, picture 147
   wall hanging, picture 326
Ethiopia 365
   drought 72
   Haile Selassie deposed 357
   human fossils found 359
Evangeline, Acadian heroine
   statue, picture 153
Everest, Mount, Asia 154
Evert, Chris, American athlete 290

Executive privilege. In government, the idea that the executive branch has certain rights—such as that of withholding information—in its relations with the other branches of government. In the United States this idea is based on the separation of powers among the executive, legislative, and judicial branches of government as described in the Constitution. Executive privilege has been invoked a number of times in American history, most recently during the Nixon administration. President Nixon claimed that to protect the confidentiality of discussions between him and his aides, he could prevent Congress and the courts from examining certain documents and tapes relating to the Watergate affair. The claim of executive privilege in this instance was denied by the Supreme Court.

Exhibitions see Fairs and exhibitions
Experiments see Science experiments
Explorer Olympics, Boy Scout sports competition 198
Explorer Scouts 196
Expo '74, exposition, Spokane, Washington 59–63, 348
   postage stamp 119; picture 56–57

Fairs and exhibitions
   Expo '74 59–63
   postage stamps 119
   World Crafts Exhibition 327
Falla, Manuel de, Spanish composer 315
Fallow deer, animal 247; picture 248
Famine
   Sahel region, Africa 73

Fast food. Basically, restaurant food that can be prepared and sold to a customer quickly. A fast-food restaurant, often part of a chain, usually specializes in such foods as chicken or hamburgers and side dishes. The term may also be used for some convenience foods. See also Convenience food.

Faye, Alice, American actress 309
Fiji 365
Fingers, Rollie, American athlete 275
Finland 365
   International Camp of the Four Winds 202
Fishing
   Eskimos 146
Five Nations, Iroquois Indians 171
Flack, Roberta, American singer 313
Flamenco, Spanish music 314–15
Flea Market, Paris, France 164–67
Flint, poem by Christina Rossetti 222
Flory, Paul J., American chemist 359
Flowers
   names of flowers 88–93
   perfume industry 173–74
Folk art
   scrimshaw 302–5
   tapestries 40–41
   World Crafts Exhibition 327
Folk dance see Folk music
Folklore
   abominable snowman 154
   Hodja, Nasreddin, Turkish folk figure 34
Folk music
   flamenco 314–15
   World Crafts Exhibition 330
Folktales
   Arabian Nights tale 49–52
   Turkish folktale 34–37
   Swedish folktale 236–42
Food
   flavorings 174
   Middle Eastern cooking 38–39, 114–15
   United Nations food distribution in Africa 352
   World Food Conference 361
Food and Agriculture Organization, United Nations
   Grow More Food program 127
Football 280–82
Ford, Gerald R., American president 354, 356, 357, 359, 361
   Trudeau, Pierre Elliott, meeting with 362
Foreman, George, American boxer 359; picture 358
Fossils
   California, human skull fragments found in 349
   Ethiopia, human fossils found in 359
   rose plants 91
Fragonard, Jean Honoré, French painter 173
France 365
   Children's Villages 138, 139
   coins 126
   Flea Market, Paris 164–67
   Giroud, Françoise, appointed to cabinet 353
   Giscard d'Estaing, Valéry, elected president 349
   Grasse, city 172–75
   nuclear test 351
   Pompidou, Georges, death of 346

Freebie. A slang term for something that is given or obtained free of charge. It is used especially to refer to free tickets to theatrical and sporting events.

French language
   Quebec 353
Frère Jacques, song 306
Fur seal, animal, picture 261

G

H

Hang gliding. A sport of self-launched flight, in which a person leaps into space from an elevated place, such as a cliff, and glides with the aid of a triangular kite or sailplane. The frame of the kite or sailplane (a single- or double-wing glider) is strapped to his or her body by means of a harness. After the launching, the person is kept aloft and in motion by air currents. Flights of more than three hours have been made, though most are much briefer. The sport is also known as sky surfing, three-dimensional surfing, earth skimming, organic flying, and slope soaring.

Hobbit. An imaginary being, small in size and having some resemblance to a human. Hobbits are gentle and good-natured, and have furry feet. Most hobbits live in holes in the ground. These creatures were created by the writer J. R. R. Tolkien in his children's classic *The Hobbit.*

L

Lander, Eric, American science student, picture 184
Langford, Bonnie, English singer and dancer, picture 183
Languages
    chimpanzee language experiments 264–65
    Middle East 14
Langur, monkey
    footprints 154
Laos 367
Leafhopper, insect, picture 257
Lebanon 367, 13, 14, 16
    Beirut International College 47
Leech, worm, picture 257
Léger, Jules, Canadian governor-general 341
Leonardo da Vinci, Italian artist
    notebooks 99
Leopard, animal 247; picture 271
Lesotho 367
Liberia 367
    stamps 116
Libya 367, 13
Liechtenstein 367
Lindbergh, Charles A., American aviator 355
Linnaeus, Carolus, Swedish botanist 88
Lin Wen-hsiung, Taiwanese athlete 277
Lion, animal 247, 253
Literature
    Arabic 19
    Nobel prizes 359
    See also Young people's literature
Little League baseball 277
Little President, The, story by Peter Ustinov 228–35
    UNICEF drawing contest 191
Little Prince, The, motion picture 332–35
Llama, animal, picture 266
London, England 351
López Michelsen, Alfonso, Colombian president 347
Lunar exploration see Moon
Lunar module, spacecraft 79
Lunar roving vehicle, space vehicle 78, 79
Luxembourg 367
Lyre, musical instrument 53

M

MacBride, Seán, Irish humanitarian 359
MacLeish, Rick, American athlete 285
Magic 322–25, 208
Magic Show, The, musical 322–25
Makarios III, Archbishop, president of Cyprus 352, 362
Malagasy Republic 367
Malawi 367
Malaysia 367
Maldives 367
    stamps 119
Mali 367
    drought 72, 73
Malta 367, 363
Mamo, Sir Anthony, president of Malta 363
Manatee, animal, picture 269
Manitoba, province, Canada
    Riel, Louis, leader of the Métis 225
Maple leaf, national emblem of Canada 156

Maple sugar and syrup 156–59
March, poem by Mary Jane Menuez 221
Mariner 10, U.S. spacecraft 64, 65, 342, 345
Mars, planet 69
Marshall, Mike, American athlete 275
Martinson, Harry Edmund, Swedish writer 359

Mascon. A concentration of heavy, dense material below the surface of the moon. Mascons, which occur under the seas, or maria, of the moon, have a more concentrated mass, and therefore a stronger gravitational pull than other parts of the moon. They produce an asymmetrical field of gravity, which causes objects in orbit around the moon to wobble slightly and thus orbit somewhat unevenly rather than in a perfectly symmetrical path. The word "mascon" comes from "mass concentration."

Massachusetts
    witches of Salem 207–13
Mathieu, Atha, American parks commission member, picture 184
Mauritania 367
    drought 72, 73
Mauritius 367
Max, Peter, American artist 119
McCartney, Paul, British musician 312
Mecca, Saudi Arabia, picture 20
Medicine
    communications satellite 85
    Nobel prizes 359
Mediterranean Sea 87
Meir, Golda, Israeli premier 346
Merchant Marine Academy, U.S. 353
Mercury, planet 65, 345
Merrimack, Confederate warship 136, 137
Meteorology see Weather
Métis, person who is part American Indian and part European 225–27
Metro Toronto Zoo, Canada 260–63
Mexico 367
    Girl Guides 202
    gray wolf 252
    handicrafts 327
    petroleum 358
    toys 130–31
Middle East 12–55
    cooking 114–15
    Palestine Liberation Organization 359
Miki, Takeo, Japanese premier 363
Miller, Johnny, American athlete 284
Minasyan, Asya, Soviet composer, picture 185
Minimum wage 346
Minor hockey, sport 292–95
Mitchell, John N., U.S. public official 358
Mohammed, Islamic prophet 14
Mohawk Indians 168–71
Monaco 367
Mongolia 367
Mongolian wild horse, animal, pictures 270–71
Monitor, American warship 136–37
Monsoon winds
    Africa 75
Monsters 154–55
Moon 76–79
    phases of the moon 66
    robot explorers 69, 71

Moonquake. A vibration of the moon's surface, similar to an earthquake. Like an earthquake, such a trembling is probably caused by a subsurface movement of a mass of rock. The movement in turn produces a fault, or fracture, at the surface.

Morocco 367
Motion pictures
  Little Prince, The 334
  music 309
Movies *see* Motion pictures
Müller, Gerd, German athlete 283
Murphysboro, Illinois
  monster sightings 155
Murray, Anne, Canadian singer 312
Muscat, Oman 30
Music 308–13
  Assyrian song 53
  flamenco 314–15
  Gould, Glenn, Canadian musician 336–38
  Minasyan, Asya, Soviet composer, picture 185
  response of plants to music 81
  songs to sing 306–7
  Tivoli Gardens, Copenhagen, Denmark 134, 135
  Tucker, Tanya, American singer 187
  Vienna Boys' Choir, picture 184
  World Crafts Exhibition 330
  Zavaroni, Lena, Scottish singer, picture 182
Musicals 309
  Gypsy, picture 183
Musk-ox, animal 149
Muslim, a believer in Islam 15
Mustang, horse 253
My Older Sister, poem by Rosamond Dauer 220
Myrdal, Gunnar, Swedish economist 359

N

Nashville, Tennessee
  Opryland 313
National Basketball Association 278, 279
National Collegiate Athletic Association 278
National Football League 280, 282
National Hockey League 285, 287
National Invitation Tournament, basketball 278
National League, baseball 276
Nauru 367
Neff, Francine I., U.S. treasurer 349
Negev, The, desert, Israel 31–33
Nepal 367
Netherlands 367
  soccer 283
  tulip 90
  Witkar, battery-powered car 86
New Brunswick, province, Canada
  Acadia 150
New France, French empire in North America 150, 157
New Zealand 367
  Kirk, Norman E., death of 355
  Rowling, William E., named prime minister 356
Nicaragua 367
  stamps 116
Niccolò Torrentino at the Battle of San Romano, painting
    by Uccello 318
Niger 367
  drought 72, 73
Nigeria 367
Nile River, Africa 16
Nixon, Richard M., U.S. president 340, 346, 351
  impeachment articles adopted by House Judiciary
    Committee 353
  pardoned by President Ford 356
  resignation 354, 11
Nobel prizes 359

Nomads, people 42–44, 15
  Africa 73, 75 ,
  camel 27
  Eskimos 146
  Indians, American 146
  Oman 30
  United Arab Emirates 45
Northern Ireland *see* Great Britain
North Korea *see* Korea, North
Northwest Territories, Canada 144, 149
  Aklavik, picture 147
Norway 368
Nova Scotia, province, Canada
  Acadia 150–53
Nuclear tests 351
Numismatics 126–27

O

OAO, or **Orbiting Astronomical Observatory** 97
Observatories, Astronomical 94–97
Oil *see* Essential oils; Petroleum; Whale oil
Olympic Games 359
  Canadian coins 126; picture 146
Oman 30, 13, 368
Onoda, Hiroo, Japanese soldier 345
Ontario, province, Canada
  Toronto zoo 260–63
  World Crafts Exhibition 327
Oplonti, ancient Roman city 98
Opossum, animal, picture 267
Orange Bowl, football game 281
Orlando, Tony, American musician 312
Oryx, animal 249; picture 248
OSO, or **Orbiting Solar Observatory** 97
Outward Bound, educational program 178–81

P

Painting 316–21
Pakistan 368
  Bangladesh, recognition of 343
  earthquake 363
Palade, George Emil, American scientist 359
Palestine 19
Palestine Liberation Organization 359, 360
Palestinian leopard, animal, picture 271
Panama 368
Panov, Valery, Soviet dancer 350
Pantomime 132; picture 133
Papua New Guinea
  stamps 119
Paraguay 368
Parent, Bernie, American athlete 285, 287
Paris, France
  Flea Market 164–67
Parseghian, Ara, American football coach 281
Peace prizes, Nobel 359
Peacock, bird, picture 256
Pee-wee hockey tournament, Quebec, Canada 292
Pérez, Carlos Andrés, Venezuelan president 344
Perfume 172–75
  roses 91

Q

R

S

Sitcom. The word used by television producers for a situation comedy, or series of programs based on a single comic idea.

T

Telemedicine. The practice of medicine by means of closed-circuit television. It enables doctors in one place to treat patients in another. Groups of patients, such as employees of a large company, receive medical information and instruction from a doctor or doctors by watching a television receiver connected to a transmitting studio located in a medical office, hospital, or medical school. Telemedicine also includes the televising of surgery or other treatment for the instruction of medical students or other observers. ("Closed-circuit" television uses a private transmission system rather than the broadcast channels available to the public.)

Transcendental meditation (abbreviated TM). A form of concentration or religious devotion with its origins in Hinduism. The mind of the person meditating is directed to a single mystical idea. The person in meditation sits motionless, with eyes closed, usually for two 20-minute periods each day, and concentrates on a passage in Sanskrit (an ancient Indian language) that has been assigned by the person's teacher. Besides spiritual benefits, the practice is said to be an aid to health by reducing tension, and to make the person more energetic and efficient and better able to deal with others.

U

Nixon, Richard M., resignation of 354
space exploration 69
stamps 116, 119
Upper Volta 369
drought 72
Uruguay 369

V

Van Gogh, Vincent, Dutch painter 316, 320, 321
Vatican City
stamps 116
Vegetables
houseplants 122–25
Middle Eastern cooking 38
Venezuela 369
coins 127
Pérez, Carlos Andrés, becomes president 344
Venus, planet 64, 69, 71
Vienna Boys' Choir, picture 184
Vietnam, North 369
Vietnam, South 369
Vincent's Room at Arles, painting by Van Gogh 320
Vladivostok, USSR 361
Volcanoes
cave formation 297
Vesuvius, Mount 98
Vulture, The, poem by Hilaire Belloc 222

W

Walton, Bill, American athlete 278
Wangchuk, Jigme Singye, king of Bhutan 350; picture 351
Warner, Steven, English actor 334; pictures 333, 335
Warren, Earl, U.S. chief justice 352
Washington, state
Expo '74 59–63
Watergate scandal, American politics 344, 358
Weather
Canadian North 144, 145
drought 72
Middle East 14
Weather satellite 349
Weaving
Harrania tapestries 40
World Crafts Exhibition 327
Westar 1, U.S. communications satellite 347
Western Samoa 369
West Germany see Germany, West
Whale, mammal 251, 305
Whalebone 304
Whales' teeth 304; picture 302
Whaling industry 304
What Are Heavy?, poem by Christina Rossetti 223
White, Barry, American singer 311
Whooping crane, bird 254; picture 255
Wild horses, animals 253; pictures 270–71
Wildlife conservation see Conservation of wildlife
Williams, Esther, American actress, picture 308
Williamsport, Pennsylvania
Little League World Series 277
Wilson, Harold, British prime minister 344, 358
Wisent, animal, picture 262

Witches of Salem, The, historical story by Elisabeth Margo 206–213
Witkar, battery-powered car 86
Wolf, animal 252
Wonder, Stevie, American musician 311, 313
World Crafts Council 327
World Cup, or **Jules Rimet Cup,** soccer award 116, 283
World Food Conference 361; picture 360
World Football League, or **WFL** 280
World Hockey Association 285, 286
World Population Conference 355
World Series, baseball 274, 275
Little League 277
World's fair
Expo '74 58–63
Worry beads 48
Wright, Mary Van Lear, American Scout 196

Y

Yarn painting 327; picture 328
Yeager, Steve, American athlete, picture 274
Yellowknife, capital of Northwest Territories, Canada 144
Yemen (Aden) 369, 13
Yemen (Sana) 369, 13
Yeti, monster 154
Yoffe, Avraham, Israeli conservationist 246
Young people's art 191–94
Boston Museum of Science drawing contest 203
Harrania tapestries, pictures 40–41
Little President, pictures 233, 234
photography 188–90
Young people's literature
Acadians, The 150–53
Guiccioli Miniature, The 214–19
literary quiz 243
Little President, The 228–35
Nasreddin Hodja and the Honored Guest 34–37
poetry 220–23
Prince and His Magic Horse, The 49–52
Twin Sisters, The 236–42
Witches of Salem, The 206–13
Youth organizations
Boy Scouts 195–98
Girl Scouts and Girl Guides 199–202
Outward Bound 178–81
Yugoslovia 369
stamps 119
Yukon Territory, Canada 144, 148, 149
Dezadesh Lake, picture 144

Z

Zaïre 369
Ali-Foreman fight 359
Zaitsev, Alexander, Russian athlete 288
Zambia 369
Zavaroni, Lena, Scottish singer, picture 182
Zebra, animal, picture 262
Zeitz, Paul, American mathematics student, picture 182
Zoo
Metro Toronto Zoo, Canada 260–63
Zoology see Animals

ILLUSTRATION CREDITS AND ACKNOWLEDGMENTS

The following list credits or acknowledges, by page, the source of illustrations and text excerpts used in THE NEW BOOK OF KNOWLEDGE ANNUAL. Illustration credits are listed illustration by illustration—left to right, top to bottom. When two or more illustrations appear on one page, their credits are separated by semicolons. When both the photographer or artist and an agency or other source are given for an illustration, they are usually separated by a dash. Excerpts from previously published works are listed by inclusive page numbers.

10 Carl Frank—Photo Researchers; Marvin Newman—Woodfin Camp; Scala; Tom Salyer—Expo '74; *Sports Illustrated* photo by Heinz Kluetmeier © Time Inc.
12 Alain Nogues—Sygma
15 George Buctel
17 Luis Villota; F.P.G.; Tony Howarth—Woodfin Camp
18 Paolo Koch—Rapho Guillumette; Luis Villota; Thomas Hopker—Woodfin Camp; Tony Howarth—Woodfin Camp; Roland Michaud—Rapho Guillumette; Thomas Hopker—Woodfin Camp
20 Gerry Granham—Rapho Guillumette; Louis Goldman—Rapho Guillumette; Aramco
21 Annan Photo Features; Marvin Newman—Woodfin Camp; Paolo Koch—Rapho Guillumette
22 Susan Rayfield—Photo Researchers
23 George Holton—Photo Researchers
24 Frank Schwarz—Lee Ames Studio
26 John Bryson—Rapho Guillumette
27 Paolo Koch—Rapho Guillumette
28 Smithsonian Institution, Freer Gallery of Art
29 Editorial Photocolor Archives
30 George Buctel
31 Louis Goldman—Rapho Guillumette
33 Louis Goldman—Rapho Guillumette
36 Susan Anderson—Publishers Graphics
39 Fred J. Maroon
40 Werner Forman Archive
41 Werner Forman Archive
42 Marvin Newman—Woodfin Camp
43 Bernard Gerin—UNICEF
45 Frank Schwarz—Lee Ames Studio
46 Dominique Lacarriere
47 John K. Cooley
48 John C. Wallner
51 Jan Pyk
53 *The New York Times*
55 Frank Schwarz—Lee Ames Studio
56– U.S. Postal Service
57
58 Tom Salyer—Expo '74
60 UPI
61 Tom Salyer—Expo '74
62 Tom Salyer—Expo '74
64 NASA
65 NASA
66 © 1973 by D. C. Heath and Company, reprinted by permission of the publishers.
67 © 1972 by D. C. Heath & Company, reprinted by permission of the publishers.
68 Howard Koslow
72 Alain Nogues—Sygma
73 George Buctel; United Nations
74 United Nations
75 United Nations—FAO
76 NASA
78 NASA
80 From *Mother Earth's Hassle-Free Indoor Plant Book* by Lynn & Joel Rapp; illustrations by Marvin Rubin, © 1973 by J. P. Tarcher. Illustrations reprinted by permission of the publisher.

82 From *Mother Earth's Hassle-Free Indoor Plant Book* by Lynn & Joel Rapp; illustrations by Marvin Rubin, © 1973 by J. P. Tarcher. Illustrations reprinted by permission of the publisher.
83 From *Mother Earth's Hassle-Free Indoor Plant Book* by Lynn & Joel Rapp; illustrations by Marvin Rubin, © 1973 by J. P. Tarcher. Illustrations reprinted by permission of the publisher.
84 NASA
85 NASA
86 David Halperin
87 *The New York Times*
89 Jane Latta; R. F. Head—National Audubon Society; Karl Weidmann—National Audubon Society; Jeanne White—National Audubon Society; Jane Latta
90 R. F. Head—National Audubon Society; Jane Latta
92 A. W. Ambler—National Audubon Society; A-Z Botanical Collection, Ltd.
92 N. E. Beck, Jr.—National Audubon Society
93 Mary M. Thacher—Photo Researchers; John H. Gerard—National Audubon Society
94 Novosti from Sovfoto; Tass from Sovfoto
95 Smithsonian Astrophysical Observatory; Cerro Tololo Inter-American Observatory
96 Australian News Bureau
97 Cornell University; National Radio Astronomy Observatory
98 Wide World
99 From *The Madrid Codices*, © 1974 by McGraw-Hill Book Company (UK) Ltd. By permission of the publisher.
100– Robert Dunne
101
102 Robert Dunne; text adapted from *Ranger Rick's Nature Magazine,* © 1974 by the National Wildlife Federation. By permission of the publisher.
103 Adapted from *Ranger Rick's Nature Magazine,* © 1974 by the National Wildlife Federation. By permission of the publisher.
104 Sybil C. Harp
105 Sybil C. Harp
106 Sybil C. Harp
107 Sybil C. Harp
108 From *Working With Odds and Ends*
109 © 1974 by Franklin Watts, Inc., reprinted by permission of the publisher.
111 © 1974 by Highlights for Children, Inc., Columbus, Ohio, reprinted by permission of the publisher.
112 Robert Dunne
113 Robert Dunne
120– Reprinted and adapted with permission
121 of Macmillan Publishing Co., Inc., from *Let's Make More Presents* by Esther Hautzig. Text © 1973 by Esther Hautzig. Illustrations © 1973 by Macmillan Publishing Co., Inc.
122 John C. Wallner
123 John C. Wallner
124 John C. Wallner

125 John C. Wallner
126 Krause Publications, Inc.
127 Krause Publications, Inc.
128– Peter Klose—Photo Researchers
129
130 Jane Latta, courtesy of Mexican Folk Art Annex, New York City
131 Jane Latta, courtesy of Mexican Folk Art Annex, New York City
133 Fritz Henle—Photo Researchers; Marvin Newman—Woodfin Camp
134 Marvin Newman—Woodfin Camp; Henry Kurtz
136 The Harry T. Peters Collection, Museum of the City of New York
140 Lisl Steiner
143 Carl Frank—Photo Researchers; American Museum of Natural History
144 Annan Photo Features
145 Ted Grant—DPI
147 Ted Grant—DPI; Canadian Consulate
149 Government of the N.W.T.
152 Nova Scotia Information Centre
153 National Film Board of Canada
155 Wide World
156 National Film Board of Canada
158 National Film Board of Canada; Canadian Consulate
161 Marc & Evelyne Bernheim—Woodfin Camp; Joyce Deyo
162 Dick Davis—Photo Researchers; John Lewis Stage—Photo Researchers
165 Gordon Gahan—Photo Researchers
166 Robert Rapelye—Editorial Photocolor Archives
168 Ray Ellis—Rapho Guillumette
171 Ray Ellis—Rapho Guillumette
172 Sabine Weiss—Rapho Guillumette
175 Sabine Weiss—Rapho Guillumette
176– 1974 Scholastic-Kodak Photography
177 Awards
178 Outward Bound, Inc.
179 Outward Bound, Inc.
180 Outward Bound, Inc.
181 Outward Bound, Inc.
182 Tyrone Dukes—*The New York Times;* James Caccavo—*Newsweek;* Wide World
183 *The New York Times;* Martha Swope; Martha Swope
184 Westinghouse Electric Corp.; Austrian Information Service; UPI
184– Ludwig Laab—*The New York Times*
185
185 Wide World
186 UPI
188 Canadian Magazine National Photo Contest; 1974 Scholastic-Kodak Photography Awards
189 Canadian Magazine National Photo Contest; 1974 Scholastic-Kodak Photography Awards
190 1974 Scholastic-Kodak Photography Awards
191 UNICEF
192 UNICEF
193 UNICEF
194 UNICEF
195 Boy Scouts of America
196 Boy Scouts of Canada